▼ AS MEDIA STUDIES:
THE ESSENTIAL INTRODUCTION

This completely updated, easy-to-use second edition of the popular AS *Media Studies: The Essential Introduction* is designed to support students taking AS Media Studies courses, whether in schools or further education colleges.

The authors have between them wide experience working in the field of media studies as teachers, examiners and authors. They introduce students step by step to the skills of reading media texts and address key areas such as media technologies, media institutions and media audiences. Individual chapters cover:

- introduction to studying the media
- reading media texts
- media institutions
- audiences and the media
- case studies of news, advertising and marketing, and the horror genre
- research and how to do it
- preparing for exams
- coursework and production guide.

AS *Media Studies: The Essential Introduction* will give students the confidence to tackle every part of an introductory media course. Specially designed to be user-friendly, it includes:

- activities and further activities
- practical assignments and exam questions
- further reading and a glossary of key terms
- case studies showing how theoretical ideas can be applied.

Philip Rayner is Senior Lecturer in Media Communications at the University of Gloucestershire and has acted as a Principal Moderator for A Level Media Studies. **Peter Wall** is Chief Examiner and Principal Moderator for GCSE Media Studies and a Chair of Examiners for Media Studies A Level. **Stephen Kruger** is a Chief Examiner for Media Studies A Level and Head of Media Studies at Holland Park School.

'Truly excellent! A veritable one-stop shop for those studying A Level Media Studies. Up-to-date, informative and user-friendly.'

Jo Wilcock, Senior Examiner VCE Media and Communication

'Explanations of the media concepts, cultural terms and theoretical perspectives are clear, concise, well illustrated and accessible to all, while the notebook sections offer deeper insights, more detail and the stimulus to engage in more depth with media theories and debates . . . The section on Media Institutions is the best I've seen.'

Julia Burton, Principal Examiner for two GCE Media units

'An ideal coursebook for students following a Media Studies course at A Level and an invaluable planning tool for the teachers who lead them.'

Les Grafton, A Level teacher, Subject Advisory Committee

'Each part is well explained, relevant and interesting. I liked the sound advice on how to study, appropriate and well-considered activities, easily digestible theory and helpful reference and resource material.'

Lesley Kerr, Queen Elizabeth School, Hexham, Northumberland

Other books for Media and Communication Studies

Media Studies: The Essential Resource
Philip Rayner, Peter Wall and Stephen Kruger

AS Communication Studies: The Essential Introduction
Andrew Beck, Peter Bennett and Peter Wall

Communication Studies: The Essential Resource
Andrew Beck, Peter Bennett and Peter Wall

AS MEDIA STUDIES:
THE ESSENTIAL INTRODUCTION

Second edition

Philip Rayner, Peter Wall
and Stephen Kruger

Routledge
Taylor & Francis Group

LONDON AND NEW YORK

First published 2001 as *Media Studies: The Essential Introduction*,
reprinted 2002 (twice), 2003

Second edition published 2004
by Routledge
2 Park Square, Abingdon, Oxon OX14 4RN

Simultaneously published in the USA and Canada
by Routledge
270 Madison Avenue, New York, NY 10016

Reprinted 2005, 2006

Routledge is an imprint of the Taylor & Francis Group

© 2004 Philip Rayner, Peter Wall and Stephen Kruger

Typeset in Novarese and Bell Gothic by Keystroke, Jacaranda Lodge, Wolverhampton
Printed and bound in Italy by Printer Trento

British Library Cataloguing in Publication Data
A catalogue record for this book is available from the British Library

Library of Congress Cataloging in Publication Data
Rayner, Philip, 1947–
 AS media studies : the essential introduction / Philip Rayner, Peter
Wall, and Stephen Kruger. – 2nd ed.
  p. cm.
Rev. ed. of: Media studies. 2001.
Includes bibliographical references and index.
1. Mass media. I. Wall, Peter. II. Kruger, Stephen, 1951– III.
Rayner, Philip, 1947– Media studies. IV. Title.
 P90.M3723 2004
 302.23–dc22   2003024476

ISBN 10: 0–415–32965–5 (hbk)
ISBN 10: 0–415–32966–3 (pbk)

ISBN 13: 978–0–415–32965–1 (hbk)
ISBN 13: 978–0–415–32966–8 (pbk)

▼ CONTENTS

▼ FIGURES

▼ PREFACE

In writing this, the second edition of *Media Studies: The Essential Introduction*, we, as authors, have become aware that since the publication of the first edition in 2001 the media seems to have assumed an even more dominant role in our daily lives. This is partly owing to the events of 11 September 2001, the subsequent 'war on terrorism' and the way in which images of these events are transmitted around the world. It is also partly owing to our society's increasing use of the Internet as a source of information, a means of communication and a provider of entertainment.

It therefore seems ironic that there is still criticism aimed at attempts to undertake any kind of critical and systematic educational study of the media and their role in our lives. In the summer of 2003 over 60,000 students sat AS and A2 exams in Media Studies and the number of applications for places on media courses in universities continues to grow. For the majority of people there is no question that an understanding of how the media work is an important part of our education, whether it be informally examined or integrated into other aspects of our education. Our own careers reflect this commitment, as we ourselves have each spent over twenty years working in the field of Media Studies as teachers, examiners and authors and like many others feel that the media play too important a role in our lives simply to be either ignored or accepted unchallenged.

We believe that studying the media, although undoubtedly important, is also fun. Consuming media texts, whether on radio, television, in the cinema or via a computer, is often a highly social activity and can be entertaining; making your own media texts through websites, video, radio or newspaper production can be extremely creative and very satisfying; developing your own interests, reading what other scholars think about the media and their products and carrying out your own research can be stimulating and satisfying. In this book we have tried to share some of these many aspects of studying the media.

The overall structure of this second edition is very similar to the first. There are three main sections: Reading the Media, Media Audiences and Media Institutions. At the end of each of these three parts there is an example (title sequences, lifestyle magazines, newspaper ownership) that illustrates how the concepts addressed in each section can be applied to particular situations. We have also included three case studies on particular aspects of the media (News, Advertising and marketing, and The horror genre). As previously, we have included a section on the essential skills that, in our experience, students need; these include how to carry out research, undertake production work and prepare for examinations.

The media are ever changing and it is only possible at any one time to capture a 'snapshot' of what is going on. This book was largely written in the summer of 2003 and by the time you read it some of the information it contains will be out of date. We have therefore included suggestions for activities and further work that will enable you, as students and/or teachers, to apply the concepts to your own particular experiences, interests and examples. This is part of the challenge and excitement of studying the media – their immediacy and spontaneity.

We hope you get as much pleasure and fulfilment out of using this book as we have had in writing it and we welcome any comments you may have regarding its content and/or structure.

Finally we would like to thank those who have helped and supported us in the writing of this second edition:

our families and partners
colleagues, friends and students (past, present and future)
Moira Taylor, Kate Ahl and the rest of the team at Routledge
Francine Koubel and all the other examiners, moderators and subject officers (past, present and future).

Philip Rayner
Peter Wall
Stephen Kruger

▼ FIGURE ACKNOWLEDGEMENTS

▼ INTRODUCTION

Although it is rather a cliché to say that the media are an important part of our lives, since the events of 11 September 2001 it has become especially apparent that media images often have a power and significance that can resonate around the world in a matter of seconds.

It has become clear that we live in a 'mediated' society (see section on representation, p. 61) in which many of our ideas about the world, our knowledge of what is happening and, perhaps most importantly, our values come from beyond our individual daily or

Figure i.1 *11 September 2001. Twin Towers burning – a view from Brooklyn Bridge. Source: Popperfoto; photo: Reuters/Sara K. Schwittek.*

immediate experience. Our ideas of the world are derived largely from the modern media, which produce and 'package' versions of events and issues in their output, and which we consume as part of our daily lives and situations. This means that the media therefore have a very strong influence on us both as individuals and as a society.

In this introduction we want to consider why we should study the media and also offer some guidelines on how to study the media. Before we study the media in detail, it is useful to consider two basic questions:

- What do we mean by 'the media'?
- Why are the media important?

The first question is perhaps more easily answered than the second.

WHAT DO WE MEAN BY 'THE MEDIA'?

Although what constitutes the media and their products may change over time, we can identify certain key characteristics that seem to apply to all media products at any time in history. These basic characteristics can be summed up in the following general statements:

- The media reach a large number of people.
- The media, although centrally produced, are usually privately consumed.
- Media products are 'shared'.
- The media are controlled or 'regulated'.
- The media rely on sophisticated technology.
- The media are 'modern'.
- The media are expensive to produce.

Let us now examine each of these in turn.

The media reach a large number of people

What counts as a 'large' number of people will vary depending upon the historical period. *The Times* used to sell about 7,000 copies a day in the early nineteenth century. This was a high circulation when we consider that there were no other major forms of media or mass communication. In July 1985 *Live Aid* was seen by 1.5 billion viewers in over 160 countries. Every day the Internet has a potential 'audience' of millions of people across the world. Most media products today are constructed to be consumed by large numbers of people.

Such large numbers of people, however, will be 'fragmented', divided up into various different groups, depending on the media concerned. They will also 'consume' the media in many different ways. Each media 'text' will nevertheless be aimed at a large number of people, in many cases many millions of people throughout the world. In Part 2, on media audiences (p. 107), we look in more detail at how this 'mass' audience is made up.

TEXT Although we usually associate this word with something that is printed or written, in Media Studies the term is used to refer to all media products. This can include television programmes and/or adverts, photographs, films either on video or in the cinema, newspaper articles (or the newspapers themselves), radio programmes and/or jingles, billboards, video games or web pages.

ACTIVITY . . .

Make a list of all the ways in which you are part of 'an audience'. Go through your list and for each occasion that you are part of an audience think about the setting, other activities that you might be doing at the same time, your companions at the time (if any) and any other factors that you think might be important. Can you identify any particular trends or patterns that might be significant or might influence your patterns of consumption?

Using the list above, consider the different types of text that you consume.

- Are they local, national or international?
- Who else might be consuming these texts at the same time as you?
- Again, are there any particular patterns or trends that you can identify?

Now carry out a more detailed survey of other people's patterns of consumption. You can design your own questionnaire or you might find the worksheet below of some help in deciding the sort of questions you might ask. (You might want to read the sections on audiences (p. 107) and research skills (p. 307) before undertaking this task.)

WORKSHEET . . .

WORKSHEET TO DETERMINE MEDIA CONSUMPTION PATTERNS

Newspapers:

- Which daily newspapers (if any) do they read?
- What sections of newspapers do they turn to first, and why?
- What sections do they never read, and why?
- What kinds of stories do they usually read, and why?
- Do they, or does someone else, buy the newspaper they read?

continued

Magazines:

- What magazines (if any) do they buy regularly, and why?
- What sections of the magazines do they read and not read, and why?

Television:

- Approximately how many hours a week do they spend watching television?
- What times of day do they usually watch television?
- What programmes do they like best, and why?
- What programmes do they dislike most, and why?
- Do they watch alone or with others?
- If they watch with others, who decides what they will watch?

Radio:

- What stations do they like best, and why?
- Approximately how many hours a week do they spend listening to the radio?
- What times of day do they usually listen to the radio?
- What stations do they dislike most, and why?
- Do they listen alone or with others?
- Where do they listen to the radio?
- What other activities (if any) do they do whilst listening to the radio?

Cinema:

- What films, if any, have they seen at the cinema in the last month?
- What films have they seen in other places – for example through DVD/video purchase or rental, satellite film channels (free or otherwise) or through video-on-demand?
- Who else watched the films with them?
- Who decided which films to watch?

Internet:

- How often do they access the Internet?
- Where do they access the Internet – at home, at college or school, or at work?
- What are the main sites that they access?
- What are the main reasons for accessing these sites – for example for information, to make purchases, to communicate with friends, to download music or for entertainment?
- What other activities (if any) do they do whilst accessing the Internet?

The media, although centrally produced, are usually privately consumed

This may appear to be a paradox, but one of the key characteristics of the media today is that, despite large audiences, consumption is still very much a personal experience. We still talk of 'family viewing'. There may be eighteen million people watching a particular episode of *EastEnders*, but the experience will largely be individual and private. We usually watch television in the privacy of our own home with perhaps one or two other people, or we may watch it alone in our bedroom whilst elsewhere in the house someone else is also alone, watching the same programme at the same time.

Many millions of people will have seen a film like *The Matrix*, yet each person's experience of the film is probably a personal and intimate one – even if we are part of an audience of 300 people all sitting together in the dark in the cinema.

We often consume music as individuals, carrying out other tasks, either at home or perhaps in the privacy of our car – in our own 'personal space'. The *Sun* newspaper may be read by over twelve million people each day, but for each person it is a private act, often carried out in a private and personal space (even in the lavatory!). Some commentators suggest that it is this sense of the media coming into our private worlds, our homes, and 'saturating' our daily lives that makes them so important.

> **MEDIA SATURATION**   A term used to describe the way in which the media today 'saturate' all aspects of our lives and the extent to which our experience of the world is dominated by the media.
>
> **KEY TERM**

Yet we need to remember that media products are constructed like a production line in a factory, whether it is the newspaper, the television show or the Hollywood film. The distribution is also very centralised, whether it is the transmission of a television news bulletin across the whole country at one particular point in time, the fleet of lorries that deliver the newspapers to the newsagents, or the distribution of a film over a period of time to be shown at cinemas, on subscription television and eventually on DVD/video.

Media products are 'shared'

The media produce texts that are both popular – hence the high audience figures – and also 'shared' in the sense that they become part of our common culture. Today we are all familiar with the expression 'Phone a friend' – even those who do not regularly watch or have never seen the television show *Who Wants to Be a Millionaire?* will know the phrase, its origin and what it means. The phrase has become part of our daily vocabulary in the way that 'Good morning, have you used Pears Soap?' was in the late nineteenth century (see p. 258). Although the level of our particular knowledge may vary, almost everyone is familiar with the stories of the *EastEnders* characters Phil Mitchell or Pauline Fowler. Media images can become a common 'language' – across the world millions of people

Figure i.2 *Papuans watching* Grease. *Source:* The Age, *Melbourne; photo:*
Jason South. Consider some of the ways in which media images have become
a common language.

know about Luke Skywalker or Harry Potter or what MTV stands for. Although many
commentators suggest that this 'colonisation' of the world's media by predominantly
American companies and artefacts is damaging, it is again a sign of the media's power
and the universality of its images. See, for example, Figure i.2, which depicts some
tribesmen in Papua New Guinea wandering around a television store and looking at
an extract from the film *Grease*.

We are all very 'media literate' and share a sophisticated understanding of the
'language' of media images that are constantly being shown, repeated and referred to
(see the subsection on semiotics, p. 28).

SEMIOTICS   The study of signs and sign systems.

The media are controlled or 'regulated'

Perhaps because of the large audiences they attract, and the power, reach and
popularity of the media, another key characteristic is the way in which the media are
seen as being in need of control or regulation. Even in cases of media forms like the

Internet, where there is some difficulty in deciding how actually to control and regulate it, there is nevertheless the desire to make rules about who has access and what is available. (See subsection on regulation of the media, p. 204.)

Consider the number of dictatorial countries in which the media are still largely controlled by the government as a means of 'controlling' the circulation of ideas and criticisms. Often one of the first things that happens in a revolution is that the national media and communications centres are taken over, so that the new leaders can 'control' the messages that are transmitted. In this way they use the media to win the 'hearts and minds' of the people. In Britain there is a continuing debate about the 'freedom' of the press and the powers of the Press Complaints Commission (PCC) and in 2003 there was a sizeable dispute between the Labour government and the BBC over the war in Iraq.

The media rely on sophisticated technology

The media need this sophisticated technology to produce and transmit the texts they create. Even in today's world in which media hardware is seemingly becoming smaller and more personalised (for example MP3 players/Walkmans, mobile phones or wristwatches with television receivers inside them), the media are still very dependent upon a highly sophisticated technology. We may perhaps take this level of technological sophistication for granted. However, it is important to consider the technology required to make the television programmes that may be seen on a wristwatch, or to download music from the Internet, or to produce 'blockbuster' films or glossy magazines.

In the recent conflicts in Afghanistan and Iraq the television news reporters' increasing use of video satellite phones has meant that we, the viewers at home, can receive live, up-to-the-minute news reports from remote parts of the world that a few years ago would have taken several days to arrive in Britain.

The media are 'modern'

The media are seen as being 'up to date' or 'modern' – or even 'postmodern' (see p. 11). Although we can trace newspapers back to the early 1700s when the *Daily Courant* (the first daily newspaper) was first printed, the media (as we understand the term today) are a very modern phenomenon. Increasingly it is part of any definition of the media that they respond to, and quickly incorporate, the most up-to-date innovations and trends such as the 'convergence' of communications, computing and telephone technologies. Today this means, among others, MP3 players, WAP/video phones, ADSL telephone lines, over 300 digital television channels (many of them interactive) and a range of digital radio stations.

The media are expensive to produce

The media, partly because of the technology required to produce and distribute texts, are expensive and so tend to be owned either by large commercial companies, often multinationals (and, increasingly, American ones), or by state-owned or government organisations. This means that the media tend to be very centralised and a few companies have a lot of power and control in particular industries. (See the section on media institutions, p. 181.) As the problems at ITVDigital demonstrate, it can be very difficult for newcomers to set up and become successful, even if they are already backed by large media companies. It is interesting to watch how 'new' media, like the Internet and dot.com companies, are being increasingly taken over by established companies that have already been financially successful in other areas of the media.

(In the section on production skills on p. 321, we offer some guidance on how to produce media images without the use of the complex, sophisticated and expensive equipment that most media companies use.)

ACTIVITY...

These 'key characteristics' (p. 2) are our own suggestions, and you may disagree with them. You can 'measure' different types of media against this list of key characteristics to test how accurate it is. Can you suggest any other key characteristics that could be applied to all media?

WHY ARE THE MEDIA IMPORTANT?

The second question as to why we should study the media is perhaps more complicated. However, here is a list of suggestions:

- The media tell us what is going on in the world.
- The media are a central part of our lives.
- The media are influential.
- Domestic media hardware has become an intrinsic part of our homes and our lives.
- The media are very profitable.

Let us look in more detail at each of these.

The media tell us what is going on in the world

The media are important because they tell us what is going on both in the world at large (for example, natural disasters, wars) and at home (for example, political and sporting events, star 'gossip'). Try to imagine what life would have been like before broadcasting. Think about what we would know (or not know) of the world without television, radio, newspapers or the Internet.

The media are a central part of our lives

We turn to the media for entertainment, to relax after a hard day's work. We use the media for information, whether it is to find out the latest cricket results, the weather tomorrow or what is happening in the rest of the world. Perhaps less willingly, we accept the media as a source of persuasion, most noticeably through advertising but also through campaigns like the 'drink/drive' ones at Christmas or political campaigns during an election.

Figure i.3 will help you think about how much time you spend being 'exposed' to the media's products every day and the different ways in which you 'use' the media. Think about how omnipresent the media have become in our lives, the extent to which the media saturate our daily lives.

The media are influential

Because the media are so much a central part of our daily lives, they obviously wield influence: however, it is not always clear what that influence is and whether it is good or bad (it is most probably a mixture of both). Often the media are blamed for many of the problems in today's society: violent films encouraging crime (see section on the

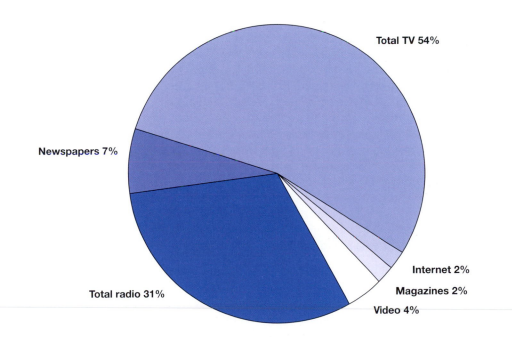

Figure i.3 *Time spent – average media day. Source:* Radio Days 2, 1999 © *Radio Advertising Bureau. How closely does the pie chart reflect your own media day?*

'effects' debate, p. 145), sexual advice in teen magazines encouraging promiscuity (see p. 162), pin-ups in 'lads'' magazines encouraging sexist attitudes, or tabloid newspapers running 'name and shame' campaigns (see section on news, p. 235).

ACTIVITY . . .

Draw up a list of your own examples to show the influence of the media. Separate your list into negative and positive influences; positive influences could include encouraging healthier lifestyles, anti-drink/drive campaigns, charity promotions, supporting national sporting events.

We need to recognise that, despite the prevalence of the media in our lives, there are other influences that are as strong or even stronger. Family, education, religion, peer groups, ethnicity all help to shape our ideas, values, beliefs and behaviour, and it is very difficult to isolate one factor and say that the media caused that to happen. (See p. 146 on the James Bulger case.)

Domestic media hardware has become an intrinsic part of our homes and our lives

One of the ways to understand the importance of the media in our everyday world is to think about the hardware we have in our homes for receiving the media's products. In Britain 99 per cent of all homes have at least one television set – although many homes nowadays have several, perhaps one in each bedroom as well as a communal one. Over 60 per cent of the population is described as being 'online', having access to the Internet through work, home or study (for comparative figures for other countries see Figure 3.8 on p. 221, <http://www.nua.com/surveys/how_many_online>). In 2003 11.7 million households in the UK (47 per cent) could access the Internet from home (see <http://www.statistics.gov.uk/cci>). Over 40 per cent of British households are now considered to be 'multichannel' homes, in other words they can receive more than just the five terrestrial television channels, In Britain there are more radios than adults: for every 100 adults there are about 120 radios. In some parts of Africa one radio is shared between, on average, eighteen adults and there are no television sets at all (often there is not even a reliable supply of electricity).

Think about the rest of the technology that today we take for granted in our homes: VHS and DVD recorders, personal stereos for CDs and mini-discs as well as cassettes, mobile phones, personal computers and MP3 players. It is hard to imagine having a car without a CD player and perhaps a digital radio. For many people it is difficult to imagine how they kept in touch with each other before the arrival of email or telephone texting.

Look around you next time you are in a town centre or on public transport and note the extent to which the media, both public and private, are present.

It is also instructive to go around your own home looking at each room and noting down the quantity and different types of media that are there. You could then work out how many telephones, television sets, computers and other media equipment there are per person in your household. Compare your results with those of your peers.

The media are very profitable

Companies and organisations such as News International, Time-Warner/AOL and Disney exist to make a profit. They do not make films or produce newspapers because they are nice people who want to help us be entertained and/or better informed; they make films like *The Matrix* or print newspapers like the *News of the World* because they know that they will make large amounts of money. (See, for example, the section on magazines, p. 151.) However, it is also important to realise that media organisations can often make mistakes and actually lose large amounts of money, for example ITVDigital, the Kevin Costner film *The Postman* or the publisher Dorling Kindersley, whose tie-in books of *Star Wars Episode 1* failed to meet sales expectations, thereby bankrupting the company and causing a takeover by Pearson/Penguin.

Look through the financial pages of newspapers to see what information is available about media companies. Access the websites of media companies to try to find out about their financial details or the amount of profit (or loss) that they make.

Postmodernism

This is a term that is used a lot, although there is still some debate and uncertainty about what exactly 'postmodern' means, the value of the term and the extent to which we are living in a postmodern society (see, for instance, the essay 'Postmodernism and popular culture' by Dominic Strinati, 1995).

According to most art historians, 'modernism' was a movement that started in the late nineteenth century and ended around the 1960s. So 'postmodernism' is a term that is used to characterise the type of society and culture that has developed in Western societies since the 1970s and into the beginning of the twenty-first century.

POSTMODERNISM The social, political and cultural attitudes and images of the late twentieth and early twenty-first century.

The idea of postmodernism is partly based on a particular view of contemporary life – a high-tech, post-industrial society dominated by the 'flow' of media images and information around the world. It is claimed that we are increasingly living in a 'world time' in which news, financial trading or sporting events are all transmitted 'live' around the world. It is possible to be at home in Birmingham on a Sunday morning and watch 'live' a Formula 1 car race as it takes place in Malaysia. We can trade money and shares around the world twenty-four hours a day. Enormous amounts of information and imagery can be distributed around the globe almost instantaneously and accessed by large numbers of people in a way that would not have been possible twenty years ago. More and more we 'borrow' from other cultures for our music, furnishings, food, clothes, and so on. What Marshall McLuhan called the 'global village' is increasingly becoming a reality.

ACTIVITY...

Try to remember how you received the news of the events of 11 September 2001. Compare your recollections with your peers. Did you watch the events as they happened on television, live from New York? Think about how quickly those images were circulated around the world and have become a universally recognised symbol, although there is perhaps some difference of opinion as to what it is they represent.

Postmodernism is said to reflect modern society's insecurities and uncertainties about identity, history, progress and truth, and the break-up of those traditional agencies, such as religion, the family or, perhaps to a lesser extent, class, that helped identify and shape who we are and our place in the world. Artists like Madonna, Michael Jackson and David Bowie are all cited as examples of postmodernism in the ways in which they have created or re-created different identities for themselves.

According to some theorists, we are made up of several shifting and fragmented identities and increasingly our identity is now defined by our lifestyle and what we consume rather than by what we produce or by our background.

Figure i.4 (right) Leigh Bowery, an Australian performance artist, was postmodern in the sense that he created different identities for himself, turned himself into a work of art, confounded 'normal' expectations about men and women. In our postmodern age identity is no longer fixed but constructed and can be manipulated by individuals. Source: Fergus Greer.

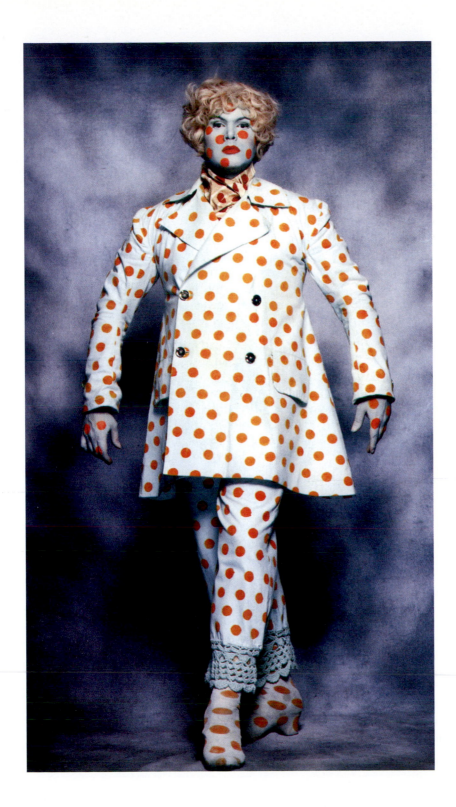

Jean-François Lyotard in *The Postmodern Condition* (1979) suggests that what he called 'meta-narratives' or grand theories, such as religion, Marxism, capitalism or science, no longer have the same importance in our lives. The concept of progress – the certainty that the developments of the arts, technology, medicine and knowledge would be moving inevitably towards a 'greater good' – is now seen to be questionable. Progress is seen by some as a way of controlling people and, using examples like CCTV or the government's reading of private emails, as 'spying' on ordinary citizens.

One of the films often cited as 'postmodern' is Ridley Scott's *Blade Runner* (1982), in which science, technology and progress are all questioned and shown in some way to have 'failed'. The world in *Blade Runner* is polluted by industry and overcrowding; only the rich escape to the 'off-worlds'. One of the key themes of the film is the 'blurring' of the differences between the real and the artificial, between the humans and the replicants. Increasingly it is no longer possible to be clear about what it means to be 'human'.

Another media text described as postmodern is David Lynch's television programme *Twin Peaks* (1990). A characteristic of postmodernism is the way in which 'high' art and popular culture are mixed together, and in Twin Peaks we can see an example of popular culture (the television 'whodunnit'/soap opera) mixed with 'high art' (the work of film director David Lynch, which includes films such as *Eraserhead* (1977), *The Elephant Man* (1980) and *Blue Velvet* (1986)). *Twin Peaks* also 'blurs' the distinction between various genres of television programme by being part cop-show, part comedy and part Gothic horror, amongst others.

Another key idea of postmodernism is that of 'simulacra', a term introduced by Jean Baudrillard to explain the way in which simulations or copies are replacing the 'real' artefacts. Examples might include theme parks, 'fake' Irish or Australian pubs or American-style coffee-houses where the 'pretend' version seems as real as, if not more real than, the actual thing it is copying. This idea can be extended to include much of television's output, where, for example, we, as 'armchair travellers', can visit countries all over the world, see exotic sights and perhaps feel that we have 'experienced' or understood these different places. 'Confessional' shows like *Jerry Springer* can also be seen as false copies that 'pretend' to offer solutions to personal problems but are actually only there to entertain the viewer. In the postmodern world, style is 'celebrated' at the expense of substance and content, while the fake and the artificial increasingly replace the real

KEY TERM

SIMULACRA According to Baudrillard, simulcra are simulations or copies that are replacing the 'real' artefacts so that increasingly reality becomes redundant and we can no longer distinguish between the real and the representation of the real.

Another useful term associated with postmodernism is 'bricolage' (see section on media intertextuality, p. 70). The term was used to describe the punk movement and the way in which punks took a variety of different objects (such as dustbin liners, safety-pins, Mohican haircuts and bondage trousers) and by combining them made a new style or fashion. Bricolage is quite a useful way of looking at certain media forms such as music videos and advertising that increasingly seem to mix together a wide range of different images that do not appear to have any connection, except that they are somehow 'modern'.

> **BRICOLAGE** The way signs or artefacts are borrowed from different styles or genres to create something new.

KEY TERM

Another film that is often called postmodern is Quentin Tarantino's *Pulp Fiction* (1994), which also mixes pieces from various different types of genre: gangster films, sporting films, comedy, for example. Part of the 'pleasure' in watching this film is its 'intertextuality', identifying the references to other types of film. An example of bricolage is the scene at the restaurant, Jack Rabbit Slim's. In this scene John Travolta is dressed as a cowboy and 'copies' his *Saturday Night Fever* dance routine surrounded by images of dead film stars from the 1950s and 1960s. Later he does 'the twist', a dance from the 1960s. The people working in the restaurant are dressed as Hollywood and rock 'n' roll stars.

Postmodernism is quite a difficult term to understand as it is still quite vague and can seem to include everything that is happening in early twenty-first-century life. However, it can be a useful tool for analysing some aspects of the media and highlighting their importance in our life today.

Media texts seem to be ever present and are increasingly invading our lives; they are, however, also fun and pleasurable. Making sense of all these different media texts and how we interact with them is a complex process. In the next section we try to identify some of the ways you can start to study the media.

HOW TO STUDY THE MEDIA

One of the key aspects of studying the media is that there are no 'simple answers'; often there is no obvious 'correct' answer at all. The skills that you are developing are the skills of analysis, interpretation and being able to argue a particular position regarding some aspects of the media. If, for example, we take the censorship debate (see pp. 207–10), it becomes clear very quickly that there is no one answer but that it is a matter of looking at various points of view, various pieces of evidence and opinion, and then coming to your own conclusion, which you can justify. Quite often you will end up raising more questions than you started out with, but often a sign of success is knowing what questions to ask. This means that studying the media can be both exciting and empowering for you as a student but also that at times it can be quite frustrating and difficult to grasp.

NOTEBOX

One of the keys to success for a Media Studies student is to develop a wide knowledge of the media 'out there'. Most of us have a few favourite radio stations, television channels, newspapers or magazines that we consume regularly. Most of us are reluctant to change or to try something different; rather we develop a routine or habit in our media consumption. However, as a media student you should take risks, try different types of newspapers, magazines, radio stations or television programmes. You might be pleasantly surprised and discover something new that you like and it will help you understand the range and variety of media products that are available to us all. Having a wide knowledge of media products will also help you to use your own examples instead of relying on those given to you in this book or by teachers. Independent thinking and the ability to transfer concepts and apply them to different examples is a characteristic of the successful Media Studies student.

Media Studies skills

Let us now look at the skills you will need to make you an effective and successful student of the media. In addition to such skills as note-taking, we will consider:

- how to look at media texts
- how to plan and get the best from your own media consumption
- using textbooks
- using the Internet
- getting information first hand.

The world is full of media texts waiting to be studied. For the student of media this provides easy access to a wide range of texts for consideration. For most people media texts exist simply as a source of information and entertainment. For the media student, however, they are also a source on which to base serious academic study. It is important, therefore, that you bear this in mind whenever you are considering a media text.

By the end of your course, it is very likely you will say: 'I can never look at a media product in quite the same way again.' So what is the fundamental shift that you need to undergo to change from being a media consumer to a media student? Well, the first step you have to take is to start thinking more deeply about the media you consume. When you go to a restaurant and eat a meal, you will likely think that it was good or it was bad: 'I enjoyed eating that' or 'That tasted awful'. A chef having an evening out eating the same meal may well have a similar response. However, because the chef understands the process of cooking and serving food, s/he will probably be thinking about the raw ingredients that were used, the cooking process, the way the food is presented and even how much profit the restaurant is making on the dish.

Similarly a media student should look beyond a superficial response to a media text in terms of pleasure and enjoyment, and be prepared to consider a broad range of issues and concepts relating not only to the text itself but also to its production and consumption. Media consumption becomes a much broader consideration of how different people consume a media product, how it is constructed, and the conditions under which it was produced.

The hard bit is to identify the difference between enjoying a media text and applying the skills you have learnt to look at the text in a more considered or academic way. In this chapter we hope to consider ways in which you might think about doing this.

General skills

Studying the media is an important skill that you, the would-be student, need to develop. Some academic disciplines define reasonably clearly how you should study. You may need to refer to books on the subject, or perhaps undertake practical or research work. In some cases it may even involve watching a video or a television programme. For the media student, however, watching television, going to the cinema, reading a magazine, or even looking at the billboard at the side of the road can all claim to be part of any study of the media.

Media Studies is an academic discipline with its own language and terminology and its own conceptual understanding. To be a good media student you need to develop a set of skills that will enable you not only to look at the media and its texts with a critical and discriminating eye, but also to grasp the principles of academic study that consider how media products are produced and consumed.

Many of the important skills you need to develop in order to study media will be very similar to the skills you need for other academic disciplines. A wide variety of self-help guides are available to help you develop these broader study skills. Some suggestions are given at the end of this chapter. Consequently our focus here will be on identifying some of the basic skills you need for media and other subjects.

Note-taking

The ability to make notes from a range of sources, such as lectures, class discussion and reference books, is a key skill for every student. Similarly, your ability to make sense of your notes from these sources over a period of time can mean the difference between success and failure.

The key to effective note-taking is to be conscientious and to stick to an organisational method that works. For many students, this means not only taking an initial set of notes, but also revisiting these notes while they are fresh and expanding or developing them in such a way that they will make sense later. Many students find that the most efficient method of doing this is to transfer handwritten notes on to a computer at the earliest opportunity. If no computer is available, then writing them up in long hand into a logical and clear format is the next best thing.

ACTIVITY . . .

Choose a topic you have covered recently, either in Media Studies or another subject. Now look through your notes and see how easy it is to retrieve information on the topic. What has the result told you about your level of organisation?

Organisation

Organisation is a skill closely linked to note-taking. The most accurate and detailed set of notes imaginable will be quite worthless if you cannot retrieve them for use when you want them.

Whatever system of storage you have, be it a computer or simple A4 binder, you need to develop a method of filing and organising your notes in such a way that you can confidently gain access to them whenever you need to refer to them. If you are able to store information on a computer hard disk, do not forget to make a back-up copy on a removable disk, especially if you are not the only person to use the computer.

The need for organisation, however, goes far beyond simply filing your notes for easy retrieval. Probably the single most effective way to improve your ability to study lies in organising your time, or 'time management' as it is often called. The simple act of drawing up a timetable or a daily action plan can help you optimise the use of your time. This can be especially important to a media student; time spent on recreational activities and time spent on study can sometimes become blurred. A visit to the cinema, for example, might well be considered a pleasurable social activity as well as a feature of your study of the media. It is up to you to try to make sure you get the best of both worlds.

Information retrieval

We live in an information-rich society. Indeed, many people see a new division within society between those who have access to information and those who do not. In general, students belong to the former category, especially when they have access to the Internet and possess the skills and knowledge necessary to retrieve information from it. However, the privilege of such access has its downside. So much information is now available through the average student's computer that it is very easy to suffer from an overload of information and data. It is important to learn how to be selective in gaining access to and retrieving information. Equally important is how to make the most effective use of the information you have obtained.

Later in the chapter we consider some of the more useful and reliable sources of information available to the media student, as well as offering some words of caution about the uses to which this information is put.

Despite some potential drawbacks, the Internet has become a real boon to students, allowing instant access to information twenty-four hours a day. For the student who has taken the trouble to learn how to use it effectively, it is a valuable short cut to rich sources of information. Compare this to the situation just a few years ago, when a student often had to wait several weeks for a library to transport a book across the country or even across the world.

Learning to discriminate

Now let us get back to some of those specific study skills that are so useful to the media student. There are a number of good habits you can develop that will help your study of the media. As you gain an understanding of some of the underlying principles of Media Studies, through using this book, for example, you will begin to realise that there are a number of key concepts that can be applied to media. For example, look at the three main areas into which this book is divided:

- Reading the media (or textual analysis)
- Media audiences
- Media institutions.

These three headings can be used to provide you with a framework for looking at any media text you encounter. For example, when you are considering a media text, you may want to ask yourself:

- How is it constructed?
- How is it consumed?
- Where was it created?

If you can get into the habit of applying these questions to media texts you encounter, you will be making an important step towards looking at them in a Media Studies context.

Second, it is important to ensure that you have some method of making a note of your responses to and thoughts about media texts that you find particularly interesting. Many media students find a diary or log in which they keep a note of these on a daily or weekly basis to be a useful method of keeping track of important aspects of their media consumption. Such information can be very useful later in your course when, for example, you may be looking for ideas for coursework or production, or perhaps some texts to illustrate an essay you are writing.

Third, it is a good idea to be thinking of ways you can preserve some of the key texts that you come across. You will probably want to keep copies of important texts that you can use as examples in essays, such as copies of television programmes, newspaper or magazine articles and radio programmes. You are also likely to come across quite a lot of material in the media about the media itself, such as a documentary about the

launch of a new magazine, a newspaper article about a new television programme, or a radio programme discussing the ethics of the press. All of these are potentially valuable sources of information and ideas that can be used in your media work. It is important, therefore, to keep a look-out for them and ensure that you either record them or save particular articles in a scrapbook.

NOTEBOX

> One important way in which you can make yourself a better media student is to select your own texts for use when you are illustrating a particular point in an essay or piece of coursework. Far too many students limit their examples to those discussed in class. Inevitably that leads to a whole class of students writing essays that are very similar to one another. If you can show you have understood a concept or principle by providing an example from a text that you have chosen, this is likely to be rewarded much more than the work of the student who has relied on the teacher's example. Indeed, if the example you choose is an appropriate contemporary text, you will have demonstrated clearly your own up-to-date engagement with a study of the media.

Planning ahead

It should now be clear just how important it is to plan your media consumption. Of course, there will be recurring texts you need to look at, for example the *Media Guardian* every Monday or a monthly film magazine such as *Empire*. Remember that these should be available in libraries, so you do not have the expense of buying them regularly and you can also look at back copies.

NOTEBOX

> Keeping up to date with key issues and debates in the media is an important aspect of your study and looking in such places as the media sections in the broadsheet newspapers is a particularly good way of doing this. A list of other recommended information sources is given at the end of this book.

Getting hold of a good listings magazine that has details of the week's television and radio programmes is an effective way of identifying useful programmes that are likely to help you with your study. Do not forget to look in some of the places you might not normally consider. Radio 3, Radio 4 and some of the local radio stations have quite a lot of speech-based output, some of which you may well find interesting, stimulating and probably quite accessible, once you have given it a try.

Some sources of information

Even though we live in an age of electronic information, books are still an important source for the media student. Indeed, many publishers believe that books are set to grow in importance and popularity as society is keen to have access to more and more information, encouraged by such innovations as the Internet.

For the media student, using a textbook is an important skill that needs to be developed. The first challenge is to find the right book. You will need to consider both the content of the book and the level at which it is pitched.

A lot of Media Studies books are aimed at students who are well ahead of A Level and are used to a much more sophisticated level of language and concepts than people at your stage of study. Unless you are prepared to spend hours wrestling with the ideas and looking up unfamiliar words, these books will not be very helpful. Also there is a wide range of media books across a variety of different media topics. Finding the best one for your needs is bound to be tricky. Here are some tips to help you select the right book at the right level.

- **Check the jacket or cover copy.** If you are browsing in a library or bookshop, read it to see if the book covers the topics you are looking for.
- **Check the contents page** to assess if it covers the right ground. You may also find information about the level the book is aimed at. Ideally you want a book that is geared to the needs of a reader looking for an introduction to the topic. You can check this further by reading half a page of the text inside the book to see how easy or difficult you find it.
- **Check the name of the writer(s).** This may also be a hint about the usefulness of the book. Is this a writer whose name you have heard mentioned in other books or in class, perhaps? You will find in the resources section at the end of this book some suggestions for further reading. Most of the authors mentioned in it have produced books that are accessible to students at your stage of study.

Once you have found the right book, the next step is to learn how to get the best from it. It is always a good idea to read the introduction to any textbook. This should tell you about the approach the writer is going to take and what s/he intends to cover.

It is unlikely that you will have the time to read a whole book, so you need to learn how to select the sections that are especially relevant for what you are doing. One device that may help here is the index. This will outline for you all the references to a particular topic. Where these are fairly detailed you will find they span several pages (for example, 68–73), so that is always a good place to start looking. Note also that most textbooks give a chapter summary at the beginning of every chapter, outlining what is covered. It is a good idea, therefore, to check each chapter in turn to see if it is likely to contain any relevant material. To help you with this, look at the section headings within each chapter as a way of navigating your way to the information you are looking for.

The next stage is to make some notes. Some students like to photocopy useful sections of books. If you do this, you need to check with your school or college that you are not infringing copyright laws. Whilst photocopying can be a useful tool, it is often much better to make some notes from the book you are using. The reason is that the process of transferring information in this way helps to reinforce your learning – not least because you need to read and understand the original before you can write down your own version, but also because it is important to learn the skill of summarising other people's ideas in your own words; taking notes will help you to perfect this skill. On a very few occasions you will want to lift direct quotations from a book. When you do so, do not forget to remind yourself they are direct quotes by putting them in inverted commas. In this way you will not forget to attribute the ideas to their original source.

NOTEBOX

Do not forget to write down all the publication details of a book you use. In the section on coursework we look at the important art of reference and writing a bibliography. Every time you use a book, make a note of:

- author
- title
- publisher
- date of publication
- ISBN (international standard book number).

It is also a good idea to make a note of the page numbers from which your notes have been taken. Don't forget, if you are using a reader or collection of essays by different people, you also need to note down the name of the individual contributor whose work you are using.

An important reason why you need to make a note of the source of your information is that when you come to use it in an essay or a piece of coursework you have to attribute it. That means that you should not try to claim that it is an original idea of your own but should acknowledge the source from which it comes. Otherwise you can be accused of plagiarism, which means taking and using other people's ideas without properly acknowledging them.

The Internet

The Internet is a great boon to all students, but for the media student it also offers some unique advantages as well as disadvantages. The chief advantage is the way it provides swift access to contemporary information. A problem with much of the information in a textbook is that it may become out of date. In a subject such as Media Studies, important issues like patterns of consumption or audience figures can change rapidly as new media products are launched and gain popularity. The Internet is an especially useful way of keeping up to date with important data. For example, a site such as <http://www.abc.org.uk> offers details of up-to-date circulation figures for a wide range of magazines.

Similarly, most of the bodies who are responsible for the regulation of the media industries (the Press Complaints Commission, or Ofcom, for example) all have useful websites. Not only do these offer background information about codes of practice and complaints procedures, but they also provide details of recent cases on which they have adjudicated. Certainly it is worthwhile bookmarking these sites, the addresses of which are given in the resources section (p. 340).

(p. 340)

NOTEBOX . . .

If you are using a computer that does not belong to you, make sure you have a plentiful supply of disks to store information. It is a good idea to reserve one disk for keeping a list of bookmarked sites that you have found especially useful. If you download information to a disk for future reference, keep a detailed note of the contents of that disk on the label so you can find it again without having to search through each of your disks in turn.

Just as you will find that the many textbooks available to you are pitched at a range of different levels, so it is with Internet sites. Many sites that deal with media-related issues are aimed at a general audience. This is especially true of many of the cinema-related sites, such as the Internet Movie Database (<http://www.imdb.com>). Other sites are directed towards students with quite a sophisticated level of understanding. Just as you will have found it necessary to dip into a textbook to find if it is useful or not, so it is with a website.

Before you do this, however, it is a good idea to learn how to use a search engine to the best effect. Search engines, for example Yahoo or Lycos, are the means by which you can enter keywords to identify what you are looking for and they will list all of the sites on the Internet that seem relevant to your search. Often this can number several thousand, so it will pay you to do some initial research into how to get the best from the search engine you have chosen to use. Click on the help icon on the home page of the search engine and it will tell you how you can use such devices as inverted commas and plus and minus signs to limit your search. It is really worthwhile getting familiar with these devices if you are going to make searches that produce a manageable amount of information for you to follow up.

One difficulty that the Internet is likely to present to you is probably also its chief attraction. Using hypertext links allows you to move quickly from one site to another in search of related information. Simply clicking on the link will transfer you immediately to a related site. The danger is that, unless you adopt a very disciplined approach to your use of the Net, you can end up skipping from site to site until you lose all sense of what it was you were originally seeking. Fortunately the back button on your browser will allow you to retrace your steps, or alternatively you can pull down the history menu and find your way back to a relevant site that way. You will get the best from your session exploring the Internet if you can avoid getting sidetracked and

Advanced Search   Preferences   Language Tools   Search Tips

Media + effects   Google Search

Search: ● the web ○ pages from the UK

Web | Images | Groups | Directory | News

Searched the web for **Media + effects**.   Results **1 - 10** of about **4,140,000**. Search took **0.23** seconds.

www.theory.org.uk -- the **media** theory site
January 2004: Web.Studies published this month / ArtLab features new material
Six new Trading Cards / **Media**, Gender & Identity site updated. ...
Description: Covers **media** studies and gender studies, with content on queer theory, gender, Foucault, Judith Butler,...
Category: Society > People > Women > Women's Studies
www.theory.org.uk/ - 6k - Cached - Similar pages

www.theory.org.uk Resources: **Media Effects**
... The whole problem with the **media effects** research is that it takes place in that
depressing corner of 'communications' research which places more value on a ...
www.theory.org.uk/ctr-eff.htm - 8k - Cached - Similar pages
[More results from www.theory.org.uk]

PSU's **Media Effects** Research Laboratory
Description: Dedicated to conducting empirical research on the psychological **effects** of **media** content, form, and...
Category: Reference > Education > ... > Penn State University > Research
www.psu.edu/dept/medialab/ - 1k - Cached - Similar pages

mass **media effects**: introduction
Mass **media**: effects research. Mass **media effects**: introduction. This ... Mass
media: effects research. Hypodermic needle: overview. Sometimes ...
www.cultsock.ndirect.co.uk/MUHome/ cshtml/media/effects.html - 22k - Cached - Similar pages

mass **media effects**: glossary
... As a result mainly of experiments by Feshbach and Singer, this idea has been developed
in **media effects** research. ... Introduction to Mass **Media Effects**. BACK,
www.cultsock.ndirect.co.uk/MUHome/ cshtml/media/efterms.html - 56k - Cached - Similar pages
[More results from www.cultsock.ndirect.co.uk]

Preteenagers Today: **Media Effects** on Children: Television
Media Effects on Children: Television. by Sam Greenspan. Bruce Spolansky had
tickets to see a taping of "The Jerry Springer Show" May 26, 1999. ...
preteenagerstoday.com/resources/articles/tv.htm - 26k - Cached - Similar pages

Mediacan: **Media Effects**
mediacan.ca > Links > **Media Effects**, Site Map. Theories ... Diffusion. Television;
Theories. Search only in **Media Effects** Search entire site.
klaatu.pc.athabascau.ca/cgi-bin/b7/main.pl?rid=222 - 9k - Cached - Similar pages

YMA - Readings & research - **Media effects** - general
Readings & research **Media effects** - general. ... Wartella, Ellen (2002)
New directions in **media** research and **media effects** on children. ...
www.youngmedia.org.au/mediachildren/ 10_01_bib_general.htm - 25k - Cached - Similar pages

An initial study of computer-based **media effects** on learners who ...
... communication technologies. Dyslexia; computer based **media effects**
on learners who have dyslexia. **MEDIA** Project. Techdis Home Page. ...
www.techdis.ac.uk/resources/beacham01.html - 7k - Cached - Similar pages

Claes de Vreese - Home (Research : **media effects**, news, public ...
A key resource for teaching and research on public opinion, **media effects**, campaigns,
media and politics. www.claesdevreese.com, Home, ...
Description: Resource for teaching and research on political communication, public opinion, **media effects**, campaigns,...
Category: Science > Social Sciences > Communication
www.claesdevreese.com/ - 8k - Cached - Similar pages

Goooooooooogle ▶

Result Page: **1** 2 3 4 5 6 7 8 9 10   **Next**

keep to a focused exploration of the topic you are concerned with. One way to do this is to set yourself a time limit; staring at a computer screen in a tired frame of mind is not conducive to getting the best from the Internet.

Finally, remember that, although the Internet is about freedom of speech and ideas, it is still necessary to acknowledge any information you intend to use in your own work. So remember to make a note of all the details, including the URL or address, just as you would when using a textbook.

NOTEBOX . . .

Warning: As well as information that you are likely to find useful, there is also an awful lot of irrelevant material on the Internet. One thing you must learn quickly is how to discriminate. In many cases it is only experience that can teach you this, so you must learn to be cautious in the early stages and keep an open mind about the value of the information a site is offering. One useful test is to ask yourself if you have come across this information source elsewhere. Another is to consider how long the site has been in existence. A site such as those of the BBC or *The Times* would clearly have credibility on both counts and could be considered a source of reliable information. If you are not sure, it is probably a good idea to start looking at some of the sites indicated in the resources section (p. 340).

ACTIVITY . . .

A contact from overseas is doing some research into British media and the bodies that regulate them. Find three website addresses for regulatory bodies that might be useful.

Other sources of information

There are a number of other ways in which information can be obtained by the Media Studies student. These tend to involve primary sources of information, which means getting information first hand, direct from someone who knows. In the section on research skills you will see how important information obtained from interviewing people can be, for example to find out about audience consumption.

Figure i.5 *(left) Google search on 'media effects'. Source: © Google Inc., Mountain View, California.*

Another useful way of finding information is going on a visit, say, to a media organisation such as a local newspaper, or a museum that exhibits media issues, or going to hear someone speak at a conference or workshop. Similarly your teacher may arrange for someone with a media interest to visit your class. Make sure that you prepare for such an event by making a list of some pertinent questions that you would like to ask. Make sure also that you get down some detailed notes, including, for example, any useful information on follow-up opportunities.

Another way of obtaining primary information is to approach an organisation or individual directly for help. This is especially relevant when you are undertaking coursework and need some special information about an organisation or its products. Before you get in touch, think carefully about what you are doing:

1   Make sure that the information you want is not readily available elsewhere, in a magazine or on the Web for example.
2   Be very specific about what you want to know. Letters that begin 'I am doing a Media Studies project on advertising' rarely produce anything more than a very general response, if any response at all. Remember that some information is likely to be commercially sensitive, so a firm may not want it to fall into the hands of a competitor.
3   Address your request to the right department or individual; the Press or Public Relations Office is always a good place to start.
4   Do not waste people's time. Media organisations are nearly always busy, so only ask for information if it is essential and there is no other way to find it. Be specific about what you want and why you want it.
5   Consider enclosing a stamped addressed envelope so that it is easy to reply.

CONCLUSION

Studying the media is a popular and enjoyable pastime. Like any other course of advanced study, it is also hard work for the student who wants to do a good job. The important issue is to make sure that you get the balance right between your own enjoyment of media texts and the task of serious study you need to undertake to ensure you succeed in the course you are taking. If you can manage to do this, then you will find Media Studies an enriching experience that will not only make your own media consumption more informed and enjoyable, but will also provide a useful skill that you can share with your family and friends.

FURTHER READING

Barrass, R. (1984) *Study!*, E & F.N. Spon.

Chambers, E. and Northedge, A. (1997) *The Arts Good Study Guide*, Open University Press.

Drew, S. and Bingham, R. (1997) *The Student Skills Guide*, Gower.

Fry, R. (1999) *The Great Big Book of How to Study*, Career Press.

Stokes, J. (2003) *How to Do Media and Cultural Studies*, Sage.

▼ IMAGE ANALYSIS

In this section we will:

- explore the use of semiotics in analysing media texts
- consider the history of semiotics and its significance as a critical tool in the understanding of how texts create 'meaning'
- look at different kinds of sign, the way we read codes and the concepts of connotation, denotation and anchorage
- identify some of the limitations of semiotics as a critical tool for textual analysis.

WHAT IS A MEDIA 'TEXT'?

As mentioned on p. 3, we usually associate the word 'text' with something that is printed or written. In Media Studies, however, the word 'text' is used to describe any media product such as television programmes, photographs, films either on video or in the cinema, newspaper articles, radio programmes, advertisements, video games or web pages.

'Texts' are, therefore, the main point of our study in understanding how media languages create meaning. One of the keys to understanding the meanings in texts is the use of codes.

CODES Rules or conventions by which signs are put together to create meaning.

KEY TERM

The English language itself is a set of codes: letters made up into words, words made up into sentences and sentences made up into paragraphs. Just as we learn to read the letters, words and sentences, so, too, we learn to 'read' media codes and languages.

We learn that sounds or images can be put together in particular sequences, working as codes to give particular meanings.

Just as there is a great variety in the forms and style of media texts, so the codes used to construct meanings are varied and frequently depend upon the form of the media text. In most cases the text will use a variety of codes – visual, audio and written – that 'fit' together in a certain way to create a particular meaning.

Look at the Tribe advertisement (Figure 1.1). We see that this is a text that is print-based but contains visual and written codes. Its exact meaning may be quite difficult to 'fix' except to say that it is an advertisement and is trying to 'sell' a product, a particular brand of cologne. In this advertisement additional meaning is given through the use of colour codes and the written text at the bottom of the advert.

Some adverts do not even seem to be trying to sell a specific product but are, presumably, just trying to make us aware of a particular company or name, for example the United Colors of Benetton campaign (see p. 277).

Most of us living in Western society at the beginning of the twenty-first century are sophisticated media consumers and will be able to 'read' the Tribe advertisement fairly quickly. We would probably normally only glance at it as we skim through a magazine. However, as media students, we now have to distance ourselves from our daily and often unreflective consumption of media texts like the Tribe illustration. Our task is to break down or 'deconstruct' the illustration into its component parts and fully to 'reveal' and understand how the advertisers have used the various signs and codes in their attempt to create a particular meaning or set of meanings.

One of the key theoretical tools to assist us in this process of deconstruction is semiology, or, as it is often called, semiotics.

SEMIOTICS

The word 'semiology' is derived from the Greek word *semeion*, which means sign. Semiology is an attempt to create a science of the study of sign systems and their role in the construction and reconstruction of meaning in media texts. Semiology concentrates primarily on the text itself and the signs and codes that are contained within it.

NOTEBOX

One of the most influential theorists of the way visual images transmit meanings was Roland Barthes (1913–80). Barthes was influenced by the structuralist work of the Swiss linguist Ferdinand de Saussure (1857–1913), who first promoted the idea of semiology in his book *Course in General Linguistics* (1983 [1916]).

Saussure saw language as a cultural creation rather than something innate, and as a social system that was ordered, coherent and governed by sets of rules. The

continued

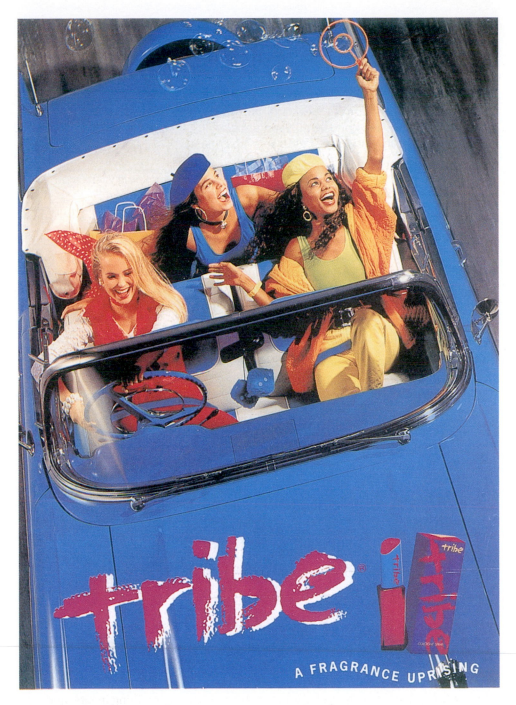

Figure 1.1 *Tribe perfume advertisement. An advertisement is usually a mixture of visual and written codes. Source: Caroline Rieger, agency for Tribe Perfume.*

American Charles Peirce (1839–1914) took Saussure's ideas and expanded them to include not just language but other 'social constructs' in society such as the way society itself is ordered, labelled and governed by sets of rules. Peirce introduced the term 'semiotics'.

Roland Barthes took these ideas still further and in *Mythologies* (1993 [1957]) applied them to areas of daily life and popular culture such as the face of the actress Greta Garbo and soap detergents advertising.

KEY TERM

STRUCTURALISM This approach argues that identifying underlying structures is all-important in undertaking analysis. In linguistics, for example, it can be argued that all languages have a similar underlying grammatical structure, which we are born with the capacity to learn. Similarly, certain social structures, such as the family unit, may be common to many cultures.

For students of the media, semiotic analysis is a useful tool in the deconstruction of texts as it helps to reveal the underlying meanings that are 'suspended' within a text. You can then take this analysis further and consider the ideologies that underpin texts and their construction.

It is important to be aware that most sign systems, like the Tribe advertisement, do not necessarily have one particular 'fixed' meaning. Part of the meaning of the sign is dependent upon the social and cultural background of the 'reader' of the particular sign system.

As part of the process of semiotic analysis we, the audience, are called 'readers' because this helps to suggest a greater degree of creativity and involvement in the construction of the text's meaning. 'Reading' is something we learn to do and is influenced to a large extent by our social and cultural background. As the reader of a text, we are likely to bring something of our own cultural and personal experiences to a text.

ACTIVITY . . .

Choose an advertisement from a magazine and show it to a range of different people. These should include people of different gender, age, ethnic and social background. Ask them what they think the text 'means'. How might you account for the different readings that you are offered by each reader?

SIGNS

The Tribe advertisement is a sign. It consists of a signifier, the printed magazine advert itself, and something that is signified, the 'idea' or 'meaning' behind the set of images used in the advertisement.

Fiske and Hartley in *Reading Television* (1978) describe the sign as being made up of two components: the signifier and the signified

signifier + signified = sign

The signifier is a physical object, for example a sound, printed word, advertisement. The signified is a mental concept or meaning conveyed by the signifier.

Peirce differentiated between three different types of signs: symbolic (or arbitrary); iconic; indexical. Symbolic signs have no obvious connection between the sign and the object. For example, the word CAT has no obvious link with a small furry animal usually domesticated as a pet. It only works because we understand the rules that say the letters C-A-T, when put into a certain order, mean or 'signify' that small furry animal. If it was a different 'we', for example a group of French speakers, then the 'rules' would be different and we would use the letters C-H-A-T to signify that small furry animal.

SYMBOL A sign that represents an object or concept solely by the agreement of the people who use it.

KEY TERM

These types of signs Peirce also called 'arbitrary' as their 'meaning' is the result of agreement amongst their users. These types of signs do not have any direct or intrinsic connection with what is being 'signified'. This means that some arbitrary signs can have several meanings that are 'contested', or about which people might not agree. The Union Jack has a variety of meanings depending upon who is using it – the British monarchy at a national ceremony, the Unionists in Ulster, the mods in films like *Quadrophenia* (1979), or a group of football supporters.

The symbol Ⓐ referring to anarchy will have different meanings for different groups of people. Think of other signs that may be arbitrary and then list all the different groups of people and the different readings that they may apply to these signs.

Iconic signs are like the religious paintings, statues, and stained-glass windows found in churches. Photographs are a good example of an iconic sign. They have a physical similarity to the objects that they 'signify'. We are familiar with iconic signs in our everyday lives, for example the use of a wheelchair to signify facilities for disabled people. Wherever we are in the world, we can usually find the men's and women's toilets by looking for the iconic signs on the doors.

Indexical signs are the signs that have some kind of direct connection with what is being 'signified'. Smoke is often used as an indexical sign for fire, and a tear running down someone's cheek can be an indexical sign for sorrow.

NOTEBOX

So why is it useful to know about these signs in order to study media texts? Let us look at some of the reasons here. Media texts are usually complex messages. Most texts are composed using all of the types of sign that we have indicated. Printed words and a spoken commentary both employ arbitrary signs to communicate with an audience. Photographs in magazines or moving images in film or on television are iconic signs, which work because of their similarity to the thing they represent. We may also see or hear indexical signs; someone sweating profusely may be an index of either extreme temperature or high levels of stress. Similarly, tears or the sounds of sobbing provide an index of grief.

An audience consuming the media by watching television, for example, is creating meaning from a complex system of signs that they have become used to 'reading'. By understanding the nature of signs and how they work, we can gain some insight into the process by which media messages are interpreted.

As you may have realised, iconic signs are especially significant in our study of the visual image, in photography, film and television. It is because iconic signs so closely relate to the object they represent that they seem so natural. In the process it is easy to forget that we are looking at a sign and confuse the sign with reality itself. As we will see in later sections, this has important implications for the way in which we read the representation of reality in the media.

John Fiske in *Introduction to Communication Studies* (1990) uses the example of a road sign (Figure 1.2) to illustrate how a seemingly simple familiar sign is in fact composed of all three of these different types of sign.

Fiske suggests that this road sign is symbolic because it is in the shape of a triangle, which, according to the *Highway Code*, indicates a 'warning'. The cross in the middle is iconic in that its shape is determined by the shape of the object that it signifies, a crossroads, and the road sign is also indexical because it is related to the physical presence of the actual crossroads further along the road.

Media texts can have several possible meanings depending upon the way in which the signs are read and the background of the individual 'reader'. This means that signs are polysemic, or are open to many interpretations. Sometimes, however, a particular or preferred meaning is indicated by the way in which the text has been produced and presented to the reader.

Figure 1.2
The road sign for crossroads combines three different types of sign. Source: Department of Transport.

The photograph used in the Dolce & Gabbana advertisement (Figure 1.3) could have many different readings and can be considered, therefore, to be polysemic. We are directed, however, towards a particular or preferred reading by the inclusion of the name of a well-known fashion company and the fact that this text would probably have appeared in lifestyle magazines such as *Company*, *FHM* or *Elle*.

It is the name Dolce & Gabbana that provides the anchorage for this text, in the same way that the wording at the bottom of the Tribe advertisement, along with the picture of the product itself, directs us towards its preferred reading.

ANCHORAGE The fixing or limiting of a particular set of meanings to an image. One of the most common forms of anchorage is the caption underneath a photograph.

KEY TERM

ACTIVITY . . .

Without the wording the Dolce & Gabbana photograph could be very ambiguous and difficult to put into context. Try putting different captions to the photograph to illustrate some of its possible meanings and suggest where else the photograph might appear.

CODES

Signs often work through a series of codes that are, like signs, usually socially constructed and, therefore, agreed upon by society as a whole. There are many different types of code at work in media texts; some of the most common are: dress codes, colour codes, non-verbal codes, technical codes.

Dress codes relate to what people wear in particular situations. If we see people in evening dress we usually make the association of glamour, wealth or sophistication.

Figure 1.3 *Dolce & Gabbana advertisement. What is your reading of this image? Once you have decided, try the activity on p. 33. Source: Dolce & Gabbana.*

Sometimes these dress codes are deliberately flouted, for example in the title sequence to *Blind Date* where a couple are seen in swimming costumes in the middle of a busy city street.

Colour codes in particular vary within different cultures. Black, for instance, is usually the colour of mourning in most Western countries, but in some Asian countries mourners will often dress in white. Red is a particularly strong colour in terms of what it signifies: depending upon the context it can mean danger, stop (as in traffic lights) or socialism. It can also mean excitement and glamour if it is included in a fashion picture of a woman, perhaps with red glossy lipstick, painted fingernails or a red dress. Part of the way in which the Tribe advertisement works is through its use of bright colours such as red, pink and blue.

Non-verbal codes are to do with gesture and body language, and again these vary from culture to culture. In some countries it is normal to shake hands every time you meet someone, whereas in other societies you may kiss on the cheeks each time you meet. In some Muslim countries on the other hand such open gestures of intimacy between couples would be frowned upon.

In a media text such as the Tribe advertisement, non-verbal codes would include facial expressions, different postures or gestures, and proxemics (the way in which the people appear close together or keep their distance).

Technical codes relate to the way in which particular texts are reproduced and the media used. This may be a photograph or a film (such as *Schindler's List*) that is shot almost entirely in black and white to convey an idea of documentary 'realism'. It may be the use of a close-up in a film or television programme to convey a character's strong emotions. (See section on production skills (p. 321) for further discussion.)

NOTEBOX . . .

Andrew Crisell in *Understanding Radio* (1994) identifies silence as an important code used in radio texts alongside more obvious codes such as words, sounds and music.

ACTIVITY . . .

Look at the Tribe advertisement again (Figure 1.1, p. 29).

- How important are the dress codes in this advertisement?
- Why does the advertisement use bright colours such as red, pink and blue?
- In what ways do you think the body language and facial expressions (the non-verbal codes) are important here?

As particular media have their own sets of codes and sign systems, we can see that the Tribe illustration 'works' in the context of a fashion magazine. It is read by (predominantly) women readers who are familiar with the signs and conventions of this type of illustration. The advertisement would work less well in a newspaper like the *Big Issue* because its 'glossy' image would not work on the recycled newsprint the *Big Issue* uses and readers would possibly not respond to the advert in the way that the advertisers planned.

Part of the 'meaning' generated by the Tribe advertisement is dependent upon (a) where it is placed and (b) who 'reads' it.

DENOTATION AND CONNOTATION

According to Roland Barthes we, the 'reader', go through various stages when we deconstruct the meaning of a sign.

The first stage he called denotation, which refers to what is actually reproduced in the text. In the case of the Tribe advertisement, the denotation consists of three young women in a car, brightly dressed, smiling and laughing, surrounded by shopping bags and with one of the women holding up a bubble blower. We may be tempted to say that the car is on a road but we cannot confirm this as, in denotational terms, we cannot see the road, we only *assume* that it is there.

KEY TERM

DENOTATION What an image actually shows and what is immediately apparent, rather than the assumptions an individual reader may make about it.

We may say that the women are fashionably dressed and are wearing jewellery and make-up. We should also notice that at the bottom of the page is the slogan 'a fragrance uprising' written in a wavy line and a picture of the product and its packaging.

The next stage that Barthes identified, connotation, is where we, the 'reader', add our own pieces of information. We fill in what is missing from the denotation stage and attempt to identify what the sign is signifying. In the case of the Tribe advert this will probably mean that we 'add' the information that this is an illustration of three fashionable, attractive, happy-go-lucky young women, who are having fun, have been shopping, and who presumably use Tribe cologne.

KEY TERM

CONNOTATION The meaning of a sign that is arrived at through the cultural experiences a reader brings to it.

We should be able to identify the various codes that are at work in this sign, particularly those to do with the clothes that the three young women are wearing, the use of primary colours in the advertisement and the body language of the three women.

ACTIVITY . . .

Look at the woman using a bubble-blower in the Tribe advertisement. Carry out a small-scale piece of research by asking various people what connotations they associate with this image.

■ Do their responses vary? If so, why?
■ Why do you think the advertisers have included this image?
■ Can you think of other ways in which the same meaning could have been created?

We may wish to add other connotations that say that the three young women seem to be reasonably affluent, that they are not working but appear to have the time to enjoy themselves. They have the money required to go shopping and drive the type of car illustrated in the advertisement. The car itself looks like an American-style convertible.

NOTEBOX . . .

The idea of alternative ways of presenting an image is also important in the analysis of moving images. For example, a director may choose to shoot someone's face in close-up. All the other possible sizes of shot, for example mid-shot or long shot, have been rejected in favour of the close-up. It can be argued that at some level we are aware of all the shots that have been rejected in order to include the one that has been selected.

There may be different connotations that other 'readers' add. It is sometimes helpful to ask what has been excluded from the image or how it might have been presented differently.

For instance, why is the car set in a kind of limbo that seems very unrealistic? Would the advertisement work better if the car were situated in a local high street? Would other models of cars work as well? A four-wheel 'off-roader'? A 'people-carrier'? Or a small hatchback like the Renault Clio or Ford Fiesta?

We also need to consider the connotations associated with the written slogan. We need to look at the words 'a fragrance uprising' and the typeface that is used. We may identify

connotations that suggest carefree, happy-go-lucky, revolutionary, stylish, sophisticated, expensive, fashionable and possibly desirable.

We have, through our reading of the connotation of the Tribe advertisement, added 'extra' layers of meaning beyond that denoted by the images themselves.

ACTIVITY . . .

Collect a selection of advertisements from various magazines and then, using the worksheet on p. 40, describe what you can see in terms of the denotative content of the advertisements. Remember that denotation only means what is there and you must be very disciplined in not adding information or assuming more than is shown. This can be quite a difficult exercise as most of us have learnt to become very sophisticated in reading in the additional information that advertisers intend us to supply ourselves.

One way of noting everything that is contained in the illustrations is to cover each advertisement and slowly reveal it bit by bit. This will help you to identify some of the smaller details that are often overlooked when we glance or skim through printed material.

Using the same set of advertisements, now describe what the connotations are. Again try to look at all the aspects of the illustrations and try to say why the advertisers put them in.

Compare your interpretation of the same advertisement with a colleague's. This can be a useful means of illustrating how meaning is not 'fixed' but is partly dependent upon the individual reading.

THE PROCESS MODEL OF COMMUNICATION

Semiotics, with its emphasis on the text and its codes and signs, can be seen as a move away from earlier analyses that saw the media as a 'process' model of communication. The model suggested that the medium used was perhaps more important than the message itself (see Part 2, on media audiences, p. 107).

(see Part 2, on media audiences, p. 107)

KEY TERM

PROCESS MODEL This model considered the audience's interaction with the media as part of a linear process – SENDER–CHANNEL–MESSAGE–RECEIVER – in which the meaning of a text was thought to be 'fixed' by the producer.

In the Tribe example, the sender is the producer of the advertisement, in other words is the agency that created it on behalf of the perfume manufacturer. The channel is that of magazine advertising. Other channels such as television and billboard advertising are also likely to have been used. The message is basically 'buy this perfume and you will be like these people'. The receiver is the reader of the magazine. The process model assumes that the message created by the sender and the message received are likely to be the same. The meaning of the message is thought to be set by the producer.

You may like to compare this idea with some of the theories about media effects (p. 145) in Part 2, on media audiences.

You can see that semiotics offers a much more sophisticated view of how media texts communicate meaning and are interpreted by audiences. However, just as the process model has been criticised for being too simplistic, so the semiotic approach has itself been criticised.

CRITICISMS OF SEMIOTICS

Critics have suggested that semiotics is not really a 'science' in the way that Barthes claimed, and that because all signs can have different meanings depending upon the individual reader's interpretation there is some difficulty in judging which interpretations are the most 'valid'.

Another weakness of semiotics is that it can sometimes be difficult to measure the effect or influence of the audience or reader in creating signs. For instance, the flowers left outside the various royal palaces after the death of Diana, Princess of Wales, could be seen as 'signifying' national mourning – but only after the event had started and had become widely publicised in the media. This seemed to create a snowball effect, whereby many people decided to join in. In this case it is difficult to say whether this 'signification' originated with people expressing their sorrow or through media manipulation of that sorrow.

Critics have also suggested that the denotation stage is not very useful because it is so artificial and all readers automatically 'add' connotations.

ACTIVITY...

Consider some of these criticisms and suggest ways in which they may be answered. Suggest reasons why you think semiotics may be a useful tool for analysing media texts.

WORKSHEET FOR ANALYSING ADVERTISEMENTS

Use the worksheet below to help you with the analysis of an advertisement of
your own choice. Consider each of the following aspects:

Portrayal of people in the advertisement:

- How old are they?
- What gender are they?
- What racial group do they come from?
- Which social classes are represented? How do you know?
- What do the clothing codes tell you?
- What are their facial expressions? Why?
- What is their posture? Why?
- What roles and stereotypes are being represented?
- How would you describe the relationship between the people?
- What other people could have been included? Why have they been excluded?

Technical codes:

- Is the illustration in colour or black and white? Why?
- How have the images been framed and cropped?
- Are all the elements of the image in focus? If not, why?
- Has anything been left out of the illustration? Why?
- How has it been lit and what is the camera angle? Are these important?

Text included in the advertisement:

- How does the slogan relate to the images?
- What other information are we given to help explain the images?
- Who is being addressed?
- What typeface has been used? Why?

Objects that are included:

- Where is the advert set? How do we know?
- What objects are included in the advert? Why?
- Does the product appear in the advert? If not, why not?
- What else could have been included but has not been? Why?
- What do the background colours and textures signify?
- What colour codes are at work?

The function of the advertisement as a whole:

- What kind of advertisement is this? Does it refer to any other advertisements or media texts?
- What is the narrative and how do we make sense of it?
- Who are we supposed to identify with?
- What is being promised by this advertisement?
- What are the values that underpin it?
- Who is in control in this image and where does the power come from?

The audience for the advertisement:

- Who is the advertisement aimed at? How do we know?
- Is any prior knowledge required to understand the advertisement? If yes, what?
- In what publications might the advertisement appear? Why?
- Whereabouts in the publication might the advertisement appear?
- Is the advertisement part of a larger campaign? If so, what are the other components of the campaign?

▼ NARRATIVE

In this section we:

- consider the significance of narrative in both fiction and non-fiction texts
- look at narrative construction and mode of address
- examine the relationship between narrative and genre.

NARRATIVE CONSTRUCTION

From our earliest days narrative is an important part of our lives. For many people, their earliest recollections relate to bedtime stories or stories told by their teacher in primary school. Another reason why narrative is so important to us is that it acts as an organising principle that helps us make sense of the world. To a child the world is a mass of unconnected and incomprehensible events, some pleasurable, some frightening, none of which makes a great deal of sense. Narrative, or storytelling, performs the important function of interpreting the world and shaping it into a comprehensible and comfortable form that allows us to see the forces of light and dark, and good and evil, battle against each other. Usually we are rewarded with the comforting outcome of the triumph of good and the reassurance of an equilibrium in which all will live 'happily ever after'.

KEY TERM

NARRATIVE The way in which a story is told in both fictional and non-fictional media texts.

As we grow up, narrative remains an important source of reassurance in a hostile universe, in much the same way as it did when we were children. Indeed, satisfying our need for narrative can in itself become associated with reward or punishment. Bad behaviour at school or at home may be punished with the denial of an end-of-day or bedtime story. Good behaviour on the other hand is rewarded with a narrative.

Narrative, therefore, plays an important role in our growing up and consequently in forming our social values.

Indeed so commonplace and natural does story-telling appear that it may seem invisible to study. Yet story-telling is a complex process with important implications.

(Tilley 1991)

ACTIVITY . . .

Watch on television a children's programme that involves some element of storytelling. Paying particular attention to the narrative, consider how conflict within the narrative is developed. What devices are used to indicate to the audience where their sympathies are expected to lie between the characters?

Clearly narrative is a powerful force not only to help us make sense of our world, but also with the potential to influence our behaviour. Similarly, for the media producers, narrative is an important tool for organising seemingly random and incoherent events into a coherent and logical form that an audience can assimilate. Consider, for example, a news story that has occurred in some remote part of the world. It may be a disaster, such as an earthquake or a famine, that has damaged the lives of many thousands of people in a terrifying way. A journalist writing a newspaper story has to explain what has happened in a few hundred words and, perhaps, a couple of photographs. Often the journalist will do this by focusing on specific detail about the impact of the disaster on the lives of individual people or families. In this way the audience has a clear point of reference with which to make a comparison with themselves or their own families. The scale of the disaster, too vast to comprehend, is understood in terms of the individual human being, with whom we, the audience, can empathise.

NOTEBOX . . .

Narrative can be used as a potent means of influencing the responses of an audience to a particular event. This is often determined by the way in which the information is presented. Certainly when we are being told about a conflict, in a western or gangster movie for example, the narrative often unfolds in such a way as to make us 'take sides' in support of one party or the other. The narrative can thus be used to position an audience in such a way as to limit the range of readings available to them from the text.

It is important to note that although the term 'narrative' is associated, through its literary origins, with fictional texts such as films and novels, it also plays an important part in non-fiction texts such as newspaper stories. Consider how the news photograph (Figure 1.4) exploits the moment of conflict between the police and the protesters to achieve its effect.

So we have seen that narrative is a means by which media producers shape and control the flow of information to an audience. At a basic level, narrative can be seen as the sequencing of information about events into a logical and cohesive structure in time and space. Indeed, it has been argued that the underlying structure of all narratives is basically the same, with variation only taking place in terms of character and setting. The Bulgarian theorist Tzvetan Todorov reduced the concept of narrative to a simple recurring formula:

equilibrium → disequilibrium → new equilibrium

A narrative starts with a state of equilibrium or harmony, for example a peaceful community getting on with and enjoying life. A firm sense of social order is established. Into this world of stability comes a force of disequilibrium or disruption, an evil outsider, intent on destroying the sense of well-being. By some mechanism such as the intervention of another outside agency, such as a lone gunfighter, the force of evil is overcome and order and harmony, in the form of a new equilibrium, are restored.

Figure 1.4 *Protesters and police in Prague at the International Monetary Fund (IMF) meeting, 2000. A photograph can be read as a frozen moment in an ongoing narrative. What do you think were the events leading up to the moment in this photograph? What do you think happened afterwards? Photo: Jorge Ordonez.*

Figure 1.5 The Evil Dead II *(1987). The horror movie is another example of a film genre in which external forces disturb the equilibrium of a community. Source: British Film Institute © Rosebud/Renaissance.*

Clearly you will see the plot of many Hollywood movie genres, for example western, sci-fi or even musical, fitting into this structure. Less obviously, the plot of the television news follows a similar pattern. The opening shot (see Figure 1.6) introduces us to the harmony of the studio as the news programme opens. The tragic events of the world news, reports of wars, famines, social unrest and political intrigue, invade our living space and disrupt the harmony. Finally we are offered a light and comic story to provide relief from this narrative of world disorder and disaster before we are returned to the newsreader shuffling papers and calmly saying good night. The equilibrium of the familiar world – our living room – is re-established, disrupted only briefly by the tragic events of the world at large. Similarly, in a programme such as *Crimewatch*, despite depicting the nightmare deeds of the criminal community, the narrative closes in the security of the studio with a familiar and friendly presenter reassuring us that we are unlikely to become victims ourselves. We may have experienced the dangers of the world, but are told that we can still sleep soundly in our beds.

In their book *Film Art: An Introduction* (1979), Bordwell and Thompson offer a technique for looking at film narrative in segments or sequences. These are called scenes, or distinct phases of the action occurring within relatively unified space and time. The segmentation allows us to see major divisions within the plot and how scenes are organised within them. This is a useful device that can be applied to a number of

Figure 1.6 *Trevor McDonald, a familiar figure on ITV News, opens the narrative of the news bulletin. Source: Sy Vin for ITV.*

different narratives in order to reveal the way in which they are constructed. Few films or broadcast texts are likely to break down into the complex narrative structure of *Citizen Kane*, however (see Figure 1.7).

As you can see, this film relies heavily on flashback as an organising principle for the narrative. Instead of presenting a chronological life of Kane, common in biopics, the structure employs elements of the detective story as each flashback signals a different phase in the investigation of Kane's life and the meaning of his dying word, 'Rosebud'.

ACTIVITY...

Using Figure 1.7 as a guide, produce your own narrative segmentation of a film or fictional television programme you have watched recently. A comedy film or situation comedy might make an interesting example. What have you learnt about the structure of the text from breaking it down into segments?

This activity should help you to understand that even seemingly simple and straightforward programmes often reveal quite complex narrative structures. It also

CITIZEN KANE: PLOT SEGMENTATION

C. **Credit title**
1. **Xanadu: Kane dies**
2. **Projection room:**
       a. "News on the March"
       b. Reporters discuss "Rosebud"
3. **El Rancho nightclub: Thompson tries to interview Susan**
4. **Thatcher library:**
       a. Thompson enters and reads Thatcher's manuscript
       b. Kane's mother sends the boy off with Thatcher
  First   c. Kane grows up and buys the *Inquirer*
  flashback   d. Kane launches the *Inquirer*'s attack on big business
       e. The Depression: Kane sells Thatcher his newspaper chain
       f. Thompson leaves library
5. **Bernstein's office:**
       a. Thompson visits Bernstein
       b. Kane takes over the *Inquirer*
  Second   c. Montage: the *Inquirer*'s growth
  flashback d. Party: the *Inquirer* celebrates getting the *Chronicle* staff
       e. Leland and Bernstein discuss Kane's trip abroad
       f. Kane returns with his fiancée Emily
       g. Bernstein concludes his reminiscence
6. **Nursing home:**
  Third
  flashback   a. Thompson talks with Leland
       b. Breakfast table montage: Kane's marriage deteriorates
       c. Leland continues his recollections
       d. Kane meets Susan and goes to her room
       e. Kane's political campaign culminates in his speech
  Third   f. Kane confronts Gettys, Emily, and Susan
  flashback g. Kane loses election and Leland asks to be transferred
  (cont.)   h. Kane marries Susan
       i. Susan's opera premiere
       j. Because Leland is drunk, Kane finishes Leland's review
       k. Leland concludes his reminiscence
7. **El Rancho nightclub:**
       a. Thompson talks with Susan
       b. Susan rehearses her singing
       c. Susan's opera premiere
       d. Kane insists that Susan go on singing
       e. Montage: Susan's opera career
  Fourth   f. Susan attempts suicide and Kane promises she can quit singing
  flashback g. Xanadu: Susan bored
       h. Montage: Susan plays with jigsaw puzzles
       i. Xanadu: Kane proposes a picnic
       j. Picnic: Kane slaps Susan
       k. Xanadu: Susan leaves Kane
       l. Susan concludes her reminiscence
8. **Xanadu:**
       a. Thompson talks with Raymond
  Fifth   b. Kane destroys Susan's room and picks up paperweight, mur-
  flashback   muring "Rosebud"
       c. Raymond concludes his reminiscence; Thompson talks with
          the other reporters; all leave
       d. Survey of Kane's possessions leads to a revelation of Rose-
          bud; exterior of gate and of castle; the end

E. **End credits**

(Source: Bordwell and Thompson 1979:87)

Figure 1.7 Citizen Kane: *plot segmentation. Source:* Film Art: An Introduction, *D. Bordwell and K. Thompson (1993), courtesy of McGraw-Hill.*

serves to suggest how narrative works across a range of texts, some of which are non-fictional. Consider, for example, how in a programme like *Jerry Springer* a narrative unfolds in each part as each of the characters adds to the conflict that is the mainspring of the show. This provides a good example of narrative flow whereby the unfolding of the narrative is carefully controlled by the production team. Real-life characters designed to provide further opportunities for conflict are unleashed and duly move the narrative forward to its climax. The show, of course, ends with Jerry Springer's homily, which serves to restore the equilibrium.

Character is an important aspect of narrative, particularly in fictional texts such as films, TV and radio drama. In soap operas, for example, certain character types consistently recur to the point where they almost become stereotypes. For example, grumpy old people and angst-ridden teenagers are to be found as stock characters across the range of television soap operas. Grouping people into different categories like this is called character typology, and it should be clear that this principle can be extended across a range of genres, such as the police series or the gangster movie.

Vladimir Propp, a Russian structuralist, studied fairy stories and established a number of character types and events associated with them. He called these events 'functions' and suggested their number was limited to thirty-one. His work has been related to Film and Media Studies, and it is possible, for example, to use Propp's theory to fit the character types in a range of texts, especially feature films.

ACTIVITY . . .

Typical Proppian characters and their functions would include:

- the hero
- the villain
- the donor (offers gift with magical properties)
- the dispatcher (sends hero on mission)
- the helper (aids hero)
- the princess (hero's reward).

Using the above list, identify these characters in any Bond or similar action/adventure film. How well can these characters be related to any other film or television programme that you have seen?

An important influence that character has on narrative is that of causality, which is concerned with the idea of cause and effect. Characters usually act out of motives. When different characters are introduced to us, we usually get to know what their motives are, for example what goals they have. These motives are likely to be the cause of events that unfold around this particular character. At the beginning of a film or drama we will find out about a character's goal; it may be to get a partner, rob a bank, control the world, murder a spouse, or perhaps all of these. These motives will drive

the character and become the cause of action within the text. Clearly this is likely to bring the character into conflict with other characters who may be acting out of different motives and are intent on achieving different goals. Conflict is central to the functioning of narrative not least because it is conflict that invites us, the audience, to take sides.

ACTIVITY . . .

As we have indicated, narrative is an important concept in non-fiction as well as in fictional texts. Consider how conflict is used as a basis for telling stories in any of the following non-fiction texts:

- newspaper articles
- television documentaries
- radio current affairs programmes.

MODE OF ADDRESS

This is an important concept in narrative study. It refers to the way in which a media text can be said to 'talk to' its audience. As such, it also has important implications for the way in which the audience responds to the text. For example, the use of a voice-over, an off-screen narrator who talks directly to the audience, is often seen as an authoritative mode of address, providing the audience with information that is incontrovertible. The authority of this voice is often further reinforced by the use of a well-known actor with a particularly distinctive voice.

MODE OF ADDRESS The way in which a particular text will address or speak to its audience.

KEY TERM

The use of voice-over is a feature of news, current affairs programmes and some documentaries, in which this commentary holds the narrative together and develops it. Similarly, voice-over is used as a narrative device in cinema. It is a distinctive feature of the genre *film noir*, for example in Fred MacMurray's commentary on the action in Billy Wilder's *Double Indemnity* (1944). Such a voice-over is an off-screen (asynchronous) voice that directly addresses and confides in the audience. One effect of using this device is to make the audience a party to information that may not be shared by the rest of the characters on screen. It therefore offers us, the audience, privileged information about what is going on. We are positioned to accept, often without question, the information being communicated by this off-screen voice. On occasions the off-screen voice may also make us wary of trusting the character, for example in the opening scene of *Taxi Driver* (1976), in which Travis Bickle reveals his conflicted personality in a tirade against humanity (see Figure 1.21, p. 105).

Make a recording of a documentary that deals with complex medical or scientific issues about which you are likely to know very little.

■ What methods does the commentary use to help the audience understand the complex information being conveyed?

Similarly, consider the use of voice-over in a feature film.

■ How far do we trust what the voice is telling us?
■ How is the off-screen narrator used to make us view the on-screen action from a particular perspective?

The issue of audience positioning is a complex one and is dealt with more fully in Part 2, on media audiences. An important effect of narrative, however, is the way in which it can be used to place or position an audience in relation to the text. In the example of *Taxi Driver*, the device is used to provide the audience with the opportunity to be party to information not shared by other characters in the film. This was an important device used in *film noir*. Not only does it provide the audience with information that assists the development of the narrative, it also gives access to the innermost thoughts of the main character, thus providing the audience with an insight into motivation and psychological make-up.

Roland Barthes explored the concept of narrative as part of his work on structuralism. He argued that narrative works through a series of codes that are used to control the way in which information is given to the audience. Two of these codes are particularly important for our understanding of how narrative functions in media texts. The first is called the enigma code. An enigma is a riddle or puzzle, and some types of narrative make extensive use of this code. An obvious example is a detective story, in which we the audience are invited to solve the puzzle of 'whodunnit' by interpreting the clues and pitting our wits against those of the fictional detective whose job it is to find the perpetrator of the crime.

KEY TERM

ENIGMA A narrative device that teases the audience by presenting a puzzle or riddle to be solved.

This is an obvious use of enigma as a narrative device. However, there are many other, less obvious, ways in which these enigmas are used. One example is the use of trails for programmes to be broadcast later on television or radio. These often rely on teasing the audience with information that can only be fully understood by tuning in to the programme itself. Similarly a non-fiction text such as the news begins with headlines, which provide cryptic details of the stories that are to follow, ensuring that the audience stays with the programme to find out the full story behind the headlines. Print media use similar devices, with newspaper headlines or magazine front covers offering brief information to invite the reader to purchase the product and consume the larger narrative within (for example 'POP STAR IN DRUGS TRAGEDY'). Similarly, advertisers often use billboards to tease us with little clues about a product, such as a feature film, to be launched on to the market.

One of the pleasures that an audience receives from consuming a media text is that of predicting the outcome to a particular narrative. Clearly this is much of the appeal of crime-based texts, in which the audience is positioned alongside the detective in trying to solve the crime or mystery.

Another code that Barthes writes about is the action code. This code suggests how narratives can be resolved through action, often on the part of the protagonist or hero. Typically a resolution is achieved through an act of violence, such as a gun battle. The action code is, therefore, often considered to be a male genre, with problems being resolved through action such as physical violence or a car chase.

ACTION CODE A narrative device by which a resolution is produced through action, for example a shoot-out.

KEY TERM

Figure 1.8 Police Story *(1985). Barthes argues that the action code sees problems resolved through action such as violence or gunplay as in this shot from* Police Story. *Source: Kobal Collection © Golden Harvest, Hong Kong, Kowloon.*

RELATIONSHIP BETWEEN NARRATIVE AND GENRE

A study of different genres in film and television will suggest that the formula requires the narrative to be closed in a different way for each different genre. For example, a soap opera will usually end with a cliffhanger, a narrative device designed to create suspense for the audience and ensure that they tune in to the next episode.

Narrative is also often recognised for the different devices it employs to engage the audience with the text. Alfred Hitchcock spoke of a device that he called 'the bomb under the table'. Here suspense is built for the audience by making them party to information not shared by the characters on screen – in this case, a bomb under the table ready to explode but about which the on-screen characters are wholly unaware.

Most narratives will move in a straight line, following the basic chronology of a story unfolding. This is often called a linear narrative because it moves in a straight line. However, in controlling the flow of information, a number of devices can be employed to realign the narrative. An obvious example is flashback, whereby the narrative allows a character to remember events that have happened in the past, usually to shed light on events 'currently' taking place within the narrative. Similarly, a complex narrative may allow events taking place in two different locations at the same time to be shown alongside each other. This is called parallel action and provides the audience with a privileged view. An extreme form of this is the use of split-screen techniques, whereby two narratives can literally be shown simultaneously on screen.

> **KEY TERM**
>
> **LINEAR NARRATIVE** A plot that moves forward in a straight line without flashbacks or digressions.
>
> **PARALLEL ACTION** A narrative device in which two scenes are observed as happening at the same time by cutting between them.

Some media texts play on the need of the audience to find logical sequencing in narratives by denying this. For example, if we are watching a film and a character we know to have been killed suddenly and inexplicably reappears, we find it hard to make sense of. Indeed the contract that we, the audience, agreed to whereby we suspend our disbelief is clearly threatened by this. *Pulp Fiction* is an example of a film that uses this device, confounding the audience by the reappearance of a character whose death we had witnessed earlier.

> **KEY TERM**
>
> **ANTI-NARRATIVE** A text that seeks deliberately to disrupt narrative flow in order to achieve a particular effect, such as the repetition of images or the disruption of a chronological sequence of events.

▼ GENRE

In this section we:

■ consider and explain the concept of genre
■ look at the function of genre in relation to audiences and the producers of media texts
■ consider the role of genre as a critical tool in the analysis of media texts.

Figure 1.9 *Robert de Niro and Ray Liotta in* Goodfellas *(1990). What clues are present in this still from* Goodfellas *as to the genre of the film? Try the activity on p. 54 to help you. Source: Kobal Collection © Paramount.*

Look at the image in Figure 1.9. Try to identify the type of film this image is taken from.

- Can you work out what sort of storyline the film is likely to have?
- Can you determine who the villains may be?
- Can you make any suggestions as to the actors or directors that might appear in this type of film?
- What else can you deduce about the film?

THE FUNCTION OF GENRE

In working out the answers to the questions above, you will have used your knowledge of genre. The concept of genre is useful in looking at the ways in which media texts are organised, categorised and consumed. It is applied to television, print and radio texts as well as to film. The concept of genre suggests that there are certain types of media material, often story types, that are recognised through common elements, such as style, narrative and structure, that are used again and again to make up that particular type of media genre.

KEY TERM

GENRE The term used for the classification of media texts into groups with similar characteristics.

An important element in identifying a genre is the look or iconography of the text. Iconography constitutes a pattern of visual imagery that remains common to a genre over a period of time.

KEY TERM

ICONOGRAPHY Those particular signs that we associate with particular genres, such as physical attributes and dress of the actors, the settings and the 'tools of the trade' (for example cars, guns).

Look at a selection of films that are currently being shown in your area and try to categorise them into different genres.

Genre is a formula that, if successful, is often repeated again and again and can be used over a long period of time. For instance in a gangster film, like the one in Figure 1.9 on p. 53 (*Goodfellas*, 1990), we expect to see some, or all, of the following elements, which will also probably have been in a gangster film from the 1930s:

Car chases	Urban settings
Guns	Mafia
Heroes	Corrupt police/politicians
Villains	Beautiful women
Violence	Italians

There are also certain actors that we may associate with this genre of films (James Cagney in the 1930s, Robert De Niro in the 1980s or currently Vinnie Jones) as well as certain directors (Martin Scorsese and Guy Ritchie).

ACTIVITY . . .

Take two examples of films of the same genre from different eras that interest you, for instance *War of the Worlds* (1953) and *Independence Day* (1996), and identify their similarities and differences. Suggest reasons for these similarities and differences.

GENRE AND AUDIENCES

Audiences are said to like the concept of genre (although we may not identify it by that name) because of its reassuring and familiar promise of patterns of repetition and variation.

The concept of genre is important in arousing the expectations of an audience and how they judge and select texts. Placing a text within a specific genre plays an important role in signalling to an audience the type of text that they are being invited to consume. Audiences become familiar with the codes and conventions of specific genres. Familiarity through repetition is therefore one of the key elements in the way audiences understand and relate to media texts.

Not only do audiences come to expect certain common codes and conventions but these can also provide a short cut that saves the audience (and the producers) time in developing a new set of conventions each time they consume a new text in that particular genre. This can be seen where two existing genres have been brought together to create a new one. For example, television docu-soaps, which combine elements of documentary and soap opera. These rely on an audience's understanding of and ability to read each specific genre – they understand how documentaries work and they understand how soap operas work; therefore docu-soaps are able to satisfy their expectations of both.

Often the promotion and marketing for new texts invite the audience to identify similarities between a text and predecessors in the same genre. The audience can then take comfort in the fact that what they are being offered is something that they have previously enjoyed and the producers hope that they will enjoy it again.

It has been suggested that proficiency in reading texts within a genre can also lead to the audience's pleasure being heightened as they recognise particular character types or storylines.

GENRE AND PRODUCERS

Producers are said to like the concept of genre because they can exploit a winning formula and minimise taking risks. The concept of genre also helps institutions budget and plan their finances more accurately and helps them to promote new products.

One of the main functions of most of the mainstream media is to make a profit. Just as a high-street retailer has to sell goods that the customers will want to buy, so a media producer has to create texts that audiences will want to consume.

One way to do this is to find what audiences already enjoy and offer something similar. Genre is an easy way of doing this. Where a formula has been proved popular with audiences it makes sense for the producer to use that formula again and to create a new product that contains similar recognisable features that it is hoped will have an immediate appeal to an established audience.

ACTIVITY . . .

How might the use of a proven formula apply to the popular music industry? Is this also the case when listening to radio music stations? Give examples.

It is for this reason that certain genres seem to be continually popular, such as hospital dramas on television. Some genres, like wildlife programmes, although popular for many years, have changed over time as technology has changed, although the codes and conventions or the presenter may have stayed the same. Indeed, genre is such a useful tool that it is now the case that small niche audiences are targeted by themed cable and satellite channels carrying programmes of just one genre. These niche audiences are groups of people with specific media interests, such as holiday, history or 'adult' programmes. This has the very real advantage of delivering a ready-made audience to advertisers marketing specific products. For example, a channel dedicated to travel programmes will clearly attract an audience in the market to buy holidays.

Other changes in genres over a period of time may be the result of changes in society itself. Consider, for example, the police series on television. The representation of police officers in programmes like *Dixon of Dock Green* (Figure 1.10a), broadcast in the early 1950s, is quite a long way removed from the way they are represented in some more contemporary programmes like *Cops*, although some might argue that there are still many similarities between *Dixon of Dock Green* and *The Bill* (Figures 1.10b and 1.10c).

The dominance of genre, coupled with the caution of many media producers, can mean that some new texts are marginalised because they do not fit into the generic conventions that audiences recognise and accept. However, there are always new combinations of programmes being produced that can be difficult to fit into a particular genre but yet are successful. For instance, where do *The Young Ones* or *Third Rock from the Sun* fit?

Figure 1.10 *Genres change over time. Consider, for example, the representation of the police in the series* Dixon of Dock Green *(top) and its contemporary counterpart,* The Bill *(bottom left and right). Sources: BBC Picture Archive and Pearson Television Ltd.*

Some texts, such as the television series *Police Story* or the films *Airplane* and *Scary Movie*, deliberately adapt or parody genre conventions and characteristics. It could be argued that texts that fail to fit into a particular genre are often the most successful. For instance, the popularity of Ridley Scott's film *Blade Runner* or the television series *Absolutely Fabulous* might result from the fact that they failed to fit neatly into audience expectations.

GENRE AS A CRITICAL TOOL

The idea of genre has been used for a long time. For example, Literary Studies categorises texts into such genres as sonnets, tragedies, picaresque novels. It was the film theorists of the 1960s and 1970s who recognised the importance of genre to Film and Media Studies. They saw genre as important because media texts are the product of an industrial process, rather than the creation of an individual, as typified by the Hollywood studio system or indeed Bollywood today!

Grouping texts according to type makes studying them more convenient, recognises the industrial constraints upon producers of media texts and also allows these texts to be looked at in terms of trends within popular culture (for example the western). Genre theory acknowledges that while an individual text may not be worthy of detailed study, a group of texts of the same genre can reveal a good deal, especially in terms of audience appeal (for example Hammer films).

Recent studies suggest that categories of programmes can be gender-specific in that they appeal particularly to either male or female audiences. Males, it is suggested, prefer factual television programmes, sport or action-based narratives, and fictions in which there is a clear resolution at the end, for instance all the villains are killed and the boy gets the girl.

NOTEBOX

David Morley in *Family Television* (1986) found that men often disapproved of watching fiction on the grounds that it was not 'real life' or sufficiently serious. He also found that men tended to define their own preferences (sport, current affairs) as more important and more 'serious'. Morley suggests that men do in fact enjoy more 'feminine' genres but are perhaps not prepared to admit it.

ACTIVITY

Select a group of males and females from a range of age groups. Using a questionnaire that you have designed, conduct some research into the popularity of a particular genre across any medium. You should be trying to establish whether consumption of genre in the media is gender-specific.

LIMITATIONS OF GENRE

1   The concept of genre can have limitations when applied to a range of media texts because of the variety and the need for constant updating of texts that are being produced. Many texts may look similar but are too different to be put together.

2   Sometimes the category becomes too generalised to be helpful. For instance, soap opera could be described as a genre because there are many common characteristics (domestic settings, continuing storylines, cliffhanger endings, familiar characters, and so on) but how helpful is it to say that *Sunset Beach* and *EastEnders* belong to the same genre? We need to be able to distinguish between subgenres within a genre, for example American 'fantasy' soap operas and British 'realism' soap operas. How would you describe Australian soap operas such as *Neighbours* or *Home and Away*?

3   Although we have used the concept of genre for all types of media text, it has been argued that genre is most useful for film and television and is of limited use when applied to newspapers, magazines or radio.

ACTIVITY

If you are interested to know more about this, research the early days of newspapers like *The Times* or the *Observer*. Look up references to 'The Radical Press', which was a series of illegal, untaxed or unstamped newspapers, including *The Poor Man's Guardian* and *The Working Man's Friend*, aimed at the working classes.

OR

Carry out a survey of the television schedules and try to categorise the main genres that appear. Also look at satellite, cable and digital channels.

■   What are the most common genres?
■   Why is this the case?
■   How can these genres be linked to particular audiences?
■   What effect does this have on shaping the schedules?

▼ REPRESENTATION

In this section we consider the important concept of representation in examining media texts. We look at:

- how the media represent to us the world at large
- the significance and accuracy of such representations
- the use of stereotyping
- how minority groups may be affected by media representation.

REPRESENTATION The process by which the media present to us the 'real world'.

KEY TERM

MEDIA REPRESENTATION OF THE WORLD AT LARGE

For many of us, the media are an important source of information about the world in which we live. Indeed, it has been argued that the media are one of the chief means by which we reach an understanding of this world. In consequence, many people believe the media are a powerful means of shaping our attitudes and beliefs.

This process by which the media can be said to interpret the world, or external reality, for us is called representation. There is a wide philosophical debate about what constitutes 'reality' and whether, in fact, reality ultimately exists. If, however, we assume, for the convenience of looking at representation, that there is an external reality, then one key function of the media is to represent that reality to us, the audience. The means by which they do this are discussed in the earlier section on image analysis, p. 27, in which we identified a series of sign systems that are used by the media to represent the world.

As we have seen, each medium, such as television or print, is composed of an elaborate system or code, by which it represents the world outside. These codes are often a complex combination of symbolic, iconic and indexical signs (see p. 31). Television, for example, uses iconic images of a world we can recognise, often anchored by spoken language to shape and limit the meanings it is communicating to the audience. The use of iconic images is an important element of the televisual message because it has the impact of making the images seem very like the world it represents. The television screen gives the audience a two-dimensional representation of the three-dimensional outside. The image can, therefore, be said to be very 'naturalised' as we have grown up to 'read' two-dimensionality as a realistic representation of what we know to exist in the outside world. A similar argument can be made about still photography. 'The camera never lies', we are told, although we all know that it can and does. Indeed the French film director Jean-Luc Godard described film as truth twenty-four times a second, alluding to the number of individual frames used to create a second of screen time.

ACTIVITY . . .

Consider a situation in which you have been involved in an argument or fight with a classmate. Imagine you are asked to describe the altercation to:

- your parents
- a close friend
- your teacher.

What factors might influence your representation of the events that took place in each of these contexts? Consider carefully how you are likely to select, edit and prioritise the information that you choose to provide.

HOW ACCURATE?

Clearly an important debate in any study of the media is about the accuracy of the representation it offers us. (The issue of realism is dealt with more fully in the section on p. 84.) What must be borne in mind is that the media offer us a representation of reality rather than reality itself. The information communicated by a media text is a constructed reshaping of the world, in the same way as in the above activity, where you will have reshaped your own experience to communicate it. There are a number of

questions that we can usefully ask ourselves when we look at examples of media representation:

- Can we trust the representation that is being made to be an accurate portrayal?
- How far have the institutional context and audience expectations determined the nature of the representation?
- In whose interests is it that the representation is made in this way?

MEDIATION The process by which a media text represents an idea, issue or event to us. This is a useful word as it suggests the way in which things undergo change in the process of being acted upon by the media.

Consider an event that takes place and is shown on television, for example a sporting fixture, protest/demonstration or concert.

- In what ways is there a difference between being at the 'live' event and watching it on television?
- Are there qualities that are present in the live event that cannot be experienced through watching television?
- Are there some things in the televisual representation that may not be experienced by being there?

ENCODING The process by which the media construct messages.

Encoding involves re-presenting ideas and events from the world outside into a form that can be decoded by an audience. As we have seen in the section on image analysis, the audience has to learn the code in order to take meaning from a media text. Once this has been learnt, however, the process of decoding media texts can make them appear extremely natural, as though the process of encoding had not in fact taken place and the audience were directly experiencing reality itself.

Take, for example, a location interview on the television news. Often this will have been filmed using just a single camera. The process of this filming is usually to conduct the interview with the camera framing the interviewee.

What you have is a highly constructed presentation of an event that most people watching television would identify as quite 'natural', simply because the audience have become so familiar with this method of presenting an interview. Note, too, that in terms of fictional dialogue in the cinema and on television the concept of shot/reverse shot is the standard or even 'natural' way of presenting two people in conversation.

ACTIVITY . . .

It is interesting to contrast the technique of shot/reverse shot with the intrusive and self-conscious production techniques employed on programmes such as *The Big Breakfast*. This programme actually highlighted the presence of the technology and production personnel in the studio by involving them in the programme. How do you think this affects the way in which the programme represents the world to us?

Not only are most media texts highly constructed representations of the world, they are also quite carefully selected. In the example above, we have considered how a constructed representation can be made to appear natural through simple convention – we are used to seeing it that way and its iconic form convinces us of its naturalness. Prior to the image ever reaching our screens, however, a process of selection has taken place that determines which aspects of the world are chosen to be represented.

As we will see in the case study on news in Part 4, a careful selection process takes place that will determine which events on any one day will be reported on television, in the newspapers and on the radio. In putting together a news report, a television news crew will then make a series of decisions about what images and information are going to be gathered by a reporter and film crew to represent a particular news item. Back in the television studio images and information will be selected (and others rejected) and then combined on an edit suite to produce a representation of the event. These processes of selection may heavily mediate the original event that took place. What we see on our evening news bulletin is a highly refined representation of an event that has taken place, selected and shaped to be represented in a particular way to the audience.

This process of selection and refinement inevitably involves a large element of simplification in order to produce a text that is clear and manageable enough for the audience to consume. A good example is television highlights of a sporting event, or a report of such an event in a newspaper. Here the process of representation will involve the selecting and highlighting of important details. Inevitably, therefore, those elements that in some way are controversial or dramatic will be included at the expense of more mundane and run-of-the-mill events. As we have noted in the section on narrative (p. 42), dramatic and controversial events usually involve conflict between people. In consequence, it is often this conflict that becomes the main focus of the media's attention in representing the world at large. In this way a violent tackle, a controversial decision or a brawl on the pitch will almost certainly be highlighted rather than an example of skilful play or sportsmanship.

Figure 1.11 Wakefield Express. *The original newspaper caption to this photo read: 'ARMED COMBAT. Huddersfield-Sheffield Giants' Karl Lovell gets to grips with Wildcats centre Tony Tatupu during the side's high-scoring encounter at McAlpine Stadium last Sunday. The Giants clawed their way back into the game and pinched it at the death with a decisive drop-goal'. Note how the language used in the original caption emphasises the sense of conflict in a sporting event. Photo: John Clifton.*

NOTEBOX

> When we consider tabloid newspapers, this highlighting of conflict is often called sensationalism. The tabloid press is accused of seeking to sensationalise events that it represents.

STEREOTYPING

An important result of the media needing to simplify in order to make a representation is in the production of stereotypes. The process of simplification in order to make events and issues more digestible for the audience in this case is extended to the representation of groups of people. Rather than representing them as individuals,

sections of the media use a kind of shorthand in the way in which they represent some groups of people. These groups of people come from all walks of life, but significantly they are often minority groups (for example, gay men or ethnic groups). What stereotyping does is to characterise whole groups of people by attributing to them qualities that may be found in one or two individuals. These characteristics are often exaggerated, and entire racial groups or nationalities become reduced to single characteristics. For example, the Jewish race and people from Scotland are both characterised as being tight-fisted.

In their book *Media Studies* (1999), Taylor and Willis consider images of youth as examples of stereotyping. They base their analysis on the work of two Cultural Studies writers, Angela McRobbie, who produced an influential study of the influence of the magazine *Jackie* on teenage girls, and Dick Hebdige, who wrote extensively about media representations of youth (see Hebdige 1988).

Youth tended over the latter half of the twentieth century to suffer from a rather negative representation in the media. From the Teddy Boy images and panics surrounding Elvis Presley movies in the 1950s, through mods and rockers, punk and the representation of 'E' and related drug culture today, youth in revolt has always provided the media with ample opportunities for negative representation of young people. Typically, much of this stereotyping has been based on the activities of one or two individuals whose activities have provided a source of newspaper headlines.

ACTIVITY . . .

- Is it possible to find media representations of youth that are positive?
- If so, where are these mostly to be found?
- Do you feel these are accurate representations?

Stereotyping is obviously a useful short cut for media producers to reproduce and represent groups of people in the media. What a stereotype allows them to do is to condense a lot of complex information into a character who not only is easily recognised but also is simple to deal with. Minor characters in films are often presented as stereotypes. The unfortunate side effect of this is to dehumanise people by denying them the complex psychological make-up that an individual possesses by reducing them to a few generalised personality traits. As Tessa Perkins has pointed out, some stereotypes are based on truths that can be observed. For example, France has produced many talented chefs and most French people enjoy gourmet food and wine. However, like the rest of us, French people are complex individuals with more to their lives than indulgence in food and drink.

An even more worrying aspect of stereotyping is the way in which it can be used to marginalise and devalue the worth of whole groups of people in society. In addition, it tends to disregard the causes of stereotypical behaviour, making the group a potential scapegoat for broader ills within a society. For example, the stereotyping of some members of ethnic minorities as living all together in crowded and substandard accommodation can suggest that, where this is the case, it is a matter of choice rather than a result of economic and social deprivation.

This use of stereotypical representation can be seen to reflect the power relations within our society; it tends to subordinate certain groups. Often this will involve some element of ridicule by suggesting that certain groups of people are intellectually challenged or more prone to criminal activity than the rest of the population.

ACTIVITY . . .

In the 1970s in America, George Gerbner produced a quantitative survey, using content analysis techniques, to investigate the representation of violence in the American media. One of his findings was that the victims of violence were often minority groups that society considered most expendable.

Make a list of groups that you feel are most often stereotyped or represented negatively. In what ways can these groups be said to be subordinate within our society, for instance economically or socially?

You may like to link this activity to the content analysis activity on p. 317.

CONTENT ANALYSIS A method of collecting, collating and analysing large amounts of information about the content of media products, such as television advertisements, in order to draw conclusions about such issues as the representation of gender roles.

KEY TERM

ACTIVITY . . .

The end of the twentieth century saw the emergence of so-called 'Girl Power'. Discuss the extent to which this phenomenon represents the emancipation of women and to what extent it can be seen as another form of exploitative representation in the interests of patriarchy (male domination in society).

Another important issue has been the under-representation of people from minority groups in the media. Certainly television representation of ethnic-minority groups and the gay community has increased in recent years. However, some would argue that this is in fact mere tokenism. This implies that the increased presence of such groups is simply to give the illusion of fairer representation, rather than being a genuine attempt to produce a more even balance. Many, for instance, would point to the relative absence of people with disabilities in the media other than in texts aimed at audiences with a disability. People with a disability have traditionally been represented in a particularly negative way by the media. Commonly they are depicted in films as evil and dangerous people intent on causing harm to able-bodied people. For example, consider some of the villains featured in Bond movies or look at the use of disability in the *Sun* front-page lead discussed on p. 244.

The representation of groups, however, is not fixed for ever, and it is possible to observe changes over periods of time. The emergence of specific groups and subcultures is often accompanied by a challenge to existing stereotypes and a challenge to the media to produce more positive representations. It can be argued that this may be linked ideologically to such things as legislation promoting equal opportunities. Some people would argue that these groups remain marginalised; it is simply that the negative representation of them becomes less overt.

ACTIVITY . . .

Consider the media representation of minority groups:

■ Do you think the high-profile media representation of openly gay figures such as Graham Norton and Julian Clary is a positive development for gay people?
■ In the programme *Goodness Gracious Me* the Asian actors direct much of the humour at their own culture and stereotypes. Do you think such a programme might have been called racist (and been censored) if the programme had featured white actors?
■ What is your reaction to the *Ali G Show*?

To some extent the work of many activist groups fighting on behalf of minorities has at least drawn attention to the extent of negative stereotyping. For example, the feminist movement on both sides of the Atlantic has served to highlight the exploitation of women through the media in such forms as page-three girls in the tabloid press, and, more recently, the emergence of 'lad culture', with magazines such as *Loaded* using images of women in an exploitative way.

Certainly it is an interesting exercise to compare some of the stereotypical representation from the recent past with today. For example, *Carry On* films or 1970s television sitcoms such as *Mind Your Language*, frequently rerun on cable and satellite networks, were much more overtly sexist and homophobic than today. However, many people would argue that the difference lies in the extent to which such negative attitudes are made manifest.

Figure 1.12 Carry On Loving (1970). Comedy films such as the Carry On series rely heavily on stereotypes and stock characters as a source of humour. What are the stereotypes in this still? Source: Kobal Collection © Rank Corporation.

Choose a group of people that you consider to have been negatively represented in the media. Can you identify any members of the group who feature in the media and can be said to present a positive representation? For example, you might like to consider Victor Meldrew or Miss Marple as representatives of elderly people.

▼   MEDIA INTERTEXTUALITY

In this section we look at the concept of intertextuality and explore its role in Media Studies through:

- ■ mimicry
- ■ parody, pastiche and homage
- ■ marketing of media texts
- ■ the treatment of fictional soap opera stories in the tabloid press
- ■ reviews of media texts in other media forms
- ■ media performers working in more than one media form.

One of the pleasures that audiences experience in the consumption of media texts is the joy of recognition. One form of this pleasure comes in recognising the reference in one media text to other media texts. This process of referencing is called intertextuality.

KEY TERM

INTERTEXTUALITY The way in which texts refer to other media texts that producers assume audiences will recognise.

MIMICRY

This interdependent relationship between texts can take a number of different forms. It often transcends both genres and media forms so that a text created in one particular medium will be used in some way in another medium. Advertising and music videos are two genres that rely heavily on the use of intertextuality to achieve a particular effect. Often this borrowing of a text to link it to a second one is stylistic. This means that a text will mimic or otherwise copy certain stylistic features of another text. Usually this is done in order to create a particular impact, although there may be instances where this borrowing may seem simply a matter of convenience to give a music video, for example, a particular look. For the reader of the image, however, the connotative power of the original text is likely to be carried through into the new text.

(a)

(b)   (c)

Figure 1.13 (a) Geena Davis and Susan Sarandon in Thelma and Louise (1991). (b) and (c) Stills from the Peugeot advertisement. Sources: Kobal Collection © MGM/Pathe, and Europ RSCG WNEK, Sally Hope agency for actress Julie Graham and Galloways for actress Annie Dunkley.

An example of this is the deliberate playing on the style and content of the film *Thelma and Louise* in advertising a Peugeot 106 car (Figure 1.13). The original film portrays two women travelling across America seeking to escape from the dominant influence of life in a patriarchal society. The women are seen as emancipated travellers seeking their own destiny in a world free from the oppression of men. The film is often regarded as an example of post-feminist cinema. By deliberately making references to the film in the advertisements, the car comes to symbolise the concept of emancipation, suggesting that any woman who buys it will be able to liberate herself in just the same way as the women in the film.

Clearly we, the audience, experience the joy of recognising the 'cleverness' of the way in which advertisers play with both the style and themes of *Thelma and Louise* in order to link their product to the film. At a deeper level, however, the connotative power and mythological status of a female road movie provides a selling point to a hatchback car. Owning the car will be a statement about lifestyle aspirations to be an independent self-assertive woman just like Thelma and Louise. Advertisers are always keen to sell the consumer a lifestyle to go with the product.

Of course, the impact of the car advertisement relies on our familiarity with the film. There may be audiences watching the advertisements who have never seen the film, as well as some who only hear about the link second hand from those who have. Much of the impact of intertextual reference is determined by our own cultural knowledge or awareness of the texts with which the link is being made.

The Peugeot example is a source of pleasure because it can be said to contain elements of parody. There is a certain tongue-in-cheek comedy about the way in which the characters in the advertisement mimic their cinematic counterparts, perhaps in a subtle way to poke fun at the original. There is perhaps also some element of self-parody in the vaguely absurd notion that owning a car can effect a new emancipated lifestyle. Intertextuality can confront us with some complex readings of media texts.

PARODY, PASTICHE AND HOMAGE

The postmodern critic Fredric Jameson has suggested a differentiation between *parody*, which aims to mock an original in a critical way, and *pastiche*, which he suggests is merely a stylistic mask. Pastiche simply uses images in an empty surface way in order to sell products. Parody for Jameson has substance; pastiche is merely a matter of imitating.

In the introduction to this book we discussed the significance of postmodernism in any study of the media. You may find it useful to look back at that section in light of some of the ideas about intertextuality. Specifically, one of the concepts mentioned is *bricolage*, the French word for 'do-it-yourself'. The word also carries a more negative connotation of 'patching up'. As you will see, there is an obvious relevance to the idea of recycling earlier texts to produce 'new' ones. For example, the idea of sampling existing pieces of music and mixing them to create new ones is typical of this notion of bricolage. Some people would argue that this recycling represents an act of great creativity, while others would suggest that it is a symptom of the fact that people have run out of ideas, what Jameson calls 'the failure of the new'.

Perhaps what is most significant is the idea that the insatiable demand for media texts in the postmodern media-saturated world requires a large degree of recycling simply to meet this demand.

Watch a segment of output from MTV or a similar music channel.

- How many of the videos that you encounter make some reference to other media texts you have come across?
- How many of these can be said to be parody?
- How many are pastiche?
- What criteria have you used to distinguish this?

Obviously, parody can only be effective through our knowledge of the text or genre of text being parodied. We take a delight in the recognition of the elements being parodied, in what is called the 'shared cultural knowledge' which enables us to enjoy through recognition the relationship between the texts.

Similarly, some texts work through the idea of homage. Homage suggests respect for a particular text, acknowledging the power and importance of the original text by imitating it. Homage is commonly experienced in the cinema, where a director may deliberately create a scene, or even a whole film, in which the intertextual elements combine to pay respect to an earlier creation. The work of Alfred Hitchcock is frequently referred to in this way, through, for example, the work of directors such as Brian De Palma. Similarly more recent examples of *film noir*, sometimes referred to as neo-noir, have paid homage to the Hollywood genre that dominated the cinema in the 1940s and 1950s.

> How can we distinguish homage from plagiarism? Consider the many films that have simply copied the successful style of others. What films have you seen that you think develop the style and themes of the original to which they relate?

MARKETING OF MEDIA TEXTS

One area of the media in which intertextuality is important is in the marketing of media texts. In order for a media product to be promoted successfully, it is often advertised extensively. Some of this advertising will naturally be placed alongside existing products of a similar nature and form. Trailers on television and radio for programmes to be shown later in the schedules are a typical example of this. Even the early evening news is used to trail programmes later in the evening by thinly disguising them as news items. Examples of this include upcoming documentary 'exclusives' and even football matches to be televised that evening.

However, it also common to find examples of new media products being promoted through other media forms. For example, trailers for new cinema releases are often shown as advertisements on television or on the radio. More subtle forms of promotion are also brought into play. Celebrity news stories in the press are often linked to the promotion of a new film or album release. Similarly, appearances by stars on chat shows, breakfast television and radio programmes are used to promote newly released texts. Increasingly, new films and television programmes are the focus of billboard campaigns. Such methods of promotion have also been used to make the public aware of new presenters on national radio stations. In all of these instances there is an intertextual relationship between one or more texts.

SOAP OPERA AND THE TABLOIDS

An interesting example of intertextuality is the way in which stories from soap operas find their way into the tabloid press. Sometimes these stories feature the actors who play the roles of soap characters. At times, however, the fictional characters themselves are featured in the print media. For example, a famous storyline from *Coronation Street* featured the wrongful imprisonment of the fictional character Deirdre Rashid. This story was taken up by the tabloid press and the *Sun* newspaper's front-page story demanded her release.

REVIEWS

Reviews of media texts appear regularly across different media forms. Cinema releases are reviewed on television in programmes dedicated specifically to the week's cinema releases. Films and television programmes are similarly reviewed in the press and on radio. Radio output itself is also reviewed in the broadsheet newspapers. In many ways, the media, it has been argued, spend a good deal of time looking at themselves rather than at the world outside, positioning themselves at the centre of their own universe.

Figure 1.14 *The* Daily Star *boasts of its status as 'The official* I'm a Celebrity Get Me Out of Here *newspaper', 3 May 2003. Source: © Express Newspapers.*

An increasingly common television genre involves programmes about the making of a particular film. These programmes are usually linked to an expensive new blockbuster film and take audiences behind the scenes of the shooting of the film. Often they include interviews with the stars and the director as another method of promoting the film.

Some genres and media forms are so popular that they have whole magazines dedicated to them. Consider, for example, the number of film magazines currently available that not only reflect but also promote interest in the cinema. There is also a range of magazines given over to television soaps. It would seem that the audience for these products has an almost insatiable desire to consume them both in televisual and print formats.

The Internet is another media form that constantly makes reference to other media. Most major newspaper and magazine publishers have a website that complements their existing publications. Film companies are able to show clips of new releases via the Internet, and in a similar way the music industry uses it to promote new music. Many individual fans also have their own websites promoting a whole range of media-related issues. Indeed the Internet has rapidly become a forum for a dynamic exchange of views, some more informed than others, across media forms on a worldwide scale. Some sites of particular interest to media students are given in the resources section at the end of this book.

Allied to this type of promotion is that of the 'spin-off'. One particularly successful spin-off is the magazine or book that emerges from the television programme. The newsagent's shelves are packed with examples, ranging from X Files magazines to cookery books. Similarly, videos of successful television series are often made available for sale or rental once the programmes have been transmitted.

MEDIA PERFORMERS IN DIFFERENT MEDIA FORMS

It is worth noting the increasing number of performers in the media who appear in different media forms. Commonly journalists are likely to write for newspapers and magazines as well as appearing in, or presenting, television and radio programmes. Working across the media provides opportunities for these performers to promote both themselves as well as the publications and programmes for which they are working. One example is Richard and Judy, who currently write a column in the Saturday edition of the Daily Express newspaper as well as presenting their Channel 4 show. In a similar vein, it is also possible to find examples of media texts that exist in, or have developed through, a number of different media forms. A comic-strip character, such as Batman, has been transformed into feature films and television programmes.

Richard & Judy

BRITAIN'S BEST-LOVED HUSBAND AND WIFE TEAM REFLECT ON THE WEEK'S EVENTS EVERY SATURDAY IN YOUR **DAILY EXPRESS**

. . . Clare Short's ludicrous antics in recent weeks, culminating in her ridiculous resignation speech, reminded me of a former colleague, a disruptive reporter who caused nothing but trouble in the office . . . She may have been an efficient

International Development Secretary but she's committed one of the most unpardonable political sins of all; she has made *everyone* feel embarrassed.

[. . .]

Typical of the English upper-middle classes to feel miffed that Posh and Becks have bought a house in 'their' part of Provence as opposed to the French villagers of Beremon who are chuffed to bits . . . I'd say to these snobby Brits . . . unpurse those lips and invite them round for drinkies by your charming pool.

(*Daily Express*, 17 May 2003)

▼ MEDIA IDEOLOGY

In this section we:

- consider the concept of ideology
- explain the nature and function of ideology
- assess its significance in studying the media.

IDEOLOGY A system of beliefs that determines how power relations are organised within a society.

BELIEF SYSTEMS

As suggested in previous sections, as humans we experience a need to make sense of the world and the events that take place in it. One important way of doing this is through our consumption of media texts. However, it is often argued that all media texts are in some way ideological. On one level, ideology is the system of beliefs that organises the way in which we view the world and the events that take place in it. It follows, therefore, that in our consumption of media texts we will be subjected to the ideological views of the producer of the text.

Ideologies come in a variety of different forms. Perhaps the most prevalent and obvious examples are the political and economic systems that govern the way in which people live their lives. Capitalism is an ideology that emphasises the importance for people in a society to be free to create wealth by setting up and running their own businesses. Marxism, on the other hand, is a belief system that considers that capitalism exploits the labour of the workers and argues that the state should own and control wealth creation and distribute it fairly among the population as a whole. Clearly these two ideologies are in conflict.

Religion, it can be argued, is an ideology in which an organised system of beliefs and values defines to people how they should live their lives and what constitutes appropriate behaviour. The stained-glass windows in a church, for example, traditionally portray a worldview and a set of values (symbolised by parables, for example) designed to instruct the local people in how to live their lives in a righteous and morally responsible way.

Today the media have to a large degree replaced stained-glass windows as sources of ideology. Media messages, as we have seen, are constructed. In this process of construction, selection and shaping take place in order to represent the world outside. This selection and shaping reflect the value system of the originator of the message. An important question we need to ask when considering the ideology that lies behind a media message is 'In whose interest is it that we perceive the world this way?'

Researchers such as the Glasgow Media Group have undertaken investigations that reveal that television news reporting on industrial disputes tends to depict strikers as a disruptive force in society that needs to be resisted. Clearly such a representation is doing a good deal of ideological work to reinforce the belief that it is wrong to take industrial action. Ideologically we are being encouraged to see capitalism as a system that is basically fair and just. Workers who exercise their democratic right to withdraw their labour to achieve social justice through better pay and conditions are seen as disruptive and antisocial. Ideologically they are seen to represent subversive forces that threaten the very fabric of society.

As the vast majority of people in this country are workers, many of whom are likely to be dissatisfied with their pay and conditions, it can be argued that such a view is in the interests of those people who hold power within our society and who benefit from keeping workers on low pay. In a democracy the people who hold power and rule over us have to do so to some extent with our consent. Forces do exist that are capable of coercing people into behaving in certain ways, the police for example, or in extreme

cases the armed forces. Generally, people have to be persuaded to allow other people to exercise power over them. Some see the media as a powerful tool to ensure the co-operation of the population in accepting the norms imposed by the ruling elite.

HEGEMONY The concept used by the Marxist critic Antonio Gramsci to describe how people are influenced into accepting the dominance of a power elite who impose their will and worldview on the rest of the population. Gramsci argues that this elite is able to rule because the rest of the population allow it to do so. It can be argued, therefore, that the ideological role of the media is to persuade us that it is in our best interests to accept the dominance of this elite.

NOTEBOX . . .

The American commentator Noam Chomsky argues that popular culture can be used to divert people's attention from real issues such as their conditions of employment; it is only the intellectual and educated classes in society, largely the professional classes, who must be persuaded to agree with the ideological values of the ruling elite.

ACTIVITY . . .

Make a list of some of the mass-media texts that could be viewed as a diversion from real issues and social conditions. Which texts do you think are aimed at Chomsky's educated classes?

WATCHING *BIG BROTHER*

Let us look at a particular example of the way in which the media can be seen to shape our attitudes in order to accept what is best for the elite in power.

The idea of 'Big Brother' has always had strong negative connotations in our society. The freedom to go about one's daily business without being spied on has been considered a fundamental human right. In his novel *1984* (which was subsequently made into a film), George Orwell offered a nightmare vision of a society in which a citizen's every move was watched, leaving little opportunity to oppose the oppressive power of the state.

Today, however, nearly every public building and every town centre has surveillance cameras that watch every move of the people who occupy these spaces. The majority of people accept the presence of the cameras, and many would argue that they serve the public good as they are an effective deterrent against crime. Clearly there has been a shift in consciousness on the part of the population from the paranoia of the Big Brother idea to the acceptance of the concept of surveillance. An important mechanism by which this change has been brought about is the media. Programmes such as *Police, Camera, Action* make extensive use of footage from such cameras. These clips are often accompanied by a commentary from a reputable media personality, such as a newsreader, extolling the advantages of the cameras in detecting crime. Commonly we are presented with a chase in which cameras, for example in a police helicopter, offer the audience a privileged vantage point from which to observe the chase, which leads to the arrest of the criminals. As the narrative unfolds we are positioned to identify with the forces of law and order as they use this sophisticated equipment to keep crime off our streets.

The ideology behind surveillance cameras is an example of how the media can be used to shape social attitudes and gain the acceptance of a population for something that may seem to be against their interests. It also demonstrates how ideologies do not remain fixed or static. In many respects, the media are part of a battleground in which different power elites fight for supremacy in terms of the acceptance of their ideas.

The concept of ideology is closely allied to that of representation. One way in which ideology works through media texts is by the simple process of repetition. This is particularly true of repeated representations across media forms, which can have the effect of naturalising a way of seeing an issue so that it seems that no other interpretation is possible.

So changed is the ideological meaning of Big Brother that it was used as the title of one of the most talked-about television programmes at the beginning of the twenty-first century. A group of people locked in a house, trying to win a prize by staying the longest, became the focus of the nation's attention. The filming of their every action provided voyeuristic entertainment for the nation and the media, beginning with the first series in the summer of 2000. Instead of Big Brother watching us, we took our pleasure from watching *Big Brother*.

IDEOLOGY AND GENDER

Our perceptions of female beauty, for example, are dominated by young, white, flawless size 10 women staring out from the covers and advertisements in magazines, and in newspapers, films and television. Similarly, as we have seen, family life is nearly always depicted as being a happy and desirable state, with married couples bringing up children. On the other hand, consider the negative representation of people who do not go out to work and earn a living. They are called scroungers and are depicted as people who live off the backs of other people who work hard for a living. Single mothers, for example, have been demonised in this way.

It can be argued that the effect of these representations is cumulative and that, as we saw with stereotypes, they deny the complexity of human existence and reduce it to a basic issue of right or wrong. This can be seen in terms of going to work and using your

earnings to support your family being 'right' and being unemployed and not being able to support your family being 'wrong'.

ACTIVITY . . .

What do you think is the ideological work of game shows and quiz programmes?

An interesting and useful way of looking at ideology is through its impact on minority groups within society. Despite the ground won by the feminist movement in the emancipation of women, it is generally accepted that we still live in a patriarchal society, that is, one dominated by men, who retain most of the power. Clearly it is not in the interest of most women to occupy a position of inferiority to men. However, the ideological work of the media is such that women are represented so as to accept this subordinate position as being both natural and inevitable and in some way 'right'. If we were to make a list of typical depictions of women in the media, we would find a preponderance of images in which women are seen in a domestic situation; as objects for the pleasure of men; and as partners to men.

An interesting comparison can be made with the way in which ageing Hollywood stars are depicted. Generally when a female star ceases to be 'young and attractive' she is seen in fewer and fewer screen roles. She is then replaced with the latest and most attractive young starlet. Male stars, however, go on well past their youth and prime, many working into their old age.

One inference we can make from this is that women in Hollywood movies are seen to be of interest only when they are young, attractive and sexually desirable. In an important essay on the image of women in the cinema, 'Visual pleasure and narrative cinema' (1975), Laura Mulvey uses ideas based on psychoanalysis to argue that the main source of visual pleasure in the cinema is the voyeuristic male viewer enjoying the image of the female body. In order for a woman to experience pleasure from the film she has to position herself in a similar role to that of a male viewer enjoying the spectacle. Ideologically it can be argued that this positioning functions in order to persuade women that by occupying a role similar to that of the women on screen they will become desirable and attractive to men, thus reinforcing a woman's subordinate position within a patriarchy.

In this way, the ideological function of many media texts is to identify for women how they should perform within a patriarchy. Magazines aimed at young girls contain articles and features on how to look attractive and suggest ways in which to develop relationships with boys. Ideologically it is clear that happiness for a young girl is to be found in the arms of a male partner. Similarly the output of both television and magazines aimed at women suggests the importance of their domestic and child-bearing roles. Women who are able to juggle the demands of a career as well as these other duties are celebrated. Men on the other hand are only expected to be successful in their jobs.

Figure 1.15 *Michael Douglas and Catherine Zeta-Jones. A 'young and attractive' female star with her husband. Source: © Popperfoto; photo: Dani Cardona.*

Angela McRobbie in 1983 made a study of a magazine called *Jackie*, which was popular with teenage girls. She wrote how girls were being introduced into the sphere of feminine consumption. It can be argued that magazines of this type work ideologically to define for their audience those domestic roles of wife and mother that they should accept and embrace.

Another ideological impact of the media is through what is known as 'moral panic'. This is basically a scare story, often with little basis in truth, which serves to persuade people of the need for drastic action to cure a social ill. Horror videos, dangerous breeds of dog, asylum seekers and the drug Ecstasy have all been at the centre of moral panic. This panic is often orchestrated by the tabloid press and has the ideological impact of people demanding immediate action, usually to ban the availability of such things, without any rational consideration of whether this is an appropriate reaction or not.

MORAL PANIC A mass response to a group, a person or an attitude that becomes defined as a threat to society.

KEY TERM

▼ REALISM

In this section we look at the concept of realism and consider its particular significance to the genre of documentary. We consider:

- the accuracy of the representation
- different types of realism
- continuity editing
- documentary film-making
- the docu-soap
- reality television.

REALISM Representation by the media of situations or ideas in such a way that they seem real.

THE ACCURACY OF THE REPRESENTATION

In previous sections we looked at the way in which the media use sign systems to provide us with a representation of the outside world. We also noted that, because of a prevalence of iconic signs in visual media such as film, television and photography, these representations of the world can appear so natural that we easily see them as real. In this way, audiences can easily overlook the process of mediation that has occurred in presenting these images to us.

In considering the issue of realism, one of our concerns is to determine just how accurately a media form such as film or television can be said to represent 'reality'. As we have noted in the section on representation (p. 61), what the media present to us is always a constructed and edited version of the real world. Any enquiry into realism must always take on board this issue. Similarly, when we look at a landscape painting

we always bear in mind the fact that it is a painting or representation rather than the landscape itself. In both the painting and a media representation we should always remember that what we are presented with is an illusion of the real world and the events that take place in it.

We can identify just how constructed and encoded the concept of realism is by considering the significance of monochrome, for example, in press photographs or film and television text. Many people find they associate black and white images with realism. For example, some types of documentary photography or 1960s British cinema, in films such as *This Sporting Life* or *A Kind of Loving*, use black and white photography to depict a gritty realism of working-class life or poverty. As most of us see the world in its full spectrum of colour, there is a fundamental contradiction in the perception of black and white being in some way more real than a Technicolor image. Obviously there is something in our reading of monochrome images that serves to make us perceive its starkness as depicting the world in a more realistic way.

To confuse matters further, it has been argued that there is not one single realism, but that realism in media texts exists in a number of different ways.

Figure 1.16 *Early episodes of Coronation Street, launched in the 1960s, are an example of filming in black and white to create realism similar to British cinema of that period. Source: © Granada Television.*

DIFFERENT TYPES OF REALISM

Some media texts may be considered realistic because they contain 'truth' from the outside world. In this way we would identify a news bulletin as realistic in so far as the information it communicates to us is based on a verifiable external reality. In consequence we could argue that the content of such a text makes it realistic. A similar argument may be made for the realism of documentary films, which like news are concerned with offering factual information about external reality. This realism is sometimes referred to as 'realism of content'.

Some media texts may contain material that has little credibility in terms of what we may know of any external reality. Science-fiction programmes or action movies are likely to contain material that we perceive as far-fetched or unrealistic. However, the construction of these texts may still be seen as realistic in so far as they are produced in such a way as to remain plausible and to contain detail that we accept as being realistic. For example, the characters, although unreal in appearance, may act out of plausible motives and hence appear realistic. We might ask ourselves the relatively simple question of whether or not we are convinced by the text.

One of the ways in which we judge a text is by its ability to represent reality to us in a convincing way. We expect some degree of verisimilitude or resemblance to things that we know from real life. For example, an anachronism such as motor vehicles appearing inadvertently in a historical drama will create implausibility and can interfere with our ability to believe what we see in the text.

CONTINUITY EDITING

An important aspect of realism in film and television is rooted in the way a text is edited. The use of continuity editing is one method of shaping a text in such a way that it appears natural or realistic. Continuity editing requires that the action on screen should appear 'continuous'. In order to achieve this, the material must be shot so that the editor can ensure that what we see appears logical, for example: matching the eye levels when using shot/reverse shot for dialogue. The editor must also observe the 180-degree rule, whereby the camera keeps to one side of an imaginary line dividing a scene. This means that the audience has a constant reference point in viewing the action. If the 180-degree rule is broken, the audience will lose this frame of reference and the sense of continuity may be destroyed.

For some critics, discussion of the issue of realism has no relevance in a world in which for many people the media themselves have come to represent the real world. The media no longer simply try to represent the real world; they have in fact replaced it. The French writer Jean Baudrillard coined the term 'hyper-real' to describe the way in which the media now dominate our perception of the outside world. For Baudrillard the world of the television represents a reality that is 'more real' than that which we can directly experience in the outside world. In this way a media representation becomes a hyper-reality, with the reality encountered in the world itself a pale shadow of this.

DOCUMENTARY FILM-MAKING

Documentary film-making is one area in which the issue of realism is important. As its name suggests, a documentary seeks to document real life. It attempts to replicate experiences in the world in a realistic fashion. So, to some extent, we assess the effectiveness of a documentary film by its ability to convince us that what we are seeing is 'real'.

As a genre, documentary has developed over a period of years but still functions by seemingly holding up a mirror to the world to show the audience what is 'out there'. Clearly this is an oversimplification, not least because there is a whole range of different types of documentary. However, one feature common to all documentaries is the fact that, like all media products, they have to be constructed. Although this construction may be undertaken in such a way as to make the text seem natural and realistic, the same process of selection and shaping has taken place as in a fictional text.

Indeed, there are important areas in which there is a clear parallel between fictional film-making and documentary. Film-makers such as Mike Leigh, for example in *Meantime* (1981), or Ken Loach, in *Raining Stones* (1993), create films that have a strong realistic or naturalistic quality. This is in part because of their subject matter. Many of their films are a celebration of the lives of ordinary people. The filmic style contrives to be naturalistic in that there is little evidence of intrusive camerawork or editing. The artifice of film-making is rendered subsidiary to the truth being told on the screen. Similarly some documentaries will use the reconstruction of events where the original footage is either non-existent or needs to be supplemented by more dramatic sequences (for instance the series *999*). There are also examples of drama documentaries in which real-life events are dramatised to enable audiences to relive the experience. Such programmes may draw on court transcripts or eyewitness testaments, *Hillsborough* (1996), written by Jimmy McGovern, being an example.

View extracts from a docu-soap and a drama documentary such as the one mentioned above.

- Which do you consider to be the more accurate representation of reality?
- What criteria have you used in arriving at your decision?
- Do you think other readers of these texts would agree with you?

There are a number of issues that need to be explored in relation to the nature of documentary and of realism. There are also ethical and ideological issues to be considered. If documentary seeks to show us some kind of truth, the process of construction is obviously going to represent that truth from a specific viewpoint. As we have seen, the use of a voice-over narrator is a powerful device not only in determining the response of the audience to a documentary, but also in positioning them in such a way as to limit the readings that are available.

Part of the popularity of documentary as a genre is the way in which it allows the audience to get inside other people's lives. We often associate it with the idea of fly-on-the-wall filming techniques, where the participants are seemingly unaware of their being characters in the unfolding drama. Reality unfolds before our eyes, and the function of the camera is simply to capture it. This is not true for a number of reasons. First, there is generally a process that takes place before filming, which is about selecting precisely what is to be filmed. The characters who feature in a documentary will be vetted for their charisma and screen presence long before a camera is ever pointed at them. What on screen seems a spontaneous process in which a film crew simply turns up at someone's house and starts filming is in most cases a carefully planned and constructed piece of film-making. A good deal of planning and preparation is likely to have taken place before the expense of committing a film crew is incurred.

It is very likely that the character featured will have been interviewed by a researcher to determine what he or she will say and do on camera. As most people, when confronted by a camera, will either freeze or ramble on for hours, some prompting as to the most appropriate responses may well be necessary. Similarly, as talking heads (mid-shots of people just talking) tend to be boring in televisual terms, it is often necessary to set up some activity in order to add visual interest. Note how often people in documentaries are filmed undertaking some domestic chore while their voice is played over the action.

A second key issue with shooting documentary is the extent to which the camera itself necessarily intrudes and determines how people will respond and react. Your own experience of using video equipment will probably tell you that people 'play to the camera'. There is evidence to suggest that the more accustomed people become to the presence of the camera, the more likely they are to forget that it is there and to act naturally. Despite this, there will always be the tendency for a person to act differently when being filmed.

A third issue is that at the post-production stage editing will probably be used to cut any of the material that does not fit readily into the narrative or is felt to get in the way of the flow of the programme.

ACTIVITY . . .

In the section on narrative (p. 42), we emphasised the importance of conflict. Consider the narrative construction of a documentary. How has conflict been presented here? Do you think the conflict has emerged naturally or do you think it may have been contrived for dramatic effect?

Most successful media texts are about people. Even when it is ideas and issues that are important, the story is usually told in terms of people. In many ways the docu-soap has become such a successful genre because it engages with the lives of people. The people featured are also ordinary enough for us to be able to relate readily to their lives. A new spin on this is the increasing use of minor celebrities in reality television shows such as *I'm a Celebrity Get Me Out of Here*. Here the appeal of the show may be seeing 'stars' of the media in situations that reveal to us their real-life vulnerability, making it easy for us to identify with them.

Figure 1.17
Phil Tufnell, winner of I'm a Celebrity 2. *Source: © Rex Features.*

Another issue to take on board in terms of documentary realism is that commonly documentaries are made from a specific standpoint adopted by the film-maker. For example, a documentary may have been made to expose some social injustice. A documentary film-maker such as John Pilger or Nick Broomfield may well be intent on offering a particular viewpoint in order to convince the audience of an argument. Clearly the editorial process is going to impact on what is represented in the film as well as the way in which that representation is made.

An extreme is the actual faking of scenes in documentary films – reconstructing an event that has taken place but filming it as though the action had been caught on camera. This may be a deliberate cutting of corners by a film crew in order to make filming easier, less time-consuming and less costly. Equally, film-makers are occasionally conned by the subjects of their documentaries, who manage to persuade them that they are something that they are not.

THE DOCU-SOAP

An interesting recent development in documentary film-making is the advent of a genre called docu-soap, which comprises elements of both the documentary and the soap opera. The common factor here is a strand that is concerned with the lives of ordinary people and the engagement of the audience with their lives. The docu-soap is an example of what is called a hybrid genre, where elements of two or more genres are fused to create a new category of media text.

> **KEY TERM**
>
> **DOCU-SOAP** A hybrid genre in which elements of documentary and soap opera are combined to create a series about the lives of real people.

As Sonia Livingstone has pointed out, one quality of the soap opera is that the perceived realism generates for us a greater sense of involvement. This is a source of pleasure for the audience in that they can readily suspend their disbelief and involve themselves in the characters and the action. Similarly, in a study of *Dallas*, Ien Ang suggests that audiences enjoy pretending that soaps are real in order to heighten the pleasure they get from watching them.

The docu-soap usually focuses on a group of people who have a common interest, for example people working for the same organisation. So, like a soap opera, it is concerned with the interaction of a group of people living or working in a community. Just as in a fictional soap, the audience is invited to engage with the lives of these people, empathising and forming allegiances with these real-life characters. Docu-soaps produce their own 'stars', who then often go on to make appearances in other programmes and in the print media.

Figure 1.18 *Maureen in the BBC docu-soap* Driving School, *one of the first celebrities created by the genre. Source: © BBC Picture Archive.*

REALITY TELEVISION

A natural extension of the docu-soap is the use of real-life characters in 'reality television'. This genre seeks to replicate or reconstruct real events. Footage shot by the emergency services, such as the police or the fire brigade, is partly used, but this is often enhanced by real people playing their own roles in the event. *Crimewatch* is a good example of people being asked to reconstruct their own roles as victims of or witnesses to crimes. Similarly, a programme such as *999* uses real people to re-enact life-threatening disasters and misfortunes that have befallen them. Such programmes clearly have a distinct audience appeal in terms of ordinary people being recognisably similar to us. The audience, therefore, is able to empathise with an ordinary member of the public in a way that they may not be able to do with an action hero or heroine. This may account for the popularity of a series like *Big Brother*, which attracted both large audiences and considerable media attention in the summer of 2000. The opportunity it presented for the audience to observe other people's daily lives in minute detail seemed irresistible to a large proportion of the population.

In making reality television programmes, the television producer is rewarded with a relatively cheap programme, using the public to act out the roles usually played by expensive stars.

FURTHER WORK . . .

1   Choose six different genres of film or television programme. For each identify the most likely generic convention for bringing the narrative to a close. Can you think of any texts that deliberately break the genre conventions in terms of narrative closure?

2   Choose two examples of fictional television series, such as soaps, and outline the main narrative characteristics of the genre.

3   Consider how the representation of a particular group has changed over a period of time. Do you think the change is positive or negative?

4   In what ways can the media be influenced to make more positive representations of minority groups?

5   How far can it be said that professional working practices in the media lead to negative representations?

6   It is argued that genre is a more useful concept to media producers than to media audiences. Do you agree?

7   Genre analysis is of little use when considering contemporary media texts. Discuss this statement by drawing on contemporary media texts to support your arguments.

8   Consider how one particular media genre has changed over a period of time. How do you account for these changes?

9   Create a publicity package for a new film or television programme that fits into an existing genre. Your package should contain a range of work including an advertisement and a press release. Identify where these will appear in order to reach the existing audience for this type of genre.

10 In what ways can narrative be said to be an important element of non-fiction texts? Support your answer with examples from at least two media forms.

11 Choose a minority group that is said to be inadequately or negatively represented in the media. Using examples, outline how the group is represented.

12 Find examples of texts that exist in different media forms. For example, think of some that started life as computer games. Why do you think these texts lend themselves so well to such intertextuality?

13 Consider how your reading of a text is affected by your knowledge of other texts from which borrowing may have occurred.

14 Assess the way in which real-life events and news stories are used as the basis for fictional texts.

15 Are there any texts created in order to oppose dominant ideological beliefs? If so, in what context are these texts likely to be found? At what type of audience are they aimed?

16 Consider some of the ways in which the media have been be used to change ideological beliefs and social attitudes.

17 All media texts are ideological. What do you understand by this statement? Illustrate your answer with examples.

18 In a media-saturated society in which media technology is playing an increasingly important role in our lives, how far do you agree with Baudrillard's notion of the hyper-real?

19 Documentaries have to be constructed in just the same way as fictional programmes. How far do you agree with this statement?

20 Imagine you are creating a marketing campaign for a film, a television series, a radio station or a magazine shortly to be launched. Decide on what you think would be appropriate promotional material. Which media would you use for advertising and promotion?

21 What do you understand by the term 'intertextuality'? Illustrate your answer with examples.

FURTHER READING

Bell, A., Joyce, M. and Rivers, D. (1999) *Advanced Level Media*, Hodder & Stoughton.

Bordwell, D. and Thompson, K. (1979) *Film Art: An Introduction*, McGraw-Hill.

Branston, G. and Stafford, R. (1999) *The Media Student's Book*, 2nd edition, Routledge.

Cohen, S. and Young, J. (1973) *The Manufacture of News: Deviance, Social Problems and the Mass Media*, Constable.

Corner, J. (1996) *The Art of Record: A Critical Introduction to Documentary*, Manchester University Press.

Fiske, J. (1987) *Television Culture*, Methuen.

— (1990) *Introduction to Communication Studies*, 2nd edition, Routledge.

Herman, E.S. and Chomsky, N. (1994) *Manufacturing Consent*, Vintage.

McRobbie, A. (1995) *Feminism and Youth Culture: From* Jackie *to* Just Seventeen, 2nd edn Macmillan.

Nelmes, J. (ed.) (1999) *An Introduction to Film Studies*, 2nd edition, Routledge.

O'Sullivan, T., Dutton, B. and Rayner, P. (1998) *Studying the Media*, 3rd edition, Arnold.

Paget, D. (1998) *No Other Way to Tell It: Dramadoc/Docudrama on Television*, Manchester University Press.

Storey, J. (1993) *An Introductory Guide to Cultural Theory and Popular Culture*, Harvester Wheatsheaf.

Strinati, D. (1995) *An Introduction to Theories of Popular Culture*, Routledge.

Taylor, L. and Willis, A. (1999) *Media Studies: Texts, Institutions and Audiences*, Blackwell.

Tilley, A. (1991) 'Narrative' in Lusted, D. (ed.) *The Media Studies Book: A Guide for Teachers*, Routledge.

Wilcock, J. (2000) *Documentaries*, Auteur.

Winston, B. (1995) *Claiming the Real: The Documentary Film Revisited*, BFI Publishing.

▼ EXAMPLE: TITLE SEQUENCES

In this section we present a case study of title sequences in film and television programmes. We draw on the concepts we have explored in the preceding chapters on media language. You may find this chapter valuable in considering how you might approach work on the close textual analysis of moving images.

Title sequences offer an interesting and rewarding area of study in our reading of media texts for a number of different reasons. Perhaps most importantly, it is their role in establishing initial contact with the audience and signalling to them what is to follow that makes them worthy of consideration. An audience receives from a title sequence an indication of the content of the text they are about to consume. As we have seen in the section on genre (p. 53), audiences usually approach a text with certain expectations.

Title sequences play a significant role in both raising the expectations of the audience and indicating how likely it is that these expectations will be fulfilled. Title sequences also signal to the audience an indication of the tone of the text that is to follow. They may suggest that it is light-hearted or serious. In doing so they have a clear function in both preparing and positioning the audience by putting them in an appropriate frame of mind to consume the subsequent text. News programmes have music that is serious and important-sounding. Comedy programmes, on the other hand, employ a lighter, more flippant style of music.

ACTIVITY . . .

Consider how music is used to indicate to an audience the nature of a text and its role in establishing the tone. Think of a situation where you have been in another room and heard the title music for a television programme. How does this impact on you?

In communist states in the Eastern bloc, solemn music was broadcast several days before the announcement of the death of an important political figure. Part of the function of this music was to prepare or position the audience in readiness for the national mourning that was expected to follow this news.

Title sequences can also be compared to magazine covers or the front pages of newspapers. All of these have the function of attracting an audience to come and consume the product that is on offer. An effective title sequence on television will call out to or hail an audience, through such devices as music, and invite them to consume the text. This invitation usually indicates the pleasures that lie in store for the audience if they choose to partake.

KEY TERM

INTERPELLATION The process by which a media text summons an audience in much the same way as a town crier would ring a bell and shout to summon an audience for an important announcement.

Louis Althusser argued that this process of interpellation is important in preparing an audience for the text they are about to consume. Part of its function, he argued, was to position the reader to be receptive to the ideological function the text was about to perform.

The idea of repetition also needs to be taken into account when we consider the functioning of title sequences. On television, many texts form part of a series that recurs over a period of time. News bulletins, for example, have individual time slots each weekday. Typically, a programme such as *Newsnight* has its own title sequence signalling to the viewer the programme that is to follow.

ACTIVITY . . .

Look at the title sequences for typical news bulletins broadcast by each of the terrestrial channels.

- What similarities do they have?
- In what ways are they different?
- What does this tell you about the style of news presentation that each adopts?

Similarly, serial programmes such as soaps, sitcoms and quiz shows all have title sequences that are immediately recognised by an audience. It is important to producers that these title sequences remain recognisable to the audience. Even programmes such as soaps, which have run over long periods of time, have maintained very similar title sequences in order to provide their audiences with the reassurance of instant recognition.

NOTEBOX

When a new series of programmes is launched, it is interesting to consider how the title sequence, although clearly individual to that programme, is likely to rely on links to other title sequences to programmes of a similar genre.

The idea of recognition is obviously not an issue with television programmes that do not form part of a series or with feature films shown both at the cinema and at home. In these cases the title sequence has other functions to perform. Besides summoning the audience and setting the tone of what is to come, these title sequences often function as the opening of the narrative that is to unfold. In this way they are likely to present a series of enigmas that work to engage us with the narrative in a similar way to a headline on the front of a newspaper. We are teased with information that invites us to involve ourselves in the narrative and to consume the rest of the text. At the same time we are promised that, through consuming the text, the enigmas that are teasing us in the title sequence will be resolved as the narrative is unravelled.

NOTEBOX

As the name suggests, a title sequence provides the audience with details of the title of the film or programme that they are about to watch. In addition, according to the particular genre of the text, it sometimes provides other information, such as details of the actors or stars, the production company and director/producer. A more detailed list of people who have contributed to the production process is usually given at the end. These are known as the end credits. Why do you think some people remain in the cinema to watch all the end credits?

When we undertake the analysis of a media text, it is always useful to have a checklist of the things we need to look for, similar to the worksheet given on p. 98. When we consider the title sequence of a television programme or film, it is important to keep in mind the function that the sequence has been designed to perform. For example, it may be a title sequence from a long-running series designed to remind the audience of a familiar programme. Alternatively you may be looking at a sequence for a film or a one-off television programme, which, as we have indicated, will work rather differently.

WORKSHEET FOR ANALYSING TITLE SEQUENCES

It is always useful to have any moving image text that you want to analyse available on video. This will enable you to watch it as many times as you wish. In addition you will be able to use the pause and slow-motion facilities on your video recorder to consider the framing of individual shots.

The following ideas may help you when you get started in your analysis of a title sequence:

- What sort of text is the sequence introducing? For example, a fictional/factual text?
- What tone is being set? Serious, light-hearted, flippant, or comic?
- What is the function of the text? Information; entertainment?
- What type of audience is being addressed? You might like to think in terms of age, gender, background, cultural experience.

Some further points to consider:

- Is the sequence live action or an animation? If the latter, why do you think this medium has been chosen?
- How has the sequence been edited? Short, fast-moving edits or long sequences? What is the effect of this?
- What does the soundtrack contribute to the sequence? You should consider use of music, voice-over and sound effects, for example.
- How long is the sequence? Is there a clear division between the end of the title sequence and the beginning of the text?
- What links does the sequence have to the text itself? How does it work as an introduction to the text? Is it, for example, an opening scene from the film or television programme?
- Is any iconography used that will be significant in the text to follow?
- How does the sequence link to other sequences introducing texts of the same genre?

CORONATION STREET

Coronation Street is the longest-running serial drama on television. It attracts an audience in the region of fifteen million viewers for each of its scheduled slots every week on ITV.

The title sequence for *Coronation Street* was revamped in January 2002. This was the fifth version of the title sequence in the show's forty-two-year history. Despite the many technical innovations in television production at the time of the revamp, it is interesting to note that the key features of the title sequence have remained very much the same as throughout the programme's history.

Clearly the main function of the title sequence is to announce to viewers that a familiar programme is about to be broadcast, rather than to entice them to watch a new one. In fact, the sequence introducing *Coronation Street* (Figure 1.19) will be familiar to the majority of the population, even those who are not regularly part of the vast audience.

The sequence itself runs for approximately twenty seconds. It is preceded by an animation that uses familiar chocolate-coloured images of the street to advertise the sponsor of the programme, Cadbury. The opening shot of the sequence is a crane shot. It creates for us an interesting contrast, with the screen split from top to bottom into three parts. At the very top of the screen we see, in the distance, a block of 1960s high-rise flats. These are separated by an area of what looks to be parkland from the back-to-back terraced houses that are Coronation Street and its immediate neighbourhood, the fictional town of Weatherfield. The camera slowly pans across the terraces, with smoke rising occasionally from a chimney, as the title 'Coronation Street' fades up. As the camera pans, a car turns into a side street and as the camera comes to rest a milk float makes its way across the screen down Coronation Street itself. The street is recognisable from the corner shop and the garish stone-clad fascia of the Duckworths' house at number 9.

Afficionados of the series may wonder how a street that is in fact a set built within the Granada Studios in Manchester can find its way into the back streets of a real Manchester suburb. Clearly in developing the new titles the producers have used computer-generated images to locate the 'fictional' set into the 'real' world.

The two types of housing shown in the opening shot are set in contrast. The brick-built terraces suggest an old-fashioned, close-knit, working-class community, while the two blocks carry with them the connotations of the alienation of impersonal life in the inner city, with all its incumbent social problems. This long shot from a high angle is important in establishing for us the inner-city context of the drama, with both its old and new architecture, as well as providing us with the name of the programme, which is overlaid on the image. On a connotational level there is a contrast between the lasting values and sense of an old-fashioned, close-knit, working-class community represented by the brick-built terraces and the decline of these same community values implicit in the images of the impersonal concrete tower blocks.

This establishing shot then dissolves into a ground-level shot of a road going under an arched bridge with a high brick wall to the right and a somewhat uninviting and unoccupied bench next to it. Through the frame of the bridge we can pick out more terraced houses, the glint of sunlight on one of them serving only to remind us of the greyness of the rest of the scene. Through the bridge a group of young boys run across the otherwise deserted street with their football. The whole scene is dominated by the bricks; the grey bricks of the arched bridge, the high brick wall and the brick-built houses beyond. There is a solidity and permanence about this gloomy environment from which the camera moves gently, almost imperceptibly, back.

As this scene dissolves into the next, the titles fade down. The next scene depicts a cobbled pathway, or ginnel, between the backs of the terraced houses, again shot from above. These are the characters' back yards, where they hang their washing and put rubbish in the bins. A black cat confronts a neighbouring feline along a wall between two houses and a blue van drives past the bottom of the ginnel. The scene then dissolves to a high-level shot above the roofs of the houses as two chimney pots fill half the screen. We see for the first time that Coronation Street is a street of contrasts; on one side Victorian terraces and on the other side bijou modern residences with token front gardens filled with greenery. We also notice that the street is one of the few remaining cobbled streets. Our eye also catches a denim-clad character walking away from the camera to the end of the street. This then dissolves to a ground-level shot of the street, showing the Rover's Return pub on the left of the screen with a board outside advertising its special deals. The director's name appears on the dissolve and as we look down the street a Greater Manchester tram runs across the viaduct at the top of the screen, left to right, before the action cuts to the first scene of the evening's episode. The movement within each shot suggests that the mise-en-scène has been carefully orchestrated to suggest real-life activity going on within the static townscape.

The music that acts as a soundtrack to these titles is an instantly recognisable tune associated with *Coronation Street* throughout the course of its history. The brass instrument playing in a minor key provides a plaintive accompaniment to the images on screen. The association of brass instruments with northern industrial life is clearly an element contributing to the effectiveness of the title sequence. Allied to the images, it presents us with a sense of timeless northern working-class life with its connotations of a down-to-earth community in which the lives of people are played out against a backdrop of industrial grime and squalor.

There are a great number of similarities between the new title sequence and those that preceded it. It remains a strong affirmation of the idea of community in what many would see as a rather nostalgic and even outmoded way. There has clearly been some attempt to enhance the sense of realism through firmly locating 'Weatherfield' within the framework of Greater Manchester. This is achieved first through the computer manipulation of the images to place this fictional stage alongside its real-life counter-parts and, second, by the presence of the tram speeding across the bottom of the street, binding the programme into the wider context of Manchester and northern culture.

It is worth noting that although the tram runs past the bottom of the street, there seems to have been little protest or even comment from the street's residents, who collectively rose in spontaneous protest when the local council sent the boys from the blackstuff to tarmac over their precious cobbles.

ACTIVITY

> Look carefully at a video of the title sequence for *Coronation Street*.
>
> ■ Why do you think there are so few people featured in any of the shots?
> ■ Why do you think dissolves have been used as transitions between each shot?

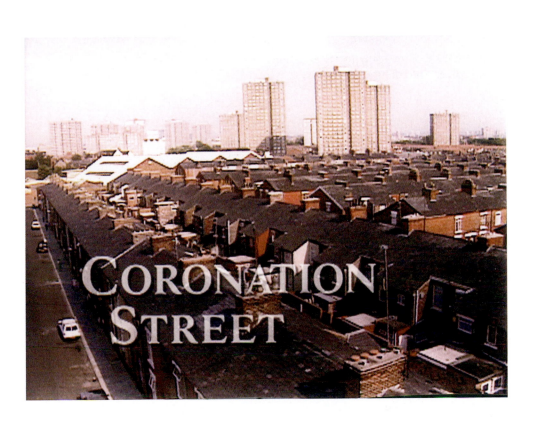

Figure 1.19 Coronation Street, *opening shots. Source © Granada Television, courtesy of Pinewood Studios.*

DISSOLVE Film term for the transition between two images whereby one 'dissolves' into the next.

NEIGHBOURS

The title sequence to *Neighbours* (Figure 1.20) makes an interesting contrast to that of *Coronation Street*. *Neighbours* is an Australian-produced soap, broadcast on BBC One at lunchtime each weekday and repeated early evening. The early-evening time slot and the preponderance of characters in their teens and early twenties have made it popular with a young audience. In fact the slot it occupies in the early evening immediately follows the end of children's television.

The programme is based on a community who live in a suburban street of an Australian city. Unlike *Coronation Street*, in which no one appears in the title sequence, *Neighbours* uses its opening credits to introduce all the major characters currently featuring in the serial.

The title sequence opens with a couple of 'dramatic' sequences from recent episodes of the soap. Each presents the audience with an unresolved narrative conflict involving characters who appear in the episode that follows. Each is a narrative enigma designed both to tease and remind the audience, and to ensure their interest in the current episode, which promises some development or even resolution of the conflicts.

Accompanying this opening is the instantly recognisable *Neighbours* theme tune. The melody, which is much more upbeat and jolly than the plaintive tones of *Coronation Street*, is at this stage an instrumental version of the well-known melody.

The reprise sequence runs for around thirty seconds before cutting to a montage of approximately twenty seconds that introduces us to the characters at play. The montage is interesting because of the way in which it employs a split-screen technique to introduce a group of central characters currently in the series. These short scenes are set outdoors, where, in contrast to the grim urban landscape of *Coronation Street*, the bright sunshine of Australia beats down on the *dramatis personae* as they relax on the lawn in family and domestic groups. The use of the split-screen technique, particularly effective in widescreen format, allows the left-hand two-thirds of the screen to be used primarily for long shots of the groups of characters, while the right-hand side picks up on close-ups of individual characters and objects in the garden such as the lawn sprinkler. The audience find themselves trying to locate the close-ups in relation to the broader picture framed opposite, rather like fitting in a jigsaw piece.

The music that accompanies this sequence contains lyrics that celebrate and idealise the virtues of neighbourliness, suggesting that *Neighbours* can 'become good friends'. Frequently, however, the subsequent narratives suggest that this is not always the case, despite the insistence that everybody needs good neighbours, a sentiment that clearly seeks to universalise the theme.

As the title comes to an end the title sequence offers us the name of the location by way of a street sign that we never see in its entirety, again offering a piece of a jigsaw that we are invited to fit together. As the title sequence draws to an end the title 'Neighbours' appears on the screen. It is interesting to note that both *Neighbours* and *Coronation Street* end by emphasising the setting of the drama and with it the connotations of communities and the people who live in them.

Figure 1.20   Neighbours, title sequence. Source: © Pearson Television.

ACTIVITY...

Now watch the title sequences of the two soaps yourself, checking for any changes in style or content that may have been made.

- How do you account for the different approaches of the two programmes?
- What do you think this tells the audience about the themes and content of the two programmes?
- What do the title sequences tell us about the way in which each programme addresses its audience?
- Do you think the audience for the two programmes is likely to be similar?
- Now consider two more soaps, such as *EastEnders*, *Hollyoaks* or *Home and Away*.
- What similarities and differences does each have with *Neighbours* and *Coronation Street*?
- What does this tell you about the nature of the programme?

As we have noted previously, title sequences for films and one-off television programmes function differently from those for a television series. The latter work through a form of interpellation which relies on audience familiarity and recognition. The title sequence of a feature film will almost certainly be new to the audience when they encounter it. It therefore needs to perform several important functions, not the least of which is to gain and hold the attention of the audience. This is especially true when a film is being shown domestically rather than at the cinema. When we watch a film at home, even by means of a rented video, it has to compete not only with other choices of media consumption (other television programmes, radio, computer games), but also with a multitude of distractions, such as the telephone or unexpected visitors.

The title sequence of a film, however, does much more than grab the attention of the audience. It is an important signalling device to show us what we can expect from the text we are about to consume.

TAXI DRIVER

Taxi Driver is arguably one of the most important films of the last century. Released in 1976, it is director Martin Scorsese's study of an obsessive loner, alienated from society by his experiences in the Vietnam War. He finds work as the eponymous taxi driver, and the opening to the movie provides the audience with an insight into the man who is to be the focus of attention in the action that follows (see Figure 1.21).

The opening shot is a cloud of steam emerging from a New York street that fills the screen. From the steam emerges a yellow cab, which drives in slow motion towards us and across our field of vision, in close-up, leaving us with the screen again filled with the steam. Both the steam from the street and the yellow cab are powerful, almost indexical, images of New York. The image is accompanied by a discordant soundtrack of percussion instruments, which adds to the eerie nature of what we see on the screen. The title credits, in the same yellow as the taxi, appear on screen against the backdrop

Figure 1.21 Taxi Driver (1976). Source: Kobal Collection © Columbia.

of the white steam and accompanied initially by the discordant music, which itself gradually develops a clearer melody, until the screen dissolves into an extreme close-up image of Travis Bickle's (Robert De Niro's) face bathed in a red light, as his eyes scan across the screen. The music has now become a mellow-sounding and harmonious saxophone solo. The scene then dissolves into a point-of-view shot through the windscreen of the cab.

The image through the screen is blurred by rain on the windscreen itself. Even when the wipers clear the screen, the image remains distorted and unworldly as we try to pick out the New York night-time street scene with its garish lighting and ghostly figures. As the scene dissolves into a clearer and closer shot of people crossing the road in front of the cab, the music again shifts from melodious sax to discordant percussion. The figures crossing the road are shrouded in the steam and bathed in the same red light, giving them the appearance of creatures of another world, perhaps even some kind of hell. The image again dissolves to an extreme close-up of Bickle's face as his eyes pan across the screen. Again his face is coloured by the same red light that pervades the night-time street. Finally the image dissolves into the dense white steam that again fills the screen, as the music hovers between the melody of the saxophone and the discordant sound of the percussion.

This opening sequence runs for a little over a minute and a half before dissolving into a shot following Travis Bickle into an interview for a taxi-driving job. On a denotational level we can read the sequence as a man driving a taxi at night through the streets of New York, On a connotational level, however, this title sequence is rich in themes and ideas that prepare the audience for much of what is to follow in the film. There are a number of images in which what we see on screen is blurred or distorted, for example the clouds of steam and the rain on the windscreen. Psychologically, Travis Bickle is a man who finds it hard to see the world clearly, at least from a moral perspective. His experiences in Vietnam have clouded his judgement. The blurred images on the screen can be read as a metaphor for the confusion that exists inside his head. Similarly the recurrence of the colour red, on two occasions on Bickle's face, suggests the anger that is pent up inside him – an anger that ultimately finds its release in a bloodbath, when Bickle decides to play the avenging angel. The music's movement between harmony and discord again suggests the volatile state of Bickle's mind, moving between controlled calmness and sudden bursts of anger.

The sequence creates a sense of weirdness: familiar images are filmed in such a way as to seem dislocated or out of context. The effect is achieved in several ways, such as the use of slow motion and the garish colours. The sequence seems to have been constructed specifically to suggest the hero's emotional and psychological state as well as to introduce us to the nature of his job and the environment in which he works.

NOTEBOX . . .

The reason that Robert De Niro's eyes move so slowly and deliberately across the screen is that the camera was over-cranked in order to shoot the scene in slow motion to create this particular effect that the director wanted.

FURTHER WORK . . .

Taxi Driver is a rich and complex film that rewards detailed study and analysis. This is not the case with many films. It is, however, still a useful and worthwhile process to look closely at the opening of a film or television programme to identify:

■ how it has been constructed
■ why it was done in that way
■ how this affects the audience's reading of the film.

PART 2: MEDIA AUDIENCES

In Part 2 we look at:

- how audiences are made up
- the ways in which audiences have changed over time and how our engagement with media forms is patterned and determined
- 'passive' and 'active' views of the audience
- some of the issues around the 'effects' debate
- some of the research that has been carried out on audience behaviour
- terms such as 'hypodermic needle theory', 'uses and gratifications', 'mode of address' and 'situated culture'.

DIFFERENT TYPES OF AUDIENCE

In one sense everyone is part of the audience in that we are all, to some degree or another, exposed to media texts. However, it can sometimes be difficult to stand back and think about the different ways in which our daily lives interact with the media. It is well worth considering the extent to which, in an average day, we will be part of many different audiences for a wide range of media. (The activity on p. 3 of the introduction will help you classify your exposure to different media forms.) This may include being part of a radio audience in the morning as we get ready for college or work, watching breakfast television or reading the newspaper, listening to music on an MP3 player, surfing the Internet, or glimpsing advertising hoardings as we travel to school or work.

Throughout the day we will be, either consciously or unconsciously, exposed to different media products – becoming part of many different types of audience. As we mentioned in the introduction, it may be as part of an audience of over fourteen million people all watching the same episode of *EastEnders* at the same time. It may be as part of an audience sitting alone in their cars listening to the same radio show, or as one of 200 people watching a film in a cinema. It can also be through the more personal and private consumption of newspapers, either local or national, or

magazines, or through the one-to-one communication of the Internet. We may work in an environment in which a radio is on in the background, or somewhere – for example a hospital or a shop – that has its own radio station.

WHY ARE AUDIENCES IMPORTANT?

There are several reasons why audiences are important. The first is perhaps the most obvious.

- Without an audience, why would anyone create a media text? What is the point of a film that no one sees?
- Audience size and reaction are often seen as a way of measuring the success (or otherwise) of a media product. One of the reasons why we say that the *Sun* newspaper is successful is because it sells over three million copies a day and is read by nearly twelve million people.
- Audiences who buy media texts are providing income for the media companies which produce them.
- Much of the media available to us, however, is free or subsidised; it is financed by advertising, and the advertisers want to know that they are getting value for money.
- In other words, they want to know which, and how many, people are seeing their advertisements.
- As the media become more central to our lives, so many people want to know how we use the media, what we understand of what we consume, and the effects that the media have on our lives.

HOW HAVE AUDIENCES CHANGED?

Concerns about the size and impact of the media on audiences, the 'effectiveness' of advertising, and how audiences interrelate with the media have been with us since the development of a 'mass' audience at the beginning of the twentieth century.

We know that the media are constantly changing, and this means that audiences, too, must be changing, partly as a result of the changes in media technology but also because of the changes in the way we live our lives and because we as individuals change. Consider Figure 2.1; it shows cinema audiences in the 1950s wearing special glasses to watch such films as *It Came from Outer Space* (1953) and *Creatures From the Black Lagoon* (1954), which were made with special 3D effects that made the monsters seem to come out of the screen to attack the audience. (If you study the figure closely you may notice that the audience is predominantly male and that there appears to be one man not wearing special 3D glasses.) Although this was seen as a gimmick in the 1950s and the films quickly disappeared, there has been a reappearance of 3D effects in recent years, especially through the growth of IMAX cinemas, where, once again, audiences wearing special glasses can see characters and objects appearing to fly around in space in front of them.

Figure 2.1 *Cinema audience wearing 3D glasses – one way in which cinema tried to compete with the increasing popularity of television. Source: British Film Institute.*

The word 'broadcasting' implies a 'mass' audience of perhaps more than thirty million people all watching or listening to the same event, at the same time, participating in the same experience. The 1966 World Cup final attracted a television audience of thirty-two million viewers, while the wedding of Prince Charles and Lady Diana in 1981 attracted thirty-nine million. The episode of *EastEnders* in which Den and Angie split up, broadcast in December 1986, attracted over thirty million viewers and was voted twenty-fourth in a millennium poll of the top 100 television excerpts. Number One was the live broadcast of Neil Armstrong and Buzz Aldrin walking on the moon in July 1969; it is estimated that over 600 million people watched this on television.

Today we have a wide range of broadcasting and press services available to us. Radio and television, in particular, have moved away from the original ideas of addressing a large 'mass' audience. Today the concept is one of narrowcasting, where programmes are aimed at specific, specialist audiences in a way that is similar to the range and variety of magazines available in a newsagent. There is now a wide range of specialist channels and stations aimed at small and specific markets that might be defined on the grounds of age (Classic FM, Disney, or Angel Radio in Havant, where they refuse to play any music recorded after 1959), gender (the digital television channel Men & Motors), interests (most obviously sports channels, but also television channels such as National Geographic, UK History or Home & Leisure) or ethnicity (radio stations such as Sunrise in London and Bradford or television channels such as PCNE Chinese, Bangla TV or Channel East, aimed at Chinese or other Asian audiences).

<table>
<tr><td>KEY TERM</td><td>**NARROWCASTING** The opposite of broadcasting. Where texts are aimed at very small, special-interest groups.</td></tr>
</table>

ACTIVITY...

Research the way people used to consume the media.

- Perhaps using your parents or grandparents, carry out a small oral history project. Ask them to talk about how they listened to the radio, watched television or went to the cinema when they were young. Is the way they watched television then different from the way we watch it now? How have patterns of consumption changed? If so, how do you account for these changes?

- The coronation of Queen Elizabeth II in 1953 was one of the most important events in introducing people to television for the first time. Try to find people who remember watching the live broadcast of the coronation and ask them how they watched it. Think also about your own earliest experiences of seeing television and 'special events'.

- You could also try to find out what the television schedules looked like in the 1950s and/or 1960s. What does a comparison between then and now tell us about the changing television audience?

This change from 'broadcasting' to 'narrowcasting' partly results from the development of new media technologies that have become, or are increasingly becoming, part of our ordinary domestic lives. These include new hardware products such as DVD and video recorders, computers and satellite and cable television receivers, but there has also been an increase in ownership of existing hardware. For instance, once upon a time it was the norm for a household to have only one television set, often placed in the living

room and usually with the furniture organised around it. Before that it was not unusual for households to have just one radio (or wireless) set that again would have been placed in the living room and the furniture arranged around it. The illustration on the cover of the *Radio Times* (Figure 2.2) represents a view of how families were thought to consume radio in the 1930s and 1940s. It might be interesting to look at the covers of current listings magazines to see what types of images are used today (see also section on media ideology, p. 78).

Figure 2.2 Radio Times *cover, 30 September 1949. The radio set was once the focal point of family entertainment. Source:* Radio Times.

Today many households have several radios and televisions spread around the house, perhaps in bedrooms as well as in the living room, maybe in the kitchen and, in the case of radios, in cars and as part of personal stereos. Part of the reason for this growth in hardware is that television sets and radios have become both increasingly cheap to buy and more compact in size. When colour television sets first came on the market, they cost the equivalent of several weeks' wages, whereas today they represent less than one week's wages. Increasingly radio receivers, television screens and MP3 players are becoming smaller and smaller and can now be incorporated into other technology such as mobile phones. As more and more of our lives become linked with media consumption and as more and more of our peers have several radio and television sets, so there can be a pressure on us as consumers to buy more and more of these products – especially when we are told that each new piece of technology is better than the previous one.

ACTIVITY...

Carry out research amongst your peers to see how many television sets, radios or MP3 players they have in their households. Work out the average number of people per radio and television set. In Britain, according to BBC figures, there are more radio sets than adults. Does your research support this claim?

OR

Consider how one particular media genre has changed over a period of time. How do you account for these changes?

Some of the changes you may have identified in the ways in which we consume media products will have come about because of the increase in services available to us. When television first started it was broadcast for only a few hours a day, mostly in the evening, and the BBC had something called 'the toddlers' truce', when television closed down at teatime, after children's television, to allow parents to put their children to bed. On Sundays broadcasting was very limited because it was assumed that most people would be going to church services or wanting religious programming.

Gradually over the years the amount and range of television broadcasting have increased. Breakfast television went on air in 1983, and now we have five domestic terrestrial channels that broadcast twenty-four hours a day. Part of the reason for this is that television companies now recognise that there are many different groups of audiences who watch television at different times of the day and want different types of programmes. Figure 2.6 on p. 119 shows how different media are used across an average day. Radio is shown to be more significant during the day but television takes over during the evening and night.

Figure 2.3 demonstrates the effects that increased competition has had on the main terrestrial television channels. In 1981, when there were only three channels available to viewers, BBC One attracted 39 per cent of the audience, compared to 26.2 per cent

Figure 2.3 *Annual % shares of viewing (individuals), 1981–2002.*
Source: Broadcaster's Audience Research Board Ltd (BARB).

Year	Channel					
	BBC One	BBC Two	ITV (inc. GMTV)	CH4	CH5	Others (Cable/ Sat/RTE)
1981	39	12	49	–	–	–
1982	38	12	50	–	–	–
1983	37	11	48	4	–	–
1984	36	11	48	6	–	–
1985	36	11	46	7	–	–
1986	37	11	44	8	–	–
1987	38	12	42	8	–	–
1988	38	11	42	9	–	–
1989	39	11	42	9	–	–
1990	37	10	44	9	–	–
1991	34	10	42	10	–	4
1992	34	10	41	10	–	5
1993	33	10	40	11	–	6
1994	32	11	39	11	–	7
1995	32	11	37	11	–	9
1996	33.5	11.5	35.1	10.7	–	10.1
1997	30.8	11.6	32.9	10.6	2.3	11.8
1998	29.5	11.3	31.7	10.3	4.3	12.9
1999	28.4	10.8	31.2	10.3	5.4	14
2000	27.2	10.8	29.3	10.5	5.7	16.6
2001	26.9	11.1	26.7	10.0	5.8	19.6
2002	26.2	11.4	24.1	10.0	6.3	22.1

Note: Shares before 1996 have been rounded to nearest whole

in 2002. ITV1, a commercial organisation whose revenue is dependent upon its ratings, had 49 per cent of the audience in 1981, whereas in 2002 this had dropped to 24.1 per cent. Since their introduction in 1991, the cable and satellite channels have built up an audience share of over 22 per cent. Other relatively new services, such as Channel Four and Channel Five, in 2002 accounted for another 16 per cent of the audience.

Today the rate of change is becoming faster and it is difficult to predict what our domestic media will look like in ten years' time. The new ADSL (Asymmetrical Digital Subscriber Line) telephone network turns an ordinary telephone copper wire into a high-speed connection for Internet, broadcasting and video-on-demand services. Over 40 per cent of households in Britain now have digital television services, many of which provide access to the Internet via the television set. Increasingly such developments as Internet-based radio services, more digital television channels and MP3 players will mean that audiences for traditionally popular 'mass' programmes will become more fragmented. The 'free' audience for programmes such as *The Premiership* or *Match of the Day* is likely to decline as more and more football clubs offer their own subscription channels, like Manchester United's MUTV, or because of the growth of 'interactive' digital channels that offer the viewer a choice of camera angles, instant replays and additional information about players and teams. Consider Figure 2.4, which lists the top digital television programmes for the week ending 16 March 2003. You will see that three of the top five programmes are football matches. Increasingly digital television channels offer additional services; for example, it is possible to select your own 'news story' on most digital news channels and travel channels offer the opportunity to book holidays as well as giving weather details from around the world.

Eventually we may rely upon the mobile phone instead of *Top of the Pops* to give us the latest record charts and we will be able to download and play the latest releases and order tickets for concerts at the same time.

This increase in choice may suit those who can afford to pay monthly cable or satellite subscription fees in addition to pay-per-view fees for films or special sporting events. However, there are some observers who are concerned that those who are less affluent may end up with an inferior and limited, but 'free', choice. The popularity of the BBC Freeview digital service suggests that there are a number of people who want access to digital services but do not want the range that is on offer via the subscription packages. BBC's Freeview can also be seen as an attempt to 'marry' new digital services with the BBC's public service broadcasting remit (see p. 210 in Part 3).

ACTIVITY . . .

Look at BARB's Top 20 multichannel programmes (Figure 2.4).

■ Can we draw any conclusions as to the most popular types of programme for satellite viewers?
■ How do the audience figures compare with those of terrestrial programmes?

■ What do you think is the attraction of these programmes for satellite viewers?

(You can access more up-to-date viewing figures at the BARB website, <http://www.barb.co.uk>.)

Figure 2.4 *BARB: Top 20 multichannel television programmes. Source: Broadcast, 4 April 2003. Source: Broadcaster's Audience Research Board Ltd (BARB).*

	Title	Day	Start	Viewers (millions)	Channel	Last week
1	Uefa Champions League Live	Wed	19.40	1.48	ITV2	–
2	Live Ford Football Special	Sat	12.00	0.94	Sky Sports 1	–
3	The Simpsons	Sun	18.30	0.91	Sky One	3
4	Uefa Champions League Live	Tue	19.40	0.84	ITV2	–
5	Buffy the Vampire Slayer	Thu	20.00	0.82	Sky One	5
6	Dream Team	Sun	20.00	0.79	Sky One	21
7	Angel	Thu	21.00	0.74	Sky One	9
8	Coronation Street Special/Hillman	Fri	20.00	0.69	ITV2	–
8	The Simpsons	Mon	19.00	0.69	Sky One	11
8	Futurama	Sun	19.00	0.69	Sky One	10
8	ER	Thu	22.00	0.69	E4	4
12	The Simpsons	Thu	19.00	0.67	Sky One	16
12	The Simpsons	Tue	19.00	0.67	Sky One	11
14	ER	Thu	21.00	0.64	E4	–
15	The Simpsons	Wed	19.00	0.63	Sky One	16
15	The Simpsons	Sun	19.30	0.63	Sky One	33
17	The Simpsons	Thu	19.30	0.62	Sky One	30
18	When Football Managers Go Mad	Sun	21.00	0.60	Sky One	–
18	Ford Super Sunday	Sun	15.00	0.60	Sky Sports 1	–
20	The Simpsons	Mon	19.30	0.59	Sky One	17

Part of the change that has occurred over the years results from the way in which the technology that produces media texts has changed. The introduction of such innovations as the 'Steadicam' or high-definition portable video-cameras has made news, documentaries and 'live' programming much more 'action-packed' and attractive to viewers. There was a vogue a few years ago for investigative programmes that used small hidden cameras to expose various malpractices. Consider, for example, the technology required to produce a programme like Channel Four's *Big Brother*, or the way in which video-phones were used in the reporting of the 2003 Iraqi and 2002 Afghan wars.

Another example of how our patterns of consumption have changed is cinema attendance in this country.

ACTIVITY...

Look at the figures for cinema attendances in Britain between 1933 and 2000 in Figure 2.5.

■ Can you suggest reasons why admissions almost halved between 1956 and 1959? Or why they have more than doubled between 1984 and 2000?

■ Consider how the cinema audience has changed. Look at the development of multiplexes and the types of film they show. How might these have helped shape the cinema audience and to what extent is such an audience similar to/different from ten or twenty years ago?

■ Find out about cinemas other than multiplexes, for example independent, 'art house' cinemas and/or clubs. What sorts of films do they show? What types of audience are attracted to these cinemas?

■ How has the introduction of video recording and DVD changed the way in which we consume films?

■ Consider the different formats that one film may appear in: the cinema version, on video or DVD, on cable or satellite television, on terrestrial television or shown on an aeroplane. Are there different audiences for different formats of the same film?

■ What effect has the introduction of DVD technology had on the market for pre-recorded videos and video players?

■ What are the differences for audiences between seeing a film in the cinema and on a television set in a domestic setting?

■ Is there a difference between the ways in which we consume a film video or DVD that is rented and one that is bought?

■ Choose a particular film and consider the way in which it is being marketed. This should provide you with clues as to the type of 'imagined' audience the producers are aiming at.

Figure 2.5 *UK cinema admissions 1933–2000. Source: Screen Digest/CAA/AC Nielsen EDI.*

Year	Millions	Year	Millions
1933	903.00	1967	264.80
1934	950.00	1968	237.30
1935	912.33	1969	214.90
1936	917.00		
1937	946.00	1970	193.00
1938	987.00	1971	176.00
1939	990.00	1972	156.60
		1973	134.20
1940	1,027.00	1974	138.50
1941	1,309.00	1975	116.30
1942	1,494.00	1976	103.90
1943	1,541.00	1977	103.50
1944	1,575.00	1978	126.10
1945	1,585.00	1979	111.90
1946	1,635.00		
1947	1,462.00	1980	101.00
1948	1,514.00	1981	86.00
1949	1,430.00	1982	64.00
		1983	65.70
1950	1,395.80	1984	54.00
1951	1,365.00	1985	72.00
1952	1,312.10	1986	75.00
1953	1,284.50	1987	78.50
1954	1,275.80	1988	84.00
1955	1,181.80	1989	94.50
1956	1,100.80		
1957	915.20	1990	97.37
1958	754.70	1991	100.29
1959	581.00	1992	103.64
		1993	114.36
1960	500.80	1994	123.53
1961	449.10	1995	114.56
1962	395.00	1996	123.80
1963	357.20	1997	139.30
1964	342.80	1998	135.50
1965	326.60	1999	139.75
1966	288.80	2000	142.50

HOW IS AUDIENCE CONSUMPTION PATTERNED AND DETERMINED?

We have already mentioned how we, as audiences, use different media at different times of the day. It is worth spending a little more time exploring the relationship between our patterns of media consumption and the routines of our daily lives. One of the measurements of the extent to which we now live in a media-saturated society is the degree to which our routine daily activities are interlinked with the media.

Many of us wake up in the morning to the sounds of a radio rather than an alarm clock. We may possibly have gone off to sleep with the same radio playing and set to its 'sleep' function. Many televisions also have the same feature, although it may be harder to imagine drifting off to sleep part way through a television programme or a film. We have also already mentioned breakfast television, which many of us now take for granted as a way of getting the latest news over our breakfast or whilst getting ready for college or work.

The programmes we watch and/or listen to in the morning often have regular features or segments that are broadcast at the same time each day. In this way we are able to measure our progress each morning by their regular appearance, for example the news headlines, reviews of the day's newspapers or spoof 'wake-up' calls made to unsuspecting members of the public.

It is interesting to reverse the equation and consider to what extent the media *organise* our daily routines rather than just fitting in around them. Some people will refuse to go out in the evening or to answer the telephone or speak to visitors until their favourite programme has ended. Mid-morning television shows encourage housewives to sit down with a cup of coffee and relax after getting the family off to work and/or school.

Schedulers for channels such as BBC Two and Channel Four assume that young people will watch their channels between 5 p.m. and 7 p.m. in the evenings, presumably as a means of relaxing after a day at school or work or as a break between day and evening activities.

ACTIVITY...

Consider your own daily/weekly routine and the manner in which the media interweave with it.

- To what extent does your own daily media consumption fit with that illustrated in Figure 2.6? How do you account for any differences?
- Consider the extent to which your consumption of the media fits around your schedule or whether your schedule is to some extent shaped by your media consumption; do you, for example, sometimes plan your activities around particular media output?

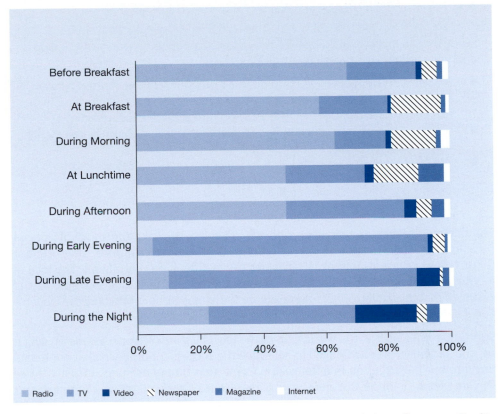

Figure 2.6 *Share of media consumption by time of day. Source:* Radio Days 2, 1999 © Radio Advertising Bureau.

If you look at the radio or television schedules, you will notice that particular categories of audiences are addressed and particular genres of programmes are featured at particular times. We are all familiar with the notion of 'peak viewing time', but it is perhaps more interesting to look at the schedules outside this period to see what types of audience are being addressed, say, between 9 a.m. and lunchtime on a weekday on the different channels or on a Saturday or Sunday morning.

Children's television, for example, is mainly broadcast in the late afternoon and early evening when schoolchildren are expected to have finished school. There are, however, also children's programmes shown on terrestrial television at other times during the week and at weekends.

Study the schedules of the terrestrial television channels and identify what groups are being addressed at particular times.

- Is there a difference between the children's programmes transmitted between 4 p.m. and 6 p.m. and those transmitted in the middle of the morning or at the weekend? When do the children's satellite channels broadcast?
- Why are Channel Four programmes such as *Frasier* or *So Graham Norton* usually broadcast after 10 p.m.?
- Does the same exercise work for radio schedules or for the schedules of cable, satellite and digital television?

Popular media such as television and the press try to make the most of special occasions like royal or sporting events or, recently, the Queen's Jubilee. They attempt to turn these occasions into rituals in which the media play a central part. The idea of a typical Christmas Day that centres around the television is one example – it is assumed that the family cannot fully celebrate Christmas without watching the Queen's Speech, film premieres and special editions of popular programmes.

Sporting events such as the World Cup or the Olympics are other occasions on which we, the audience, are encouraged to celebrate the success (or otherwise) of our teams through our participation in a 'television event' that often has special theme tunes (*Nessun Dorma* for the 1990 World Cup is perhaps one of the best-known examples) and a special presentation studio for links and interviews. The normal schedules may be changed to highlight the importance and uniqueness of the occasion. There will probably also be special 'souvenir' editions of television listings magazines or newspaper supplements in which we can get background information and keep a record of the progress of the events.

One of the reasons that media companies like to turn these occasions into rituals is that by packaging them in this way they hope to attract larger audiences than normal. These packages can then be sold on to advertisers. Another reason is that, as pay-per-view becomes increasingly available, it is a way of making these broadcasts look 'special' and worth paying extra money for. This is increasingly the case with sporting events such as world championships in, for example, cricket, rugby, boxing or golf.

- List all the different media texts that you have consumed in the last week. Divide your list into those texts that you had to pay for individually (cinema, newspapers, magazines, books and so on) and those that were available to you free of charge (television channels and radio stations, for example). Are the services provided by the BBC free?

■ Compare the prices of the television licence and the various costs of digital television and radio packages.

WHO IS THE AUDIENCE?

Many commentators suggest that in any text there is an implied audience, that the producers of media texts have a 'typical' audience member in mind when they start to create a text. (Look at the section on production skills (p. 321) – you are asked to do the same thing in terms of your target audience.)

Ien Ang, in *Desperately Seeking the Audience* (1991), discusses the manner in which media producers and institutions view audiences as an 'imaginary entity', as a mass rather than as a set of individuals. They will, however, often have a 'typical' audience member in mind when they produce their texts.

Figure 2.7 The Royle Family. *The Royle family entertain us, the audience, while they themselves sit round the television being entertained. Source: © BBC Picture Archive.*

Trainee ILR (Independent Local Radio) presenters were supposed to have had an imaginary person, 'Doreen', whom they were told to consider as the 'typical listener'. Presenters were told about her age, her likes and dislikes, her habits, her household and her husband. They were told that Doreen is 'typical'. She is educated and intelligent but may only listen to the radio with half an ear and does not necessarily understand long words or complicated discussions. They were told that this does not mean that Doreen is stupid and should be talked down to, but that they should make sure that she understands and is engaged with what is happening on the radio. They were encouraged to address Doreen and her husband personally, as if they knew them.

Academic research, however, has produced another version of this 'imaginary entity'. In *Understanding News* (1982), Hartley identified seven types of what he called 'subjectivities' that are used by media producers to help define the social position of the individual audience member and to engage with him or her:

- self-image
- gender
- age group
- family
- class
- nation
- ethnicity.

Fiske, in *Television Culture* (1987), added four more:

- education
- religion
- politics
- location (geographical and local).

However, Hartley acknowledged that sometimes these categories can get mixed up or can conflict with each other; for instance, some notions of nationhood and some types of ethnicity (Hartley 1982: 69). It is also not clear to what extent these subjectivities are equal or whether in particular circumstances some may be more influential than others.

These categories are useful in identifying the way in which individual members of mass audiences are identified both by themselves and by media producers and advertisers. Fiske, talking about television, says that it 'tries to construct an ideal subject position which it invites us to occupy, and, if we do, rewards us with . . . the pleasure of recognition' (Fiske 1987: 51).

ACTIVITY . . .

Using the subjectivities above, try to deduce an 'ideal viewer/reader' for particular programmes/publications. Consider what clues to this type of person there are in programmes such as *Newsround* or *The Bill*.

'TELEVISION DOESN'T MAKE PROGRAMMES, IT CREATES AUDIENCES' (JEAN-LUC GODARD)

Advertising is important to a whole range of media products because these products are financed by advertising revenue or are subsidised by the revenue that advertising brings in. The media therefore spend a lot of time and money looking at the circulation and ratings of their products.

Even if you pay for some media products, the advertising can still have subsidised the price and made the product cheaper for you to buy. Take a local weekly newspaper such as the *Wiltshire Times*, which costs 40p a copy and is probably considered a good buy for that price. It will have lots of local information, stories and photographs. However, if we look through the *Wiltshire Times*, we see that nearly 40 per cent of it is made up of advertisements, either for such products as cars, computers or shop goods, or for job vacancies, private car sales and other services (classified ads). One of the reasons why people buy this newspaper is to obtain the information contained in the advertisements. If we want to buy a new car, find somewhere local to live, or see what is on at the cinema, we can look through the advertisements in our local paper and see what is available.

The cover price of the *Wiltshire Times*, 40p, probably represents about 15 or 20 per cent of the true cost of printing an edition of the paper. Without the advertising the reader might have to pay about £3 a copy, and at that price it is unlikely that the *Wiltshire Times* would sell many copies. A few years ago there was an enormous growth of free local newspapers that were financed purely through their advertising revenue. The *Wiltshire Times* has a circulation of about 19,000, but the company that publishes it also publishes several other local free newspapers, whose circulation varies between 20,000 and 60,000.

ACTIVITY . . .

Investigate the local newspapers that are available in your area.

- List those that are paid for and those that are free.

continued

- Either contact the companies that publish them or, using reference books such as *Benn's Media*, compare circulation figures and advertising rates. The websites <http://www.jicreg.co.uk> (the Joint Industry Committee for Regional Press Research) and <http://www.newspapersoc.org.uk> (the Newspaper Society) both have a lot of information about local newspapers and it is possible to get readership reports on your own local newspaper through the JICREG website.
- Can you identify any connections between the advertising rates of your local newspaper and the size and profile of its circulation?

Similarly, if you buy magazines you are certainly not paying the full cost of producing those magazines. The advertising revenue is probably paying up to three-quarters of the production costs.

The attraction for the advertiser is that these media outlets provide an opportunity to advertise their products to particular social groups of people. In relation to the *Wiltshire Times*, it is a group of people defined by the particular area in which they live. The newspaper will probably have a lot more additional information about its readers in terms of demographics – age, social class, gender, income – similar to the 'subjectivities' that Hartley and Fiske identified. The newspaper will have spent a lot

Figure 2.8   *The proportions of income that different types of publications obtain from advertising and from sales. Source: Student Briefing no. 6, Advertising Association.*

Type of publication	% from advertising	% from sales
National quality dailies (e.g. *The Telegraph*)	75	25
National popular dailies (e.g. *The Sun*)	46	54
National quality Sundays (e.g. *Sunday Times*)	76	24
National popular Sundays (e.g. *Mail on Sunday*)	53	47
Regional dailies and Sundays (e.g. *Manchester Evening News*)	73	27
Regional paid-for weeklies (e.g. *Hereford Times*)	85	15
Consumer magazines	38	62

of time and money trying to identify and categorise its readers so that it can then 'sell' these readers to its advertisers.

You may think that this does not apply to the BBC because it does not take advertising. Certainly it is true that at present on its terrestrial services the BBC does not have 'paid-for' advertising, but it is moving into other types of services and many BBC programmes are already available on digital channels available via subscription, and many of its magazines, for example *Top Gear* and *Gardeners' World*, carry commercial advertising.

Figure 2.9 *Top 20 television programmes for all terrestrial channels, 2000. Source: Taris-Taylor Nelson Sofres/BARB.*

	Title	Channel	Date of transmission	Audience (millions)
1	Coronation Street	ITV	1 Mar	19.0
2	EastEnders	BBC One	1 Mar	18.4
3	Who Wants to Be a Millionaire?	ITV	19 Jan	15.9
4	Heartbeat	ITV	23 Jan	15.2
5	Euro 2000: England v. Portugal	ITV	12 Jun	14.9
6	Euro 2000: England v. Romania	BBC One	20 Jun	14.6
7	Inspector Morse	ITV	15 Nov	13.7
8	Emmerdale	ITV	22 Mar	13.3
9	One Foot in the Grave	BBC One	20 Nov	12.8
10	The Vicar of Dibley	BBC One	1 Jan	12.5
11	Casualty	BBC One	2 Dec	12.3
12	Seeing Red	ITV	19 Mar	12.3
13	Stars in their Eyes	ITV	12 Feb	12.1
14	The National TV Awards	ITV	10 Oct	12.0
15	A Touch of Frost	ITV	1 Jan	11.9
16	Garages from Hell	ITV	1 May	11.5
17	The Bill	ITV	4 Feb	11.5
18	Hero of the Hour	ITV	3 Dec	11.2
19	I Don't Believe It	BBC One	20 Nov	11.2
20	The Full Monty	ITV	29 Nov	11.1

Note: Only top-rated episodes of each series are included

The BBC is also in competition with the commercial channels in an attempt to prove its popularity and to justify the licence fee. If the BBC's audience share falls below a certain level, the criticisms of its licence fee increase. (See public service broadcasting (PSB), p. 210.) This was a particular problem in 1999 as few of the top ten programmes in terms of audience share was made by the BBC.

One of the reasons for the debate over the position of *News at Ten* was not because ITV wanted to give viewers a better news programme or evening's entertainment but to allow ITV to get better ratings for the time slot so that it could charge advertisers more money. If *News at Ten* remained in its original slot, ITV had to break its 'adult', post-watershed programmes at 10 p.m., and often viewers did not return to the film or programme after *News at Ten*. In effect 'peak viewing' ended at 10.30 p.m. With the main evening's news programme moved to 6.30 p.m., ITV could start its 'adult' programmes at 9 p.m. or 9.30 p.m., and audiences would stay with the film or drama through to its end at 11 p.m. This in effect extended peak viewing time by half an hour and allowed ITV companies to charge higher amounts for advertising space at 10.30 p.m., 10.45 p.m. and 11 p.m. Although the audience for *ITV's Nightly News* was one million less than that for *News at Ten*, the audience for ITV between 10 p.m. and 10.30 p.m. rose by over one million. These new viewers were mainly younger and more downmarket, belonging to the C2DE social grades (see p. 130 for classification of social grades). Although generally advertisers prefer to reach ABC1 audiences, they are also keen to reach young viewers in their late teens and early twenties as they are considered to have a large amount of 'disposable income'.

The BBC, although not driven by the financial need to attract advertising revenue, had a similar problem in that *The Nine O'Clock News* interfered with its main evening schedules. It was therefore very keen to move into the gap created by the move of *News at Ten*. However, since *News at Ten* is back at its old slot, at least for some evenings, there is now a direct clash between the two channels.

ACTIVITY . . .

Read the section on news (p. 235) and then consider your own consumption of television news.

- Do you ever watch it?
- If so, is it a conscious decision to find out what is going on in the world or just because you could not be bothered to switch over/off?
- Which news bulletin(s) do you watch?
- Are there some news bulletins that you feel are more directly aimed at you?
- What types of audience do the other bulletins address?
- Are the news items of interest to you?
- If you could choose your own news items, what would they be and to what extent would they differ from what is usually presented?

Being able to identify both the size and type of their audience is very important for both the BBC and commercial media. There are various organisations who carry out this research and whose findings are sold to media companies. Some of this information is also available to the public; BARB's tables of weekly top television programmes are published in *Broadcast* magazine (see Figure 2.10) and some are available on their website <http://www.barb.co.uk> (see the section on BARB in research skills, below).

Currently BARB measures the audiences for the five terrestrial channels and all the digital channels. According to BARB, its ratings are based on the use of 5,250 panel homes, of which 1,600 currently have multichannel television. As the way we consume television is changing with the introduction of many more digital channels, 'narrowcasting', 'time-shifting' (recording programmes and watching them later) and the 'shuffling' of programmes (when they are repeated several times a day or over several days), television companies and BARB will need to develop ways of measuring much smaller but more specialised audiences.

Both NRS (National Readership Survey) and ABC (Audit Bureau of Circulation) carry out a similar function for the newspaper and magazine industry, producing circulation figures, but using different methods. ABC measures the sales of newspapers and magazines, whilst NRS interviews a sample of approximately 40,000 people about their reading habits. RAJAR (Radio Joint Audience Research) also uses the sample method and compiles both BBC and commercial radio listening figures. All these organisations have websites that contain up-to-date figures as well as explaining how they carry out their research (<http://www.nrs.co.uk>; <http://www.abc.org.uk>; <http://www.rajar.co.uk>). Another industry-based organisation that offers detailed information regarding newspaper circulation and readership is JICREG – the Joint Industry Committee for Regional Press Research (<http://www.jicreg.co.uk/about/index.cfm>).

Figure 2.10 BARB Top 50 network programmes for week ending 29 June 2003. Source: BARB.

		Title	Day	Start	Viewers (millions)	% Share	Viewers (MCH)	% Share (MCH)	Broadcaster/ producer
1	1	EastEnders	Mon	20.00	11.91	53.24	6.14	52.29	BBC One
2	4	Coronation Street	Mon	20.30	11.76	48.18	5.65	45.15	ITV1 Granada
3	2	EastEnders	Fri	20.00	11.43	53.40	5.89	52.61	BBC One
4	7	Coronation Street	Fri	19.30	11.24	55.52	4.50	43.20	ITV1 Granada
5	9	Coronation Street	Sun	19.30	11.24	56.27	4.34	43.31	ITV1 Granada
6	6	Coronation Street	Wed	19.30	11.19	57.72	5.31	53.93	ITV1 Granada
7	3	EastEnders	Thu	19.30	11.09	57.41	5.77	57.01	BBC One
8	5	EastEnders	Tue	19.30	10.77	56.66	5.42	54.51	BBC One
9	8	Emmerdale	Mon	19.00	9.23	47.70	4.38	42.42	ITV1 YTV
10	16	Emmerdale	Fri	19.00	8.25	45.21	3.30	35.35	ITV1 YTV
11	10	Emmerdale	Thu	19.00	7.84	46.19	3.69	42.40	ITV YTV
12	11	Emmerdale	Wed	19.00	7.83	45.00	3.57	40.54	ITV1 YTV
13	18	National Lottery – In It To Win It	Sat	20.10	7.46	42.43	3.17	35.29	BBC One 12 Yard Prods
14	17	Spooks	Mon	21.00	7.39	31.48	3.26	26.66	BBC One Kudos
15	15	Emmerdale	Tue	19.00	7.37	44.39	3.31	38.34	ITV1 YTV
16	12	Holby City	Tue	20.00	7.31	36.49	3.56	34.21	BBC One
17	30	The Royal	Sun	20.00	7.16	31.92	2.45	21.96	ITV1 Granada
18	20	The Bill	Wed	20.00	6.97	33.56	3.08	28.67	ITV1 Thames
19	35	Fortysomething	Sun	21.00	6.54	29.09	2.15	18.41	ITV1 Carlton
20	26	The Bill	Thu	20.00	6.39	30.76	2.78	25.50	ITV1 Thames
21	23	Bad Girls	Thu	21.00	6.36	29.68	3.01	26.23	ITV1 Shed Productions
22	51	A Touch of Frost	Fri	20.30	6.35	29.38	1.70	15.24	ITV1 YTV
23	25	My Family	Fri	20.30	6.31	27.73	2.79	24.16	BBC One DLT and Rude Boy

24	36	*Born and Bred*	Sun	20.00	6.17	27.66	2.15	19.36	BBC One
25	14	*Rogue Traders*	Thu	20.00	6.14	30.89	3.32	31.15	BBC One
26	27	*Ultimate Force*	Wed	21.00	6.13	28.67	2.73	23.97	ITV1 Chrysalis TV
27	39	*Wish You Were Here?*	Sun	19.00	6.02	38.75	1.93	24.01	ITV1 Granada
28	38	*Ten O'Clock News*	Mon	22.00	5.75	26.74	1.94	17.18	BBC One
29	32	*The Darling Buds of May*	Mon	21.00	5.73	24.44	2.25	18.40	ITV1 YTV
30	21	*Big Brother*	Mon	22.00	5.70	26.59	3.04	26.98	C4 Endemol
31	28	*The Trouble With Sleep*	Tue	21.00	5.68	25.90	2.59	22.50	BBC One
32	24	*Big Brother*	Fri	22.00	5.67	26.68	2.94	25.54	C4 Endemol
33	55	*BBC News*	Sun	22.00	5.62	26.91	1.61	14.82	BBC One
34	19	*Big Brother*	Tue	22.00	5.38	26.26	3.17	28.74	C4 Endemol
35	44	*Ten O'Clock News*	Thu	22.00	5.36	26.84	1.80	16.93	BBC One
36	37	*Crimewatch UK*	Thu	21.00	5.19	24.27	2.03	17.74	BBC One
37	22	*Big Brother*	Wed	22.00	5.01	24.94	3.02	28.09	C4 Endemol
38	45	*Ten O'Clock News*	Tue	22.00	4.91	23.71	1.78	15.98	BBC One
39	59	*Murder in Mind*	Sun	21.00	4.85	21.53	1.54	13.19	BBC One
40	40	*Only Fools and Horses*	Sat	21.00	4.84	25.59	1.92	19.43	BBC One
41	33	*Bargain Hunt*	Thu	20.30	4.81	22.35	2.24	20.04	BBC One
42	31	*Changing Rooms*	Mon	20.30	4.73	19.44	2.28	18.25	BBC One Endemol
43	65	*Ten O'Clock News*	Wed	22.00	4.69	23.31	1.45	13.42	BBC One
44	24	*Big Brother*	Fri	20.30	4.69	20.65	2.94	25.54	C4 Endemol
45	52	*The Sketch Show*	Sun	22.05	4.67	24.27	1.69	16.56	ITV1 Avalon
46	34	*Holiday Airline*	Tue	20.00	4.55	22.95	2.16	20.93	ITV1 LWT
47	42	*Question of Sport Out-takes Sp*	Tue	22.35	4.52	29.34	1.89	22.29	BBC One
48	29	*Big Brother*	Thu	22.00	4.51	22.84	2.48	23.70	C4 Endemol
49	53	*The Vicar of Dibley*	Sat	21.30	4.48	23.40	1.66	16.48	BBC One Tiger Aspect
50	50	*The Vice*	Tue	21.00	4.38	19.90	1.70	14.74	ITV1 Carlton
		Averages			6.79	33.48	2.99	28.27	

Figure 2.11 shows the top twenty 'paid-for' weekly regional newspapers taken from the Newspaper Society's website.

■ Study these figures and suggest reasons why the majority of these newspapers have increased their circulation when there is an increasing amount of competition amongst news sources.

■ Why do you think there is a column headed 'Actively purchased'? You might wish to carry out research on the readership of your own local newspaper, for example asking local people if they buy a 'paid-for' local newspaper and, if so, why.

■ You might look at local competition for newspapers in your area. Are there free news sheets available and, if so, who owns them?

Read the section on news (p. 235) and investigate how local people get their local news.

According to the Radio Advertising Bureau all commercial radio stations have a clearly defined core target audience – those who are at the centre of its market and who, it is hoped, will become station 'loyalists'. Around this core are other, secondary, listeners.

All of these organisations use the same categories for classifying audiences. These are based on the National Readership Survey's social grades used in advertising and market research. This divides the adult population of Britain into six grades and identifies the types of occupation that each grade represents and the percentage of the population that fits into that particular grade:

A	Higher managerial, administrative or professional	3%
B	Intermediate managerial, administrative or professional	15%
C1	Supervisory or clerical, junior managerial, administrative or professional	23%
C2	Skilled manual workers	28%
D	Semi-skilled and unskilled manual workers	18%
E	Casual labourers, unemployed, state pensioners	13%

Sex and age are also important. Age is generally divided into the following categories:

< 15

15–24

24–35

35–55

55 >

(For more detailed information on how the National Readership Survey categorises the British public, see its website (<http://www.nrs.co.uk/newindex5open.cfm?flag=dem>).)

Figure 2.11 *Top UK regional paid weeklies ranked by circulation.*
Source: ABC.

	Newspaper Title	Circulation	% change	% actively purchased	% full rate sale
1	Kent Messenger	62,171	+7.49	100	100
2	West Briton	51,694	+0.79	100	100
3	Essex Chronicle	48,462	−2.61	91.7	91.7
4	Derbyshire Times	43,206	+1.44	100	100
5	Western Gazette	42,755	+1.46	99.9	99.9
6	Barnsley Chronicle	42,540	+2.98	100	100
7	Hereford Times	42,353	+1.23	100	100
8	Cornish Guardian	41,633	+1.10	100	100
9	Isle of Wight County Press	40,553	+1.03	100	100
10	Kent & Sussex Courier	39,775	−2.32	98.6	98.6
11	Surrey Advertiser	39,565	−4.88	100	100
12	Chester Chronicle	39,536	−4.00	92.3	92.3
13	Cumberland News	38,454	+1.41	100	100
14	Chichester Observer	37,678	−1.23	100	100
15	Warrington Guardian	37,235	+1.63	100	100
16	Mansfield Chad	36,485	+6.44	99.8	99.8
17	Doncaster Free Press	35,818	+8.95	100	100
18	North Devon Journal	35,687	+1.36	100	100
19	East London & West Essex Guardian*	35,113	N/A	96.4	96.4
20	Darlington & Stockton Times	33,655	+2.72	88.3	88.3

* January–December 2002

(Average net circulation July–December 2002)

Figure 2.12 National newspaper circulation (Guardian 14 April 2003). You can access more up-to-date circulation figures from the ABC website at <http://www.abc.org.uk>. Source: ABC, permission: Guardian

	March 2003	March 2002	% change	March 2003 (including bulks)	October 2002– March 2003	October 2001– March 2002	% change
Dailies							
Sun	3,521,144	3,379,508	4.19	3,521,348	3,533,439	3,404,783	3.78
Daily Mirror	1,997,846	2,089,539	–4.39	1,997,846	2,061,241	2,105,273	–2.09
Daily Star	849,689	755,040	12.53	850,043	805,986	724,671	11.22
Daily Record	514,488	566,420	–9.17	517,248	521,701	573,169	–8.98
Daily Mail	2,341,999	2,318,023	1.03	2,427,032	2,361,164	2,361,119	0
Daily Express	888,145	852,252	4.21	932,560	919,261	866,187	6.13
Daily Telegraph	910,725	952,622	–4.40	926,500	920,766	961,322	–4.22
Times	622,592	657,113	–5.25	655,484	631,713	665,882	–5.13
FT	453,282	469,521	–3.46	472,969	430,688	459,038	–6.17
Guardian	396,849	382,057	3.87	412,341	389,957	395,105	–1.30
Independent	189,664	191,826	–1.13	223,867	185,571	194,910	–4.79
Sundays							
News of the World	3,849,013	3,970,726	–3.06	3,849,189	3,915,457	3,983,122	–1.70
Sunday Mirror	1,603,578	1,762,500	–9.02	1,603,578	1,663,232	1,765,962	–5.82
People	1,107,048	1,320,256	–16.15	1,107,048	1,151,394	1,323,766	–13.02
Daily Star Sunday	437,766	N/A	N/A	437,766	478,116	N/A	N/A
Sunday Mail	619,546	662,170	–6.44	621,956	631,870	674,869	–6.37
Mail on Sunday	2,312,905	2,277,898	1.54	2,399,222	2,303,805	2,294,078	0.42
Sunday Express	859,290	812,482	5.76	924,047	883,634	814,387	8.50
Sunday Times	1,365,988	1,368,608	–0.19	1,382,778	1,377,133	1,382,908	–0.42
Sunday Telegraph	704,964	753,255	–6.41	716,362	735,409	763,864	–3.72
Observer	430,791	422,470	1.97	455,387	443,382	434,358	2.08
Independent on Sunday	182,719	193,809	–5.72	222,238	181,105	195,092	–7.17

Figure 2.13 *Radio listening share. (You can access more up-to-date listening figures from the RAJAR website at <http://www.rajar.co.uk>). Source: RAJAR/RSI.*

Radio channel	October–December 1998 %	October–December 1999 %
All BBC	48.5	51.3
All BBC Network	39.1	40.5
BBC Radio 1	10.6	10.9
BBC Radio 2	13.1	12.8
BBC Radio 3	1.3	1.3
BBC Radio 4	10.5	11.0
BBC Radio 5 Live	3.6	4.4
BBC Local/Regional	9.3	10.8
All Commerical	49.3	46.7
All National Commercial	9.3	8.3
Atlantic 252	1.4	0.6
Classic FM	3.7	4.3
Talk Radio (now Sport)	1.6	1.5
Virgin Radio (AM only)	2.6	1.8
All Local Commerical	40.0	38.4
Other Listening	2.2	2.0

ACTIVITY . . .

Carry out your own research to test the validity of the information contained in Figure 2.14, p. 134. Try to account for any differences you may find.

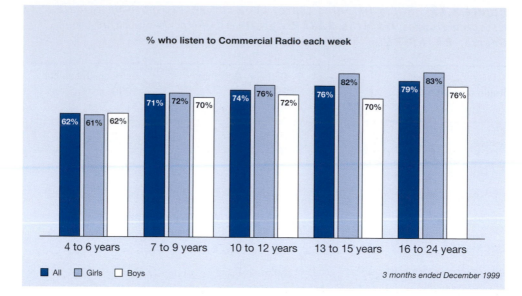

% who listen to Commercial Radio each week

4 to 6 years: 62% / 61% / 62%
7 to 9 years: 71% / 72% / 70%
10 to 12 years: 74% / 76% / 72%
13 to 15 years: 76% / 82% / 70%
16 to 24 years: 79% / 83% / 76%

■ All ☐ Girls ☐ Boys

3 months ended December 1999

Figure 2.14 *Young people's radio listening increases with age. Source: RAJAR.*

The statistical information provided by organisations such as BARB and RAJAR is then supplemented by more detailed and qualitative data about audiences (see section on research skills, p. 307). This is often carried out by advertising or marketing companies for particular broadcasters and media companies, and focuses on the audience's lifestyle, their habits, opinions and sets of values and attitudes. Advertising companies claim that they can segment audiences on the basis of 'socio-economic values' such as:

- **Survivors**   Those who want security and like routine
- **Social climbers** Those who have a strong materialistic drive and like status symbols
- **Care givers**   Those who believe in 'caring and sharing'
- **Explorers**   Those for whom personal growth and influencing social change are important.

These socio-economic groups may be given a variety of names (Mainstreamers, Aspirers, Achievers and Reformers is another version), but they are all based on the work of the American psychologist Abraham Maslow and his idea of a 'Hierarchy of Needs' (see Figure 2.15). Maslow suggested that we all have different 'layers' of needs and that we need to satisfy one before we can move on to the next. In other words, we all start at the bottom of Maslow's hierarchy, having basic *physiological* needs such as food and shelter for our survival. We can then move up the hierarchy to the level of *safety* needs, probably to do with having a regular income, from a job for example, that guarantees us a regular source of food and shelter – perhaps being able to pay the rent or mortgage. The next level is to do with belonging to a *social* group, whether it be our

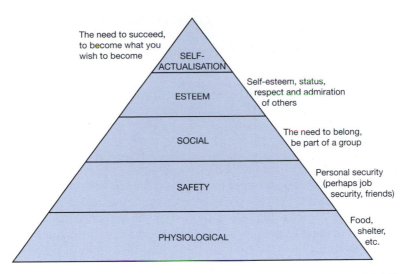

The need to succeed, to become what you wish to become — SELF-ACTUALISATION

Self-esteem, status, respect and admiration of others — ESTEEM

The need to belong, be part of a group — SOCIAL

Personal security (perhaps job security, friends) — SAFETY

Food, shelter, etc. — PHYSIOLOGICAL

Figure 2.15 *Maslow's 'Hierarchy of Needs' (from Maslow 1943). Original theory in* Psychological Review, *50: 370–96.*

family, work colleagues or peer group. In fact most of us belong to a variety of different social groups, for example as students, family members, social groups, work groups and so on. Our *esteem* needs are to do with wanting to gain the respect and admiration of others, perhaps through the display of status symbols such as expensive consumer goods. Maslow argues that many people stop at particular levels and only a very few reach 'self-actualisation' at the top of the hierarchy. These are the people who are considered to be in control of their lives and to have achieved all their goals.

Advertisers are increasingly using ideas like Maslow's and are combining both demographics and lifestyle categories in an attempt to be more effective and efficient in the way in which they target particular groups of people. They are trying to sell their products in a way that meets the target audience's perceived needs.

ACTIVITY . . .

Some commercial media organisations may be willing to let you have media packs or out-of-date rate cards. You could then use these to plan a campaign for a new product. (See case study on advertising, p. 257.)

We must get away from the habit of thinking in terms of what the media do to people and substitute for it the idea of what people do with the media.

(Halloran 1970)

The history of audience research is a story of the shift from the view of the audience as passive to one that views the audience as active in its relationship with media texts

Some of the earliest academic studies of media audiences appeared in the 1920s and 1930s and looked at what we understand as the 'mass media' – cinema, radio, popular magazines and newspapers – as they became increasingly available to the majority of people in Europe and America. In these early studies the audience itself was seen as a 'mass' audience – a mass of people, all together, consuming the same product and receiving the same 'mass' message. This seemed to be particularly effective when the Nazis in Germany and the Communists in the Soviet Union used the media as a propaganda tool. They appeared to be successful in making their ideas dominant and 'injecting' large numbers of people with their messages.

The Frankfurt School was made up of German Marxists who, in the 1930s, saw the success of Nazi propaganda and later, in 1950s America, of commercial television. They thought that the media were a force for pacifying the population and restricting and controlling public and cultural life by injecting a 'mass culture' that functioned as a distraction from the mundanity of ordinary daily life. Members of the Frankfurt School, including Theodor Adorno and Max Horkheimer, suggested that the American culture industries, in particular commercial television and popular cinema, moulded people into a standardised, passive state of being that allowed them to be easily manipulated. Although in America most of this manipulation was carried out by advertising and the drive for consumerism, they suggested that, as had happened in Germany, mass media could also be used to manipulate people into accepting particular political ideas such as capitalism. They believed that these culture industries worked against democracy and restricted people's choices and actions.

NOTEBOX

This view of the media seemed to be reinforced by Orson Welles's *The War of the Worlds*, broadcast on American radio in 1938. The programme, based on the book by H.G. Wells, was broadcast as part of a regular weekly drama slot but was produced to sound like a series of news reports and newsflashes about the invasion of America by Martians. The programme appeared to include interviews with people in authority such as politicians and police officers and contained instructions for people to evacuate their homes. Many people did in fact believe that the broadcast was a real emergency and did drive out of New York State. The

programme caused considerable panic and also attracted considerable criticism and complaints for being 'too realistic'. It is a good example of the power and 'authority' that the media had at the time in the minds of radio listeners. Many commentators have suggested that today we are too sophisticated to make the same mistake but a spoof broadcast of the BBC programme *Ghostwatch* on Halloween in 1992 fooled many viewers into believing that they were seeing real paranormal experiences on television.

In Britain there has been a series of exposés about fake documentaries of the re-enacting scenes in docu-soaps and actors pretending to be 'real' people on chat shows such as *Vanessa*. The campaign to 'name and shame' paedophiles by the *News of the World* is also perhaps a reminder that we still give the media too much authority and credence.

With the introduction of commercial television and in particular advertising, the idea of 'injecting' the audience with a message seemed even more relevant. It was thought that advertisers could make people buy particular products or brands of products merely by repeating the message often and loudly – the 'hard sell' approach. Vance Packard in *The Hidden Persuaders* (1957) identified many of the ways in which advertisers attempted to manipulate audiences. C. Wright Mills in *The Power Elite* (1956) suggested four functions that the media perform for audiences:

- to give individuals *identity*
- to give people goals, *aspiration*
- to give *instruction* on how to achieve these goals
- to give people an alternative if they failed, *escapism*.

However, studies of the various political advertising campaigns in America in the 1940s and 1950s suggested that the audience was not so passive and did not just accept what the advertisers or the programme makers said. Rather, in terms of political advertising, audiences focused on those messages that reinforced their existing beliefs and tended to dismiss those that contradicted their established ideas. This suggested that audiences in fact selected the messages that they wanted to hear and ignored others. The media's effect seemed to be one of reinforcement rather than of persuasion.

This research led to a view that audiences, rather than being simply a 'mass', were composed of different social groups, with particular sets of social relations, and a variety of cultural norms and values. Several American researchers, including Paul Lazarsfeld and Elihu Katz, concentrated on providing evidence that audiences were not simply one large, gullible mass but that messages put out by the media were in fact being received by a complex mixture of different groups and that media texts were themselves mediated by these social and cultural networks. The audience was now being seen as playing an active role in the interpretation of the meaning of particular media texts.

USES AND GRATIFICATIONS THEORY The idea that media audiences make active use of what the media offer. The audience has a set of needs, which the media in one form or another meet.

Uses and gratifications theory was an important shift in the study of how audiences interacted with texts and was developed by Blumler and Katz in 1975. Through a series of interviews with viewers, they identified four broad needs that were fulfilled by viewing television:

Diversion	A form of escape or release from everyday pressures
Personal relationships	Companionship through identification with television characters and sociability through discussion about television with other people
Personal identity	The ability to compare one's own life with the characters and situations portrayed and to explore individual problems and perspectives
Surveillance	Information about 'what's going on' in the world.

ACTIVITY . . .

Other uses and gratifications research developed models about how viewers use quiz shows for four main gratifications:

1 **Self-rating**   To see how well I do
2 **Social interaction** To watch/share/compete with others
3 **Excitement**   To see who wins and what they win
4 **Education**   As a source of knowledge.

■ Design and carry out your own research to see if this is correct.
■ Think about other genres or other media and suggest ways in which uses and gratifications theory may be applied.

Uses and gratifications theory is seen to have some merit as it supposes an 'active' audience that to some extent provides its own interpretation of the text's meaning. However, as a means of understanding the relationship between the audience and the creation of meaning, it can appear to be rather simplistic and limited in relation to the complexity of how we the audience/reader actually work with a text. One of the main problems with uses and gratifications theory is that it assumes that the media somehow identify these needs on behalf of the audience and then provide the material to meet or gratify them. An alternative interpretation could be that we the audience

create these needs as a response to the material provided by the media, and that in fact we could have many other needs that are not identified, or met, by existing media texts.

ACTIVITY...

Look at the data produced by BARB (Figure 2.10, pp. 128–9) or access its website (<http://www.barb.co.uk>) for the most popular television programmes. Try to identify the main uses and gratifications that these programmes may provide for viewers. Design a questionnaire and test your theory.

In fact many of our 'uses' and 'pleasures' can be seen to be 'making the best' of what is available and putting it to our (the audience's) use, which may be different from the one that the producer intended. For example, consider the unexpected popularity and fashionableness of many cheap daytime television shows, such as *The Weakest Link* or *Ready Steady Cook*.

> **SITUATED CULTURE** A term used to describe how our 'situation' (daily routines and patterns, social relationships with family and peer groups) can influence our engagement with and interpretation of media texts.
>
> **KEY TERM**

In Media Studies there is a lot of debate and research about how the reader/audience consumes and makes sense of particular texts. There have been specific studies by researchers such as David Morley (1980), who researched the way families watched television programmes like *Nationwide*, Dorothy Hobson (1982) on viewers of *Crossroads*, David Buckingham (1987) on *EastEnders'* audience, and Christine Geraghty (1991) on the relationship between women and soap operas.

It is worth thinking a little about the differences in the ways we tend to consume different media. Tunstall in *The Media in Britain* (1983) has suggested that the way in which we consume the media can be divided into three levels: primary, secondary and tertiary.

> **PRIMARY MEDIA** Where we pay close attention to the media text, for instance in the close reading of a magazine or newspaper, or in the cinema where we concentrate on the film in front of us.
>
> **KEY TERM**

SECONDARY MEDIA Where the medium or text is there in the background and we are aware that it is there but are not concentrating on it. This happens most often with music-based radio but also when the television is on but we are not really watching it; maybe we are talking with friends, eating or carrying out some other activity. This could also include 'skimming' through a magazine or newspaper, waiting for something to catch our eye.

TERTIARY MEDIA Where the medium is present but we are not at all aware of it. The most obvious examples are advertising hoardings or placards that we pass but do not register.

If we compare our consumption of films and television, there is an obvious difference between the two in that television is generally part of what Raymond Williams (1974) described as a 'flow'. By this Williams meant that television was a constant stream available to us in the home that we can turn on or off at will, like a water tap in the bathroom or kitchen. Sometimes we have it on as background or, as it is suggested that many elderly people do, have it on as 'company'. On other occasions we may turn the television on in order to 'share' our watching with others, particularly with sporting events or perhaps soap operas. This may be a way of sharing companionship or, like *The Royle Family*, a way of being a family.

This, Williams suggested, means that our reception of television programmes, and the media in general, is mediated through our domestic, situated culture. It means that *who* we are, our sense of our own place in the world, our views and beliefs, as well as *where* we are in terms of our social location, all influence our responses to the media.

Watching a film, in contrast to television, is generally a more carefully chosen and focused activity. A visit to the cinema requires a series of conscious decisions such as deciding to go out to the cinema, choosing who to go with, at what time, to which cinema or multiplex and which film to see. Watching a DVD or video also involves a set of deliberate choices such as deciding which DVD or video to rent, paying money, putting aside the time to watch the film, perhaps choosing particular companions to watch it with. Even a film on television is often chosen in a much more deliberate way than the rest of the television's 'flow', which is often watched 'because it is on' rather than as the result of a series of deliberate choices.

ACTIVITY...

Think about the last time you went to the cinema. List the series of decisions that you had to make. How did you make your decisions? Refer back to some of the earlier activities in this section that are about patterns of film consumption. How do you and your friends consume this medium?

DAVID MORLEY'S *NATIONWIDE* STUDY

In 1980 David Morley and Charlotte Brunsdon investigated how different audiences responded to, and made sense of, *Nationwide*, an early-evening BBC programme. Their research suggested that audiences brought a complex set of knowledge and experience to the programmes that they were consuming. This, alongside other factors such as gender, ethnicity and class, was, Morley suggested, an important part of the way in which audiences 'consume' and 'understand' texts and 'create meaning'.

IEN ANG'S *DALLAS* STUDY

In 1985 Ien Ang looked at readers' reception of *Dallas*. Ang put an advert in a women's magazine in Holland asking about viewers' reactions to and reasons for watching *Dallas*. Of the forty-two replies that Ang received, she identified three different types of response:

- **The ideology of mass culture** suggested viewers liked the programme because it was successful and was a high-profile piece of American popular television culture.
- **The ironic or 'detached' position** represented viewers who would watch it knowing that it was 'bad' but wanting to see what it was other people were watching.
- **The ideology of popularism** is based on people's everyday routines and experiences and the 'pleasure' that they get from watching *Dallas* even though they may recognise that it is 'trash'.

(See also the section on Ang on p. 121.)

Researchers have also looked at the way in which the media 'address' or 'position' their audiences in relation to an event, person or idea. (See section on narrative, p. 42.) Audiences can be positioned by the viewpoint used both verbally and visually to create a relationship between the text and its audience. Expressed verbally, this can include words like 'I' used by the narrator or broadcaster, 'you' when addressing the viewer or listener, and 'it' or 'they' when referring to an event, third person or idea. Visually this positioning can be maintained by using camera angles, where the camera follows the action in a particular way or follows a particular person. Editing the flow and sequencing of shots can also position the audience to the extent that they become observers who see more than the participants and are spectators placed outside the action. For example, this occurs in a crime drama where the audience is given 'privileged' information about who committed the crime, or in a soap opera where someone is lying or has a secret.

The modes of address used in broadcasting are often informal, conversational and open-ended because they are consumed in the private domestic world of the home. (See Figure 2.16.) To create the necessary sense of intimacy, presenters talk to the audience as if they were individual members whom they know personally (see discussion on 'Doreen', p. 122). Although these modes of address are largely motivated by the producers' sense of their audience, sometimes they are determined by the institution's own sense of itself. For example, the BBC might consider itself to be representing the nation at a time of crisis and therefore may present its material in a particularly solemn and dignified manner (see section on mode of address in Part 1, p. 49).

Figure 2.16 *Radio listening locations. Source:* Radio Days 2, 1999; *permission:* Radio Advertising Bureau (RAB).

	Ever listen %	Listen most often %	Favourite %
Listening places			
At home	81	57	56
bedroom	48	17	18
living room	48	18	18
kitchen	47	20	17
bathroom	10	1	1
garden	8	0	0
study	3	1	1
garage/shed	2	0	0
In the car	44	24	24
At work	24	17	16
Listening situations			
Having breakfast	39	10	10
Doing the housework	36	20	19
Driving to work	34	20	19
Getting ready for work/school	27	7	6
Whilst at work	27	19	18
Radio alarm (on waking up)	25	5	4
In bed at night	18	5	7
Having lunch	15	1	2
Doing DIY	12	2	2
Having evening meal	6	1	1

AUDIENCE PARTICIPATION

'Real people' are increasingly appearing on television. Once upon a time it was only certain privileged types of people (politicians, experts, presenters) who appeared on our screens. If the public were seen, they were tightly controlled and mediated through

the use of presenters (as in documentaries) or a quiz-master. (Even the early quiz and entertainment shows relied upon various types of 'expert' or personality – for instance the BBC's *What's My Line?*, *Juke Box Jury* or *Brains Trust*.) It was largely with the introduction of more American-type quiz shows on ITV in the 1950s that 'ordinary people' started to appear in front of cameras and then usually only to answer a well-rehearsed and tightly controlled set of questions.

Today, however, the public, ordinary people, are increasingly the stars of the shows. They may appear as the victims in humorous or emotional situations such as in *You've Been Framed* or *Surprise Surprise*, or in fly-on-the-wall documentaries such as Paul Watson's *A Wedding in the Family* (2000). A recent popular genre has been the 'makeover' show, where ordinary people change their looks (*What Not to Wear*), their homes or gardens (*Home Front* or *Changing Rooms*) or even find new partners (*Blind Date* or *Street Mate*). Another recent popular genre involving 'ordinary' people comprises the various property shows (*Location, Location, Location, Escape to the Country, Get a New Life*), in which people, usually couples, are given help in finding new homes to buy either in Britain or abroad.

Docu-soaps have turned 'ordinary people' into stars and personalities – for example Maureen from *Driving School* (see Figure 1.18, p. 91). Ordinary people also appear in the various 'real-life' programmes that may contain actual footage or reconstructions, such as *Jimmy's, It Happened to Me, Condition Critical or Police, Camera, Action*. They may also appear in programmes like *Video Nation* talking directly to the camera, or recounting their experiences in history programmes like *The People's Century* or *Out of the Doll's House*. A recent popular genre has included programmes such as the BBC's *Castaway*, ITV's *Survivor* and Channel Four's *Big Brother*, which 'isolate' ordinary people somewhere and then record their experiences of being together.

There are many possible reasons for this increase in ordinary people appearing on television. One explanation is that they are a lot cheaper to use than professional entertainers and presenters. They may also help the audience at home identify with the participants and the programme and they may help to encourage audience loyalty through their familiar situations and characters.

ACTIVITY...

Look through the television schedules and identify those programmes that make a feature of incorporating 'ordinary' people.

- Can they be divided into different types of programmes?
- Ask members of your family and friends whether they like this emphasis on 'ordinary' people on television.
- Can they identify what the attraction is of these types of programmes?
- Are the schedulers successful in using these types of programmes to attract audiences?

continued

OR

Other people's pain, grief and misfortune make good television. However, as the television seeks to fill more and more broadcasting hours and programme makers chase audience ratings, are there limits to what 'reality' can be presented on screen?

OR

In what ways are popular genres like docu-soaps and game shows important in determining television schedules in Britain?

OR

Why do you think docu-soaps are so popular? Use examples to illustrate your answer.

GENDERED CONSUMPTION

There has been much research on how gender affects our consumption of the media. Studies such as Hobson (1982) and Gray (1992) suggest that women prefer 'open-ended' narratives like soap operas whereas men prefer 'closed' narratives like police dramas (see section on narrative, p. 42). Soap operas are considered popular among women because they conform to what Geraghty (1991) calls 'women's fiction' and have certain common conventions:

- They have strong female lead characters.
- They focus on the private, domestic sphere.
- They deal with personal relationships.
- They contain an element of fantasy and/or escapism.

(See section on genre, p. 53.)

Other research, such as Radway's (1984) study of a group of readers of romantic novels and Stacey's (1994) work with women cinema-goers from the 1940s and 1950s, also explores this notion of escapism or 'utopian solutions'.

KEY TERM

UTOPIAN SOLUTION A term taken from R. Dyer (1977), who suggested that entertainment genres are popular because of their fantasy element and the escapism that they provide from daily routines and problems. He suggested that particular genres such as musicals or westerns offered particular types of utopian solution.

These studies suggest that women audiences welcome romantic texts as a means of reasserting positive aspects of their lives. Radway suggests that heroines in romantic

novels are seen as victorious because they symbolise the value of the female world of love and human relationships as being more important than fame and material success.

Males are considered to prefer factual programmes such as news and current affairs, although, as Morley (1986) notes, many men may watch soap operas but are not prepared to admit it. Mulvey (1975) suggests that most Hollywood films are based on the idea of a male viewer and that the camera shots and editing are 'positioned' from a male perspective. This she calls the 'male gaze', which automatically positions women as passive and as objects.

All this research suggests the complex nature of the relationships between audience and media text. As you will have read in Part 1, texts are polysemic (see p. 33) in that they have a variety of meanings, and the audience is an important component in determining those meanings.

THE 'EFFECTS' DEBATE AND MORAL PANICS

There has long been concern about the supposedly bad effects that popular culture may have on 'ordinary' people. This concern has grown with the increase in 'mass media' and the availability of cheap fiction books, popular magazines, the cinema, popular music, television and, more recently, the Internet.

In the 1950s American comics such as *Tales from the Crypt* or *Haunt of Fear*, with their depictions of violence, were seen as dangerous, so a law was introduced called the 1955 Children and Young Persons (Harmful Publications) Act to control which comics were allowed to be on sale in this country.

In fact we can trace panics about the effects of the media back to the introduction of newspapers in the eighteenth century, when a tax or stamp duty was put on newspapers by the government to make newspapers so expensive that only rich people could afford to buy them.

The term 'moral panic' comes from *Folk Devils and Moral Panics* (1972) by Stan Cohen. Cohen looked at the media reaction to the fights between mods and rockers at various seaside resorts in Britain during the mid 1960s. His term 'moral panic' came to mean a mass response to 'a group, a person or an attitude that becomes defined as a threat to society'.

Once a threat has been identified, a panic is then often created through press coverage, particularly the tabloid press, and is then taken up by other newspapers and/or television programmes. Newspapers may start campaigns claiming 'something must be done' and then politicians may become involved, offering support to the campaigns, and often legislation is introduced as a result.

In recent years we have had panics over refugees 'flooding' into Britain from Eastern Europe seeking asylum, as well as over dangerous dogs, illegal raves and video nasties. As a result of these 'panics', legislation has been introduced to try to control dangerous dogs, make rave parties illegal, control the activities of asylum seekers and the classification and distribution of certain types of video. One topical 'moral panic' was the 'naming and shaming' of paedophiles by the *News of the World* (see p. 235).

The moral panic over video nasties such as *Driller Killer*, *Zombie Flesh Eaters* and *The Texas Chainsaw Massacre* in the early 1980s led to the Video Recordings Act of 1984, which limited the kinds of videos on sale in this country (see section on regulation of the media, p. 204). Other moral panics can be more subtle, for instance the campaigns over unmarried mothers who, it is claimed, get pregnant for the welfare benefits, or the panics about supermodels and 'heroin chic', which, it is claimed, encourage young girls to diet and can result in anorexia.

Perhaps the most well-known case is the murder of James Bulger in 1993 and its association with the film *Child's Play 3*. In this case neither the prosecution nor the police presented any evidence to support the supposition that the two boys who had killed James Bulger had actually seen (yet alone been influenced by) this film.

The two boys came from socially and environmentally deprived backgrounds. Jon Venables had been referred by teachers to a psychologist because at school he banged his head against a wall to attract attention, threw objects at other children and had cut himself with scissors.

Even if it had been proved that the two boys had seen *Child's Play 3*, it is difficult to know how the court could have separated the influence of this video from all the other factors that made the two boys who they were. It was the judge in the case who, in his summing up, made the connection, which was then taken up by the tabloid press and MPs. This eventually led to the law being changed so that the British Board of Film Classification now has to take into account the influence of videos as well as their content.

There has been a large amount of research to try to identify the effects of the media on audiences, particularly in relation to violence. However, such research tends to be either inconclusive or contradictory (see, for instance, Barker and Petley 2001). Part of the problem with any attempt to prove the effects of watching violence or sex on television, video or film is trying to isolate the effect of the media from all the other factors that are involved in shaping us as individuals – family, home, education, religion, peer groups, and so on. In America there were several cases of supposed 'copycat' killings after the release of the film *Natural Born Killers*. In fact many of those convicted of murder already had a history of violence before seeing the film.

Two of Britain's worst murder cases were the shootings of schoolchildren and their teacher in Dunblane by Thomas Hamilton in 1996 and the murders of elderly women carried out by the doctor Harold Shipman over a number of years. In neither case was there any suggestion or evidence at all that Hamilton or Shipman had ever watched any violent videos.

Much of this 'effects' debate seems to assume that somehow if we, the audience, watch a violent film then we will carry out violent acts. This seems very simplistic in view of the complicated relationship that we, as audiences, have with the media. The most we can possibly say with certainty is that people with violent tendencies may watch violent videos, but that does not mean that everyone who watches violent videos is (or becomes) violent.

What do you understand by the term 'moral panic'? By referring to one or more specific examples, illustrate how the media can be said to be responsible for creating moral panics.

One of the panics today is focused around access to the Internet. Over 60 per cent of adults in this country now have access to the Internet, and it is available in schools and public libraries. There does perhaps need to be a debate about how media like the Internet are controlled and monitored, but perhaps the real difficulty lies in deciding who should be in charge of regulation. Many people are probably fully in favour of censorship – as long as they are the ones who make the decisions! (<http://www.nua.com/surveys/how_many_online> is a website that provides worldwide data about access to the Internet.)

AND FINALLY . . .

Let us return to *The Royle Family* (Figure 2.7, p. 121) as this programme highlights many of the key themes in this section on media audiences and how audiences interact with media texts. In one episode of the situation comedy, the family members settle down after Sunday lunch to watch the BBC's *Antiques Roadshow* but instead of admiring the antiques they bet on how much they are valued at, and the family member who is nearest takes the winnings.

This episode is a good example of how the fictional family members are using a programme as a means of both entertainment and diversion from the mundane routines of daily weekday life as well as bringing themselves together as a family and sharing in the experience of betting on the antiques in the *Antiques Roadshow*. Their particular use of the programme, to see who can best guess the value of the antiques, is their own 'negotiated' meaning of the programme, but one that is shared by all the members of the family. Their 'situated culture', the family together, affects the meaning of the programme, and their social background affects their interpretation of what the notion of 'antiques' means – not something to own but a way of sharing pleasure and winning money.

We could also say that in fact the members of the Royle family are making quite an astute comment on the *Antiques Roadshow* itself – middle-class people bring out their antiques and pretend surprise when told how much they are worth – but actually the money 'value' of the antiques is the whole point (and attraction?) of the programme. So really we could say that the Royle family is getting to the hub of the programme and exposing its hypocrisy.

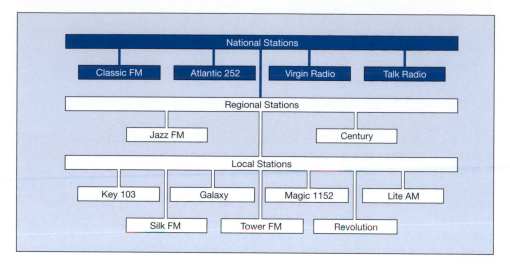

Figure 2.17 *Targeted station programming, Manchester. Source:* Radio Days 2, *permission RAB.*

1   Write a detailed clarification of the information contained in Figure 2.6 (p. 119), 'Share of media consumption by time of day'. Analyse the ways in which the media might be said to organise the everyday lives of its audiences. Your analysis could be based around one specific individual or could be discussed in more general terms.

2   Figure 2.17 contains a diagram of the commercial radio stations available in the Manchester area. Create a similar diagram for your own area and include the BBC stations.

■ For each station draw up a profile of the 'core' audience. You will be able to make some judgements about the core audience from the types of programmes, the types of advertisements and the shows where listeners are in contact with the station. You can use Hartley's and Fiske's 'subjectivities' (p. 122) but you should also try to research demographic information. (You could contact the stations themselves to check how accurate your profiles are.)

■ On what basis are the different listener audiences segmented?

■ Are there any particular groups not catered for? Why do you think this is? If so, draw up a design for a radio station that would meet the needs of this group. Consider the types of programmes, presenters, advertisers and promotional material that this station would need.

3   Working as a group, imagine that you have been asked by a film company to provide the outline for a new film aimed at audiences between the ages of eighteen and twenty-five. Draw up an outline that includes:

■ the main situation or narrative of the story and its dramatic potential
■ descriptions of the main characters, any major supporting roles and the relationships between them
■ ideas for two or three main settings, explaining their visual impact, the reasons for using them and any technical difficulties that they may present
■ the opening sequence of the film (both in terms of sound and images), explaining how it will attract the audience's attention. (You may wish to read the section on title sequences, p. 95.)

Then explain the ways in which you think the film will appeal to its target audience and suggest ways in which the film could be marketed. You may wish to present your outline to other students and ask them to choose the one most likely to be commercially successful. You may also consider filming the opening scene on video.

4   Using a selection of examples from a range of different genres in either radio or television, discuss the role that 'ordinary people' have in contemporary media texts.

5   'The media have become a central part of everyday life.' Discuss this proposition using specific examples.

6   Examine the ways in which social and cultural factors influence how audiences use and interpret media texts.

7   Explain what is meant by the term 'the active audience'. How useful is it as a concept for understanding how audiences interact with the media?

FURTHER READING

Ang, I. (1985) *Watching Dallas: Soap Opera and the Melodramatic Imagination*, Methuen.

Barker, M. and Petley, J. (eds) (2001) *Ill-Effects: The Media/Violence Debate*, Routledge.

Buckingham, D. (1987) *Public Secrets: EastEnders and its Audience*, BFI Publishing.

Fiske, J. (1987) *Television Culture*, Methuen.

Geraghty, C. (1991) *Women and Soap-Opera*, Polity Press.

Halloran, J. (1970) *The Effects of Television*, Panther.

Hartley, J. (1982) *Understanding News*, Methuen.

Hobson, D. (1982) *Crossroads: The Drama of a Soap Opera*, Methuen.

Miller, T. (ed.) (2002) *Television Studies*, BFI Publishing.

Moores, S. (1993) *Interpreting Audiences: The Ethnography of Media Consumption*, Sage.

Morley, D. (1980) *The Nationwide Audience*, BFI Publishing.

Radway, J. (1984) *Reading the Romance: Women, Patriarchy and Popular Literature*, Verso.

Williams, K. (2003) *Understanding Media Theory*, Arnold.

Williams, R. (1974) *Television: Technology and Cultural Form*, Routledge.

▼ EXAMPLE: MAGAZINES

In this section:

- we apply some of the theories about audiences to magazines
- we concentrate on 'lifestyle' magazines and in particular those aimed at women readers.

Estimates of the number of magazine titles available in Britain vary between 8,000 and 10,000, of which about one-third are consumer and lifestyle magazines, the remainder being professional and business publications or 'giveaways'. It is also estimated that over £3 billion was spent on magazines in 2000.

Figure 2.18 shows the top ten magazines as measured by their circulation, but only one, *What's on* TV, is 'actively purchased'; in other words all the others are given away free in one form or another. It is interesting to speculate whether magazines such as the Sky or AA magazines or the periodicals for companies such as Asda or Safeway would be so popular if readers had to pay for them. Do you think people actually read these free magazines? If not, how are they consumed? Why do you think these companies seem to be prepared to give away magazines for free?

ACTIVITY...

Carry out a survey about people's magazine-reading habits. You could look at:

- what magazines people read
- how much they spend on magazines
- how they choose which magazines to buy
- when and where they read them
- why they read them or, if they do not read magazines, why not
- which parts of the magazines they read first

continued

- which parts of the magazines they find least interesting
- how much influence they think the magazines have on their 'lifestyle'; for example, do the features or advertisements influence the products they purchase?
- their 'history' in terms of magazine-reading – what magazines and/or comics have they read in the past?

Do any patterns emerge? Is there any significant difference between the sexes in terms of magazine consumption?

Figure 2.18 *Top 10 magazines ranked by overall total average net circulation/distribution. Source:* PPA.

	Title	% actively purchased	December 2002
1	*Sky Customer Magazine* (formerly *Skyview Digital*)	0	5,795,091
2	*AA Magazine*	0	4,961,341
3	*O Magazine* (Group)	0	2,498,361
4	*Boots Health & Beauty*	0	1,895,208
5	*Safeway Magazine*	0	1,748,316
6	*Asda Magazine*	0	1,740,533
7	*What's on TV*	100	1,630,850
8	*O Magazine* (Pay-monthly edition)	0	1,498,288
9	*The National Trust Magazine*	0	1,471,352
10	*The Somerfield Magazine*	0	1,379,290

'LIFESTYLE' MAGAZINES

This is one of the most popular and competitive areas of the magazine publishing market. Although, as Figure 2.19 shows, the top five 'actively purchased' magazines are all television-related, over the past ten years it is lifestyle and celebrity magazines that have shown the biggest increase in the number of titles available, the number of copies bought and the amount of advertising revenue that they bring in.

(You can get more up-to-date information on magazine circulation, plus other facts and figures, from the Periodical Publishers Association website at <http://www.ppa.co.uk/magad/data_trends/circulation/index.htm>.)

Figure 2.19 *Top 20 magazines ranked by UK/RoI actively purchased circulation/distribution. Source: PPA.*

	Title	Net circulation/distribution per issue, December 2002
1	What's on TV	1,630,850
2	Take a Break	1,193,666
3	Radio Times	1,157,518
4	BBC Pre-School Magazines (Group)	1,012,020
5	TV Choice	902,241
6	Reader's Digest	899,221
7	Now	611,130
8	That's Life	592,268
9	FHM	587,382
10	Woman	620,450
11	Saga Magazine	1,204,669
12	TV Times	566,809
13	Heat	547,441
14	Chat	543,094
15	OK! Magazine	568,942
16	Glamour	507,754
17	Woman's Own	503,124
18	Woman's Weekly	433,945
19	Bella	422,617
20	TV Quick	417,618

'Lifestyle' is a very broad category that can include *FHM*, *Gardener's World* and *Woman's Own*. However, all these magazines are trying to do the same thing, using a consumerism based on particular lifestyles to deliver particular groups of audiences to advertisers. It is interesting, for example, to carry out a simple contents analysis of the most popular lifestyle magazines to determine the amount of advertising that they contain. This advertising will not only include the glossy advertisements and double-page spreads at the front of the magazine but also the smaller advertisements that often appear at the back of these magazines. It is not unusual to find that over 40 per cent of a lifestyle magazine is devoted to advertising in one form or another.

On p. 110 we talked about 'narrowcasting': as new magazines come on to the market they are increasingly trying to narrow down the market and provide advertisers with more and more specific reader 'profiles'. Like most newspapers (see p. 124), the revenue that lifestyle magazines get from advertising is far more important than the income they receive from the cover price and individual sales. According to the *Guardian Media Guide*, more than 80 per cent of adults, and 84 per cent of women, read a consumer magazine. It is estimated that women spend £230 million a year on monthly 'glossies' and that the magazines receive another £190 million from advertising.

Consider what the term 'lifestyle' means. What is it that these magazines offer their readers? On the surface they seem to offer information and advice about certain types of 'lifestyle': what products to buy; where to buy them; the types of goods and services that might be available to someone leading that particular 'lifestyle'. However, as Lazarsfeld and Katz suggest (see p. 137), the relationship between audience and text is often much more complex and more intimate, offering a range of 'uses and gratifications' for the reader.

Lifestyle magazines often offer their readers not only advice but also a sense of identity and possibly companionship and reassurance. They appear to share with their readers the problems and issues of other similar people who also read the magazine. *FHM*, for example, includes a 'Things we did this month' on its editorials page that appears to offer a shared camaraderie between the producers and the readers in the magazine's 'laddish' attitudes and activities. As well as providing entertainment and escapism, male lifestyle magazines appear to offer guidance and instruction on how to live a particular lifestyle. Through both their articles and their advertisements the magazines offer aspiration in a variety of different spheres, such as relationships, careers, material possessions or fashion and looks. Some commentators suggest that magazines such as *FHM* and *Loaded* seem to offer specific groups of people (perhaps heterosexual men between eighteen and thirty years old) 'commodified' guidance on how to express a particular type of masculinity, often requiring the purchase of a wide range of consumer goods from grooming products and fashion items to holidays, gadgets and other electronic equipment. Other commentators, such as Whelehan (2000), see magazines such as *Loaded* as participating in a misogynistic backlash against 'new' definitions of male sexuality that have evolved as a result of feminist critiques, the advent of the 'new man' and increased male gay iconography. David Gauntlett, on the other hand, is more positive about the role of men's lifestyle magazines. Writing on the website associated with his book *Media, Gender and Identity*, Gauntlett says that

> In the analysis of men's magazines . . . we found a lot of signs that the magazines were about men finding a place for themselves in the modern world. These lifestyle publications were perpetually concerned with how to treat women, have a good relationship, and live an enjoyable life. Rather than being a return to essentialism − i.e. the idea of a traditional 'real' man, as biology and destiny 'intended' − . . . men's magazines have an almost obsessive relationship with the socially constructed nature of manhood. Gaps in a person's attempt to generate a masculine image are a source of humour in these magazines, because those breaches reveal what we all know − but some choose to hide − that masculinity

is a socially constructed performance anyway. The continuous flow of lifestyle, health, relationship and sex advice, and the repetitive curiosity about what the featured females look for in a partner, point to a clear view that the performance of masculinity can and should be practised and perfected. This may not appear ideal – it sounds as if men's magazines are geared to turning out a stream of identical men. But the masculinity put forward by the biggest-seller, *FHM*, we saw to be fundamentally caring, generous and good-humoured, even though the sarcastic humour sometimes threatened to smother this. Individual quirks are tolerated, and in any case we saw from the reader responses that the audience disregards messages that seem inappropriate or irrelevant or offensive.

(<http://theoryhead.com>)

There is more discussion available on the role and value of men's and women's lifestyle magazines on the Gauntlett website, for example 'Are magazines for young men likely to reinforce stereotypical, "macho" and sexist attitudes in their readers?' by Lucy Brown, available at <http://www.theory.org.uk/mensmags.htm>.

ACTIVITY . . .

- Re-read the section on representation (p. 61) and then conduct an analysis of the ways in which either men or women are represented in magazines such as *FHM*, *Loaded* or *Cosmopolitan*. It would be particularly interesting to consider how women are represented in men's magazines or vice-versa. This can be done by looking at the images of men and women in the magazines, starting with the front covers but also looking at the articles and editorials to see how the opposite sex is discussed as well as considering images contained in the adverts. You might then wish to compare your conclusions with a colleague who has looked at a different genre of magazine to see if there is any difference in the ways in which men's and women's magazines represent the opposite sex.
- Do what extent do you agree or disagree with Gauntlett's argument that magazines like *FHM* are 'fundamentally caring, generous and good-humoured'? What evidence would you use to support your views?

One of the attractions of lifestyle magazines is that they are usually a secondary media (see p. 140) and require little effort or concentration to consume. They are designed to be 'browsed' through, with regular features signposted and articles and advertisements designed to attract the reader's attention. These magazines will possibly be kept until the next edition arrives and so may be left lying around a home for some time. The magazines will therefore be looked at several times by the same reader or glanced through by new readers. Readers may have different patterns of reading magazines; perhaps when they do not want to be disturbed and can go somewhere quiet, or perhaps in the mornings over a cup of coffee.

The readership of a magazine, therefore, is important as well as its circulation. Magazines aimed particularly at one market may have a significant number of readers from another market, for example EMAP claims that 30 per cent of *FHM*'s readership is female. Another large 'cross-over' readership is men who read women's magazines. Sometimes this is done 'secretly', as often men are reluctant to admit that they enjoy reading some of the features of women's magazines or they may only admit to reading the problem pages. There may be an element of titillation and vicarious pleasure from gaining glimpses of other people's sex lives. Sometimes this reading may be more open, for example letters from the opposite sex regularly appear in both men's and women's magazines and some women's magazines have included sections aimed specifically at male readers.

ACTIVITY

Ask a selection of your peers how they 'consume' magazines.

- Do they have a particular pattern to how and when they read?
- Does it vary for different types of magazine?

You may wish to ask them if they read magazines aimed at the opposite sex.

- Do men 'confess' to reading women's magazines? Which ones? Which, if any, particular aspects of the women's magazines do they look at?
- Do women read men's magazines? Which ones? Again, which particular features interest them?
- Are women or men influenced by the articles supposedly addressed to the opposite sex?

It might also be interesting to ask men and women if they buy magazines for their partners and, if so, which ones and why.

Lifestyle magazines are primarily consumer magazines that aim to make a profit by 'selling' particular types of audience to advertisers. The magazines are literally offering their readers a 'lifestyle' – in other words, a model on which to base their lives at this particular moment and the goods necessary to accommodate it. To do this successfully, magazines need to be able to make their readers identify with the lifestyle on offer but at the same time offer them slightly more than they may already have. The magazines offer both guidance and aspiration: 'You, too, can be like this if only you do this/buy that'. The way this works for successful magazines is to have a clear sense of the target audience, Ang's 'imaginary entity' (p. 121), and to adopt an appropriate mode of address.

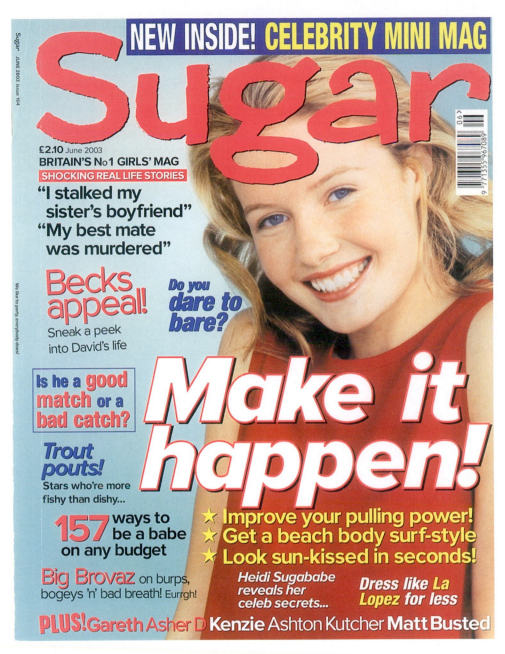

Figure 2.20 Sugar *cover. Source:* Sugar *magazine.*

'THE MOST FUN A GIRL CAN HAVE WITH HER CLOTHES ON!': TEENAGE MAGAZINES

As Figure 2.21 shows, *Sugar* is currently the most successful teenage girl's magazine, and it was recently bought by Hachette Filipacchi, which is a subsidiary of Hachette Filipacchi Medias, publisher of over 222 titles worldwide. In the UK the company also owns *Elle*, *Red*, *B*, *tvhits!*, and both *Inside Soap* and *All About Soap*.

Bliss and *J-17* are notionally in competition with each other but are in fact both owned and published by EMAP. They are both very carefully aimed at separate, distinctive niche markets defined by age. EMAP claims to be a media company 'whose purpose is to create "must-have" entertainment and information that can be delivered to every home and business within defined communities' (see <http://www.emap.com>). Apart from publishing and business event management, EMAP owns eighteen radio stations and seven television channels.

ACTIVITY...

EMAP is a good example of the way in which media companies attempt to create synergy. Conduct research into the radio and television stations that are owned by EMAP, which also publishes magazines such as *Smash Hits*, *Kerrang!* and *Q*.

- To what extent do all these different media complement each other?
- To what extent do they represent EMAP's attempt to address 'defined communities'?
- How would you define these particular communities?

Figure 2.21   *ABC: Teenage lifestyle magazines. Source: ABC.*

Sorted by total average net circulation per issue (total) on 9 April 2003

Title(s)/(Publisher)	
Sugar (Hachette Filipacchi (UK) Ltd) 01–Jul–2002 to 31–Dec–2002	321,258
Bliss (EMAP Elan Ltd) 01–Jul–2002 to 31–Dec–2002	260,102
J-17 (EMAP Elan Ltd) 01–Jul–2002 to 31–Dec–2002	143,308
Cosmo Girl (The National Magazine Company Ltd) 01–Jul–2002 to 31–Dec–2002	142,073
Mizz Specials Series (IPC Media Ltd) 01–Jul–2002 to 31–Dec–2002	136,827
Mizz (IPC Media Ltd) 01–Jul–2002 to 31–Dec–2002	129,654
Shout (D.C. Thomson & Co. Ltd) 01–Jul–2002 to 31–Dec–2002	101,010

© Copyright

Although the style of contemporary popular 'teen mags' may have moved away from the photo-stories of *Jackie* and *My Guy*, much of the content deals with similar issues, albeit in a more up-to-date manner. McRobbie (1983), writing about the ideology underpinning *Jackie*, noted that it socialised female adolescents into a 'feminine' culture:

[*Jackie*] sets up, defines and focuses exclusively on the personal, locating it as the sphere of prime importance to the teenage girl. It presents this as a totality – and by implication all else is of secondary interest to the 'modern girl'. Romance problems, fashion, beauty and pop mark out the limits of the girl's concern – other possibilities are ignored or dismissed.

(McRobbie 1983: 743)

McRobbie suggests that magazines such as *Sugar*, *Bliss* and *J-17* can be seen to offer reassurance and guidance to adolescent readers who are still learning about themselves. These magazines offer advice, entertainment, amusement and escapism and speak to their readers in a language that they understand.

As McRobbie suggests, however, it is important to question the extent to which teenage readers accept or challenge this reading of these magazines. For example, research by Keynote, a market research company, suggests that although readers are more influenced by these magazines than they are by their parents, television and friends play a more important part in promoting ideas about how to live.

Teenage Magazines – Executive Summary

The teenage magazine market, while potentially very lucrative, also tends to be very volatile. Population trends are currently working in favour of the market, which also benefits from the fact that many teenage girls are keen readers of magazines, which can have an important influence on the habits and attitudes of this age group. On the more negative side, however, young people are notoriously fickle in their tastes, and magazines need to work hard to keep their loyalty.

After a boom in the mid-1990s, the second half of the decade saw very mixed fortunes for the teenage magazine market. Overcrowding in the market followed the rush of new titles that appeared after the launch of Attic Futura's *Sugar* in 1994, and sales have been slipping since 1997. Among the factors which have been cited to explain this have been: the changing face of the pop music industry – currently, there are no big stars to replace the sales-generating success of Boyzone and the Spice Girls; and the phenomenon of 'getting older younger', which means that those in their mid to late teens are increasingly switching their allegiance from teenage titles to those aimed at an older age group.

The overall market is segmented into fashion/lifestyle and pop/entertainment titles. The former is the largest sector in terms of numbers of titles, and has gained share over the past 3 years in both volume and value terms.

Despite the fact that circulations have been falling for many magazines, successive rises in cover prices have meant that sales revenue has shown reasonable growth; this is particularly important for teenage magazines, which are less able to attract large amounts of advertising than the glossy titles aimed at older women. This is partly because teenagers' own disposable incomes, although increasing, are generally low, and partly because of their incomes advertising to young people is a sensitive area, and likely to attract controversy. However, there are signs that things are becoming more promising at the older end of the market, with high-spending advertisers, which are already beginning to target US teenagers in the hope of capturing early loyalty, reportedly showing an interest in the UK market.

Magazine publishers are having to spend a great deal of marketing effort in maximising copy sales, including extensive use of covermounts, and initiatives such as events and exhibitions, which help put magazines and their advertisers in touch with the hard-to-reach teenage market.

The rapid growth in mobile phone ownership among teenagers, and with it the increasing popularity of text messaging, is beginning to be exploited

by teenage magazines as a means of finding out about, and keeping in touch with, their readers. Brand extensions – through product licensing and the extension of magazine brands into other media – are being utilised within the teenage magazine sector, as in other parts of the magazine market.

Although the Internet is undoubtedly very important to teenagers, attempts to combine teenage magazines and the online world have so far met with limited success. This is partly because of the difficulties presented by the teenage market for those seeking revenue through e-commerce – and there are also concerns about sexual explicitness and safety, especially in relation to the chat room elements of some teenage sites.

During 2000, a number of fast moving consumer goods (FMCG) companies attempted to set up their own teenage magazine-style sites, several of which were closed soon afterwards. These experiences have caused some teenage magazines to hold back for the moment on their own plans for online development.

The mid-1990s peak in the teenage magazine market coincided with a good deal of adverse publicity concerning the sexual content of magazines aimed at young women in their early-to-mid teens. The industry has taken steps towards self-regulation in this area, and the content of most magazines has been toned down. Teenage magazines have recently been enlisted by the Government to help in their campaign to reduce the number of teenage pregnancies by carrying advertisements and advertorials.

The exclusive research conducted for this report indicated that a very high proportion of adults are aware of the strong influence exercised by magazines. The balance of opinion seems to be that explicit articles about sex should not be encouraged in teenage magazines, and at present a relatively small proportion think that magazines take a responsible attitude to issues such as teenage pregnancy and drugs.

Despite the current problems in the teenage magazine market, a number of new launches have taken place or are planned. There is a move away from sex-based content towards a focus on celebrities; there are also attempts to capitalise on the fact that high-end advertisers are showing an interest in capturing the loyalty of young women, with planned teenage versions of glossy adult titles. Both of these trends are also apparent in the US teenage magazine market.

The sales revenue is forecast to rise only modestly over the next 5 years, and there will no doubt be more magazine closures. However, in the long term, teenage magazines are in a strong position to benefit from trends such as cross-media strategies and the growth of online brands.

(<http://www.keynote.co.uk>, April 2001)

J-17 and Sugar

According to EMAP, *J-17 is* 'for girls with attitude. Alongside sex, snogs and advice in *J-17* confidential, to cutting edge street style, sorted careers info, cool celebs and text message fun – it's the original teen mag and the best!'. *J-17* used to have a circulation in excess of 300,000 and a readership of nearly three times that, but has recently lost out to competitors such as *Bliss* and *Sugar*. All three magazines are targeting readers in the twelve to sixteen age range – those who aspire to the maturity that being seventeen years old seems to offer.

Research by *J-17* suggests that 'appearance and image are very important' for teenage-girl readers and that they are 'the highest spenders on toiletries/cosmetics within the youth market'. *J-17* readers, for example, wash their hair on average 4.4 times a week and in 1998 spent £6 a month on hair care and £19.55 a week on clothes, usually bought from places like Top Shop, Tammy, Miss Selfridge and River Island.

Advertising in *Sugar* and *J-17* reflects this profile, with an emphasis on health and beauty products, fashion and music but also quite a lot of confectionery. Articles include 'how to cope with your parents' and 'how to stop smoking' as well as fashion tips, star profiles, show-biz gossip and horoscopes, and are all presented on high-gloss full-colour paper.

Most of *Sugar* and *J-17's* readers are under the legal age of consent, and a major part of these magazines' attraction is their 'problem pages', where readers can not only 'speak for themselves' but also read about problems and issues that may feature in their own lives and that they may have difficulty in discussing with their peers or family. The mode of address is personal, friendly and intimate. It is this area of the magazine that is perhaps the most 'reassuring', saying to its readers 'you are not alone, others are having similar problems and fears'. Typical letters might read:

> I am not yet 16 and my boyfriend is several years older than me. We have been together for a year and been having sex for several months. He has asked me to take part in a bondage session with him and his friends. I like having sex with him but the thought of being tied up scares me. What should I do?

> Recently I was caught by my mum snogging with my boyfriend. Now she says that she doesn't like us being alone together, and that I'm acting like a slut. But I haven't any plans for sex and I don't understand why my mum doesn't trust me.

These types of feature have been the focus of a 'moral panic' (see p. 145) over the last few years. There have been accusations that these magazines condone under-age sexual activity and seemingly endorse sexual promiscuity as well as offering a 'guide' to different sexual practices. There have been calls for magazine editors to curb such sexually explicit content, although the editors and publishers have argued that they offer 'responsible' advice that their readers may otherwise not receive. For example, *Sugar* has advice pages focusing on 'You and your life', 'You and your heart' and 'You and your body' as well as advice on where to buy condoms and adverts asking 'Should I let my friends control my sex life?' *Sugar's* website offers advice on sex and relationships:

So when you do decide you are ready to have sex and don't want to get pregnant – or catch a sexually transmitted infection – make sure you use a condom. Don't be afraid to say no if you're not ready to have sex. It's your decision. If your guy thinks you're special, he'll wait. And remember, you can get confidential advice from a clinic or your doctor, even if you're under 16.

(<http://www.sugarmagazine.co.uk>)

Figure 2.22   'Over to you', from Contents page of Sugar. *Source:* Sugar *magazine.*

ACTIVITY . . .

Figure 2.22 is taken from the contents page of *Sugar* and identifies some of the ways in which magazines like *Sugar* try to promote a more personal mode of address. They also represent opportunities for readers of magazines like *Sugar* to interact with the magazine and become more involved with the products and lifestyle the magazine promotes. The keynote research suggests that they are key elements in the success of teenage magazines like *Sugar*.

Conduct some research that looks at teenage girls' magazines, especially:

■ the use of websites, email and text messaging to encourage readers to become more involved and to provide the magazine's producers with more demographic information (for example, *Sugar* asks its readers to text in their date of birth, their postcode and the make and model of their phone; this gives the marketing department useful information when trying to sell advertising space)

■ the use of 'covermounts' to provide extra 'value' to encourage readers to purchase, or stay loyal to, the magazine. What types of products are most frequently on offer? What assumptions do they make about the magazine's readership?

continued

■ What 'brand extensions' can you find (for example the ways in which magazine titles are used to promote other activities such as pop concerts or exhibitions)?

More!

More! is one of EMAP's most profitable titles and has a circulation of around 250,000 sales per issue and a readership of about 500,000 per issue. The target age of its readership is sixteen to twenty-four, of which 48 per cent are ABC1 and 75 per cent single. Its main rival is probably *19*, which has a circulation of about 110,000. *19* was owned until recently by IPC, which was Britain's largest magazine group; however, in 2001 IPC was bought by AOL Time Warner, the world's largest media group.

According to the editor, *More!* is

> the favourite magazine for every up-for-it young woman because it's all about fun, flirting and looking gorgeous. With its cheeky humour, hunky men, sex advice and red-hot celebrity gossip, *More!* shoots straight from the hip. And with its must-have fashion, beauty and entertainment info, *More!* is everything a sassy young woman wants from her life in a handy magazine. It's the most fun a girl can have with her clothes on!

The magazine claims that '1% of *More!* readers go out 3–4 nights in an average week. Their ideal night out is round a friend's house for a good natter and make-up session, then to the local warm-up before going to a club to check out the totty.'

The style and contents are similar to *J-17*, but the products are perhaps a little more 'upmarket' (L'Oreal rather than Cote's Puzzel) and the articles are a little more 'serious' (teenage disappearances rather than parental unfairnesses).

The title itself is quite interesting – *More!* More what – sex? fashion? advice? The *More!* editorial team would probably reply 'more fun'. What that means is suggested by the strap-line 'Eye-Popping! Pant-Busting! Bed-Busting! The sex that changed YOUR lives' on the cover of the issue of 27 January 1999 and the regular 'Position of the Fortnight' or 'Men Unzipped' features.

According to Taylor, magazines such as *More!*, *Sugar* and *J-17* are offering their readers a positive representation of themselves, 'reassuring the girl she is not alone or unusual'. There is a 'theme of taking control of their lives, and living for themselves' (Taylor 2000: 9–12). It is also a representation that shows that teenage girls are mature, independent, sensible and trustworthy – values that perhaps many of them feel are not recognised by the 'adult' world. Part of the mode of address is to reinforce a sense of belonging and a type of solidarity against the unfairness of the world 'out there', a world that will not let them do want they want. According to Taylor, magazines such as *More!*, *Sugar* and *J-17* provide a teenage girl with 'a learning experience within the privacy of her own bedroom, whereby she can see and understand her peers, without feeling embarrassed

or ashamed. Quite simply the teenage girl can learn about herself, and grasp the meaning of everything that is happening to her' (Taylor 2000: 14).

It would be interesting to speculate about the extent to which the people who work for these magazines and speak the language ('Let *J-17*'s Sarra guide you through her four types of lovin' . . .' (July 1999)) in print actually live out the lifestyles that *J-17* and *More!* represent.

'SHE'S A WOMAN WITH RESPONSIBILITY . . . AND A HANGOVER': WOMEN'S MAGAZINES

Like McRobbie, Ferguson (1983) analyses women's magazines and the extent to which they are concerned with the practices and beliefs of a 'cult of femininity'. According to Ferguson, these magazines not only reflect the role of women in society but they also offer guidance and socialisation into that role. Ferguson suggests that women's magazines attempt to 'promote a collective female social "reality", the world of women' (1983: 185). Top-selling magazines such as *Woman*, *Woman's Own*, *Bella* and *Glamour* offer both guidance and membership into this 'cult of femininity'. (See also section on ideology and gender, p. 81.)

> This is a world founded on conformity to a set of shared meanings where a consciously cultivated female bond acts as the social cement of female solidarity . . . Through the selective perception and interpretation of the wider world from the viewpoint of the 'woman's angle', the editors of these sacred oracles sustain a social 'reality' that is 'forever feminine'.
>
> (Ferguson 1983: 186)

These magazines can be seen to offer a representation of the 'ideal' in terms of the self, home, family, career, relationships and lifestyle.

To gain some idea of how the 'world of women' is represented, it is useful to look through the contents pages of some of the magazines.

Glamour is the most successful of these magazines. Owned by Condé Nast, it has a circulation of around 500,000. According to its media pack, *Glamour* is for 'successful, independent, modern women who know how to have fun, how to dress and how to spend'. *Glamour* is aimed at 'successful ABC1C2 women aged between 18–34' and it claims that 32 per cent of its readership will have a degree or above. *Marie Claire* was owned by IPC before the company's takeover by AOL/Time Warner and it has a circulation of approximately 400,000 per month. The magazine targets ABC1 women aged eighteen to thirty-five.

Red was launched in February 1998 and is owned by Hachette Filipacchi. It has a circulation of around 195,000 and is aimed at ABC1 women aged thirty or over. According to its media pack, a typical reader will be a working professional (possibly in PR or the media) with a high disposable income, aged between twenty-eight and thirty-eight (what it describes as 'middle youth'), be urban based and living in a long-term stable relationship. The typical reader's interests will be fashion, travel,

Figure 2.23 *Examples of contents of a selection of magazines.*

Woman's Own	Marie Claire	Red	Glamour
Fashion	Fashion	Fashion	Fashion
–	Fashion and Beauty	–	–
Features	Features	Features	Features
–	Features	–	–
Beauty	Beauty	Health & Beauty	Beauty
–	Fashion and Beauty	–	–
Good Health	Health	–	You, You, You
Offers	Special offers	Special offers	–
Cookery	–	Food	–
Regulars	Regulars	–	In Every Issue
Showbiz	Ideas	Home & Garden	Outside
–	Entertainment	–	–
–	–	Travel	Backbite
–	Lifestyle	–	–
–	–	–	Contagious
–	–	–	Personal Call

entertainment, dining out, reading and yoga. She will be intelligent and articulate and read the *Evening Standard* and the *Guardian*. She will holiday in Florence, Bali or the Lake District and shop at Josephs, Whistles, Jigsaw and Kensington and Notting Hill designer boutiques. *Red*'s mission statement states that

> *Red* is the first magazine to speak your language. We believe in middle youth. We believe in enjoying ourselves. We believe that style, passion, and humour should fuel all our interests – whether it's fashion, food, interiors, entertainment, travel or gardening.

ACTIVITY...

Compare the contents pages of a selection of women's magazines such as *Glamour*, *Red* or *Woman's Own* or men's magazines such as *FHM*, *Loaded* or *GQ*.

- Is there a similar set of accepted subjects?
- What do the topics in men's or women's magazines suggest about their readers and the readers' role and place in society?
- How do these topics relate to ideas about stereotyping and ideology?

OR

How far do you think it is possible for audiences to resist the ideological messages of media texts such as these?

Ferguson (1983) suggests that new magazines are launched either to offer competition in an existing market or to try to identify a new 'niche' for women – a particular set of experiences, age or income not as yet targeted. This diversification explains why new magazines are constantly coming on to an already crowded and competitive market.

As overall the number of magazine-buying women is not increasing, both new and established titles have to fight to build and maintain their position in the market. One of the main ways of doing this is to try to appear 'different' whilst simultaneously offering the same benefits as the competition.

ACTIVITY...

Spend some time at a large newsagent looking through the range of magazines on offer.

- Identify the main categories of magazine type.
- Select one particular genre and list all the various titles.
- Are some newer than others? What (if anything) do the new titles offer that the old ones lacked?
- Look at the worksheet at the end of this section (p. 174) and carry out an analysis of one of the magazines.

OR

Monitor the success of the titles mentioned above.

- Are they all still in production?
- How do their circulation figures compare to those of their competitors?
- To what extent do they succeed (or fail) in being 'different' from their competitors?

Ferguson suggests that each women's magazine is targeted at a distinct group, such as teenagers, housewives, young single women, mothers, brides or slimmers. There are therefore magazines that specialise in almost every stage of a woman's life, offering a 'step-by-step' guide, tips for survival and of course products to purchase. Originally women's magazines focused on romance, marriage and household management. However, since the 1970s, Ferguson suggests, the 'Independent Woman' has emerged, who is 'urged to achieve her full potential outside the home as well as within it'. Frequently this is represented as sexual independence or, perhaps more recently, as a 'ladette' culture promoted by certain magazines and personalities.

According to Ferguson, this range allows a woman to choose the 'kind' of woman she wants to be:

- The *New Woman* reader is 'gutsy, glamorous and irreverent, embracing the philosophy that there's no right way to live and no single way to be . . . She's a woman with responsibility . . . and a hangover'.
- The *Elle* reader is 'spirited, stylish and intelligent, she expects to be successful at everything she does. She takes the lead and breaks the rules'.
- The *Red* reader 'spends as much time in the morning at Harvey Nichols as she does in the afternoon at the garden centre'.
- The *Elle Decoration* woman is 'well educated, successful and heavily involved in work, she enjoys life in a diverse and cosmopolitan environment'.

However, as much as these magazines may say 'Get out there and show the world you are someone in your own right', Ferguson suggests that they also say 'Remember you must achieve as a wife and mother too'.

ACTIVITY

Stereotyping provides media producers with a useful short cut in representing groups of people. What do you think are the dangers of stereotyping? Support your argument with examples.

Ultimately lifestyle magazines must leave their readers with a positive feeling otherwise they may not return and buy the next edition. The July 2000 edition of *Red* carried articles

on the menopause and troubled relationships with mothers, but the final paragraph of the editorial read:

> We haven't forgotten that it's summer, that the sun is shining and it's the season for feeling good. The rest of this issue is packed with sunshine, lighting up fashion (pure gold), homes (gorgeously shabby, in a very chic way), food (delicious salads), not to mention lighting you up too, with our power-packed nutrition feature 'Eat Yourself Happy'. We hope that you do just that. And, while you're at it, check out the 'Sun Beauty Special' pages for the lowdown on the best fake tans as well as the make-up to give you that authentic sun-kissed glow. Then there's all the latest news on health, fitness and feelgood treatments . . .

This paragraph serves several functions. It reassures the reader that not all of the magazine is going to be 'serious' and 'depressing'. It helps to reinforce the sense of 'personal address' ('we', 'you') by the manner in which it is written and the accompanying photograph of the editor smiling. It uses colloquial language (sufficiently everyday to appear like speech, for example 'while you're at it' and 'gorgeously shabby'). It advertises other features in this month's edition; in fact it manages to mention nearly all of the magazine's content.

The editorial in *Woman's Own* (April 1996), written by a man, is perhaps more 'mainstream', although the word 'gorgeous' still turns up:

> Families are special. The letters you send to us here at *Woman's Own* remind us just how important they are.

> Which is why Julie and Mick Seale's story is so heart-warming. The couple were refused IVF on the NHS because Julie was too old at 36. But then a mystery man stepped in and paid for private treatment, and now the Seales have a gorgeous boy to make their family complete . . . It's good to know there are still some people in this world doing things for purely selfless reasons.

ACTIVITY . . .

Re-read the section on genre (p. 53) and choose a genre of magazines, for example teenage, women's, 'lads'. Analyse a selection and identify the extent to which they share a common iconography (p. 54) and/or mode of address (p. 49).

'ALL THE GOSS, ALL THE NEWS, EVERY TWO WEEKS': *INSIDE SOAP*

Increasingly brand names are being used across different media, and magazine 'tie-ins' with popular television programmes, such as the *X-Files* or *TOTP*, are seen as a means of cashing in on established names. Other magazines that tie in with television

Figure 2.24 *Cover of* Inside Soap, *fortnight ending 23 May 2003.*
Source: courtesy of Inside Soap *magazine.*

programmes are magazines that focus on soap operas, such as *Inside Soap* and *All About Soap*, both published by Hachette Filipacchi.

Inside Soap describes itself as 'the definitive voice on the nation's favourite shows and their celebrities' and has a circulation of over 237,000. It describes its readers as the 'right type': youthful, keen shoppers, brand aware and responsive to advertising.

Advertising consists of a mixture of consumer items such as soap powder, mobile phones, chocolates, a Celtic eternity ring, a Marilyn Monroe porcelain doll, catalogue shopping, health and beauty products to help reduce weight, and sanitary towels. A typical edition of about eighty pages will have about nineteen full pages of advertising plus several other pages of smaller advertisements. As advertisements cost approximately £4,000 per full page and the cover price is £1.40, it seems that *Inside Soap* produces an income of around £400,000 per edition.

The magazine is produced in a glossy full-colour format with a high proportion of photographs of soap-opera stars or scenes from the programmes. The design is made up of small, easy-to-digest pieces, or full-page spreads. Photographs accompany all the features although these vary in size and position on the page. Most of the photographs are 'head-and-shoulder' shots of the actors either in or out of role. There is a lot of colour, with the dominant colours being primary reds and blues. The contents are largely gossip or synopses of the latest storylines. Many of the stories focus on the fictitious lives of the soap characters, discussing them as if they were real people. There is little involvement with the outside world; *Inside Soap* seems to offer information, relaxation and escapism. The overall style suggests something that is accessible, easy to read and understand. It does not require much concentration, the only requirement being a familiarity with television soap operas, their stars and stories.

The magazine also includes photographs of the various *Inside Soap* staff who are responsible for particular features, for example 'Let Andy know what you think about the soaps'. Readers therefore have the opportunity to contribute through features like 'Soapbox', where they can write or email in with comments or questions:

> When the Marsdens first arrived in *Emmerdale* they appeared to be a close-knit family, and the relationship between Ronnie and his wife seemed strong, especially when they thought she was ill. So where has Ronnie's urge to run off with another woman come from? Come on *Emmerdale* – be a little more imaginative. Can't we have a soap family having even a week or two of happiness?
>
> (*Inside Soap*, 23 May 2003)

> I am a fan of *Neighbours* and I've noticed that there's one song they always play in the background in the coffee shop. I think it's called *One Good Reason*. Am I right, and can I buy it somewhere?
>
> (*Inside Soap*, 23 June 2000)

Each issue's star letter wins a prize of £30, and there is a prize crossword and other competitions to enter. Other regular features include horoscopes, recipes, historical moments from soap operas, and television schedules for the various soap operas (see Figure 2.25).

Inside

**Inside Soap**

Issue 231 ★ 10 – 23 May 2003

Jessie talks romance – see p40

COVER PHOTO: BBC/ALAN STRUTT

This fortnight...

What a very bad lad *EastEnders'* Dirty Dennis Rickman is turning out to be! Having seduced Kat Slater, this fortnight Den Jnr turns his attention to not one, but two, other Walford ladies (see p12). But do keep reading *Inside Soap*, because we've had a sneak preview of the next few weeks' antics – and you won't believe who Dennis hooks up with next! Talking of bad 'uns, this fortnight *Corrie*'s Joe Carter reveals his true colours when he lets Karen McDonald in on his big secret! (see p18). With all this plotting and passion, it's a good job there are still nice, wholesome things in the soaps. The only problem is, you've got to wade through all those hours of bitching and betrayal to find them. Hey it's a hard job, but somebody's got to do it!

Steven

Steven Murphy, Editor

While there's bad news about baby VJ's health, it doesn't stop the little lad enjoying his christening – see p28

It's handbags at dawn in Brookie – see p15

Inside Soap is published by **HACHETTE FILIPACCHI** 64 North Row, London W1K 7LL Tel: 020 7150 7570 Fax: 020 7150 7683 www.hf-uk.com soapbox@insidesoap.co.uk

Editor Steven Murphy	**Art Editor** Simon Lambert	**Australian Correspondent** Jason Herbison	**Sales Executive** Rebecca Lemon Tel: 020 7150 7286	**Chairman** Kevin Hand	**Hachette Filipacchi Médias** 149-151, rue Anatole-France Levallois-Perret 92534 France	**Publishing Director International Editions** Alain Deroche
Deputy Editor Wendy Grandller	**Deputy Art Editor** Tanya Goldsmith	**Publisher** Grace Stewart	**Production Co-ordinator** John Morecraft	**Finance Director** Radhika Radhakrishnan	**Chairman and CEO** Gérald de Roquemaurel	**Deputy Directors International Editions** Fabrizio Lo Cicero
Features Editor Allison Maund	**Designer** Richard Atkinson	**Product Manager** Amanda Fry Tel: 020 7150 7560	**PR Manager** Sue Asbury Tel: 020 7150 7171	**PA to Executive Office** Michelle Mars	**CEO International** Jean-Paul Denfert-Rochereau	Alexandra Hamden
TV Editor Claire Brand	**Picture Editor** Ally Randell	**Advertising Manager** James Hawker Tel: 020 7150 7263	**Press Officer** Jess Blake	**Colour Separations by** Rival Colour	**Associate Deputy International CEO** Alain Chastagnol	**International Co-ordinator** Angela Smeaton
Writer Adrian Lobb	**Deputy Picture Editor** Sam Martin	**Senior Sales Executive** Tala Eagle	**Syndication Manager** Peggy Panaglotopoulou Tel: 020 7150 7510	**Printed in Britain by** Quebecor	**Deputy CEO International** Jean de Boisdeffre	**Subscription Enquiries and Back Issues** Tel: 01858 435362
Junior Writer Andy Baker	**Production Editor** Karen Larsen	**Advertising Manager** Tel: 020 7150 7293	Tel: 020 7150 7170	**Distributed by** Marketforce Enquiries: 020 7633 3300 www.marketforce.co.uk	**Editorial Director Of International Editions** François Vincens	
Editorial Assistant Sarah Ellis	**Sub Editor** Helen Williams					

Figure 2.25 *Contents page of* Inside Soap, *fortnight ending 23 May 2003. Source: courtesy of* Inside Soap *magazine.*

The Brand

- Circulation – 237,242 (July–December 02)

- An authoritative and entertaining fortnightly soap fix, which takes its readers behind the scenes of their favourite TV shows.

- *Inside Soap*'s most effective selling tools – its front cover and content – continue to lead the way

- Our success is built on our ability to come up with new angles on storylines

- We add a 'not seen on TV' element of gossip and intrigue to the nation's favourite shows

- Appealing to the voyeuristic nature in us all, *Inside Soap* is for some pure indulgence and escapism, whilst for others it is a quick fix providing them with all the latest gossip and hot news from the wonderful world of soap

- Successful brand extensions include The *Inside Soap* board game and The *Inside Soap* Awards

The Reader

- The *Inside Soap* reader is female, aged between 25 and 55. She loves the soaps and wants to be first with all the news, and latest events. She loves to gossip with her friends and soaps play and important part in that. She is a young mum, and her children are a big part of her life. She leads a busy life running home, and looking after her kids, therefore the soaps and *Inside Soap* are all part of her valuable 'me' time

- *Inside Soap* is read by 974,000 adults every fortnight

- With five consecutive increases *Inside Soap*'s readership has almost doubled in the past four years

- 81% of *Inside Soap* readers are female

- Mass market, not downmarket, 58% of *Inside Soap* readers are ABC1C2

- 49% are married

- 38% work full time

- Appeals to all ages but with a core reader age of 31

- As a bi-weekly title *Inside Soap* has proved that, even with the new competition of celebrity titles, consumers still want *Inside Soap* as their regular purchase and essential guide to the Nation's favourite shows

Figure 2.26 *Generic presentation for* Inside Soap *from 1999.*
Source: courtesy of Inside Soap *magazine.*

Choose two different types of magazine and compare and contrast their contents and the way in which they address the reader. You should consider:

- the amount and style of editorial
- the amount and type of advertising
- the way in which particular lifestyles are represented
- the ways in which readers may address the magazine.

You may also wish to carry out a semiotic analysis (p. 30) of the covers to identify the ways in which the magazine is constructed to meet its particular target audience.

You could contact the magazines to see if they will provide you with any information regarding their circulation and/or readership. (Most magazines have a media pack that contains this information.)

You could also carry out a small readership survey. Your findings can be written up as a report or presented to the rest of your group.

WORKSHEET FOR ANALYSING MAGAZINES

Consider the following features.

The title of the magazine:

- Why is it called that?
- What are the significant words?
- What connotations do they have?

The publisher of the magazine:

- Who publishes the magazine?
- What other magazines (if any) does it publish?
- What other media interests (if any) does it have?
- How much does the magazine cost?
- How often is it published?
- What is its circulation/readership?
- Does the magazine have a website?

The target audience for the magazine:

- What type of reader is it targeting?
- How do you know this (look at types of articles and advertisements)?
- How does the reader 'interact' with the magazine?

The cover of the magazine:

- Analyse the images on the cover; the types of facial expressions, body language, clothing, and so on.
- What do they tell us about the target audience for the magazine?
- What else appears on the cover?
- Why are particular items in the magazine featured?
- Explain why particular typefaces, types of graphics, colours and other notable stylistic features are used.
- Does the cover look similar to other magazine covers? If so, why? If not, how does it look different?

The 'style' of presentation of the magazine:

- What do you notice about the magazine's presentation?
- Does it look cheap or expensive?
- How does it compare with other similar magazines?
- How does it use colour, print style, artwork and other visuals to convey an overall effect?

The 'mode of address' of the magazine:

- How does it address its readers?
- How and when are readers allowed to address the magazine?
- What types of articles/features does it contain?
- What subjects are covered?

The advertisements that appear in the magazine:

- What are the main types of products being advertised?
- What is their price range?
- Who are they aimed at?
- Why are these products featured particularly?
- What percentage of the overall magazine is taken up with advertisements?
- How do the models featured in the advertisements relate to the target audience?

continued

Representations in the magazine:

- How are men and women represented? (Look at both the images and the text.)
- Are there conflicting representations? If so, why is this?
- How do these representations relate to the readership?
- Is there a limited range of representations for men and women? If so, what are they and why?
- What groups do not appear in the pages of the magazine? Why?
- Are celebrities featured in the magazine? If so, what kinds of celebrities? Why have they been chosen?

The competition for the magazine:

- What other titles are in competition with it?
- What are their circulation/readership figures?
- How much do they cost?
- What are the similarities/differences?

Finally:

- What do you think are the reasons for the magazine's popularity (or otherwise)?
- What does the magazine offer its readers?
- What 'values' or ideologies are implicit in the magazine?

The effects that the Internet may have on magazine sales and consumption are not yet clear. Some publishers are concerned that there may be a similar situation to when television became popular in Britain and newspaper sales fell. Internet websites can offer high-quality images, interactivity beyond the pages of the magazines themselves, more buying potential and a mix of video and audio. Therefore magazine publishers are increasingly looking for ways to offer their particular brand across a range of media – radio, television and new media. However, this means more than just putting a (paid-for) magazine on to a (free) website. The online version must generate income either through additional advertising revenue or through retail sales of goods and services aimed at the magazine's particular niche reader.

1   You have been commissioned to design a pilot issue of a new magazine aimed at teenagers. The company you are working for is part of a larger group that already has several teenage titles and will need convincing that there is an opportunity to launch a new title, so your magazine must be distinctive but meet readers' needs and expectations. You may wish to work as a group and allocate different tasks to different people as in a real magazine production process.

■ You need to decide upon the target audience and, using Hartley's and Fiske's 'subjectivities' (p. 122), draw up a profile of a 'typical reader' that also includes 'lifestyle'. Choose a name and price for the magazine. You could create a media pack for your magazine.

■ Design a front cover.

■ Consider what types of products and brands the readership would be interested in and then make a list of possible advertisers and cross-promotional features. Consider how you would 'sell' the magazine and its readers to potential advertisers.

■ Draw up a list of the types of articles and features that should be included in the magazine. For the pilot you may wish to write up one or two of the features and design some advertisements. You could also write an editorial, from the editor to the readers, explaining what the new magazine offers them.

■ Produce an advertising campaign for the launch, detailing where the advertisements for the magazine will appear. Again you may wish to produce a finished version of one of the advertisements.

■ Consider what else, if anything, you should be doing to convince your company of the viability of the new magazine.

You will need to work to a deadline and justify all your decisions and choices.

2   Imagine that a new magazine has been developed as a spin-off from a television programme.

■ First consider what may be a suitable programme source, who the target audience is and what the content of the magazine should be.

■ Then design a page to appear in an existing magazine that advertises the new magazine to its potential audience.

■ Detail the reasoning behind your design and content choices.

3   'The most important factor that shapes a publication is its readers.' How does this apply to magazines such as those discussed in this section?

continued

4   There has been a recent expansion in the range of women's and men's magazines available to consumers. Explain how and why this expansion has taken place.

5   Write a review of a magazine (preferably one that you do not normally read) and post your review on the Web at the US-based site <http://www.smartgirl.com>.

6   Discuss, using examples, the extent to which magazines influence gender identities.

7   Figure 2.27 contains the RAJAR figures for London radio stations, both national and local and BBC and commercial. It also gives details of the changes in the number of listeners between 2002 and 2003. Using the RAJAR website (<http://www.rajar.co.uk>), draw up a similar table for your area. Which stations are most popular? Why do you think this is? Which stations are least popular? Again suggest reasons for this. Which station has gained the most listeners and which has lost the most listeners? Again suggest possible reasons. Compare your findings with those for London. How do you account for any differences?

Figure 2.27   *'Who we are listening to . . .'. Source: RAJAR.*

	Number of listeners March 2003	Number of listeners March 2002	Change on year %
Radio 1	10, 343,000	10, 541,000	−1.88
Radio 2	13, 234,000	12,898,000	+2.60
Radio 3	2, 096,000	2,132,000	−1.69
Radio 4	10, 034,000	9, 948,000	+0.96
5 Live	6, 415,000	6, 436,000	−0.33
Classic FM	6, 872,000	6, 838,000	+0.49
Capital FM	2,413,000	2, 695,000	−10.47
Heart 106.2	1,849,000	1, 608,000	+0.05
LBC 97.3	441,000	384,000	+14.84
Capital Gold	1,037,000	1, 285,000	−19.3

Note: The 2003 figures for LBC 97.3 FM compared with last year's LBC 1152 AM audiences

FURTHER READING

Ferguson, M. (1983) *Forever Feminine: Women's Magazines and the Cult of Femininity*, Heinemann.

Gauntlett, D. (2002) *Media, Gender and Identity*, Routledge.

McRobbie, A. (1994) '*More!* New sexualities in girls' and women's magazines' in Curran, J., Morley, D. and Walkerdine, V. (eds) *Cultural Studies and Communications*, Arnold.

— (1995) *Feminism and Youth Culture – From* Jackie *to* Just Seventeen, 2nd edn, Macmillan.

Nixon, S. (1996) *Hard Looks* (*Masculinities, Spectatorship and Contemporary Consumption*), St. Martins Press.

Stokes, J. (1999) 'Use it or lose it: sex, sexuality and sexual health in magazines for girls' in Stokes, J. and Reading, A. (eds) *The Media in Britain: Current Debates and Developments*, Macmillan.

Whelehan, I. (2000) *Overloaded: Popular Culture and the Future of Feminism*, The Woman's Press.

Winship, J. (1987) *Inside Women's Magazines*, Pandora.

In this part of the book we:

■ investigate the ownership of media institutions and the power that some of these institutions hold over potential consumers of media products
■ look at the way media institutions are regulated and consider future developments in the media world.

ACTIVITY...

Look at the logos in Figure 3.1

■ How many logos do you recognise?
■ Which areas of the media do you associate them with?
■ Who owns these organisations?
■ What country are they primarily based in?

ISSUES OF OWNERSHIP AND CONTROL

As we mentioned in the introduction, wherever you go in the world it is almost impossible to avoid the media. There are few areas in the world that do not have some kind of newspaper (even if it is only a news-sheet). There is barely a country that does not have a television station, and if it does not have one of its own, then it is certainly possible to receive pictures broadcast from a neighbouring country (although in some countries this might be considered an offence).

The media have, in many ways, challenged our conventional notions of national identity. We can watch television from many different countries, listen to foreign radio stations, read overseas newspapers and now, with even more ease, access as many websites as we wish from all over the world through the Internet. And of course other countries can consume British media products.

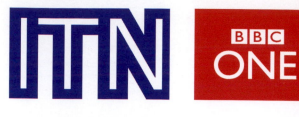

Figure 3.1 *A selection of corporate logos. Source: ITN, CNN, BBC One and BBC Two, Turner Broadcasting and TCM.*

Undertake a survey of what non-British media you can access. Although there will be much American and Australian media available, it might be more interesting to try to find examples of media produced in other, less obvious, countries: for example, there are African, Arab and Asian television and radio channels available through satellite television and many newsagents in large cities will have European newspapers and magazines, some of which produce editions in English.

You might wish to re-read the section on representation (p. 61) and consider how these 'foreign' texts represent Britain, the English, Welsh and Scots.

Marshall McLuhan and Quentin Fiore wrote in their book *The Medium Is the Massage* (1967) that we live in a 'global village'. They suggested that time and space are vanishing, and that people from all over the world can communicate with one another simultaneously, as if they all lived in the same village. The debate about the worldwide political and cultural changes that have occurred as a result of a process known as 'globalisation' is one that is alluded to throughout this book and is an important part of Media Studies.

This process of globalisation involves the idea that the world has shrunk, notably as a result of new technology and the media, and that the populations of virtually every country in the world now have almost instant access to cultures and societies that were once so far away from us that they were just considered 'foreign'. Now we can all see, hear and read about much of what goes on in the world. It is also important to note that part of this process involves the idea that we are now becoming a world audience as well. A successful mass-media product often has to have an appeal to worldwide markets if it is to make serious money. But it is important to realise that the globalisation debate is essentially a debate that is still current – an example of this ongoing debate is the role of the media in the collapse of Eastern European communism.

When the Berlin Wall came down in 1989 many commentators suggested that one of the major factors in the wave of protest that had occurred in Eastern Europe around that time was that a population that had previously been denied access to all things Western had, in the previous decade, been able to listen to and above all watch Western media broadcasts. This meant that they were finally able to see what it was about capitalism and democracy that their political masters had been denying them for decades.

It is suggested that many Eastern Europeans liked what they saw and this was an element in the political struggle that then developed. Of course the issue still remains that what they saw on television might not necessarily have been a true reflection of the reality of Western democracies. Consequently, there does seem to be an element of disappointment and anti-climax taking place in some former Eastern European/Communist countries as they discover that the reality of the Western lifestyle is not quite the same as the one portrayed in the Western media.

NOTEBOX

Some media commentators would suggest that media globalisation offers a vast 'window on the world' that has allowed media consumers to embrace the world and all that it offers in terms of differing cultures, politics and viewpoints. Others suggest that we have become overloaded with information and that our reaction to so much input is to retreat behind closed doors and shut off our minds to so much information. Has so much choice simply become too much choice? What is your view?

As we mentioned in the introduction, it is important to remember that media texts are not fortunate accidents and that often profit is the motive in producing them. The vast array of available media artefacts is not simply the product of circumstance and a few altruistic people. Undoubtedly there are some media texts produced by people who feel that they have something to say or who anticipate a gap in the market that should be filled. But as a general rule, people with money have not announced that a newspaper or magazine is needed because they feel sorry for our lack of awareness of what is going on in the world. Nor are they concerned that we have too much leisure time. In fact the vast majority of media texts are produced by media institutions that are becoming richer and more powerful by the day as the demand for their products increases.

It is possible to make many generalisations about media institutions. There can be little doubt that there is the potential for enormous profits in the media world. There is equally the potential for financial disaster. But perhaps the most difficult aspect of the media world to come to terms with is the fact that there are no set rules or patterns to follow. There is not a science to running a media institution (nor is there a science to studying a media institution). What may work for one company will probably not work for another. But certain ideas about media institutions remain constant.

On the one hand there is the 'conspiracy theory' of Media Studies. This is the popular and common idea that a small group of multimedia tycoons is busy trying to take over or amalgamate with every other media company available so that in the end this group will end up with more power to control what we know about the world, with all that this implies politically and socially. Often supporters of this theory will cite Rupert Murdoch as someone who is trying to control the world, rather like the villain in a James Bond film.

Yet there also exist many people in all media fields who remain committed to the notion of choice and independence. Organisations such as the Voice of the Listener and Viewer (<http://www.vlv.org>) and the Campaign for Press and Broadcasting Freedom (<http://www.cpbf.org.uk>) see the wave of deregulation that has taken place, in this country in particular, as not necessarily being in the public interest. They therefore argue strongly for an element of public service broadcasting (PSB) to be preserved.

There is also the perhaps rather naïve point of view that sees some parts of the media as a collection of committed and hardworking people who want us to be informed, educated and entertained. This group of people, if they find it difficult to broadcast their products, will set up as independent companies, probably beholden to no one but themselves – often in opposition to the media majors. A perfect example of this is the number of websites that have been created since the invasion of Iraq in early 2003. There can be little doubt that mainstream reporting of the conflict in most of the press and television in both the USA and the UK tended to follow the government line in both countries. An oppositional point of view is now available on the Internet. At the sites below it is possible to read articles and look at photographs and documentary footage that has not been published or broadcast in the mass media. Sites such as

<http://www.informationclearinghouse.info> and <http://www.alternet.com> are well worth examining and, as media students, subscribing to.

Neither of the two views cited above is accurate. There are no hard and fast rules that can be applied to the media anywhere in the world, although it is the case that countries do exist in which the government owns or controls the major mass media (television and radio in particular). In situations like this the media are often used purely for propaganda and informational purposes. It is interesting to note that when such governments are threatened by public uprising or military coups one of the first targets for the protesters is these very same radio and television stations – which demonstrates how important control of the media can be. This was, for instance, the case in Yugoslavia in 2000, when Slobodan Milosevic refused to accept the result of the election and people took to the streets. Their two targets were the government buildings and the radio and television stations. In 2003 in post-Saddam Iraq the coalition forces set up an American-based television service and there was an enormous expansion of independent newspapers and radio stations expressing views that had been suppressed by the previous government. This was after both radio and television stations had been specifically targeted in bombing raids on the major cities of Iraq.

One of the issues that has to be dealt with by those who study or take an interest in the media is the fairly obvious fact that much of the media is largely in the hands of multinational companies. Companies such as Time Warner, Sony, News International and Viacom are major players on the world media scene. In Britain there is a small number of companies that dominate the media industries but compared to American and Japanese companies they are relatively small.

The media world undergoes many changes in ownership. At the time of writing there are:

- only five major record companies in the world
- a rapidly shrinking ownership of mobile-phone companies
- domination of the worldwide cinema ticket sales by Hollywood and Bollywood
- only one commercial terrestrial television company running almost all of the ITV network
- heavy competition for ownership of ISPs (internet service providers) on the Internet.

ACTIVITY...

Keeping up to date with changes in media ownership can sometimes be difficult. However, you can find up-to-date information on what media companies own by accessing the 'who owns what' section of the website <http://www.cjr.org/owners>.

- Research the changes in ownership of the institutions outlined in this chapter.

continued

- What were the reasons for the buying and selling (or indeed mergers) that have taken place?
- Is it possible at this stage to predict future outcomes?
- Are there any media institutions that now seem particularly vulnerable?
- Is it possible to suggest why this is so?

NOTEBOX . . .

There are a number of ways in which you can keep an eye on media ownership. This will involve reading the business news in any of the quality broadsheet newspapers, looking out for articles in magazines about the media, listening to media programmes on radio, watching television programmes about the media (for example *Feedback* on Radio 4, occasional items in *The South Bank Show* on ITV). It is important that you monitor as closely as possible who owns what; who sells and who buys. There is a great deal of movement in the ownership of media institutions.

Keep a scrapbook. Cut interesting articles out of magazines and newspapers and file them away carefully. Record any programmes that look as if they might be useful. You may never keep up, but you should develop a fascinating overview.

Not all media companies are large players but historically a pattern has emerged. Whenever a new technology is invented or discovered, companies have been formed, or existing companies have been forced to try to take advantage of the benefits and profits that the new technology offers. However, it is often the case that no one is quite sure what those benefits might be, and that there is no guarantee that profits will be made. For instance, when CDs first came into production little was done to prevent the assumption that they would last forever and that anyone who owned vinyl records should therefore replace all their collection in the new CD format (for many serious collectors this involved a major financial outlay). The majors then started to reissue their back catalogue of records in CD format. Other smaller distributors also began to purchase the rights to less popular performances and remarket and reissue these on CD for serious collectors and 'completists'. This has meant that certain artists have had their careers revitalised by the existence of a new format. Very much the same is now happening with the arrival of the DVD to replace the video cassette.

Each new technology has been hailed as an improvement on existing technology, a boon to consumers and a way for producers to get rich (often fairly quickly). Risks have been taken, some companies have fallen by the wayside, but others have survived and prospered. For instance, all the major American film studios started off as small independent companies. Each found a particular niche for itself. Warner Bros, for instance, were famous for the realism of many of their films, whilst MGM were famous

for the escapist nature of their product. Both managed to build on their success. However, there were those film companies who were not able to respond quickly enough to the demands of the audience, or indeed to the threat of new technologies. These companies no longer exist (RKO Radio Pictures, to name but one). Embracing new technology seems to be the most effective way of responding to it.

A good example of this is the way that the major record companies have eventually responded to the 'illegal' downloading of music files off the Internet. Outlawing this activity through the courts has not prevented it happening – indeed has probably given it free and extra publicity. Eventually many of the majors have had to set up their own download sites, where, for a small payment, music files can be downloaded legally. If you can't beat them, then join them.

The potential for riches in the media world is enormous, but equally the potential for financial ruin is also rather large. This same phenomenon can now be seen with the advent of the Internet. Everyone who wants to jump on board, particularly some large multimedia companies which see some of the benefits that the Internet offers (new channels for advertising, promotion and sales) but who also want to secure a larger market share than their competitors, whilst knowing that future financial benefits might be slow in arriving. The Internet has also become a place for small entrepreneurs to start up companies. If successful, they may make a profit or indeed be bought out by the majors at considerable financial gain to the owners. The medium has potential and, whilst no one is quite sure where it will go, everyone wants to be on board. However, the collapse of some major Internet companies demonstrates that there is just as strong a likelihood that the Internet will not end up being the money-making machine that some people hoped it might become.

A reshuffling is taking place – a series of mergers, amalgamations and takeovers – as the major media players tackle the advent of new media technologies and their effect on the global media landscape.

ACTIVITY . . .

During the period of your course you should also keep a watchful eye on the Internet. Yet again the major source of your research should be the business news in the quality broadsheet newspapers. However, it is important to keep an eye on developments on the Net itself.

- What are the major ISPs?
- Who owns the major ISPs?

Keep a close watch on the way that the major ISPs make themselves known to the market. It is now simply done by television and press advertising.

- What new developments can each ISP offer you as a possible user?
- What are the drawbacks to using the Net in this country and how are the ISPs trying to get around these problems?

continued

In the 1950s both the American film industry and the British radio industry dismissed television as a medium that would not last. In America they then tried to combat it by making films that could only be seen at their best at the cinema. This goes some way to explaining why there were so many 'epics' made in the 1950s – large-scale Biblical stories as well as a multitude of big-budget musicals. These were initially popular but then audiences grew tired of too many similar products and as a consequence these companies watched their revenues dwindle as audiences decided they preferred to stay at home. It was only later that the successful and more thoughtful film companies (and producers) realised that television networks, as well as movie theatres, needed product. They then diversified into television production as well.

Nowadays, almost every television programme we see, particularly those of American origin, has the logo of a major film and television production/distribution company at the end of its final reel. Thus Fox, Columbia TriStar, Warner Bros and Paramount are all involved in large-scale film production as well as in production for television. In the UK the situation is very different. Many television productions on all channels now increasingly derive from small independent television production companies. This is the direct result of a shift from in-house production in the years preceding the late 1980s to the external sourcing of production, which in turn is the direct result of the deregulation of broadcasting that took place under successive Thatcher governments.

Today, a proportion of television programmes are spin-offs from successful films (for example *Stargate SG* and *Buffy the Vampire Slayer*) and there has developed a recent trend for producing film versions of successful television programmes, particularly of the 1950s and 1960s (for example *Lost in Space* and *ScoobyDoo*).

This is part of the process by which certain popular texts, such as *Buffy* or *Star Trek*, become brands that can be marketed and used to sell a range of related (branded) products.

ACTIVITY . . .

It is interesting to note that four American companies named above – Fox, Columbia TriStar, Warner Bros and Paramount – are still players in the media

world yet have all, at one time or another, had periods when their future might have been in doubt.

Research the history of these companies and try to establish what went wrong at various periods in their existence – and what has gone right for them so that they are now in their present powerful positions. Is it the case that they have simply been lucky? Or have important policy decisions been taken during the past fifty years that have safeguarded their positions?

- How are they now planning to maintain their positions as major players in the media?
- What is threatening their position at present?
- How do you think they will respond to these threats?

HORIZONTAL AND VERTICAL INTEGRATION

The principle motivating this process seems to be to take over or merge with those companies which are in the same area as you. This is what is known as vertical integration. One example is the ITV network, once thirteen separate companies, which is now just one company, ITV, following the merger of Carlton and Granada at the end of 2003.

HORIZONTAL INTEGRATION   This involves the acquisition of competitors in the same section of the industry. It might be possible for one company to seek to control all of the market – a monopoly position – but most capitalist countries have laws to prevent this happening.

KEY TERM

ACTIVITY . . .

The ownership of newspapers and radio stations in the UK is another area in which control is slowly shifting into the hands of fewer companies. Using the *Guardian Media Guide* or some of the websites listed at the end of this section, investigate the following:

- Who owns the national daily newspapers?
- Who owns the Sunday national newspapers?
- Who owns all the UK radio stations?
- What are the benefits for companies who own several newspapers or radio stations?

continued

If you control exhibition, then it follows that to increase power and profit you should as quickly as possible move into the area of distribution and production. This has happened in the film business, where, in particular, the American film-production studios rapidly moved into distribution (thereby gaining control over product made by smaller and less powerful rivals) and then, when legally possible, into exhibition.

This is far less the case in television in the UK, where, as mentioned previously, both the BBC and ITV, and particularly satellite and cable channels, now buy in or commission productions made by independent production companies. Television companies can be seen to operate much more like publishing houses, where the commissioning editor has an important role – indeed Channel Four creates no in-house programming.

By and large, in certain areas of the media, companies will want to control the three main areas of production, distribution and exhibition. This is called vertical integration. Many companies, given the opportunity, want to maximise potential profits by cutting out the interference of other people. Why make a product for someone else to sell?

KEY TERM

VERTICAL INTEGRATION This involves the ownership of every stage of the production process (production + distribution + exhibition), thereby ensuring complete control of a media product.

An example of vertical integration is the Fox Entertainment Group. This is an American company that is now 83 per cent owned by Rubert Murdoch's News International. If at one time during the late 1970s and early 1980s Twentieth Century Fox was a Hollywood film company that had perhaps seen better times, it is now (again) one of the major mass-media companies worldwide. Famous originally as a film-production company, Fox Entertainment now produces, develops and distributes television and film programming through its Fox Filmed Entertainment and Twentieth Century Fox units. It also owns the Fox Television network in the USA, has interests in cable television channels and major-league sports teams, and owns a chain of cinemas in the USA. But it does not end there. News International is also a worldwide media organisation with part-ownership of many satellite and cable channels across Europe and Asia. The company owns several newspapers, notably in the USA, Australia and the UK.

The advantages of this global ownership are many. A film produced by Twentieth Century Fox can be shown in Fox-owned cinemas, publicised in News International newspapers, then shown on Fox-owned television channels. All media associated with

Fox can give the product publicity in one shape or form. (It is interesting to note that Fox became joint producer of the film *Titanic* at a point when it was about to become known as the most expensive film ever made – and perhaps a financial disaster. The very fact that it received such notoriety before its release is now seen as a very clever 'hype' – it became a film that everyone wanted to see, and the rest is history.

A media product can therefore be sold, publicised and marketed to an audience through many different media, and blanket coverage is possible if a company has ownership of the following media:

- films
- videos
- soundtracks
- television stations
- radio stations, newspapers and magazines
- the Internet.

The same principles of vertical integration are present in the cinema industry. Why make a film – which has an average cost of around US$30 million – and then let another company exhibit the film and make money from a product in which you have invested heavily? It makes obvious business sense to create the product, distribute it and exhibit it as well. You then have control of the product from the moment of its inception to the end of its lifespan and are therefore likely to make a far greater profit.

Multiplex cinemas grew from the principle of vertical integration. A multiplex cinema can have as many as thirty different screens in one building. Immediately there are benefits to the owner in terms of costs. Only one or two projectionists are needed and a minimum number of staff (who may well be working on the kiosks as well). Heating, lighting and cleaning costs can be kept to a minimum and even advertising costs kept low. The major point is that if people arrive to see a film and it is sold out they do not go away cursing their bad luck. Having made the effort to get to the cinema the

likelihood is that they will see another film that is showing at the multiplex instead. At the same time they are likely to buy food and drink at vastly inflated prices. This is similar to what happens in the supermarket. Few people go into a supermarket and only buy a loaf of bread – even if that is why they entered the shop in the first place.

The implications of vertical integration in the cinema industry reflect what occurred in the example of the high street. The owners of multiplexes are in danger of suffocating the opposition. What future has a small, locally run and owned cinema when the competition down the road has so much to offer and can also control the product – despite monopoly laws?

Consider, also, the choice for the consumer. On one level the multiplex offers a wide range of films, though a particularly popular film can be shown on several screens at once and only one print of the film is actually needed (there need only be a slight time delay between screenings). But what happens to a film that might not be quite so popular and is perhaps a risk in terms of profitability? It makes sense for the multiplex owner not to bother showing such a film, since the job is to make money, not necessarily to cater for the minority film-goer. There are of course independent cinemas in existence in the USA and other countries. But even they have to make a profit to continue their existence. It can be argued, therefore, that a system that appears to offer more choice can often lead to less choice.

In terms of issues of ownership, what this implies is that decisions about what is available to media audiences rest in the hands of a few media companies. They, of course, have to answer to their shareholders and the financial institutions that have invested in them. Film companies, like all media companies, are not altruistic and have never pretended to be. They may take risks, but their responsibilities to investors and shareholders suggest that they are very unlikely to do so.

It is also interesting to note that some multiplexes have a policy of devoting one screen (from the many available) to foreign-language or minority-interest films. However, the evidence seems to be that the audience does not go to the multiplex to see these films but prefers to go to the local art-house or independent cinema to see them. It is interesting, though, that many multiplex cinemas in cities with a large Asian community are now devoting several screens to the exhibition of films from Asia, with considerable success.

This suggests that the process of distribution and exhibition is rather more complicated than many might like to think. Big is not necessarily bad. Much has to do with the nature of the audience (see Part 2, media audiences, p. 107).

Key institutions to remember:

- the majors – international media conglomerates
- the medium-sized – usually nationally based media companies
- the independents – those that have established their own niche market, such as small art-house cinemas, independent radio-production companies
- the alternatives.

ALTERNATIVE MEDIA

Alternative media organisations exist as a counterpoint to everything that has been mentioned above. Not everything in the media world is about market domination, large-scale target audiences and enormous profit.

Companies and organisations do exist that attempt to make a positive virtue out of being small and, perhaps most importantly, out of being independent. Although a typical media organisation is, almost by definition, run on hierarchical grounds, beholden to investors and shareholders, organisations do exist that are organised on democratic principles, where all workers have a say in the policy and direction of the company. A primary example of this was the London listings magazine *Time Out*, which originally operated on these grounds. All employees had a stake in the company, and everyone who worked there was essentially paid the same. A problem surfaced when the magazine started to become very successful – at which point the owner decided to rationalise the pay structure, returning to a more conventional format. This resulted in the formation of an alternative listings magazine in London, called *City Limits*, started by disgruntled ex-members of the *Time Out* staff. This magazine continued to be run on a co-operative basis but foundered within a decade of its formation, essentially because the circulation figures were never high enough to attract serious advertising revenue.

If an organisation is run on essentially democratic grounds, and has a policy of independence, then the genuine voice of an artist or writer is more likely to flourish. This is nowhere more true than in the music industry, particularly in the UK. Here pop music has flourished and with it the creation of, for example, girl and boy bands – many of which seem to follow a well-worn formula. A band or musician/singer who produces material that does not 'fit' the major record companies' notion of what should or should not be released may not get a contract and might never be heard. Thus independent record labels – small, with low budgets and few overheads – have given artists the opportunity to produce material. There might not be such a large publicity machine working for them, nor instant access to radio and television play, but there is an audience out there who have rejected the product of the mass-media organisations and keep a lookout themselves for product to purchase, often through the medium of music fanzines.

INDEPENDENTS Companies (usually relatively small ones) that maintain a status outside the normal big-business remit and therefore tend to focus on minority-interest products.

This is also true in the world of football. For years football fans have paid their money at the gate, supported their team and developed a sense of ownership. After all, the gate money is vital to the economic stability of a football team. Yet the run-of-the-mill football programme is frequently an anodyne affair – glossy pictures, many advertisements, but rarely any genuine discussion of football, the team or financial affairs. The increase in the number of football fanzines was very much a phenomenon of the 1990s. It reflects many people's dissatisfaction with the typical football programme or magazine available on the mass market – a product that cannot help but be tied to the sponsors' and the owners' point of view and is unlikely to rock the boat or court controversy.

ACTIVITY . . .

Take two media products, one mass market and one significantly alternative – for instance a football magazine and a football fanzine, or a mainstream music paper and a music fanzine.

- What are the differences?
- What are the similarities?

Concentrate particularly on:

- the content
- the style
- the political stance (if any)
- the nature of the editorials
- the nature of the advertisements
- the quality of design and layout
- the target audience.

GLOBAL MEDIA ECONOMY

There are very few homes without a television in the majority of countries in the world. (Of course in countries such as the USA and now Britain it is not uncommon for homes to have at least two televisions – and often one in each bedroom.) Even in countries where televisions are rare, the main local meeting place will often possess one that everyone can watch as a communal activity.

The communications technology available in the world today is partly responsible for this sense of global shrinkage, although there are still areas of the world in which the technology barely exists. It remains very much the case that the use of most media technologies is confined to developed nations and certain elites within developing nations.

Satellite and digital technology allows us to see instantly live events taking place on the other side of the globe. The Internet has made it possible to communicate directly and cheaply across the world, if access to a telephone line is available. But it is not technology alone that has created this 'global village'.

Since the events of 11 September 2001 the demand for information about news and events is now more global than it ever used to be. This is a demand for information not only about news and politics but also about other areas of human activity such as sport and entertainment. The world of the domestic or parochial television or radio station is changing very rapidly as media institutions, in order to deal with world-wide audience demands, have discovered that they need to look beyond their own borders.

Again money plays a big part. Take, for example, US television and film production. An American film or television series is made for an American audience on what often amounts to a tremendously well-organised and efficient conveyor-belt/studio-system production line, after much money has been spent on research and testing audience satisfaction with the product. Test audiences tell the producers whether they like, or even understand, the product. Characters are removed if test plays suggest they are not popular. It is not uncommon for the ending of a film to be changed after testing. Yet the majority of American film and television products make their money on the domestic front. It is important to remember that the production costs, based on what in many cases amounts to a factory system, are relatively cheap – relatively considering the size of the American audience in the first place.

However, a television company in any other part of the world will often find it cheaper to buy American ready-made programmes than to make them itself. Again the notion of the loss leader comes into play here. In the first instance these non-American companies can purchase the product relatively cheaply, especially if it is an old pro-gramme (*Star Trek* and *I Love Lucy* are perennial favourites). However, should that programme prove to be popular, then the next series will not be quite so cheap (a striking example of this is the escalating price of the television series *Friends*).

It is also worth noting that nowadays many products come in packages. If the television company in question wants to purchase a very popular American series that all its rival networks are also interested in buying, then it will often have to purchase other less successful or less popular series made by the same producers at the same time. Naturally, once a television company has bought a series, it will show it anyway. If it is not a great ratings winner then it can be used as early-afternoon or late-night filler material.

There are two reasons why some governments are worried by this trend. On one level this process can have a retrograde effect on the home market in terms of

developing domestic production, talent and culture. On another level there can be social and cultural consequences – an issue in Media Studies that is called 'media imperialism'.

ACTIVITY . . .

First of all, monitor closely the programming on British terrestrial television in one week and where possible note the nationality of the programmes. Then do the same for a collection of channels on cable or satellite television.

- How many programmes in one week on British television are produced in this country?
- Of the rest of the programmes on television, how many are made in Europe and how many are American product?

It is interesting to repeat the process with films showing at cinemas in your local area. Do the results of your research surprise you? Are the results of your survey a matter for concern?

MEDIA IMPERIALISM

Media imperialism is a very important issue in Media Studies. It is very easy to say that American media products are the best because they are what audiences want to watch.

But if I *Love Lucy* can be seen on a television screen somewhere in the world at any given time of day – and the same can be said of *Star Trek* – then this can be seen to have serious cultural and social effects, particularly in countries where there is next to no home-produced material being read, seen or listened to by the indigenous population (see Part 2, media audiences, p. 107).

Both socially and politically there are problems with a diet of media programming that is predominantly American, or indeed from any country other than one's own. If the indigenous population consumes nothing but a diet of American media – be it film, television, music or whatever – then there is a grave danger that it may well buy into an image of America and a way of life that on the surface seems very attractive (a realisation of the American dream) but that encompasses a version of history and culture that is often inaccurate and politically deceitful.

Figure 3.2 *A Japanese couple walk past a bus advertisement featuring David Beckham, Yokohama, south of Tokyo, 22 December 2002. The advert was created by a unit of Vodaphone Group plc to promote the company's third-generation (3G) mobile phone service. Source: Popperfoto, Reuters/Issei Kato.*

ACTIVITY . . .

- Why should an audience outside the Americas or Europe watch a diet of American war films and not believe that the Americans won the war single-handed?
- A diet of American rock videos gives what sort of impression of the American way of life?
- Can you think of some American media products that are directly critical or questioning of the American dream and the American way of doing things?

Some media thinkers suggest that the inability of the Soviet leadership to prevent the ordinary population from consuming a media diet that was becoming more Western every year was an important contributing factor to the collapse of many Eastern-bloc governments. (However, it is important to add here that for years the Soviet bloc was fed a diet of political, social and cultural propaganda that suited its own regime.)

If there are political and social concerns about the spread of media imperialism, there are also very profound cultural concerns. In fact the French are so worried about the cultural effects of the dominance of American, and other non-indigenous, media products that they have actually produced legislation to protect their own culture and language, which they saw disappearing under the influx of foreign cinema, music and other products. Thus French radio stations have to play a fixed percentage of French material in every hour of broadcast, and French cinemas have to show a fixed quota of home-produced films every year as well.

If the major concern has been historically that of American culture dominating the world, then it is interesting to note a new development in the media world. This is the merger between multinational media companies to form giant media conglomerates.

ACTIVITY . . .

The Universal/Vivendi/Seagram/Canal Plus merger

Initially Universal – a large American television and film company – was taken over by Seagram, which was once one of the largest drinks companies in the world. Media analysts were unsure of the motive behind the purchase at the time and many people were unaware of the fact that Universal was also a large player in the music world.

Early in 2000, Vivendi, a French media company, stepped in and merged with Universal-Seagram. Then in December 2000 it merged again, this time with the French television and film group Canal Plus, to form Universal Vivendi. This then became the world's number two in the communications sector after the merger between AOL and Time-Warner in February 2000.

Investigate this merger. Look carefully at what each company in the merger has on its books. Now look at what the combined company owns and possesses.

■ In what way do the various strands complement one another?
■ Is the merger part of a disturbing trend towards large multinational media companies, or should it be welcomed?
■ What are the advantages for a company as large and as diverse as this on the media stage?
■ What, if any, are the possible pitfalls?
■ Is this perhaps a case of Europe hitting back?
■ Which of the four major parts of the merger do you think are the winners in the merger? And the losers?

What is most interesting about this particular deal between Universal/Vivendi/Seagram, announced in the last week of June 2000, is that it should have happened at all.

On one level we are looking at the global economy writ large, except that in this instance it was not the American company that was trying to expand and develop, but a European company that was once a small-time player but is now expanding and, in the opinion of some experts, biting off more than it can chew.

This is no longer a case of cultural and media imperialism – there is no way that French culture will suddenly make inroads into American. It is an example of a European company looking outside the confines of Europe at trends in the media world, and also anticipating the likely needs of the consumer over the next decade or so.

At the time of writing Vivendi is about to become a part of the NBC. As has been stressed in previous parts of the section, there are no hard and fast rules to running a large multimedia company. Vivendi overstretched itself (partly because of the ambition of an inexperienced chairman) and paid the price financially. It is interesting to note that at the time of writing AOL-Time-Warner is clawing its way out of financial trouble – the ambitions of AOL were never met and less successful parts of the company are slowly being sold off to balance the books. Thus the WarnerVillage group of cinemas have been sold in the UK, as have their chain of WarnerVillage multiplex cinemas in Australia. (Ironically, once more financially stable, it may not be long before the media experts at AOL-Time-Warner suggest that really the company should reinvest in exhibition in the UK and Australia.)

ISSUES OF CONTROL

We have outlined above the process by which major media conglomerates seemingly have a stranglehold over much that media audiences are consuming. Although the emphasis above is on the film industry, this is also the case in many other media industries. And, as has been noted above, few media companies are satisfied with simply sticking to one particular medium, as is demonstrated by the increasingly cross-media composition of many of the very large companies.

For example, the Walt Disney Corporation has interests in television and film production (ABC Entertainment Television, Buena Vista Motion Pictures Group and Miramax), theme parks (including Disneyland, Euro-Disney and the Epcot Center), publishing companies, a cruise line, Internet companies (go.com) and professional sports franchises (the Mighty Ducks NHL team). Division ABC Inc. includes the ABC television network in the USA, nearly a dozen television stations, and shares in nine cable companies (including the Disney Channel). We have also noted above the fact that there are certain disadvantages and advantages inherent in this situation, both for producers and audiences.

It is in this area that the works of Noam Chomsky are particularly relevant. Noam Chomsky is an American intellectual who has written many books about the media and is particularly interested in the social and political implications of the mass media and their ownership. The basic premise of much of his writings on the media is as follows:

- Society is made up of two different classes of people.
- The top 20 per cent represents the professional class, those who feel they have a stake in the decision-making processes in society, such as judges, lawyers, teachers

and intellectuals. Many of these people have a genuine interest in politics and the rudiments of power that are associated with their positions. They like to think that they have some influence on the way things are run and governed. It is also the case that this group is (in general) the one with the most financial clout in society. They represent the dominant ideology in American society.

- Then there is the remaining 80 per cent, whose main function is to work and follow orders, usually at the bidding of the top 20 per cent. Their interest in politics tends to be minimal, as long as they are housed, fed and have enough money to finance their leisure time.
- The top 20 per cent, the group with the money and power, is also likely to contain those individuals who are involved with or who actually own the media and have a strong influence on their texts and content. This is one of the ways in which hegemony can be seen to work. (See key term 'hegemony' on p. 80 and also section on media ideology, p. 78 for more about Chomsky's ideas.)

Chomsky argues that the media, especially the large multimedia concerns, have one prevailing motive apart from profit and that is what he calls the 'Manufacture of Consent'. Essentially, Chomsky argues, the media today are involved in a two-pronged process.

The first process is to ensure that the top 20 per cent are satisfied, and this is achieved by maintaining their position as policy-makers, in control of some of the rudiments of power. The issue is one whereby the media help to keep the government on a path that keeps this elite content and feeling that their position in society is of some worth, whilst continuing to promulgate the lifestyle and political attachments of this elite. Most of the media are therefore inevitably interested in maintaining the status quo, as, frequently, is the power elite.

Broadly speaking, this means that much of the time the government and the elite are involved in an alliance – but only when it suits them. Obviously issues can and do arise on which the government and the elite disagree. For instance, towards the end of the Conservative government in the middle of the 1990s, even normally sympathetic newspapers turned against the Tory party, particularly in the area of personal morality and sleaze. This can be seen as an example of the media acting as the spokesperson for this elite and 'taking on' the government. But by and large the media can wield a considerable amount of power because, certainly since the Second World War, every government has been dependent on the media to get into office. Not for nothing was Rupert Murdoch's *Sun* able to boast that it had won the election in 1992 for the Tories. And indeed the same newspaper certainly also helped the Labour Party get into power in 1997.

A more recent example of the complex relationship between the government and the media in Britain can be seen in the reporting of the Iraq war in 2003. The media were allowed a considerable amount of access to the activities of the military in Iraq. Many reporters were 'embedded'; in other words they joined the military and lived and worked alongside them. This meant that the journalists and film crews had access to military activities and could often report from the front line. However, it also meant that the military were able to keep watch on the media and to some extent control what they saw and could (or could not) report on. There was some criticism that these embedded reporters, especially those from the American media, were not as objective or as critical of military action as they should have been.

On the other hand there was strong disagreement between the Labour government and the BBC over the reporting of the war and in particular the way in which the war was justified by Tony Blair. This argument mainly revolved around the BBC reporter Andrew Gilligan, the suicide of the Iraqi arms expert Dr David Kelly, the 'dodgy' dossier, used as the basis for going to war, and the role of Alastair Campbell. The government also accused the BBC of being anti-war in some of its reporting, but, as Figure 3.3 shows, research carried out by media academics at Cardiff University suggests that the BBC was less prone to be critical of the government and the war than was Channel Four.

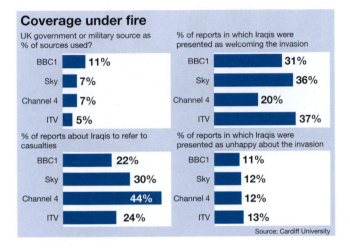

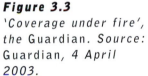

Figure 3.3
'*Coverage under fire*', *the* Guardian. *Source:* Guardian, *4 April* *2003.*

But what is the position of the remaining 80 per cent? Chomsky would argue that part of the hegemonic function of the media is to keep them happy – a concept called 'bread and circuses' – with a diet of celebrity gossip, sport, soap operas and light entertainment that they can read and watch without too much challenge. This could be seen as a rather cynical view, certainly one that might make us feel rather uncomfortable. On the other hand, the counter-argument would suggest that this is a very generalised view that shows no understanding of the pressures under which those in the media world work – it also in itself seems quite elitist at times, assuming as it does that the 80 per cent are in fact compliant in every way – which is not always the case.

Thus it can be seen that the media – and the mass media in particular – have vested interests: in broad terms, to maintain the ideological status quo, to link arms with the government (whenever possible) and to make money. Chomsky argues that this process is a form of control in a democratic society.

This process can happen in a number of different ways; it is of course not enough simply to feed people a diet of gossip, soap opera and sport. This is necessarily a very simplistic account. There is an underlying assumption here that the audience is a

Figure 3.4 *Television cameramen atop a truck film the distribution of food and supplies to Iraqi people during the Iraq war. Source: Baltimore Sun; photo: Elizabeth Malby.*

homogeneous group who all consume the media unthinkingly, and believe every word that they read or hear. (Much media effects research would refute this assumption – see Part 2, media audiences, p. 107.) One particular area that is worth some examination is the news. (See, for example, the case study on news (p. 235) in Part 4.)

As we discuss elsewhere in the book, news does not just happen, nor is it readily available to us when and where and how we want it – though we are certainly given the impression that that is the case. The concept of mediation is important to the study of all media, and the news is no exception. A process of news selection takes place in all forms of news media, and this selection is based on the agenda that the particular organisation wishes to follow. While we may well be witnessing the depoliticisation of the news in this country (in the sense that few newspapers now proclaim their political allegiance quite so clearly or boldly as might once have been the case), it is still true that each news organisation has a target audience and an agenda that will appeal to that audience and also appease the owner/shareholders. We cannot therefore automatically accept that what we are told or shown is necessarily what is going on (see also the section on realism, p. 84).

Whilst it is easy to accuse Chomsky of paranoia and of seeing conspiracy every-where in the media, the fact remains that the media-spin placed on events is now such that few thinking individuals ever take the news at face value. Chomsky himself cites the example of the genocide that took place under Pol Pot and the Khmer Rouge in Cambodia during 1975–9, events that were heavily reported in the Western press, whilst a similar genocide taking place in East Timor when Indonesia invaded the island in November 1975 was barely mentioned. Chomsky suggests this is because Indonesia had been armed by many countries in the Western world and also because the island of Timor occupies a strategically important place in the south-eastern part of the Pacific Ocean. Equally the Kosovan crisis involved much press vilification of Serbian military activity (but little analysis of the roots of the troubles) and a very sympathetic treatment of the actions of NATO at the same time. Chomsky suggests that there was a series of political and cultural reasons why this was the case.

ACTIVITY...

On any given day, you should purchase every daily newspaper, watch as many different news broadcasts as possible on the television, and also listen to as many radio news broadcasts as you can.

- Analyse the content of each as fully as possible.
- Is there any truth in what Chomsky is suggesting?
- Is there any evidence on one given day to suggest that there is one type of news for those who read the quality press and watch serious news broad-casts, and a different type altogether in the less serious press and broadcasts?
- What stories are present in the first group of media and ignored by the latter?

continued

- To what extent are the media guilty of ignoring 'important' stories in favour of light-hearted gossip and celebrity news?
- Is it indeed possible to avoid the 'serious' news altogether?

REGULATION OF THE MEDIA

There are dangers inherent in a media structure that has no rules. Those dangers are fairly obvious. At a basic level there are laws relating to media that must be obeyed.

But there are also concerns about an unfettered media industry for a variety of reasons:

- the laws of monopoly
- worries about media ownership and control
- the notion of competition
- the protection of minority interests and notions of fair play
- the understanding that cross-media ownership can act against the interests of the consumer.

In fact our media industries are more regulated than many in the rest of the world. The burgeoning of new media has had an interesting effect on the rules and regulations that govern media industries in this country.

For example, we might consider governments' attempts to take some kind of a grip on the World Wide Web. For many years now there have been few, if any, regulations affecting the Internet. The content of and access to the Internet have, on the whole, been unregulated – something that has caused great concern to many governments. In America, as a result of concern about children having access to unsuitable material, certain sites are now accessible only to people who have signed up to an age certifier/ security system, based on credit card details. But although this system ostensibly protects minors from material of an unsuitable sexual nature, it is still the case that anybody can set up a website and the Net is now so vast that the origin of a site deemed dangerous or unsuitable might be very difficult to trace.

The last few years have seen more and more governments becoming concerned about the fact that political extremist groups, or groups advocating illegal activities, can communicate across the Web without difficulty. In Britain the government has responded to what it sees as a genuine threat from political extremist and potential terrorist groups. All Internet service providers (ISPs) now have to keep a log of the activities of their subscribers, and the police can now apply to a magistrate to 'tap' into any website address – very much like phone-tapping – to monitor a suspect group or individual. This means that ordinary email is no more secure than a postcard sent by mail – though the government claims that law-abiding citizens have nothing to fear from such policing of the Internet. Yet it does have implications in terms of freedom of speech.

Much of this concern from government is the result of yet another 'media panic' caused, in the main, by the stories that have been published in the press about football hooligans organising acts of violence abroad, particularly during Euro 2000, through the Internet. Equally, the Columbine massacre, as it is now called, which occurred in April 1999, is said to have been inspired in part by some sites on the Web, though this has yet to be proved and still belongs to the 'folklore of the Web'.

But the difficulty is that if we were to look for any logic or repeating pattern in the regulation or control of any particular medium (for example film or television), then we would be unlikely to find it. There are various reasons for this:

1   Successive governments have differing policies and attitudes towards the media.
2   There is a basic understanding that governments tend not to undo the work of previous governments except in special circumstances – and certainly the regulation of media ownership is considered a bit of a political hot potato.
3   There is a PSB (public service broadcasting) organisation (the BBC) that it is clearly in the government's remit to maintain (see below for more details on this). The government has to be seen therefore to be acting even-handedly when dealing with commercial companies.
4   Most media industries are relatively new, and we are finding out more and more about them as they develop. Most governments tend to adopt a 'wait and see' position, preferring to leave things alone unless issues or problems are raised.

Yet, as we mentioned in the introduction, the fact remains that all media in this country are regulated in one way or another, for the very reasons listed above. What is interesting is that most of the media have in a sense imposed regulatory systems upon themselves. This is particularly true of the newspaper and film/video industries, which are regulated by the PCC (Press Complaints Commission) and the BBFC (British Board of Film Classification), respectively. Whilst it is true that this process has in the main been down to government pressure or a groundswell of popular opinion, it nevertheless seems to have beneficial results.

There is of course an (uneasy) relationship between these regulatory bodies and government. The self-regulatory bodies have always tried to keep one step ahead of any legislation (thus the PCC and the privacy of individuals), whilst even the regulatory bodies set up by governments in the past have frequently been at odds with the government over particular issues such as ownership of media industries. This is now becoming so complicated that the government is having trouble keeping up with it. As media companies merge, take over and buy into one another, so it becomes harder to know who owns whom. This is happening even more now that the ownership of media companies crosses borders.

NOTEBOX

When BSkyB attempted to buy a controlling interest in Manchester United Football Club the government intervened to prevent the takeover on the grounds

continued

that there would be a clash of interests when the question of football coverage on television came up for discussion and auction later on in the year. However, in the past few years there have been many examples of media organisations buying as many shares in football clubs as they are allowed (Granada buying into Liverpool Football Club, NTL buying into Newcastle United, for instance).

ACTIVITY ...

What are the possible advantages that exist for a media company buying into a football club?

- Why do you think the government intervened when BSkyB tried to buy a controlling interest in Manchester United?
- What are the possible advantages to the consumer of a media company owning a football club?
- What could be the disadvantages?

There can be little doubt that the regulation of media industries in this country is becoming less and less rigorous. There was once a cosy system in television broadcasting whereby the BBC and the ITV network transmitted to the whole country. Written into their charters were certain stipulations. The BBC had to broadcast a certain proportion of news and factual programming and even ITV was forced to do the same. Thus farming programmes were produced in the Anglia region, for example. However, during the late 1980s the Thatcher government sought to shake up broadcasting, believing that deregulation would free up finance, increase competition and, by extension, viewer choice. This resulted in the Broadcasting Act of 1990, and the awarding of television franchises to the companies which passed a quality threshold with the highest bid. Television in this country is now much freer of government and regulation, but whether the promise of viewer choice has actually been delivered is a matter of continuing debate.

Where there were once thirteen different ITV companies across the country, each with its own regional programming (admittedly mostly at off-peak times), now these companies exist in name alone, most having been swallowed up by two major ITV companies, Carlton and Granada. In October 2003 these two companies were given permission to merge, which essentially means that ITV is now almost entirely owned by one very large company. Whilst this certainly represents an opportunity to cut costs and seems popular with shareholders, the overall effect for television audiences has yet to be seen and will be something worth monitoring over the following decade.

The face of television in Britain has changed radically in the past decade. Where once there were two channels available, now there are over 100 on the two main English

digital platforms, and with a movable dish and a non-generic receiver the list of channels available rises to way above 1,000. Since so many of these channels originate from outside this country, it not possible to regulate them. The only thing a government can do if it objects to the content of a channel is to make it an offence to watch it, which involves enforcing legislation that makes it illegal to sell or possess the appropriate viewing cards (essential to watch many channels on cable/satellite television). Therefore, in many ways, attempts at regulation (or censorship) are futile. It can therefore be argued that the lessening of regulation in this country signals the acceptance of a new way of broadcasting. The government has a vested interest in prolonging the life of the BBC and ITV companies in the same way that it fights to preserve other British industries, for example fishing, in the context of globalisation.

So on the one hand we have regulation of the industry from without, but on the other hand we have self-regulation, from within.

BRITISH BOARD OF FILM CLASSIFICATION (BBFC)

The BBFC is an interesting case in point. Originally set up by the film industry itself to bring uniformity to standards of film censorship imposed by the many disparate local authorities in 1912, the BBFC has become a regulatory body with an ambiguous relationship with the industry and the audience. This is a pattern that is common to most regulatory bodies.

No entertainment organisation wants to become involved in legal battles because litigation is notoriously expensive and the publicity that court cases attract can backfire. At the same time all entertainment organisations have a genuine sense of what audiences might want and they also have to make a profit. A film, especially one made in the USA, has an average cost of US$30 million and rising, which is a considerable investment.

The essential role of the BBFC is to classify films and videos, assessing their suitability for public and private viewing across various age ranges. There is a range of certificates that can be given to film and video material. This system is particularly helpful for the exhibitors of films (the cinemas) because they feel safe in showing material without the threat of legal or other action being taken against them in terms of the nature of the material being shown. However, there have been times when this was not the case. *Crash*, a film directed by David Cronenberg and released in 1996, was banned by Westminster City Council despite being given an 18 certificate by the BBFC. Members of the Licensing Committee decided to ban the film from cinemas in their area because they felt that it was an immoral film that might actually inspire 'corrupt and depraved' behaviour in those who saw it. (It is interesting to note that since that time the film has been shown repeatedly on one of the Sky movie channels without a whisper of protest being heard.) Cinemas within the Council's boundaries simply did not show the film.

At the heart of all classification undertaken by the BBFC is the attempt to protect children from material that might be harmful to them, and also to protect the public at large from material that might deprave, harm or corrupt. This obviously pertains, in the main, to material of a sexual or violent nature.

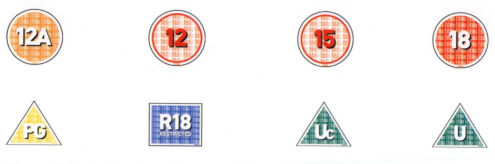

Figure 3.5 *BBFC classification symbols. Source: BBFC,
<http://www.bbfc.co.uk>.*

Five points of interest:

1   The nature of the classification system has changed over the years. As a result of increasing liberalisation, films such as *The Texas Chainsaw Massacre* (see Figure 3.6), which have been unavailable for decades, have received certificates to be shown at cinemas and released on video. Indeed, *The Texas Chainsaw Massacre* was shown on Channel Four in October 2000 as part of its horror weekend. In the last few months certain films, which only a few years ago would have had to be censored because of their hardcore sexual nature, have been granted an R18 certificate.

2   The BBFC has often been seen as the mouthpiece of the government, and certainly there is a great deal of communication between the BBFC and the Home Office, though the BBFC maintains that the Home Office has never interfered in its classification of a film or in the creation of guidelines. However, in the light of events highlighted above, there are times when the BBFC takes on the politicians. The then Home Secretary Jack Straw was said to be more than upset by the liberalisation of the R18 certificate and wanted to make changes to the Video Recording Act as a result of his concern over the BBFC's classification decisions.

3   Classification is not the only issue. There have been occasions when the BBFC have refused a film or video a certificate because it breaks their guidelines. This in turn has led to a debate about the nature of classification and whether it should be read as a form of censorship. Here one should mention the fact that some films containing hardcore scenes have been passed for exhibition in a foreign language (for example *Romance* and *The Idiots*).

4   The nature of the job is such that there are in fact no formal qualifications needed to be a classifier. However, classifiers tend to be well-educated professionals. There is no evidence that any members of the film industry's target audience (for instance eighteen to twenty-five year olds for a horror film) sit as classifiers. The BBFC says it recruits from the late-twenties age group upward because it thinks that the level of maturity required to assess some of the very disturbing material viewed by classifiers has not yet been acquired by a lower age group. However, films are tested, usually by distribution companies, with target audience screenings to see how well they are received.

Figure 3.6 *Poster advertising* The Texas Chainsaw Massacre (1974). *Source: Kobal Collection © Entertainment Film Dists Ltd.*

5   Recently we have seen the introduction of the 12A certificate. This was a direct consequence of parental and exhibitor unhappiness at the discovery that the film *Spiderman* was going to be granted a 15 certificate – thereby preventing its natural audience from having an opportunity to view the film. It is interesting to note quite how many films have been granted this 12A certification since – there has clearly been a response to public pressure and an awareness that what children might see on the television (or indeed on video/DVD) is treated in a far more liberal manner by parents and guardians than by members of the BBFC.

ACTIVITY...

Every major medium in this country has some form of regulation protecting the public in one way or another. Several of the existing regulators were replaced by one unified body at the end of 2003. OFCOM was formed by the Communications Act of 2003 and information about its duties can be found on the website <http://www.ofcom.org.uk>.

Contact each body, either by phone or via its website. It is important to find out exactly what each body has been set up to do, who sits on each board, whom they represent and what powers they have.

Ultimately there are several important questions:

■   Are audiences protected?
■   From what?
■   Who protects them?
■   Do you consider that the rights and interests of media audiences and the general public are protected satisfactorily?

PUBLIC SERVICE BROADCASTING (PSB)

The concept of public service broadcasting (PSB) was adopted in this country in the 1920s. The most obvious example of a PSB organisation is the British Broadcasting Corporation (BBC), which was founded in 1926 initially as a radio service, though it was later to involve the new medium of television. The fundamental principle behind the PSB was to provide a service for all members of the community, with what Lord Reith, Director General of the BBC in the 1920s, called a duty to 'inform, educate and entertain'. For the payment of a yearly licence fee the public received a national radio service, which was joined by a television service after the Second World War. Originally, all households that owned a radio had to buy a licence. Later, ownership of a television meant the purchase of a television licence was obligatory as well. Nowadays the two licences have been merged into one – but it is still a legal requirement to have a television licence if a household owns a television set.

What is interesting about the concept of public service broadcasting is the philosophical stance underpinning it. In a media world in which often the central concern

is profit, shareholders and aggrandisement, there can still exist, and be room for, an organisation created to serve a nation, not to make money from the nation, financed by a licence fee and, in theory, available to all.

It is important to note, however, that the notion of performing a public service is not unique to the BBC. All terrestrial television organisations have written into their charters an element of public service – usually that they should provide some kind of news programme and an element of educational programming, although it is important to note that these regulations are very much looser than they were when the first commercial television station started broadcasting in 1956.

It is also important to note that PSB is not unique to this country. It exists in one form or another in most European countries. Even the USA, where television is dominated by powerful networks showing advertisements as often as they can, possesses PSB channels. However, these channels tend to be funded by sponsorship and donations from members of the public rather than by a general licence fee.

One of the central arguments for the continued existence of PSB channels is that they represent something that is very important – namely that the public are not a homogenised audience who want to watch only what is popular.

Commercial television is bound to its owners and shareholders. It is financed by advertising. Therefore the onus on all commercial television channels is to gain as large an audience as possible. This then makes their programmes attractive for advertisers, who, on the whole, want to show their advertisements to as large an audience as possible. A popular programme attracts a large audience, who will then see the advertisement. Thus the concern is to make and broadcast popular programmes, especially during peak viewing hours. Of course there are times when audiences are necessarily small, such as the period between lunchtime and tea-time, when most people are at work or indeed at school. However, advertisers have responded to this by targeting audiences quite specifically. It is now the case that adverts on commercial television in the afternoon are aimed directly at the most likely television audience at this time, namely retired people or mothers and their pre-school infants.

The problem with this is that commercial television ends up beholden to three masters – the audience, the advertisers and the shareholders. The primary concern becomes to produce programmes that will gain the maximum number of viewers. And the evidence suggests that, in order to do this, schedules tend to become full of soap operas, quiz shows, docu-soaps and the new popular genre of reality television shows such as *Big Brother* and *Fame Academy*.

ACTIVITY . . .

Examine the current television schedules and attempt to identify which programmes or segments of programmes fall into the category of education/information and which fall into the category of entertainment.

continued

- Do any patterns emerge?
- Are some channels more educational or entertainment than others?
- Suggest reasons for this.

Underpinning the concept of PSB is the belief that all members of the community have a right to programming that appeals to them. And of course soap operas and game shows do not appeal to everyone. If fourteen million people are watching *EastEnders*, then an equal if not larger number are not. This is not to say that popular genres do not have a place in PSB but that a balance needs to be struck between entertaining popular programmes and those that might not have such a direct appeal but that still have a potential audience. Since the PSB channel does not have to gratify advertisers and shareholders, the opportunity arises to make and show programmes that are not necessarily going to be large ratings winners. (Indeed all minority interests have to be catered for under the remit of PSB, which is essentially true of BBC One as well as of BBC Two and Channel Four.)

This then presents a dilemma, which has been highlighted by the arrival of non-terrestrial broadcasters. The choice of television programmes now available to viewers (especially those who have signed up to satellite or cable television) is large, and expected to become even larger. Yet members of the population who possess non-terrestrial television have to pay for the privilege. Many of those people now find that they no longer watch any programmes presented by the BBC. So, not surprisingly, there is a groundswell of opinion that, if they do not watch BBC programmes, why should they continue to pay their licence fee? This has increased pressure on the BBC to produce programmes that will attract a large audience, if only to justify the payment of the licence fee. The conundrum then turns full circle as people who are committed to the notion of public service television start to complain because, they would argue, public service broadcasting is simply becoming a replica (and perhaps not a very good one) of commercial television, which of course is ostensibly free.

There has been a response to this debate, however. It is now possible to purchase a set-top digital receiver for your television that allows viewers to watch approximately thirty channels with no further payment. This is known as Freeview. Some of the commercial digital channels are available as well as some new channels from the BBC such as BBC Three and BBC Four.

Inevitably this has sparked off a further debate, with some critics arguing that the BBC should not be spending money on services that are very similar to those offered by other commercial channels. BBC Three, for instance, is designed to appeal to a predominantly teenage audience – an audience that is in theory already well catered for. And the news that viewing figures are poor has not necessarily helped the BBC's case. Viewing figures for BBC Four are worse, although the argument about this channel seems a little less vociferous. (See section on digital broadcasting, p. 214.)

It should be noted here that of course commercial television is not free. Millions of pounds are spent by companies in this country every year producing and showing

adverts on television. It can be argued that ultimately we, the consumers, pay for those adverts in the cost of the products that we are being enticed to buy.

There are two other debates currently circulating around the notion of public service broadcasting. This concerns 'segmentation' and digital channels.

SEGMENTATION

The way we watch television and listen to the radio is changing (see Part 2, media audiences, p. 107). There was a time when there was only one television channel, and even by the end of the 1970s there were only three.

Television was then akin to a community experience, particularly during peak hours. There was an unwritten agreement that if, for example, a serial was showing on one channel, then the other two would show programmes of a very different nature. Interestingly it was the BBC who realised that audiences for different types of programmes tended to be very different and fairly intractable in their choices. Thus the creation of Radios 1, 2, 3 and 4 in 1967, each catering for four very different types of listener. (It could be argued that this was also the first time that middle-aged executives realised that there was a youth market.)

This variation in audience make-up is now very much reflected in the format of British television on the non-terrestrial services. There are few channels on satellite and cable (other than the existing five terrestrial channels, which it must be remembered are broadcast on satellite and cable) that attempt to cater for everyone with a varied diet of programming over any given day. Channels are now devoting themselves to particular areas of viewing material – a process known as 'segmentation'. For example, there are channels devoted to sport and channels devoted to films. But it has become even more subject-specific than that. The present diet available on satellite/cable television includes health channels, home-shopping channels, sci-fi channels and channels aimed specifically at minority groups such as the Chinese Film Channel and Zee TV.

Whilst none of these channels yet has an audience that can compete with the numbers of viewers that watch the five main terrestrial channels, they are very attractive to advertisers because they allow them to target very specific audiences. And, even if some of these audiences are small, they are in the high-income bracket or have a high disposable income – teenagers, for example.

If audiences know the genre of programme that they want to watch, then a channel that gives them an assortment of programmes is no longer attractive. There is evidence to suggest that in fact the amount of channel-hopping that takes place in one evening is actually quite small. Once you are watching the sci-fi channel you are unlikely to change unless there is a specific programme that you want to watch on another channel. This is one reason why BBC audiences are under threat. Viewing habits are becoming more dominated by genre. And as the take-up of digital television increases – and all television will be digital by 2010 – the problem is likely to get worse.

DIGITAL BROADCASTING

As stated above, by 2010 all television broadcasting will be digital (and it is very likely that the date for the switch-off of analogue broadcasting may be brought forward). Public service broadcasting organisations will have to respond to this fact.

For all the reasons outlined above, it is clear that the BBC in particular will have to change with the times. There is consumer dissatisfaction with its output, and the role of a channel showing a judicious mix of programmes is changing. In August 2000, Greg Dyke, then the Director General of the BBC, outlined a series of proposals to see the BBC into the digital age. These have broadly been put into place but already there has been heavy criticism of them. The 'ideals' of public service broadcasting are seen to be under threat. Critics have been quick to point out that the two entertainment channels seem to be simply replicas of the many entertainment channels already available, whilst the other more highbrow channel will be watched by few, and perhaps positively avoided by many. Minority-interest programming will be 'ghettoised'.

Others would argue that the proposals are as inevitable as the changes that are taking place in the broadcasting environment. The licence fee does not cover the cost of the BBC's television and radio programming. Already the shortage of funds has been highlighted by the dramatic loss of several sporting fixtures that up until a few years ago could be watched free of charge on the BBC, such as Test Match cricket and English international football matches. The large investment in television, particularly by satellite and cable companies, has been reflected by the enormous sums these companies are prepared to pay for sporting fixtures. It seems inevitable that, to pay for this investment, audiences not only will have to subscribe to certain satellite/cable channels but may well soon have to pay an extra amount to watch particular major sporting fixtures.

This is already the case on some digital channels with the advent of pay-per-view (PPV) television. At present this mainly occurs for recently released films, but certain sporting fixtures, notably boxing and wrestling, have also been transmitted as PPV events. And digital television allows for each premiership football club to own and run its own television channel to show its own fixtures. Sport on Sky has had a great deal of investment money put into it by News Corporation (Rupert Murdoch's holding company) and is seen as a loss leader to get audiences to subscribe to Sky channels. Once we could watch the occasional game on the BBC for nothing; now we have to pay £28 a month for the privilege and so we have a dish or cable fitted and suddenly there

is a welter of choice – the supermarket principle yet again. Certainly when it first started there was a slow take-up for satellite television, but the sports channels have been cited as a reason why subscribers signed up, and the satellite industry now seems to have taken off with a vengeance.

However, there does seem to be a slight freeing up of premium sporting fixtures at the moment – certainly government intervention in this country and by the EEC is attempting to ensure that certain 'important' fixtures are broadcast on terrestrial television, but it remains to be seen whether this will actually work – especially in the light of the ITV Digital fiasco!

Yet the fact remains that no one is given a licence to print money. There is a risk factor. Even Sky has only just started to make a profit – and that after many years of loss-making, which could only happen because Rupert Murdoch had sufficient capital to allow it. Note that ITV Digital could only allow its own losses to go so far and then shareholder anger forced its hand and it had to close down. Over the years it has been interesting to watch the number of digital channels that have come and then gone again. Examples include Adam Faith's Money Channel, P-Rock and CNX.

CONVERGENCE

There can be little doubt that changes in communications technology in the past decade have taken many by surprise. Ten years ago some people might have owned a cordless phone at home and used a computer at work. Nowadays mobile phones are everywhere and computers rule the office. Most communication now takes place by email, and the five terrestrial television channels have numerous competitors.

Convergence means that the new media technologies are all coming together. However, not so very long ago, a typical home would have had one television set, a radio and a telephone. It is very unlikely that these were even in the same room – the commonest scenario being a television in the sitting-room, radio in the kitchen and telephone in the hall. People who spent a long time on the phone were considered slightly eccentric (usually women, as a stereotype, talking to their friends). The radio was still really a source of information and the television was watched when there was a good programme on. Things are now very different.

Most hardware is now multi-functional. The television is digital and interactive. There is the potential to have over 1,000 channels beaming into your sitting-room, or more if you possess a movable satellite dish. This is very different from the era when the choice was between four (later five) terrestrial channels. Pay-per-view television is already in existence, at present featuring mainly films and sporting events, but it is likely that the menu will widen considerably over the next few years.

More interesting is the interactive aspect of media technology. Television has now become a medium through which one can shop, bank, and even send and receive emails through a telephone cable link-up. This works both ways. The phone has become a piece of hardware through which one can still talk but can also send text messages, voicemail, emails and connect to the Internet. The radio is still a radio, but few units are simply just radios – most are again multi-functional, including cassette decks and CD players, or at the very least alarm clocks that wake you up to a radio programme.

Thus hardware has become another example of vertical and horizontal integration. If you own the hardware, or make it as multi-functional as possible, then the audience can gain access to your product with greater ease. And if it is accessible then it is much more likely to be so accessed.

But the implications are far greater than this. The computer, accessed by wide-bandwidth telephone cables, is very much at the centre of the new technological revolution. To put it another way, we are now living in the digital age, which of course springs from the computer.

THE CHANGING MEDIA WORLD

One of the difficulties in studying or writing about the media is that the media world is constantly changing. This change may be fairly superficial, for example in terms of what is this week's most controversial television programme or is the current best-selling 'lads'' magazine. Often, however, these changes are the result of developments in technology, and the rate of these technological changes is speeding up. One of the biggest changes taking place today in the media is the development of the Internet.

It is foreseeable that soon you will be able to download a film from the Internet at home and then play it back to yourself on a virtual-reality headset, played through your phone, whilst on a train journey, for instance.

The technology exists now to download music from the Net. Some musicians have used this technology to allow interested audiences to download their music (either as a taster or because they believe in providing free public access to media products), and there is a movement that supports the idea that the Net should belong to the people and freedom of access is their right.

However, there are several test cases currently taking place relating to copyright laws and the Net, since it is becoming easier by the day to download music that would otherwise cost money if bought at a record shop. Obviously the artists and record companies involved are concerned about the loss of revenue that such downloading represents. Are we looking at a total sea change in both conditions of consumption and the nature of that which we consume?

The technology now exists for programmes to be downloaded to your television through phone lines. This means that viewers are able to watch whatever they like whenever they like. This technology is still in its infancy.

Sky has produced a piece of hardware, called Sky Plus, that sits on the television set and enables viewers to skip over adverts and even pause 'live' television. It has the capacity to record over thirty hours of television from a maximum of ninety channels. But more interesting is the fact that viewers can key in certain words and the box will then automatically watch out for programmes featuring these words. Thus viewers can select programmes they want recorded or search for different types of programmes, or indeed particular actors or genres.

- What are the possible effects of the digital age in terms of our viewing habits?
- Is television as a community activity a thing of the past?
- How will scheduling differ in the future?

What all of this means is that the nature of our media consumption – and of television consumption in particular – will change. If viewers felt overwhelmed by choice at the outset of digital technology, it now seems as though the shoe is on the other foot and it is the consumers who are potentially about to take control.

Figure 3.7 attempts to show the strengths and weaknesses of various media in terms of their portability (seen as a strength), their cost and their interactivity and demands on attention. Do you think interactivity is a strength or weakness? What about 'demands on attention'?

Figure 3.7 *Which media are under threat and why? Source: Michael Svennevig, 'A neglected medium? The future of radio', University of Leeds.*

Medium	Portability	Demands on attention	Choices available	Interactivity	Cost
Radio	High	Low	Wide	Low	Low
Newspaper	High	Medium	Wide	Low	Medium
Magazine	High	High	Wide	Low	High
Terrestrial television	Low	Medium	Limited	Low	Low
Cable/satellite	Low	High	Wide	Medium	High
Video recorder (VCR)	Low	High	Wide	High	High
Video on demand (VOD)	Low	High	Wide	High	High
Internet/Web	Low	High	Wide	High	High
Future Internet/Web	High?	Variable?	Wide?	High?	Low?

Notes: The basic premise is that the greater the difference in attributes between a medium and its rivals, the more likely that medium is to have a loyal audience/user base. Radio on this basis faces its main threat from print rather than from television-based media. In turn, the latter face the threat of the VCR and VOD.

THE INTERNET

The Internet has been described as a giant car-boot sale or an enormous feast with over 600 million potential guests (see <http://www.nua.com/surveys/how_many_online>). It is estimated that there are over 400 million easily accessible web pages available at present, plus several million more 'subscription' pages. In Britain it is estimated that by 2010 nearly 90 per cent of the population will have Internet access either at home, at work or through their schools and colleges.

NOTEBOX

The Internet was developed in America in the 1960s by the military, who wanted to protect the information contained on their computers. They worked with people from universities, who soon took over the idea as a means of exchanging ideas and information. The Internet as we know it today came about through a variety of technological events that took place during the 1990s. These included the development of a common 'language' for computers to talk to each other and exchange data, the upgrading of telephone lines (which is still going on in Britain) to enable data to be sent quickly and easily from one computer to another, the availability of cheap, fast, domestic computing systems and software such as those of Intel, Apple Mac and Microsoft, and the growth of computer-literate people who could understand and use the software. Once the potential of the Internet was understood, large companies such as Compuserve in America and Freeserve in Britain became involved and spent millions of pounds developing it as a consumer tool.

Increasingly we can talk of the Internet in the same way that we discuss other media forms; television, radio, newspapers, magazines, and so on. The Internet also shares the same issues about who controls it, who owns it and how much it costs to access it.

In fact no one really owns the Internet, which is possibly part of its attraction. However, increasingly companies from the 'old' media are moving in and either setting up their own sites or buying up newly formed companies. For example, one of the earliest web-browsers was Netscape, which was bought by AOL (which merged with Compuserve), one of the biggest ISPs (Internet service providers). AOL then merged with Time-Warner, one of the world's largest media companies. It is often the established companies, such as Time-Warner, EMAP or News International, who can afford the cost of setting up new websites, especially when they can see the opportunity for 'synergy', where the same or similar products can be sold or cross-marketed in more than one medium. Today all 'old' media brands also have websites.

There have been opportunities for new companies to be established through the Internet. There has been a lot of publicity about dot.com companies such as lastminute.com or the company revise.it, founded by two twenty-year-olds, which 'publishes' GCSE revision guides. The company is said to be worth millions of pounds, but access to the site is free. Like many websites, this one hoped to make its money by charging advertisers who wanted to target its particular group of 'surfers', in this case fifteen- to sixteen-year-olds. However, as many dot.com companies have realised, it is quite difficult to make money through the Internet and in recent years many companies have either gone bankrupt or have cut back on their web-based services. Friends Re-united, revise.it and lastminute.com are some of the new companies that have been successful. Websites set up by media companies tend to be subsidised by the companies' other, more profitable, activities; however, the BBC website (<http://www.bbc.co.uk>) and Guardian Unlimited (<http://www.guardian.co.uk>) have been relatively successful.

Issues about control are in many ways similar to the 'old media' issues: for example, how do you measure the effects of material on the Internet and separate it from other influences? The main problem in terms of control is that the Internet is spread across the world and different countries have different laws. In France, for example, it is illegal to buy Nazi memorabilia, but in America there are sites that claim under the US Freedom of Information Act the right to sell such merchandise. Is a French citizen who accesses an American site to buy this memorabilia breaking the law? There has also been a lot of debate regarding the downloading of music from websites such as Napster and Karai using MP3 players.

Cases like Gary Glitter's have also highlighted the way in which the Internet can be used by members of subversive or illegal groups such as paedophiles. It is certainly true that the Internet is used by extreme right-wing groups as much as it is by left-wing groups or anti-war protesters. We may agree with one group and not the other, and this may affect our view as to whether the Internet is a 'good thing' or not. The McLibel case is a good example of a small group of people who used the Internet to subvert the power of a large American multinational company. Although they lost the legal case and McDonald's was awarded damages, the 'McLibel 2' movement is considered to have 'defeated' McDonald's by publishing its evidence against McDonald's on the Internet and so winning the public relations battle and gaining many supporters worldwide (see <http://www.mcspotlight.org>). Increasingly, following 11 September 2001, governments are trying to introduce laws that allow them to access private email accounts in the same way that they might tap telephone lines or intercept ordinary mail. Some countries, including China and Saudi Arabia, have tried to make accessing the Internet illegal, but with limited success. In China the government has traditionally been able to control what news is available to the Chinese people. However, the Internet allows unauthorised sites to distribute reactionary information. Websites in China now have to be licensed by the government, which has closed down illegal websites. However, these then move to other countries where the Chinese government has no jurisdiction over them (see, for example, Human Rights in China at <http://www.iso.hrichina.org/iso>).

The Internet is still very new, and it is a little difficult to anticipate how it is going to grow or what effect it will have on our lives over the next ten or fifteen years. As we have already discussed, one of the biggest developments will be the convergence of computer technology, telephone communications and television. Already it is possible

to access the Internet through your digital television and mobile phone. Soon the computer will stop being a piece of office furniture and move into the living room. Eventually we may have one piece of hardware, an information appliance that will provide voice telephone, email, fax, DVD/video and audio 'webcasts' and web surfing as well as the 'traditional' television channels. Some people now refer to the telephone as a 'portable data apparatus'. As the technology improves and Internet connection speeds increase, the quality of the images we can download will likewise improve. We can already download films from the Internet, place them on recordable DVD and then play them on portable DVD players wherever and whenever we want. The 'in-flight' movie could be the one that we decided to bring along instead of relying on the airline's selection.

Many of these new forms of communication will be two-way or interactive as the telephone line will allow us, at home, to send signals back to the producers of these products. Increasingly television companies are using the interactivity of digital services to get the audience to participate in choosing the winners of, for example, *Big Brother* or *Pop Idol*, or express our opinion on a political question. Television companies are keen to introduce these additional services as they are profitable; for example, Endemol (the company that makes *Big Brother*) and Channel Four made considerable amounts of money through their viewers' use of expensive telephone call charges when voting contestants out of the *Big Brother* house. Sporting events on television often allow us to select different camera angles, additional pieces of information or, in the case of the BBC's Wimbledon tennis coverage, the matches we want to watch.

It is hard to speculate on the extent to which this interactivity will affect the ways in which we consume the media. However, new hard-drive player/recorders are said to offer the potential for each consumer to organise and select his or her own particular menu of entertainment. These machines contain a computer hard-drive that stores up to thirty hours of television digitally and when played back it can skip advert breaks. Like a VCR, this technology can record live or pre-programmed television and can also suggest particular programmes based on the owner's viewing habits. It is connected to the telephone so can send viewing information back to marketing firms. Instead of 'broadcasting', these new recorders will mean 'narrowcasting' – in effect making the 'old' mass audiences increasingly fragmented. (See Part 2, media audiences, p. 107.)

Much of this technological revolution is driven by companies who see it as an opportunity to sell us consumer products – games consoles, online services (both for goods and for services), 'edutainment' software on CD-ROM or DVD, and interactive and subscription services that we may be willing to pay extra for – as well as the hardware necessary to access them. The companies will be targeting those who can most easily afford to buy these new products. Those who cannot afford the new hardware or subscription charges will perhaps be excluded, and we will develop a 'digital underclass' or 'information-rich/information-poor' societies.

Currently most countries in the world have some kind of Internet activity, but it is only used regularly by about 5 per cent of the world's population – those who live in affluent, developed societies – and most of these users are white, male professionals.

Figure 3.8 *How many people are online? Source: Nua Internet Surveys © Nua Ltd.*

Africa	6.31	million
Asia/Pacific	187.24	million
Europe	190.91	million
Middle East	5.12	million
Canada and USA	182.67	million
Latin America	33.35	million
World total	605.6	million

The science of estimating how many are online throughout the world is an inexact one at best. Surveys abound, using all sorts of measurement parameters. However, from observing many of the published surveys over the last two years, we can make an educated guess as to how many people in the world were online in September 2002. The number is 605.6 million, or approximately 10 per cent of the world's population.

However, these statistics need to be considered as a percentage of the population for each area, for example in Europe and the USA over 60 per cent of the population are online. In Africa, although the number online has doubled over the last five years it is still less than 1 per cent of Africa's population, and this varies considerably between such extremes as South Africa (with over 10 per cent of its population online) and Ethiopia (with less than 0.1 per cent of its population online). Ethiopia has a population slightly larger than that of Britain but has only one ISP (Internet service provider), and that is state-owned. In Britain there are at least 245 ISPs, most of which are commercially run.

FURTHER WORK . . .

1   Three questions follow that involve research and analysis:

- Do we have reasons to be concerned by the increasing trend towards multinational media?
- Technology continues to move faster than we can keep up with. Where might we be in twenty years' time?
- Is the notion of a mass audience, viewing the same text at the same time, becoming outdated?

2   Consider the impact of legislation and equal-opportunities policies on media representations.

FURTHER READING

As has been noted several times above, probably the best sources of information about media institutions are specialist websites or the quality broadsheet newspapers and their websites. All of the newspapers have business sections, which is where you will find regular and frequent reference to media institutions. Many of the Sunday newspapers also have a media section that always contains valuable information. It is vital, however, that you file the information in some shape or form.

Websites

There follows a list of important websites, which are regularly updated and will keep you abreast of what is happening in the world of media institutions:

<http://www.bfi.org.uk>
Website of the British Film Institute – contains invaluable information.

<http://www.cjr.org/owners>
Columbia Journalism Review – with up-to-date information on media companies.

<http://www.cpbf.org.uk>
Campaign for Press and Broadcasting Freedom – very critical of the dominance of commercial interests in the media.

<http://uk.imdb.com>
Internet Movie Database – contains virtually everything you want to know about film.

<http://www.media.guardian.co.uk>
Online version of the *Guardian*'s Monday media supplement.

<http://www.mediachannel.org>
This has an American flavour but fascinating analyses of contemporary media issues. Many links to other sites as well.

<http://www.mediauk.com/directory>
Details the media scene, with links to websites of all the main television and radio stations, magazines and newspapers.

<http://news.bbc.co.uk>
This is a good general news website and contains information about business and media companies both in Britain and throughout the world.

<http://www.raynet.mcmail.com>
Contains essential information on marketing.

<http://www.thestandard.com>
This is essentially an economics website but with a very large media section.

There are many, many more sites available – far too numerous to mention – but part of the enjoyment of the Internet is discovery. Virtually every media organisation now has a website. The easiest way to find them is to type the name in the search section of your search engine and see what happens!

<http://www.google.com>
This is undoubtedly the fastest and most rewarding search engine to date.

Further information on regulation can be obtained from:

OFCOM (<http://www.ofcom.gov.uk>)

British Board of Film Classification (<http://www.bbfc.co.uk>)

BBC (Producers' guidelines) (<http://www.bbc.co.uk/info/editorial/prodgl/chapter6.shtml>)

British Video Association (<http://www.bva.org.uk>)

Advertising Standards Authority (<http://www.asa.co.uk>)

Press Complaints Commission (<http://www.pcc.org.uk>)

Books

Curran, J. and Seaton, J. (1997) *Power Without Responsibility: The Press and Broadcasting in Britain*, Routledge.

Franklin, B. (ed.) (2001) *British Television Policy: A Reader*, Routledge.

—— (2003) 'Media institutions and production' in O'Sullivan, T., Dutton, B. and Rayner, P. *Studying the Media*, Arnold.

Williams, K. (1998) *'Get Me a Murder a Day': A History of Mass Communication in Britain*, Arnold.

▼ EXAMPLE: NEWSPAPER OWNERSHIP

A NATIONAL INSTITUTION

The *Daily Mail* is a well-known media product: some would call it a national institution. It has a circulation of around 2.5 million copies each day and it is common to see people reading a copy on the bus, train or tube on their way to work in the morning.

The *Daily Mail* is a highly influential media product. It does little to disguise its political and cultural allegiances, which are support for a right-of-centre Tory party, and its concern to represent the interests of 'Middle England', the conservative property-owning middle classes.

ACTIVITY . . .

Monitor the front page of the *Daily Mail* for the next couple of weeks.

- Decide how many of the headlines and front-page stories suggest a right-wing bias and whether there are examples that could be used to demonstrate that it also has different viewpoints.
- Do you think a newspaper should report and present news in this way?

The *Daily Mail* is an example of a national newspaper, which means that it circulates throughout the country rather than to one specific geographical area as do some local or regional papers. The news it covers will therefore be of interest and concern to people across the United Kingdom. The *Daily Mail* is also an example of a tabloid newspaper. The words 'tabloid' and 'broadsheet' are used to describe the size and shape of a newspaper. A tabloid newspaper is half the size of a broadsheet, so both formats can be printed on the same press. 'Tabloid' and 'broadsheet' are also used to signify different approaches to news coverage. Broadsheets are seen as serious-minded newspapers, appealing to professional and managerial classes, while the tabloids are generally seen as more downmarket, appealing to people with jobs in clerical and manual occupations. Clearly this is quite a crude distinction, but a readership profile comparing *The Times* and the *Sun*, for example, would support this demarcation.

Figure 3.9 *National readership survey, January–June 2003. Source: Newspaper Marketing Agency, <http://www.nmauk.co.uk/nma/do/live/cribsheetdailymail>.*

	Readership	Cover %	Profile %
AB Adults	1,919	16.3	32
ABC1 Adults	3,933	15.6	66
ABC1C2 Adults	5,084	14.6	86
C1 Adults	2,014	15.0	34
C2 Adults	1,151	11.9	19
DE Adults	849	7.1	14

The breakdown above of the *Daily Mail* readership, however, shows a significant number in the AB social groups and only 14 per cent of the readership being manual workers. The *Daily Mail* can be seen, then, as a quality tabloid with a readership similar to that of many of the broadsheets. Indeed the paper insists that it is in fact a 'compact' newspaper rather than a tabloid, with all the downmarket connotations that such a nomenclature bears.

Perhaps one reason for this profile is the way in which the *Daily Mail* targets its audience. Figure 3.10 shows a list of the supplements that the *Daily Mail* publishes on different days of the week.

Figure 3.10 *Daily Mail features by week.*

Monday	*Self*	Alternative health and well-being issues
Tuesday	*Good Health*	Healthcare, including new treatments and health-related innovations
Wednesday	*Money Mail*	Personal finance advice
Thursday	*Femail Magazine*	Fashion, style and beauty
Friday	*It's Friday*	Weekend guide, highlighting the theatre, culture and art
	Books on Friday	Literary section
Saturday	*Travel*	Holiday and travel news
	Weekend	Includes personality profiles, cookery, wine, gardening and television pages

Consider carefully the features detailed in Figure 3.10.

■ What sort of reader do you think that are aimed at?
■ Do any other newspapers have similar daily features?
■ How do the features in other newspapers differ from those in the *Daily Mail*?

It has been suggested that if current circulation trends continue the *Daily Mail* will become the country's most popular newspaper by the end of the decade. Much of the popularity of the newspaper is put down to the editor Paul Dacre, who took control in 1992. The editor of a newspaper is obviously an important and powerful figure. The *Daily Mail* stance in representing the values of Middle England can be seen, however, to make this man even more of a powerful figure, especially at a time when traditional right-wing politics represented by the Conservative Party are in disarray. Indeed it has been argued that Dacre's *Daily Mail* represents the real opposition to the New Labour government; certainly there is evidence to suggest that senior Labour politicians do attempt to avoid antagonising the newspaper unnecessarily.

NOTEBOX . . .

The editor is usually the most powerful person in a newspaper's hierarchy, although in some cases it is argued that an editor may be a mere puppet doing the bidding of the proprietor, a view commonly expressed about Rupert Murdoch's News International titles. With power, however, comes responsibility, and it is nearly always the editor who is held responsible when things go wrong. Editors in extreme cases can be sent to prison if their newspapers transgress the law.

Newspapers such as the *Daily Mail* are usually organised into departments responsible for such things as advertising, production and distribution. The news content is the responsibility of the editorial department under the direct control of the editor. The editorial department will consist of smaller sections with specific responsibilities, such as the features department. The main news-gathering operation is controlled by the news editor from the news desk. S/he is responsible for deciding which stories need to be covered and assigning tasks to individual journalists. As is illustrated in the case study on news (see p. 235), many of these tasks will be diary jobs, known about well in advance.

Where possible stories will be covered by full-time journalists, known as staff reporters. However, where this is not possible, because a story is too remote from the nearest staff reporter, a newspaper such as the *Daily Mail* will use agency copy from a large news agency such as Reuters or the Press Association. It may also buy in a story from a local freelance journalist or 'stringer', who will be paid 'lineage', a fee for each line of copy that is used in the newspaper. Similarly photographs will be provided variously by staff photographers, agencies and freelancers.

The design and layout of a newspaper is the responsibility of the sub-editors, or 'subs'. Working under the direction of a chief sub, the subs will check a reporter's copy for accuracy, both of fact and grammar, before providing a headline and laying out the page, using an on-screen page-make-up programme.

The editor has the major, and final, say over which stories are included and how prominently each is displayed. The front-page lead is clearly the most prominent story, with inside pages having less-important stories.

ACTIVITY . . .

For this activity you will need to get access to all the major national newspapers published on a particular date.

■ Check the front-page lead of each newspaper. Are all of them featuring the same story or is there a range of different stories?
■ Where one or more newspaper is featuring the same story, in what ways is their coverage of it different?.

A BRIEF HISTORY

The *Daily Mail* is a newspaper famous for being controlled by powerful press barons. Harold Harmsworth and his brother Alfred published the first edition on 4 May 1896. Both were soon afterwards made baronets, Harold taking the title Lord Rothermere and Alfred the title Lord Northcliffe. Early editions of the *Daily Mail* introduced innovations that are commonly found in modern tabloid newspapers. These included large front-page headlines, shorter and simplified stories, sports coverage and features sections, including those targeted at women. The brothers soon acquired other titles, including the *Daily Mirror* and *The Times*, and soon became such influential figures that they were invited to join David Lloyd George's government. Northcliffe died in 1922 and it was left to Rothermere to look after the press empire. He formed a political allegiance with another mighty press baron, Lord Beaverbrook, owner of the *Daily Express*, and under his control the *Daily Mail* moved sharply to the right with its support for Oswald Mosley and the National Union of Fascists. Rothermere also met Hitler on several occasions and was supportive of Neville Chamberlain's policy of appeasement towards the great dictator.

Today the title is still under the control of the Harmsworth family, with Jonathan succeeding as the fourth Lord Rothermere, following in the footsteps of his father who is credited with doing so much to increase the circulation of the paper.

Interestingly there has been an ongoing rivalry between the *Daily Mail* and the *Daily Express* after a fall-out between Beaverbrook and Rothermere, perhaps fuelled because traditionally both newspapers have vied for the same middle-class Tory readership. The *Daily Express* has, however, repositioned itself of late and is generally considered to be less right wing and more supportive of Tony Blair, to the point where Richard Desmond, the newspaper's owner, made a contribution to Labour Party funds. Desmond, who acquired the *Daily Express* in 2000, was also a publisher of softcore magazine titles such as *Asian Babes* and *Mega Boobs*. The rivalry turned particularly nasty in 2002 when Paul Dacre in a press interview described Richard Desmond as a 'pornographer' and an appalling man. The *Daily Express* retaliated by publishing articles about the Rothermere family's own chequered past.

PRESS REGULATION

As we have seen in Part 3, on media institutions (p. 181), all media organisations are subject to some degree of regulation. Newspapers are, however, a special case. The 'freedom of the press' has been for many years a rallying cry in support of democracy and this concept has done a lot to preserve the newspaper industry from many of the regulatory controls imposed on television and radio. It would be a brave government that tried to impose further restrictions on the press.

The regulation that does exist can be categorised into legal and self-regulatory controls. An example of a legal control is the law of libel. If a newspaper publishes a story, found subsequently to be untrue, that is defamatory because it lowers someone in the estimation of right-thinking members of society, then it has committed libel. The person who has been defamed has redress through the courts and is entitled to damages if the court finds in his or her favour. The main defence against libel is that the story as published is in fact true.

The problem with the libel laws as they stand is that because the loser in the case is likely to have to pay the costs of both sides usually only the very rich can afford to take the risk of starting a court battle with a newspaper. One rich person who took on the *Daily Mail* and won was Nicole Kidman. In July 2003 she received 'substantial damages' after claiming in court that a *Daily Mail* article accusing her of adultery with Jude Law was untrue. She argued that the false accusations had caused her 'considerable embarrassment and distress'. The *Daily Mail* agreed to apologise and pay court costs.

For members of the public who do not have the wealth of a Hollywood star to back their grievances, newspapers regulate themselves through a voluntary code through the Press Complaints Commission (PCC) (see p. 205). However, the PCC, which has a heavy representation on its adjudication panel from the newspaper industry itself, is often seen as a rather toothless mechanism for regulation, especially as it has no power to impose fines. One occasion when the *Daily Mail* found itself on the wrong side of the PCC was when a complaint was made by Tony and Cherie Blair about the intrusion of

the *Daily Mail* in publishing an article about their son Euan's application to Oxford University that was in breach of the PPC code of practice relating to schoolchildren. The Commission concluded its adjudication as follows: 'The Commission therefore considered that the article was an unnecessary intrusion into Euan Blair's time at school and that it had only been published because of the position of his parents. The complaint was therefore upheld.'

In addition to the libel laws there are a number of other legal statutes that impact upon what a newspaper can and cannot report. These include the Official Secrets Act, which prevents the publication of information (usually official papers) that might jeopardise state security. The government of the day can also after consideration issue a 'D Notice' to editors of newspapers suggesting that in the interests of the state security information might be withheld. Newspapers seldom breach a D Notice. One increasingly problematic area legally for newspapers relates to the reporting of information about people who are likely to be charged with criminal offences. Clearly a newspaper is able to write about the arrest and charging of a person accused of a crime. However, many are tempted to publish further background information that is likely to interest their readers. The danger is that in doing so the newspaper may influence the trial of the person when it takes place ('prejudice a fair trial') because the jury might have read information that would prejudice them in coming to a fair verdict. In extreme cases a newspaper may even be prepared to pay those involved in a trial to secure the rights to their stories once the verdict is announced.

An increasing pressure on newspapers comes from the availability of information via the Internet. In the case of footballers accused by a young girl of rape in a London hotel, newspapers such as the *Daily Mail* were unable for legal reasons to name the team involved, although this information was circulating freely on bulletin boards on the Internet. Interestingly, however, there was significant pressure on Internet service providers to restrain a number of their websites from disclosing the information, presumably from a fear that they too might be held in contempt of court and face prosecution in the same way as a print source.

OWNERSHIP

As we have mentioned in Part 3, media institutions, p. 181, many well-known media texts are produced by larger organisations or groups often with international interests. The *Daily Mail* is no exception. It is part of a larger group called Associated Newspapers, which is in turn part of a larger group called the Daily Mail and General Trust Ltd, or DMGT.

ACTIVITY...

Check a newspaper or other source for the listings of these companies on the stock market and then conduct an Internet search to find out what financial information you can about them.

Associated Newspapers publishes several well-known national titles in addition to the *Daily Mail*:

Mail on Sunday	The *Daily Mail*'s sister paper, published on Sundays with a circulation very similar to that of the *Daily Mail*
Metro	A free sheet distributed in London, Birmingham, Newcastle, Leeds, Sheffield, Manchester, Glasgow and Edinburgh by readers picking up copies at rail and bus stations, giving it a daily circulation in the region of 800,000
Loot	A classified advertising paper with editions published in several major cities
Evening Standard	Currently London's only evening newspaper, although Richard Desmond has plans to launch a free evening rival provocatively called the *London Evening Mail*.

Each of the above titles also has an accompanying website. The relationship between a newspaper and its website is often a complex one. A newspaper publisher will not want to give away free via the Web what it currently expects readers to pay for. Websites in consequence tend to be scaled-down versions of editions of newspapers, often with ancillary features geared towards supporting advertisers. An interesting example is the *Evening Standard*'s website This is London (<http://www.thisislondon.co.uk>). In addition to offering a news service, the site provides key lifestyle and cultural information about the capital. Many of the facilities, such as restaurants and cinemas, are regular advertisers in the print publication.

ACTIVITY . . .

Visit the website of any national or local newspaper. Check out precisely what is on offer.

■ How do you think the website can be compared with the print edition of the newspaper?
■ You might also like to consider websites that provide searchable archives of the newspaper's editorial content, such as Guardian Unlimited (<http://www.guardian. co.uk>).

One of the reasons that newspapers have invested so heavily in new media technology is to ensure that they are future-proof against some of the rapid changes taking place in media technology. There is a distinct possibility that newspapers will one day be delivered electronically rather than as hard copy. Websites represent one way by which this might be done. This desire to ensure survival in the competitive media market also means that newspaper groups often seek to diversify into other media and into other media-related activities.

Typically DMGT has diversified its interests over a number of years. In addition to Associated Newspapers, it also controls Northcliffe Newspapers, which publishes 106 regional newspaper titles across the UK. DMGT Radio has commercial radio interests both in this country and in Australia, where it controls more than thirty stations. The Daily Mail Group also controls the Teletext service, which provides information via Channels ITV, Four and Five. Overseas interests include newspaper titles that have been acquired in Spain, Greece and Ireland. The group, which has a turnover of nearly £2 billion a year, also controls DMG Media, an exhibitions business, and the DMG Information business services division.

According to its website:

> The success of many of the Group's businesses is inextricably linked with understanding and engaging with the communities that they serve, and this allows them to identify needs and to campaign effectively on the issues relevant to their customer base. This principle is as relevant to the *Daily Mail*, serving the whole of the United Kingdom, as to the *North Devon Journal Herald*, serving the population of Barnstaple in Devon, and to 6KG, one of our two radio stations serving the remote mining town of Kalgoorlie in Western Australia.
> (<http://dmgt.answerbank.co.uk/pages/client0/annual_report/csr.htm>)

As you will see, such an ownership profile is typical of many modern media organisations in that it has both diversified into different media forms and looked to extend its interest multinationally.

A TYPICAL EDITION

It is a useful exercise to look closely at at least one edition of any newspaper that you are studying. There are a number of ways in which you might do this, either qualitatively, by making detailed textual analysis of all or some of the paper, or quantitatively, such as by conducting a content analysis, for example by counting the amount of space given over to different types of coverage. This latter method is particularly effective if done over several editions or as a comparative analysis of two competing titles. Below we look at the edition of the *Daily Mail* published on Friday, 3 October 2003, using the qualitative method. Our focus is on the news stories rather than on features, entertainment or sport.

The front page has a headline in 72-point upper-case letters declaring 'WOMAN RAPED IN OFFICE OF LORD FALCONER'. This is an evocative (provocative?) headline in a numbers of ways. First, the sexual content, in this case an attack on a woman, is a tabloid formula encouraging readers to buy a newspaper. Second, the reference to Lord Falconer, the Lord Chancellor and a member of the New Labour cabinet, suggests, without being explicit, misdemeanour at the heart of government. Interestingly the front page is balanced with a full colour 'splash' of a young girl who has just died of cancer. We are invited to look inside to read the girl's 'heart-rending and inspiring poems'. It is as though we see two opposing sides of human nature encapsulated on one page. At the top of the page, next to the *Daily Mail* masthead, there is a promotion for a free return flight to the USA, a common device to attract and retain readers used by most of the national press. Between the dateline and the price the *Daily Mail* styles itself 'Newspaper of the Year' (*Daily Mail*, 3 October 2003).

The inside pages of the edition make interesting reading. Typical headlines and stories include:

- **Back from Hell** The story of a 'respected headmaster' acquitted of assaulting a student by forcing a dead fish into his mouth.
- **Extra Police? So Where Are They When You Need Them?** The story links the boast of David Blunkett, Home Secretary, to the Labour Conference that there are more police on the beat to the shooting of a woman in a jeweller's shop in Nottingham.
- **Brave Little Evie's Legacy of Verse** The story trailed on the front page here runs as a hallmark *Daily Mail* double-page spread illustrated with pictures of Evie, her family and the poems she wrote.
- **How Could They?** A story and accompanying picture of a cocker spaniel thrown into a river with a weight around its neck. The opening paragraph reads 'It is a picture which will shock and dismay every dog lover in Britain'. Also lower down the page is a story about bottled water entitled 'Food poisoning peril'.
- **Grammars Face the Axe for Doing So Well** A story reporting that a local council may switch star pupils to failing comprehensives.

These five stories seem reasonably typical of those that the *Daily Mail* reports on a regular basis. It is worth noting here that, as is pointed out in the section on news (see p. 235), a process of selection has taken place. From all the news stories that the newspaper might have printed, it has selected these. In fact one could argue that they have been specifically selected to support the particular ideological stance of the newspaper. Certainly each story individually suggests to the reader a dangerous world in which we live. Not only have we lost all respect for authority, but even the good things in life such as grammar schools are being jeopardised by mindless bureaucrats who are also incapable of protecting us from gun crime on our own doorsteps. Ideological messages often work cumulatively. One story in isolation might have a limited impact on an audience, but collectively a group of stories each painting a similar picture of the world is likely to influence the way in which the audience see things.

Notice also that the headlines of each story provide a particular ideological viewpoint from which the reader is invited to see what is going on in the world. Not only have the stories been selected but the way in which we should interpret them is being suggested for us by the spin put on the story. 'Back from hell' aligns us emotionally with the headmaster, who is portrayed as the victim of the judicial system, which has supported 'a boy who has a history of behavioural problems' over a 'respected headmaster'. The illustration, in the form of a four-column close-up of the smiling headmaster with an inset of his wife and daughter, goes to support the implication that he is a straight-forward family man and presumably an upholder of the *Daily Mail*'s virtues of decency, law and order, and family values. In narrative terms he is pitted in opposition to the forces of disorder, represented by the 'tearaway' who has already been 'excluded from another school'. Pleasingly for the *Daily Mail*, on this occasion the forces of darkness have been defeated.

Obtain a copy of the *Daily Mail* and analyse in a similar way the news coverage on the front and inside pages.

■ How far do you feel that these stories have been selected and presented in order to support the ideological position of the paper?

■ Now look at one story in detail and explain how you think it has been written from a specific ideological viewpoint.

■ You may then like to consider how the same story has been covered in another newspaper with a different ideological perspective, such as the *Guardian*.

FURTHER READING

Curran, J. and Seaton, J. (1997) *Power Without responsibility: The Press and Broadcasting in Britain*, Routledge.

Keeble, R. (2001) *The Newspapers Handbook*, 3rd edn, Routledge.

Media Guardian – published as a supplement to the *Guardian* every Monday and online (see below).

Private Eye – the satirical magazine's 'Street of Shame' column offers a less-than-glamorous view of the national press.

Websites

Most national, regional and local newspapers have their own websites, with variable degrees of sophistication and interactivity. Guardian Unlimited (<http://www.guardian.co.uk>) is particularly recommended as a resource.

The Evening Standard site This is London (<http://www.thisislondon.co.uk>) is an interesting example of a website that combines news and lifestyle interest for the capital.

Information about the *Daily Mail* and its associated companies can be found on:
<http://www.associatednewspapers.com>
<http://www.dmgt.co.uk>

Similarly information about the Murdoch empire can be found on:
<http://www.newscorp.com>

Other useful sites include:
<http://media.guardian.co.uk>
<http://www.pcc.org.uk>
<http://keywords.dsvr.co.uk/freepress>
<http://www.nuj.org.uk>

▼ CASE STUDY 1: NEWS

In this section we:

■ consider the nature of news and its sources

■ look at the role of news in the output of television, radio and print media, and the competition that exists between and within these media forms

■ consider issues of representation in the news and examine what powers exist to control and regulate news output

■ look at how technology influences news output and examine the future of current news output in light of new media technologies.

WHAT IS NEWS?

News is information about contemporary events. It informs us about what is going on in the world at large. In the media it is an important commodity as it is a way of attracting an audience of people keen to be informed about the events taking place in the world in which they live.

News, it can be argued, also performs the important function of helping people make sense of the world they live in. Not only do the media tell people what is going on, they also seek to interpret these events in such a way that they make sense to people. As we will see, this gives media producers an important power in relation to the audience. Not only the selection of events that are reported but also the way in which these events are presented can have a powerful impact on the attitudes of both individuals and society as a whole.

NOTEBOX

On 23 July 2000, the front page of the *News of the World* alleged under the headline 'NAMED SHAMED' that there were 110,000 child sex offenders in Britain, one for

continued

each square mile. Alongside a photograph of the recently murdered schoolgirl Sarah Payne, the paper stated that the police monitoring of 'these perverts' was inadequate and announced it was revealing 'WHO they are and WHERE they are . . . starting today'. One consequence of this was that mobs took to the streets hunting down named offenders and in a number of cases attacked innocent people.

News also has an important regulating function in the lives of an audience. News is presented by the media at regular intervals. News bulletins on the radio are hourly, national newspapers are published each morning, and television news on the terrestrial channels is broadcast at specific established time slots. When unexpected and 'important' news events occur, these may disrupt and replace existing broadcasting schedules in order to focus exclusively on an important event and the world reaction to it. The events of 11 September 2001 in New York are clearly a prime example of this, with saturation coverage of the destruction and its aftermath dominating the media. The death of Diana, Princess of Wales, in a car crash in Paris in 1997 is another example of the media focusing almost exclusively on a single event. As we have seen, it led commentators to ask how far the media were reporting a spontaneous outpouring of national grief and how far the saturation coverage by the media had engineered this response.

This regularity of news dissemination, occupying prime-time television slots, and the idea that other media events can be displaced by it reinforce to us the important role of news in the media. The very nature of the way in which it is used by the media signifies that we, the audience, must be aware of its importance and take it seriously.

ACTIVITY . . .

Consider the role of television news in the evening television schedules.

- Why in the past have the major terrestrial channels avoided showing the news at the same time as each other?
- Why do they now compete in the same time slot?
- How might an audience be influenced by news bulletins in planning an evening of family viewing?
- What sort of events do you think are considered important enough for broadcasting schedules to be disrupted to report them? Suggest two or three examples of such events.

On television, there are a number of other prompts that suggest the news is important and has to be taken seriously. Consider, for example, the type of music that introduces news bulletins, the nature and status of news readers and the way in which the studio has been designed. Notice also the way in which news readers use phrases like 'that's the way it is' to conclude the news bulletin, suggesting that the representation of the world we have been shown is definitive or the only way in which it can be seen.

SOURCES OF NEWS

Part of the mythology that surrounds the news is that news is always unexpected. In many ways the media are happy to nurture this myth by implying that the job of a reporter is to rush to the scene of an event that has just happened and find out the facts to tell the audience. On occasions this may be the case; events do happen without warning. Such incidents as accidents on the roads, railways or at airports cannot be predicted. Similarly, natural disasters such as floods or earthquakes often happen with little warning.

The vast majority of items that are reported as news, however, are predictable events that the news media know about in advance. This enables them to ensure that a journalist is in place ready to cover an event in advance of its happening. A visit by a senior political figure such as the prime minister is a good example of such an event. Generally such visits, for example to open a new hospital, are planned many months in advance. The news media have prior warning and put the visit into their diary of upcoming news events. In some sectors of the industry, reporters call such events 'diary jobs'. There is obviously plenty of opportunity for pre-planning the news coverage of such events. Television cameras can be positioned ready to ensure that the optimum visual advantage is obtained. In the same way press photographers can ensure they are well placed to get a photograph of the action.

Indeed, some events are so well prepared for that they even become stage-managed. The major political parties ensure that the news media have access to their annual conferences to guarantee that the messages given to the party faithful who attend the conferences also reach the wider electorate in the country as a whole. In political terms, a party may go to some lengths to ensure that positive aspects of its policies are reported in detail while unpopular policies or political gaffes are given much less prominent coverage. Ensuring that coverage is of the type the party wants is the job of the spin doctors, who are basically public relations (PR) officers whose job is to ensure a positive public image.

PR and spin are not limited to politics. Increasingly, commercial organisations and even individuals such as celebrities are employing people to ensure that a positive image of them is promoted in the media. The PR guru Max Clifford, for example, looks after the media profile of a number of major and minor celebrities and openly admits to manufacturing stories that will gain publicity for his clients.

Examine an edition of a newspaper or news bulletin on the radio or television. Make a note of each story and decide whether the news media had advanced warning of the story or whether it happened unexpectedly. Explain how you are able to differentiate.

A number of devices are used by the PR industry to ensure that organisations and individuals get their point across to the media. The most popular and probably the most economical is the press release. Press releases are sheets of information, often written in the form of a news story, that are sent to news media. They usually give details of newsworthy events, such as the launch of a new campaign, often with either a photograph or the opportunity for the press to take a picture. A well-written press release can often be used with little rewriting by a journalist, especially in a small local newspaper.

NOTEBOX . . .

Most large organisations provide access to their press releases through their websites. It is a useful exercise to visit a site such as Virgin to look at the press releases it has issued to publicise the activities of the different interests within the organisation to the media.

Another weapon in the armoury of the PR office is the news conference. News conferences are often called by organisations such as the police when they want to publicise a major criminal investigation. Often news conferences are screened directly on to television news bulletins, with television, print and radio journalists all seen being briefed and asking questions. In a similar way, the lobby system in Parliament is used by reporters to receive briefings about the activities of different government departments. The press secretaries of ministers have become powerful figures in the manipulation of the news media, especially the prime minister's former Director of Communications and Strategy, Alastair Campbell, whose name became synonymous with the role of spin doctor.

KEY TERM

SPIN DOCTOR A person who tries to create a favourable slant to an item of news such as a potentially unpopular policy.

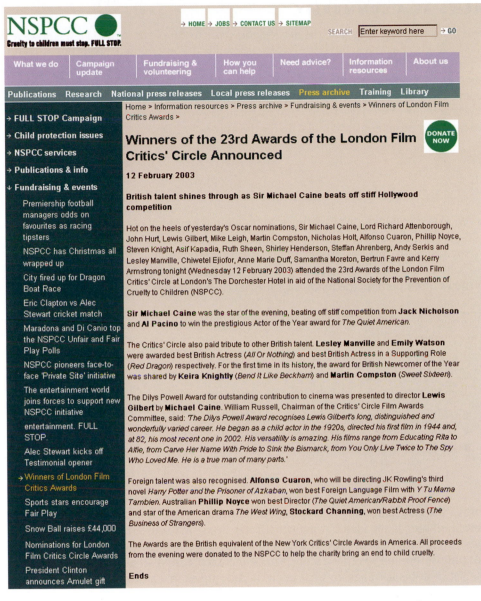

Figure 4.1   *London Film Critics' Circle Awards press release from NSPCC website. Source: NSPCC Media Office.*

Manipulating and even setting the news agenda in this way is called news management. For many people who rely on public recognition for their success, keeping a high media profile is important. In fact, it has been argued that there is no such thing as bad publicity; negative stories in the press are still a way of keeping celebrities in the public eye, even if this involves revealing intimate details of their private lives.

NEWS AS A COMMODITY

Every day we need news, and the news media need to supply us with it. News, however, has to fit into packages, the size of which is usually predetermined. News bulletins run for a fixed length of time, and newspapers generally have a similar number of pages each day. Obviously the amount of news available is likely to vary from day to day. Some days there will be more news than can be used, and items may have to be discarded. On other days, events that might not normally warrant much attention will be reported prominently to make up for the absence of news.

Weekends and holidays are times when limited amounts of news are available. This is partly as a result of the fact that such sources of news as Parliament and the law courts are not sitting or people are away on holiday. In fact, the summer holiday is known in news circles as 'the silly season', as the lack of more serious news often permits the reporting of trivial or silly stories.

ACTIVITY . . .

Consider the output of news on a particular day.

- How would you rate it as a 'news day'?
- Were there lots of stories available or a limited number?
- What evidence do you have for your answer?

One of the issues prompted by the need to decide on the content of newspapers and news bulletins is the idea of what constitutes news. Why are some events considered more important than others? The idea of news values is important here. News values not only determine whether a story is to be included, they also determine how high up the list of items it comes, or what position it occupies in a newspaper.

ACTIVITY . . .

In a newspaper the most important, or lead, story makes front-page headlines. In television and radio bulletins the most important story is given priority by being first in the running order. Compare two newspapers and two news bulletins for the same day.

In 1973 Galtung and Ruge undertook a study of news stories. They identified that certain items of news are more likely to be reported than other items and, similarly, some items of news are likely to be given more prominence than others. A full list of factors they identify can be found in *Understanding News* (Hartley 1982), in a chapter in which the selection and construction of news are given detailed consideration.

It is useful to look at some key factors that can determine whether an event is considered newsworthy. Events that take place close to home or are culturally relevant are more likely to be reported than events that happen in remote parts of the world (Galtung and Ruge call this 'meaningfulness'). A train crash involving a few injuries that happens in this country may well be given more prominent coverage than a disaster involving injury or even death to many hundreds of people in Asia, for example. Similarly, events that happen to important people will be reported in much greater detail than events that occur in the lives of ordinary people. For example, a story about a cabinet minister caught speeding will be given much greater prominence than a story about a media student (unless he or she is a close relative of a cabinet minister).

ACTIVITY...

Another important factor that determines whether a story is reported or not is the element of surprise or unexpectedness it contains. Consider a news bulletin and decide which stories have been included because of the element of surprise that they contain.

Many of the key decisions about what gets reported relate to the way in which the news-gathering operation is organised and to the professional working practices of workers employed in this branch of the media industries. A key figure in the news-gathering operation is the news editor. News editors are common to both print and broadcast media. Their function is to take charge of the news desk and to act as a filter or gatekeeper in determining which stories will be reported. They have to decide, for example, which diary jobs to despatch reporters (and film crews or photographers) to cover. They also decide which of the many hundreds of press releases that the organisation receives are worthy of being used or followed up. Pictures and stories from freelances and news agencies will also be vying for attention. A news editor needs to have a good news sense to decide how best to use the resources at his or her disposal.

In making the decision about what stories to cover, the news editor will need to employ his or her own professional judgement and experience. However, there will be other factors and pressures that will influence the decision that is made. These will include an awareness of what competitors might be doing. It will not look good if a story given extensive coverage in one newspaper or one news bulletin is wholly omitted by another. Similarly there may be pressures from a newspaper proprietor either to include or omit a particular item for political, business or even personal reasons.

The desire for an exclusive is just one example of the competition that exists between news media. On television, for example, news bulletins play a key role in the scheduling of prime-time evening viewing. The fact that news bulletins have regular slots means that they act as important regulating factors in establishing viewing patterns. Audiences tuning in to an early-evening news bulletin may well continue to watch a particular channel. Similarly, the main evening news fulfils an important function in dividing the evening between family viewing and the more adult viewing possible after the watershed.

It has been argued that this function of news in terms of scheduling means that there is pressure on producers of news programmes to make them entertaining so as to attract and retain viewers. This has led to charges that the presentation of news has been 'dumbed down' to make it appeal to as wide an audience as possible. Indeed it has been suggested that television news has become increasingly 'tabloid', with shorter news items on Channel Five and BBC Three, for example, appealing to a youth audience supposedly with a limited attention span.

An interesting development in television news presentation is the increased reliance on audience interactivity through such methods as email and, perhaps more significantly, text messaging. The latter is an especially popular means of communicating among younger people and by encouraging its use news programmes hope to encourage participation among younger viewers.

The word 'tabloid' comes from the print news media and refers to the down-market newspapers such as the *Sun*, the *Mirror* and the *Star*. These papers are also referred to as the 'red-top' newspapers owing to the colour of their mastheads, where the title of the newspaper is displayed. This distinguishes them from other newspapers with a tabloid shape, such as the *Daily Mail* and *Daily Express*, which are considered to appeal to a more sophisticated readership.

The red-top newspapers are identifiable by a number of features:

- They are generally easy to read, featuring lots of short stories with small amounts of text, and require a short attention span.
- They rely heavily on pictures and illustration to support the text.
- The stories they contain tend to be trivial and rely heavily on information about celebrities.
- They tend to sensationalise news stories by exaggerating what has taken place.
- They pander to populist opinion, for example by encouraging xenophobic attitudes to foreign countries and their peoples.
- They are responsible for the creation of moral panics, for example by stirring up public outrage over such issues as paedophiles.

TABLOID A compact newspaper, half the size of a broadsheet, designed to appeal to a mass audience. Tabloids, particularly at the lower end of the market, are associated with sensationalising trivial events rather than with comprehensive coverage of national and international news.

KEY TERM

Look in detail at one tabloid newspaper.

- How far do you think the above qualities are evident in the paper? Find examples that either do or do not support each of the above assertions.
- How far do you think it is true to say that television news bulletins exhibit similar qualities?
- Do any radio stations have bulletins that can be called tabloid?

NOTEBOX . . .

An extreme example of a red-top newspaper campaign was the edition of the *Sun* dated 13 September 2003, in which the front-page lead story headlined 'Hook Scandal, Wife's £1000-a-week-dole' featured the London Islamic preacher Abu Hamza alongside a picture of him raising his artifical hooked hand. He was described as a 'fanatic', whose family was 'raking in £1000 a week' and living in a five-bedroomed house costing £550,000. It was alleged that housing benefit paid for the Georgian council house that his wife, from whom he was separated, lived in.

Inside the paper the article continued on page 4, headlined 'We work hard to live here . . . they get it free', and below this was a 'Wanted' poster featuring a £1,000 reward for information on the whereabouts of 'Captain Hook'. The *Sun* was offering £1,000 to the reader who could lead the newspaper directly to 'the bile-spouting Islamic extremist'.

When we asked permission to reproduce the front-page lead and the reward box in this textbook our request was declined by News International, particularly after seeing the context in which it would be reproduced. Our description about the distinguishing features of red-top newspapers, particularly the statement that tabloids were associated with stirring up public outrage over such issues as paedophiles and creating moral panics, was regarded as sufficient reason not to grant permission.

Do you think our list of distinguishing characteristics of red-top newspapers hits the mark?

It is also interesting to note that competition exists not only within media forms but also between media forms. Television, radio and print media all compete to supply audiences with the commodity of news. This competition is further intensified by the arrival of other means of delivering news, such as the Internet.

A key quality of news is that it is contemporaneous. This means that it is reported soon after it has happened. Clearly, for television and radio, which have several bulletins a day, it is far easier to be contemporaneous than for a newspaper, which tends to be limited to a single daily edition. If news is important enough, broadcast media can interrupt existing programmes to bring it to the audience. Print media cannot currently compete with this, although as many newspapers develop their own websites they now have an electronic means of their own to ensure audiences are up to date with the latest or 'breaking' news.

BREAKING NEWS   A news story, the details of which are unfolding as the news is being reported.

It is interesting to consider how newspapers have responded to the challenge of competing with broadcast and electronic media for audiences for the news. Had they simply been content to report what had been broadcast on television the day before, their sales would have declined sharply. Instead, newspapers seek to engage their audiences with other strategies in order to ensure that sales remain buoyant.

BROADSHEET   A large rectangular newspaper, such as the *Daily Telegraph* or *The Times*. Broadsheets are usually associated with serious journalism, reporting important events at home and abroad. They are targeted at an upmarket, professional readership.

ACTIVITY...

Outline what content other than news you are likely to find in a national newspaper. Consider both broadsheet and tabloid newspapers. What items do they have in common? What are the major differences?

News is often categorised into different types of story. What we normally think of as 'news' is probably more accurately called 'hard news'.

HARD NEWS   News that is important and is happening at the time it is reported. A rescue attempt on a cross-Channel ferry, the death of an important national figure or a rise in mortgage interest rates could all be classified as hard news.

Human-interest stories are another popular type of news story. It can be argued that most stories that are reported involve people and therefore have an element of human interest. A human-interest story is one that has a particular appeal because of our interest in other people and the way in which they live their lives. Stories about the adventures of lottery winners are a good example of human-interest stories. Much of the appeal of these stories is that the audience may like to imagine how they might behave in a similar situation.

The arrival of twenty-four-hour news broadcasting in the form of Sky News and BBC News 24 has also made 'breaking news' an important phenomenon. With a news channel on air twenty-four hours a day, there are likely to be many instances of this, and it is interesting to watch a news story develop as more details become available to reporters. One consequence of these rolling news channels is that there is now an even greater demand for news in order to fill the output of these channels throughout the whole day. This can lead to saturation coverage of the type discussed earlier in relation to 11 September 2001 and the death of Princess Diana. A question exists, however, as to the extent to which this demand for information can lead to the media creating or at least demanding news to fill their bulletins. The murder of two young girls from the village of Soham in the summer of 2002 led to such saturation coverage. It was argued that twenty-four hours a day media coverage put pressure on the police to the extent that the media played a part in shaping the way in which the investigations were carried out.

Many types of news form a category in their own right. Sports, political or business news are typical examples. These categories usually have their own section in a newspaper or news bulletin. Similarly, broadsheet newspapers often break news down into sections according to its geographical location: home news, European news or world news, for example.

ACTIVITY . . .

Why do you think that sports news occupies a position at the back of newspapers and the end of news bulletins? What impact do you think the positioning of sports news in this way has on the audience consuming the text?

KEY TERM

FEATURE In newspapers this is generally an article that concerns itself with a topical issue while not having any hard news content.

Newspapers also make use of their format to include features as part of their news content. Features often provide the public with the opportunity to read in greater depth about the background to a topical news event or issue.

ANATOMY OF A NEWS STORY

Like all media texts, news stories are invariably constructed according to established conventions. These vary between media forms, but it is interesting to note that certain conventions exist in all the media. You may find it useful to look back at the section on narrative (p. 42), in which we suggested that narrative was an equally important aspect of non-fiction texts as of fictional ones.

A news story relies on a narrator controlling the flow of information to the audience in much the same way as in a fictional narrative. Most news stories begin with a hook designed to grab the attention of the audience and make them want to know more about what is to follow. Headlines are used in both print and broadcast media to do just this. They create an enigma that the audience is required to resolve by consuming the information provided in the remainder of the text. A good headline will provide just enough information to attract an audience but leave them wanting more information, for example 'POP STAR IN DRUGS SCANDAL'.

The narrative conventions of news reporting require a hierarchical structure to the story itself. By this we mean that the most important point generally comes first. The first paragraph (or 'intro') by convention offers the most important piece of information. Indeed, some journalists would argue that the first paragraph should sum up what the story is about and that subsequent paragraphs exist simply to elaborate on this information. A good intro, therefore, might almost be considered a complete news item in its own right. In a print news item, the intro is often given visual priority by the use of a larger point size, or bold text, or both.

Another quality that is common to news items across media forms is the way in which information is broken down into manageable portions. In a print news story the paragraphing is generally much shorter than in an academic essay, for example. This means that the reader is able to digest the information easily as it is provided in manageable portions.

> **KEY TERM**
>
> **SOUNDBITE**   A snappy and memorable quotation that can be easily assimilated into a broadcast news story (for example, Tony Blair's 'Education, education, education').

NOTEBOX

> Notice the use of quotations in newspaper stories and how these are set out. Each newspaper has its own style book that provides journalists with a list of rules about what is acceptable in terms of how stories are written. Quotations are especially important to news stories because they provide an authentic voice that supports what the story is saying and at the same time provide an element

continued

of human interest. On radio and television interviews are used as a means of providing quotations to support the story.

The importance of good quotations is clear from the concept of the soundbite. Politicians are keen to use effective soundbites in their speeches as they know that the news media will want to include these in their reports. Tony Blair's 'Education, education, education' soundbite in one of his election speeches is one example.

Pictures are an important aspect of news stories, except in the medium of radio, of course. A good picture can often mean that a news story may well have far more prominent coverage than a similar story with no pictures. This is especially true with television news, where often stories that do not have good visual support are placed much lower down in the running order.

ACTIVITY...

Watch a television news bulletin and consider its use of images.

■ How far do you think the availability of visuals has influenced the running order of the items?
■ Do you think any stories would have been given greater prominence if there had been better visual support?

OR

The radio equivalent of pictures is called 'actuality' and consists of sound recordings of events taking place. Consider how important to a radio news bulletin is this use of actuality.

KEY TERM

ACTUALITY Recordings of images and sounds of events made on location as they actually happen for inclusion in news reports or documentaries.

An important issue in the study of news coverage is the extent to which the news media give us an impartial view of the events they report. For many people, television and radio news are seen as being objective media. This may be partly because of the requirement in the BBC and Independent Broadcasting Authority charters, which define the public service responsibilities of television broadcasters to maintain balance and

impartiality. The idea of balance implies that both sides of an argument should be represented. So in the reporting of a parliamentary debate, for example, both the government's view and that of the opposition should be included. Indeed, this notion of debate is central to the way in which broadcast media report most issues that involve controversy. Similarly, the media should not be seen to favour one particular viewpoint, especially in terms of the major political parties. In many ways the animosity between the Labour government and the BBC in the summer of 2003, which ultimately led to the Hutton Enquiry, came out of a concern on the part of the Blair government that the BBC had not been objective and balanced in its coverage of the government's information on the issue of Iraq's potential to use weapons of mass destruction.

No such requirement to maintain neutrality in the coverage of political events exists for the press. The *Sun* newspaper, for example, openly instructs its readers how to vote in general elections. In fact, the support of Rupert Murdoch's News International papers was seen as essential by the Labour Party if they were to win the general election in 1997. Famously, at the previous election, Neil Kinnock's Labour Party lost partly on the strength of a damning headline in the *Sun* suggesting that, if Labour won, the last person to leave the country should turn out the lights. A newspaper like the *Daily Mail* makes little secret of its support for the Conservative Party. However, the change in the political landscape, with the Labour Party increasingly representing the interests of the centre ground of British politics, has meant a good deal of realignment of traditional allegiances. In consequence it is dangerous to offer a simplistic view of a Tory press opposed to everything a Labour government may seek to do.

ACTIVITY...

Look at two tabloids and two broadsheets.

- Can you determine which political parties these papers support?
- Who owns each newspaper? Do they own any other newspaper?
- Look at a recent issue of each paper. Can you find any particular stories relating to the main British political parties or political figures that you think reveal political bias?
- Examine closely the choice of vocabulary and note any particular words or adjectives that are positive/approving and any that are negative/pejorative.

NOTEBOX...

An organisation that has done a lot of research into the concept of bias in news reporting is the Glasgow Media Group. In 1976 it published *Bad News*, which suggested that the reporting of such issues as industrial relations was not

continued

unbiased. The Group argued that such reporting very much favoured the employers rather than the striking workers. The organisation published another study in 1980, entitled *More Bad News*, which further supported this view.

REGULATION CONTROL

As we have seen, the news media are a powerful means of disseminating information. Television news is for a large proportion of the population the main way they find out what is going on in the world. One in four of the population looks at a copy of the *Sun* newspaper daily. Clearly the news media can exert a considerable influence over the way in which people view the world and the opinions that they hold. It follows, therefore, that there needs to be some accountability or even control over what is published or broadcast. Balanced with this need, however, is the importance of media free from government control, which are able to play a key role in the democratic process. At times, it may seem that these two requirements are difficult to reconcile.

It is important to realise that there are restrictions and controls over what the news media can report. Some of these are enforced by law and are called legal or statutory constraints; others are voluntary constraints set up by the industry itself. The latter is an example of what is known as self-regulation.

One important form of statutory control is the law of libel. Libel covers any form of media that can be considered permanent, for example print, television or radio, as opposed to a transitory medium such as the unrecorded spoken voice. If anyone publishes information that can be considered to be untrue and damaging to the reputation of another person, then that other person can take out an action for libel. One of the main defences in a libel action is to demonstrate that the information stated is in fact true. The onus, however, is on the defence to prove this.

Unfortunately for most people, taking libel action against another individual is too costly even to contemplate. Doing so for most people against a large and powerful media institution would be financial suicide. The reason for this is that in a libel case the losing side is usually required to pay the costs of both parties to the action. With legal costs easily running into many thousands of pounds, a libel action cannot be readily contemplated by any but the wealthiest.

NOTEBOX

Elton John v. the *Sun*

There have been many famous libel actions over the years. Probably one of the best known was when the singer Elton John took out an action against the *Sun* newspaper, which had made a series of allegations about his personal life. Elton

John was eventually awarded damages of £1 million and received a front-page apology in the newspaper. The *Sun* had printed front-page allegations on 25 February 1987 that smeared the character of Elton John. When challenged by Elton John's lawyers for a retraction and an apology, the paper doubled the pressure with a headline on 27 February that said 'You're a liar, Elton'. Once it was proved that the stories printed were uncorroborated allegations contributed by a rent-boy paid by the *Sun*, and who told the *Independent Magazine* 'I would give the *Sun* a line and they would print it up. It was a manufactured story', the newspaper was forced to pay damages. Their printed apology was the headline: 'Sorry Elton'. (Source: Hansard.)

Fortunately for the less affluent, it may not always be necessary to have recourse to law in order to obtain justice from the news media. A good example of the regulation of the media is the Press Complaints Commission (PCC). The PCC was set up in 1991, formed on the basis of the old Press Council. It was the result of an enquiry into the press conducted by Sir David Calcutt. The newspaper industry was required to set up the Commission, the function of which is to deal with complaints by members of the public into what is published in newspapers and the conduct of journalists. The PCC published a code of conduct (see overleaf) that has been subsequently updated and consists of sixteen points. Any complaint made to the Commission must relate to one of the points in this code of conduct.

Complaints made to the Commission are investigated, where appropriate, by the sixteen members of the PCC. These members are both representatives of the newspaper industry and members of the public. The members of the Commission issue an adjudication and, if they feel that a newspaper is at fault, they can order the publication of the adjudication in the newspaper.

What they cannot do is hand out any other kind of punishment, such as a fine, to the offending publication. In consequence, the PCC has been described as a toothless tiger that does little more than pander to the interests of the newspaper industry. Many people argue that proper controls are needed if the newspaper industry is to behave responsibly. Arguments have been put forward, for example, for a privacy law that would protect people from unwanted media intrusion. This would prevent paparazzi from stalking people in order to obtain photographs without their consent. Another legal change that has been mooted is the introduction of a law giving people the right to reply when they have been attacked in a newspaper. Such a law would confer on people an opportunity to reply to comments and criticisms made against them in the press.

Governments, however, are understandably reluctant to curb the freedom of the press by introducing such legislation. Antagonising the press unnecessarily may not be in their best interests. Many would argue that, despite its inadequacies, self-regulation may be the most effective system to ensure a press that, whilst free to pursue matters of public interest, will behave ethically and responsibly towards the public.

CODE OF PRACTICE

Ratified by the Press Complaints Commission – 1 December 1999

All members of the press have a duty to maintain the highest professional standards. This code sets the benchmarks for those standards. It both protects the rights of the individual and upholds the public's right to know.

The code is the cornerstone of the system of self-regulation to which the industry has made a binding commitment. Editors and publishers must ensure that the code is observed rigorously not only by their staff but also by anyone who contributes to their publications.

It is essential to the workings of an agreed code that it be honoured not only to the letter but in the full spirit. The code should not be interpreted so narrowly as to compromise its commitment to respect the rights of the individual, nor so broadly that it prevents publication in the public interest.

It is the responsibility of editors to co-operate with the PCC as swiftly as possible in the resolution of the complaints.

Any publication which is criticised by the PCC under one of the following clauses must print the adjudication which follows in full and with due prominence.

The Public Interest

1   The public interest includes:
   i)   Detecting or exposing crime or a serious misdemeanour
   ii)   Protecting public health and safety
   iii) Preventing the public from being misled by some statement or action of an individual or organisation
2   In any case where the public interest is invoked, the Press Complaints Commission will require a full explanation by the editor demonstrating how the public interest was served.
3   There is a public interest in freedom of expression itself. The Commission will therefore have regard to the extent to which material has, or is about to, become available to the public.
4   In cases involving children editors must demonstrate an exceptional public interest to over-ride the normally paramount interest of the child. . . .

1   Accuracy
   i)   Newspapers and periodicals should take care not to publish inaccurate, misleading or distorted material including pictures.
   ii)   Whenever it is recognised that a significant inaccuracy, misleading statement or distorted report has been published, it should be corrected promptly and with due prominence.
   iii) An apology must be published whenever appropriate.
   iv)   Newspapers, whilst free to be partisan, must distinguish clearly between comment, conjecture and fact.
   v)   A newspaper or periodical must report fairly and accurately the outcome of an action for defamation to which it has been a party.

(Press Complaints Commission 1999)

Other categories of the code of practice include:

Opportunity to reply	Reporting of crime
Privacy	Misrepresentation
Harassment	Victims of sexual assault
Intrusion into grief or shock	Discrimination
Children	Financial journalism
Children in sex cases	Confidential sources
Listening devices	Payment for articles
Hospitals	

The full text of the code can be found at <http://www.pcc.org.uk>

NOTEBOX ...

All of the bodies responsible for media regulation have their own websites, a list of which is given in the resources section at the end of this book. It is useful to visit these sites, not only for background information but also to look at some of the adjudications, or decisions, they have made about issues raised by the public.

An organisation called the Campaign for Press and Broadcasting Freedom (CPBF) also has some useful information about topics relating to media freedom and regulation, as well as issues of ownership and control. It has a useful website (details in the resources section) and also publishes a newsletter (also available online), called Free Press, which contains news and comment on media-related issues.

THE FUTURE OF NEWS

In recent years the way in which news is delivered to audiences has undergone considerable change. As we have seen, we now have dedicated twenty-four-hour news channels, making television news available on tap for audiences. No longer do we have to wait for a news bulletin broadcast at a specific time to catch up with the day's events. The advent of youth-oriented news programming has had an impact on the way in which news is presented to us, with a much more informal and relaxed approach to presentation.

Perhaps one of the most fundamental changes that is taking place, however, concerns the influence of technology on the way in which we access information. As we noted in the introduction, society is now very much divided between groups of people who are information-rich and those who do not have ready access to information technology. One of the basic divides is access to the Internet. People who are able to access the Internet not only have news available to them on demand, but are also able to choose the news that they want to consume. This can be achieved in several ways, including the simple customising of a browser to provide specific categories of news, for example sport, financial or showbiz. Similarly, it is possible to obtain news direct from the source by accessing celebrity websites to find information about what the

stars are up to. Footballers involved in transfers have taken to breaking the news on their own personal websites. By setting up their own websites, celebrities seek to control the way news about them is presented.

NOTEBOX . . .

It is interesting to note the way in which both television and radio use websites to play a supporting role in their presentation of news. Commonly presenters refer audiences to linked websites, for example when additional and detailed information that cannot be included in a bulletin is available.

As technology develops or converges so that access to the Internet is readily available through television sets, so the way in which we consume news is likely to develop further. It looks certain that the mass audience for news, along with the mass audience for such programmes as soaps, is set to decline. In its place we may well see the development of individualised and perhaps even interactive sites in which people are able to call up the news that they want to hear and avoid the news that they do not. One of the categories that Galtung and Ruge suggested for news values was negativity – the idea that bad news is good news. With the growth of customised news media, it may well be that many people will wish to screen from their lives any suggestion of the bad things that happen in the world. On digital satellite television, the Sky News service already allows viewers to gain access to 'news on demand', a sub-menu that provides the audience with the opportunity to tune in to a range of live events, such as conferences or major 'happening' news stories.

FURTHER WORK . . .

1   Collect press stories about a celebrity who has been negatively reported in the tabloids. Create a mock-up of a website for that celebrity that would present a more positive representation.

2   What information is provided by the British press other than news? Provide examples from a range of newspapers.

3   How fair is it to say that most newspapers no longer consistently support either of the two main political parties?

4   In what ways has the presentation of television news changed in recent years? How do you account for such changes?

5   'Radio news is just television news without pictures.' Discuss with reference to the news output of at least two radio stations.

continued

› News	› Entertainment	› Sport	› Business	› Video Reports
› Latest headlines	› Latest headlines	› Latest headlines	› Latest headlines	› Latest summary
› Picture stories	› Picture stories	› Picture stories	› News by sector	› Regular news
› Politics	› Music	› Football	› Personal finance	› Light news
› Quirkies	› Television	› Live cricket	› Tourist rates	› Sporty news
› Royals	› Tickets	› Formula One		› Quirky news

News search: ⬜ go

Ananova: The home of breaking news

Huntley 'agitated'
Police officer tells court that Ian Huntley "became agitated" as he gave a statement hours after girls went missing. More

Quirky stories
Check out the latest quirkies from around the world, including news of animal madness, unlucky people, sex life and bad taste.

A 24-year-old man has been arrested in connection with the death of skydiver Stephen Hilder. More

William Hill make Sam evens favourite to win Pop Idol with Chris looking the most likely to be up for eviciton this week. More

Jagger 'needs help for incurable lust'
Jerry Hall says her ex-husband Sir Mick Jagger 'needs help' for his womanising ways. More

Stan the manager?
Southend hold talks with former England player Stan Collymore over a return to Roots Hall as player-manager. More

News latest

Revolution scientists say 'let them eat cake'
Man arrested over skydiver death
Prada Boys gangsters jailed for 39 years
Intellectual apartheid' teacher denies sex attacks on pupils
More news - More UK stories - More world news

Entertainment latest

Sam clear favourite to win Pop Idol
Keira had belly pierced at 13 - thanks to mum
Horror role for Ally McBeal star
Kat jilts fiance for Alfie in front of 16 million viewers
More entertainment news - TV listings

Sport latest

Oldham could lose Zola
Melligan joins Doncaster Rovers
Elliott keen on permanent move
Preview: Stalybridge v Barnet
More sport news - Football - Cricket

Quirkies at a glance

Man swallowed 200 live worms in record attempt
Girl gets tongue stuck to freezer
Council house tenants set to get £25,000 'good behaviour' prize
Grannies hotting up for curry
More quirkies - Bad taste - Sex life

Figure 4.2 *An example of virtual news on demand.*
Source: Ananova.com.

6   What do you understand by the term 'dumbing down'? Is this an accurate description of recent developments in television news coverage?

7   'The tabloid press are concerned only with sensationalism at the expense of reporting real news.' How far do you agree with this statement?

8   Most newspapers, both national and local, now have their own website. (For examples see the resources section, p. 340.) By carefully comparing an edition of a newspaper with the website, consider the relationship between the two. Consider what advantages each might have for:

■   the newspaper industry
■   the audience.

Do you think that one day websites will replace newsprint?

FURTHER READING

Allen, S. (2000) *News Culture*, Open University Press.

Hartley, J. (1982) *Understanding News*, Routledge.

Keeble, R. (2001) *The Newspapers Handbook*, 3rd edn, Routledge.

Schlesinger, P. (1987) *Putting Reality Together: BBC News*, Methuen.

Selby, K. and Cowdery, R. (1995) *How to Study Television*, Macmillan.

▼ CASE STUDY 2: ADVERTISING AND MARKETING

In this section we look at:

- the historical context of advertising
- the 'marketing mix'
- covert advertising
- audience targeting
- regulation and sponsorship
- the effects of advertising
- political 'spin'.

INTRODUCTION

According to the Advertising Association over £17 billion is currently spent in Britain on advertising each year, either on buying 'space' to show the advertisements or on their production. This money not only finances a wide range of media texts (magazines, radio and television, websites, newspapers, and so on) but also means that a vast number of advertisements are made and then seen by people in Britain. Advertising is therefore an important part of the media, not only in terms of what it finances and the effect that this may have on the content of other media products but also in its own right in terms of the advertising texts themselves, their content and their possible effect on audiences.

The advertising market share breaks down as follows:

Television	47 per cent
National papers	18 per cent
Magazines	16 per cent
Radio	7 per cent
Local papers	6 per cent
Outdoor	5 per cent
Cinema	1 per cent

(Source: *Media Guardian* 2002, from AC Nielsen MMS, April 2001)

ADVERTISING: INSTITUTION HISTORY

Advertising is considered to be one of the oldest forms of media. There is, for example, evidence of professional advertising at Pompeii, the Roman city that was destroyed in AD 79 by an eruption of Mount Vesuvius. Pub and inn signs, which date back to the Middle Ages, are a means of advertising their wares and attracting customers.

The series of advertisements for Pears Soap (Figure 4.3) is interesting not only in that they represent some of the most successful nineteenth-century advertisements but also because they show that advertising techniques have not significantly changed over the past hundred years. Like advertisements today, the Pears campaigns show that advertising is largely about image and association rather than providing clear information about the products themselves.

For instance, part of Pears' success was based on the company's catch-phrase 'Good morning! Have you used Pears soap?', which became an automatic response to the phrase 'Good morning'. Most of the Pears advertisements use images of children to represent traits such as innocence, youthfulness, freshness and cleanliness. This connotation of children is still prominent in advertisements today, particularly in those advertisements to do with cleaning products such as soap and washing-up liquid.

The exception in the Pears series is the advertisement with the (male) shopkeeper/ chemist apparently 'recommending' Pears. Today the (male) expert is still a popular advertising ploy, although it is sometimes used in a humorous (or ironic) way. The fact that Pears soap won a prize is also featured in one of the advertisements. The advertisement with the boy blowing bubbles was in fact originally an oil painting, 'Bubbles', that became very popular and was purchased by Pears to use in its advertisements.

ACTIVITY...

Try to research 'old' advertisements, perhaps from the 1940s or 1950s, and identify ways in which advertising has (or has not) changed over time. You could look, for example, at the British sites <http://www.advertisingarchives.co.uk> and <http://www.hatads.org.uk/trust.htm> or the American site <http://www.adflip.com>, which contains an archive of American advertisements.

- What do you think are the reasons for any changes that you have identified?
- What similarities can you identify?
- Talk to people of different ages to see what advertisements (if any) they remember and why they remember them.
- How effective are catch-phrases, theme tunes or jingles in helping people remember particular advertisements or products?

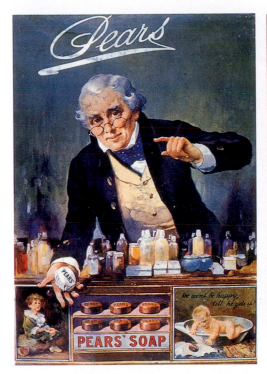

Figure 4.3 *Early Pears soap advertisements. Source: Mayfair Cards of London.*

THE 'MARKETING MIX'

Today advertising is only one part of the marketing mix that may also include public relations, sponsorship, events, tie-ins, use of celebrities, news management and product-placement among other more covert techniques. This advertising and marketing process involves a lot of people working at different stages of production. There is a great demand for research into consumer habits, needs and desires as well as the development of particular products and brands. This 'marketing mix' is often categorised as the four Ps: Product, Price, Promotion and Place.

Product

Most advertising is concerned with selling something – a product – although usually it is the brand rather than the product that is being sold. Brands are different from products. An example of product is instant coffee, but within the product there is a range of different brands – Gold Blend, Kenco, and so on – each of which tries to have a separate image and identity to distinguish itself from other brands of instant coffee. Generally, particular brands are aimed at particular groups of consumers. Often one company, for example Nestlé, will have a range of different brands of the same product that look as if they are in competition with each other but are in fact trying to target different segments, or niches, of the instant coffee market. Increasingly advertisers talk of giving different brands different 'personalities'.

Product can also include the packaging, whether it is the particular typeface used by a newspaper such as the *Guardian* or the way in which a company's logo appears on all of that company's material. Brands are often re-packaged in an attempt to change their image; for example, until the 1980s Lucozade was a medicinal drink given to invalids and was sold in large glass bottles. Through re-packaging, changing to small cans or bottles, and using the sports personality Linford Christie, Lucozade became seen as a youth-orientated 'sports' drink, the reverse of its original image. The German wine Black Tower has also recently been re-packaged in an attempt to give it extra 'value' and a more upmarket image that is supposed to appeal to a particular niche market.

> **KEY TERM**
>
> **NICHE MARKET** A small target audience with specific interests, for example DIY, classic cars or royalty.

ACTIVITY . . .

Advertisers often try to sell the same products to different people in different ways. Choose a particular product (cars, trainers, jeans, instant coffee, shampoo,

washing powder, for example) and then select four particular brands of that product (for instant coffee these might be Gold Blend, Kenco, Café Hag and Nescafé; for washing powders they might be Ariel, Persil, Bold and Radion). Then analyse the different ways each brand is targeted towards its particular audience segment.

Consider:

- how each brand has its own 'unique' or special image
- the particular audience profile for each brand and how it is different from the other brands.

Then:

- select individual advertisements and using semiotic analysis (see p. 30) identify how their target audience determines the construction of the advertisements
- identify how each advertisement is placed in the media to reach particular target groups.

Packaging can also include the way in which merchandising is used to promote a brand's image. Pop groups will often have T-shirts, posters and other merchandising that can be sold to fans to help reinforce the band's particular image. Merchandising is an increasingly important part of a film's promotion, from the release of the soundtrack album to a tie-in with a fast-food chain such as McDonald's. Increasingly films are marketed as 'event' films – films that everyone feels that they should see, in particular those members of the potential cinema audience who perhaps only visit the cinema once or twice a year.

ACTIVITY...

When you next go to the cinema, or indeed when you next watch a video/DVD, you will probably see a teaser – a sort mini-trailer for a film that is due to be released at cinemas some time in the future – usually a summer or Christmas blockbuster. The teaser will be short, often consisting merely of a short sequence from the film (which may not even have been edited properly yet).

Once you have noted the teaser, you should then monitor as closely as possible the way in which the film is advertised in the period leading up to its release in this country. This will involve watching out for trailers, posters, articles in newspapers and magazines, features in programmes on television or the radio, and indeed even on the website of the company that is handling the film. A worksheet is provided below.

WORKSHEET FOR ANALYSING THE MARKETING OF FILMS

Before the film is released:

- How is the film first brought to our attention?
- Do you, at an early stage, feel that it is a film that you might want to see when it is finally released? Why?
- What sort of publicity does the pre-release activity engender?
- What, if any, covert marketing takes place? For example, do the stars appear on television chat-shows? Are there articles and photographs in newspapers regarding the film and its particular features – for example the amount of money spent on special effects?
- Is the film sold on its genre, stars or director?
- Does it remind you of anything else you have seen or have heard about?
- What other media texts are associated with the film – for example a theme song released as a single, or a soundtrack album?
- Where are the posters and other publicity material to be found?
- Does the positioning of the publicity tell you anything about the likely audience for the film?

When the film is released:

- What sort of release pattern does it receive?
- Does it simply arrive at your local cinema or is there some kind of localised campaign to announce its arrival?
- Do local radio stations, record shops and other organisations get involved in the marketing of the film?
- How much publicity is available in the newspapers, both national and local?
- How much of the pre-release activity is created simply by word of mouth – perhaps a free preview to an invited audience who will then, it is hoped, tell all their friends about it?

Price

Price is linked to a product's value. Value can mean different things to different people; for example, some people may value having the most up-to-date hi-fi equipment and so be prepared to pay more for particular items; others may value 'freshness' or a product that is environmentally friendly. One person may place great value on having clothes that have a certain designer label, whereas another person will be unwilling to pay the extra money that, for example, a pair of Dolce & Gabbana jeans costs. Often companies use advertising and marketing to try to add value to their brands in order to increase their profit. For example, in the case of Lucozade, mentioned on p. 260, the added value was seen in terms of health and vitality and enabled the producers of Lucozade to sell the product at a higher price than before.

Another aspect of price is the way in which consumers are seemingly offered a 'special deal' or bargain, perhaps through discounts such as 'introductory offers' or 'three for the price of two'. The 'giveaways' on the front of many lifestyle magazines can also be seen to come into this category.

Promotion

The promotion and marketing of a brand or product is often done using covert advertising techniques such as sponsorship, product placement or public relations. For example, Orange's sponsorship of the Glastonbury pop festival is seen by the company as a good way of getting its products known to a large group of potential customers. Covert advertising is therefore any type of promotion that is not direct advertising but is an undercover or stealthy way of raising the image or profile of a brand or name and helping it to become recognisable and memorable to its target audience.

Companies are keen to sponsor particular events that develop a positive association for their products. Recent examples have included tobacco companies sponsoring sporting events such as Formula 1, and NatWest Bank's sponsorship of test cricket. Sponsorship of television programmes has been allowed in Britain only since the 1990 Broadcasting Act. It is the role of Ofcom to ensure that sponsors do not exert too much influence on the editorial content of the programmes they sponsor and that the sponsorship is clearly signalled to viewers. There are certain types of programme that cannot be sponsored, for instance the news. The most popular programmes for sponsors are, not surprisingly, those programmes that attract the biggest audience, for example Cadbury's sponsorship of *Coronation Street* or Domino Pizza's sponsorship of *The Simpsons* on Sky. Other sponsorship deals may target specific groups; for example, Playstation 2 presumably sponsors the Worldwide Wrestling Federation because of the programme's audience profile.

Place

Place is where a product or brand is both made known and made available to consumers. All brands are aimed at specific target audiences and advertising and marketing try to bring these brands to the attention of their potential customers. The brand must also be available for purchase by potential customers. This may mean using particular outlets, such as shops or websites, aimed at the target audience or it may mean direct selling via mail-order.

Direct-mail advertisers spend a lot of time trying to target the correct people. In addition to buying lists from other organisations, they use 'geo-demographic' databases that combine geographic information with population information. The Acorn Classification of Residential Neighbourhoods categorises people by their postcodes, making assumptions about income level, social grade and so on by the street, road or avenue in which people live and the type of housing found there. Britain's post-codes are divided into different groups varying from Higher Income to Poor Council Estates.

Direct-mail advertisers also use people's names to make assumptions about age. For instance, people called Violet, Ethel, Arthur or Cyril are assumed to be old-age pensioners, whilst those called Sharon, Tracey, Gavin or Daniel are probably in their late teens or early twenties. Names can also provide clues as to the social grade and disposable income of people.

Research amongst advertising companies suggests that it is important to have adver-tisements placed not only in the correct commercial break or publication but also in the correct position within that particular commercial break or publication. Most magazines and newspapers have higher rates for particular spots such as the inside covers or back pages but will also have different rates for right- or left-hand pages or for different sections of the publication. On radio and television, being the first in a sequence of advertisements in a commercial break is often viewed as the most effective positioning. On television, particular advertisements will often appear at both the beginning and end of the commercial break to try to create more 'impact'. Increasingly, themed digital television channels enable advertisers and sponsors to target particular niche groups in the same way that magazines target readers interested in, for example, cookery, cars or holidays (see section on segmentation, p. 213).

COVERT ADVERTISING

'Product placement' is the term for the placement of particular brands of products in high-profile situations, for example the character Rachel from *Friends* working for Ralph Lauren and Ralph Lauren himself appearing in episodes of the show. One of the best-known examples is the accessories that feature in the *James Bond* films (Omega watch, Aston Martin or BMW cars, Smirnoff vodka, to name but a few). Companies will pay film producers to have their products featured in films. It is now an established part of the financing of Hollywood films, and there are companies whose dedicated job it is to guarantee product placement in films for particular brands.

Product placement on British television is supposed to be banned, but the days are gone when the BBC covered brand labels with sticky tape to hide the real name of the product. There have been suggestions that certain brands do appear in programmes. It could be argued, however, that if a programme such as *EastEnders* is to appear realistic, then perhaps a packet of Kellogg's Cornflakes should be seen on the kitchen table at breakfast time. There has also been considerable debate about the BBC showing sponsored sporting events and so covertly carrying advertising. As nearly all major sporting events need sponsorship money it is almost impossible for television companies to avoid promoting the companies; however, the BBC has used its influence in the past to have cigarette or alcohol sponsorship of sporting events such as snooker banned.

Another means of covert advertising, celebrity endorsement is often used to give a particular brand or product 'added value' or particular ideological meaning by associating it with well-known stars or personalities. Many sports stars such as David Beckham command large sums of money not only for their sporting skills but also through their sponsorship of particular products. According to some commentators, David Beckham's move in 2003 from Manchester United to Real Madrid was as much about marketing and his commercial value to prospective sponsors such as Nike and Adidas as it was to do with his quality as a professional footballer. Before his move Beckham already had sponsorship deals with both Adidas and Pepsi, as did Real Madrid, whereas Manchester United was sponsored by Nike, rival to Adidas. Real Madrid will now take 50 per cent of all David Beckham's future endorsements.

Part of Beckham's appeal for Real Madrid was that both they and their sponsors Adidas could use the Beckham image in the profitable Asian market, where Beckham is very popular. In effect the football star and the football club are both brands, brands that complement each other and are being sold to fans around the world.

Beckham is seen as a lifestyle product, as someone who epitomises the fulfilment of a certain dream of success. According to an interview in *The Times*, Simon Fuller, the former Spice Girls manager who is now responsible for promoting the Beckhams, 'the Beckham brand is about aspiration and family values, the couple who came from nothing to achieve their dreams'. Simon Fuller has also said that when the Beckham children are older they may likewise take part in commercial projects that give out the image of a solid, clean-cut and highly desirable family (*The Times*, 24 July 2003).

Part of David Beckham's success is that he can be seen as an 'ordinary' person, someone like us, who has managed through his talent not only to acquire lots of money but also to marry a glamorous wife, own a large house in the country and be a good father. He is estimated to be worth around £200 million and has had a range of personal sponsorship deals with companies including Pepsi, Vodafone, Brylcreem, Police sunglasses, Castrol and Marks & Spencer (see Figure 4.4). Despite this wealth and lifestyle, Beckham is still seen in some way to be ordinary (like you and me), living out our fantasies for us; if he can do it, so can we! He has also managed to retain his image as a male role model despite claims that he wears Victoria Beckham's underwear and the fact that he has been photographed wearing a sarong.

Figure 4.4 *David Beckham arrives at a photo call to launch his new range of clothes for Marks & Spencer, 19 September 2002. Source: Popperfoto/Reuters/Ian Hodgson.*

Part of the success of any star or celebrity is their use, and manipulation, of public relations. Like spin doctors (see p. 288), public relations figures such as Simon Fuller, Max Clifford and Mathew Freud control media access to their clients, ensure that any publicity or story is positive and offer guidance and advice on how their clients should present themselves before the media. This may involve mediating between celebrity magazines, such as *Heat*, *Hello* and *OK!*, that want to feature a celebrity's new home or wedding, or vetoing which restaurants, parties, premiers and so on the celebrities will attend. Publicists may also approve the questions and photographs that are used in a feature and may, in some cases, agree the words a publication uses about their clients. Not all publicity is successful, however. Anthea Turner received much criticism for her wedding photographs, which showed her and her husband eating Cadbury's new Snowflakes. Known as 'flakegate', it is now impossible to get permission to reproduce any of those photographs for books such as this one. David Beckham too is very cautious about how his image is used and there are strict controls on when and where his image may be reproduced.

ACTIVITY...

Try to find examples of how celebrities such as the Beckhams are marketed and promoted. Look for images and/or stories that reflect their 'ordinariness' (for example as a mother and father) as well as their 'extraordinariness', not only as a footballer and singer but also, again, as a mother and father (for example David taking time off from training at Manchester United because baby Brooklyn was ill). Think about where and how these stories appear.

- Why are they part of the news agenda?
- What are their 'news values'?
- Why would tabloid newspapers and celebrity magazines want to feature these stories?
- In what ways do these stories identify the Beckhams as a particular brand and as being different to other similar celebrity couples?

Try to identify those stories that might have been 'planted' by PR companies and those that might have occurred as part of normal news-gathering.

Apart from the youth market, which is most directly addressed by stars and celebrities such as the Beckhams, the 'grey' market is also increasingly important to advertisers as the British population's average age increases and more people are living longer and have greater disposable incomes.

Below is a report produced by Key Note, a firm that specialises in market intelligence. Read the report and then try to find examples of where the 'over-40s consumer' is being targeted. The report highlights certain key products, for example 'functional food' and 'new tourism'.

The Over-40s Consumer

One of the most important demographic changes facing the UK – and indeed all industrialised countries – is the ageing population, with people living longer and healthier lives.

Social groups such as empty nesters and post-family are also on the increase, which gives the over-40 population as a whole a higher level of disposable income and more leisure time than ever before.

The traditional image of a middle-aged or elderly person does not fit a person of similar age today. Today, those in middle age are self confident, more in control of their lives, and reject aspects that society overall attributes to growing old. These 'modern old' consumers are flexible and enjoy change, and as a result there is a high level of acceptance of new products and services. Personal development is high on the agenda of such consumers, who are very aware of political and social issues, and look for creative personal challenges and new experiences which they believe will enrich their lives.

However, it is vital to understand that this consumer sector cannot be bundled into one group under the heading 'the ageing consumer'. Although this group shares common traits, within it there are many diverse sub-groups. The over-40s group consists of many generations, which have diverse opinions and attitudes due to the social and political conditions they have faced. For example, the generations that experienced World War Two and the hardships that came with it are very different from the generation that experienced The Beatles, hippies and flower power. Trends evident among those aged over 60 today will have changed radically by the time those who are currently aged between 40 and 50 reach that age. This makes it extremely important for marketers to be aware of lifestyle shifts if they are to develop effective marketing strategies and identify new emerging market segments.

The growing expectation among over-40 consumers that food and beverages, in addition to providing nutrition and refreshment, will also make them healthier and help ward off the chronic conditions often associated with ageing, is giving rise to new markets in the food and beverage industry. As a result of these new opportunities, functional food and 'nutraceuticals' containing ingredients said to grant health benefits beyond basic nutrition and refreshment, are currently proving particularly attractive to this consumer group.

Over-40 consumers are looking to avoid suffering the same health conditions that afflicted their parents and maximise their well being. As a result, there has been a rapid surge of interest in fitness, self-care and nutrition. At the same time, these consumers have adopted a fast-paced and demanding lifestyle that leaves little room for compromise, and have specific expectations that they are reluctant to change. The most important are the requirements for convenience, information, taste and innovation.

The success of functional foods can be attributed to many factors: their ability to deliver a lifestyle benefit to consumers without dramatically changing behaviour patterns; the increasing cost of healthcare; government encouragement towards self-health maintenance; consumer health awareness and choice; industry seeking new opportunities; scientific evidence of health benefits of certain ingredients; and improvement of ingredients, products and processing technology.

The UK functional food market is relatively underdeveloped, with the main obstacle to greater success being legislation. Despite that, looking at trends within the industry, Key Note predicts that the functional foods market will continue to grow.

Another sector of the industry facing change due to trends among over-40 consumers is the travel industry. New trends provide the industry with new opportunities. Over-40 consumers comprise several sub-groups, which have very different travel expectations. The reason is that this large group contains several generations with diverse needs, and it would be unwise to consider all consumers aged over 40 as 'mature travellers' without investigating the nature of current trends.

Although the tourist industry is still dominated by package holidays, companies are increasingly turning to creating holidays for a consumer who is environmentally aware, individualistic and flexible, and who will not be satisfied with a standardised, mass-market product. There are indications that the number of consumers who create their own itineraries by researching the possibilities via the Internet or with the help of travel agents or operators is increasing rapidly.

The holiday has become an extremely personalised experience, with the industry having to take into account various preferences of the consumers who comprise this lucrative market. Over-40 consumers who belong to the 'new tourism' era want more than beaches, a tan and nightlife from their holidays. Those in this group relish independence and have the need to personalise their holidays. Most importantly, they have the know-how necessary to do so successfully.

The travel industry is suffering in the aftermath of the terrorist attacks on the US on 11th September 2001. This may have sparked off long-term repercussions, the true extent of which the industry can only speculate [on] for the time being. Whether consumer confidence in air travel can be restored to its former level, and whether consumers can be encouraged to take holidays abroad, depends on the future political and economic environment.

However, in the long term Key Note forecasts a bright future for this specific market. As many people remain concerned about flying, it is very likely that the domestic holiday market will expand and thrive. The success of the market depends on how the industry responds to the present situation. The introduction of more competitive and attractive products, as well as increased advertising and promotion, will definitely stimulate interest in travel among consumers aged over 40.

(Key Note, <http://www.keynote.co.uk>)

Consider the travel programmes on television and look at how they are addressing the type of audience described by Key Note. Take into account which celebrities are featured in the holidays; for example, Richard Whiteley from *Countdown* recently took a trip to Bangkok for the BBC's *Holiday* programme. He is the host of the Channel Four tea-time quiz, which is supposedly popular with the 'grey market' television audience. Thora Hird often used to appear in advertisements shown in the commercial breaks in the mid-afternoons recommending different types of walk-in baths and stair lifts.

- What other types of adverts are shown around programmes such as *Countdown* that are aimed at this type of audience?
- Which other celebrities are seen on television either in advertisements or in the programmes themselves promoting certain types of lifestyles, products or brands to the over-40s market?
- Can you identify other examples of the ways in which interest in travel amongst over-40s consumers is being stimulated through the introduction of 'more competitive and attractive products' and increased advertising and promotion?

There is also an increasing number of magazines aimed at the affluent ageing consumer. Re-read the section on lifestyle magazines (p. 152) and consider how these types of magazines promote a particular lifestyle and what, if any, codes and conventions they have in common with each other.

Measuring 'success'

The final stage in any advertising or marketing process is to carry out some kind of research to check how successful the campaign has been and to see if it is getting the correct message across to the target group in the most effective (and economical) way. One of the best indicators of this is, of course, increased sales. Gold Blend claim that the sales of their coffee rose by 40 per cent over the five years of their romantic soap-opera series of advertisements.

It is claimed that sales of the Renault Clio rose by 300 per cent over the three years that the 'Papa and Nicole' series of advertisements ran. Some twenty-three million people are supposed to have watched the first broadcast of the final advertisement, in which Nicole runs off with Bob Mortimer. This example of intertextuality (see p. 70) is a direct copy of the ending of the film *The Graduate*, ironically a film that many of those twenty-three million would have been too

young to have seen in the cinema. These advertisements were shown only in Britain because they played on British ideas of 'Frenchness'. They seem to have become part of our popular culture as well as an interesting example of representation (see p. 61).

We tend only to hear about the successful campaigns such as those mentioned above (and others such as Levi 501s, Guinness, and so on). The failures are usually kept very quiet.

Another measurement of the 'success' of an advertisement or marketing campaign is to measure its 'impact'. This is often done by asking viewers and listeners what advertisements they can recall recently having seen or heard.

In 1981 Saatchi & Saatchi carried out the 'Ironing Board Study', in which they asked 300 housewives to bring their ironing to the researchers' homes. The housewives thought that they were trying out a new starch, but the advertising agency played a radio tape in the background during the fifteen minutes that they were asked to iron. The radio tape was specially created and contained a mixture of advertisements and programming. At the end of the session the housewives were questioned about the starch but then also 'spontaneously' asked questions about what they remembered hearing on the radio. The most successful advertisements were recalled by about a third of the housewives, the least successful by about a tenth. This and other research suggests that listeners do 'take in' messages from the radio even when concentrating on other activities. However, in general television is seen as the most effective in terms of recall.

NOTEBOX

It is worth spending some time thinking about the criteria for 'successful' advertisements. In a television poll held in 2000 of the 'greatest' television advertisements, the Guinness 'Surfing' advertisement came top. It is interesting to speculate why so many people thought that it was 'great'. It certainly caused a lot of comment, but many people seemed unable to explain fully what the advert was about. Perhaps this is the key to its success – the polysemic nature of its message (see p. 33). Second in the same poll were the Smash 'Martians' advertisements. It would be worth trying to measure the extent to which the success of either of these advertisements will have significantly increased the sales of their respective products.

Some adverts win awards but do not increase sales. The 'Talking Creatures' ('Creature Comforts') advertisements that made Aardman Animation so popular in the 1980s were advertisements for electricity but, according to Aardman, are frequently referred to as 'those gas advertisements'. There are very few advertisements that are totally successful in the sense that they are liked by members of the advertising industry, win awards, catch the popular imagination and increase the sales of the product. Jack Dee's 'widget' advertisements with the penguins for John Smith's beer is one such example, as it both won awards and increased the sales of the beer. (See <http://www.btaa.co.uk/flash. html> and <http://www.radioacademy.org/markprom/pams2002/pamawards.html> for recent award-winning advertisements).

Increasingly advertising is aimed not just at boosting sales but also at maintaining public awareness of existing brands in the face of increasing competition from new products and services.

ADVERTISING AND AUDIENCE

Much of the success of advertising depends upon getting the right advertisement in front of the right audience. Much of the research discussed in Part 2, on media audiences, reflects advertisers' concerns to target the correct audience.

In Part 2 we looked at some of the ways in which advertisers try to identify or categorise audiences. In the advertising world there are new methods being developed constantly as advertisers try to become more sophisticated and accurate in their targeting. (See, for example, Figure 4.5.)

The cinema is also a good source of effective advertising because the advertisers will have an idea of the age make-up of the audience by the type of film being shown – whether it is a certificate 12A comedy such as *Dumb and Dumber* or an 18 certificate such as *Secretary*.

Figure 4.5 *Harnessing the effectiveness of radio for young adults*

Why is radio so valuable for reaching young adults?

■ 78% weekly reach

■ 16 hours a week spent listening

■ trusted more than any other medium

■ . . . and more . . .

Radio reaches a high numbers of young adults

Commercial radio has consolidated its domination of 15–34s –78% are tuning in each week, rising to 93% across a four-weekly period.
Average time spent listening each week is 16 hours per listener.
Commercial radio accounts for a dominant 61% share of total listening amongst this audience, giving it a strong 20-point lead over the BBC. (*Source: RAJAR to December 2001*)

Listening amongst young adults continues to grow

Since the beginning of 1999 total time spent listening to Commercial Radio by 15–34s has grown by 7%. (*Source: RAJAR*)

Weekday evenings is the fastest area of growth for Commercial Radio – up 17% across the same period, reflecting a longer-term trend in the relationships young people are having with media. (*Source: RAJAR*)

This is also the best time to reach younger listeners – 15–24s are most receptive 8–11 p.m. Monday–Friday, when they experience high levels of engagement and enjoyment. (*Source: ROAR 2001*)

Young adults spend more time with radio

Radio occupies a large proportion of media time, particularly for young adults – 16–34s spend 35% of their media day with radio, 12% more than adults on average. (*Source*: Radio Days 2)

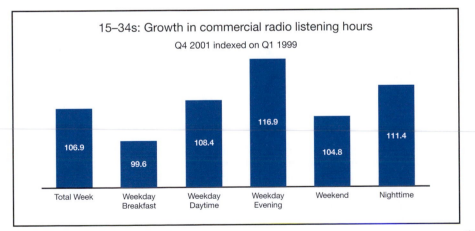

continued

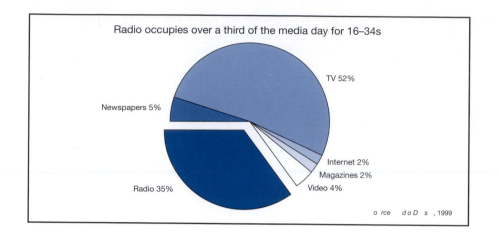

Radio is a trusted medium for young adults
Radio listeners have a very close, personal relationship with their station, hence they trust what they hear on the radio much more than what they see on television or read in the newspapers.

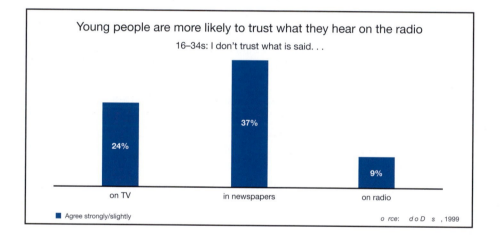

Young people feel that the advertisements on radio are more personal and relevant to them and also that they are more likely to 'stick'. Radio advertisements bring brands to life by adding character and, importantly for this audience, are good at generating hype. (*Source: ROAR 2001*)

[. . .]

Radio is intrusive
Radio has low advertisement avoidance levels – a study by Initiative showed that advertisements on radio are less actively avoided than in other media. The challenge for reaching young adults then is to exploit this lack of avoidance by ensuring the creative approach is one that appeals to them.

Radio is a real-time medium – listeners sit through the advertisements, making them a captive audience. Hence advertisements can reach the 'out of market' audience as well as those that are 'in-market' for your product, whilst scheduling advertisements at certain times of the day enables you to reach your audience at a relevant time.

Radio complements young people's busy lifestyles

As an auxiliary medium, radio allows listeners to tune in whilst doing something else – this is important for young adults where competition for their media and leisure time is high. Radio is the perfect accompaniment to many 'youth' activities, such as doing homework, getting ready to go out, playing video/computer games.

Internet usage is particularly high amongst young adults and radio provides the perfect accompaniment to this – half of 15–34s are regular users of the Internet, with this age group being over 60% more likely than the average adult to visit a station's website and to listen to the radio online. (*Source: RAJAR to December 2001*)

More than half of young adults listen to the radio in the car. (*Source: RAJAR to December 2001*)

Despite the fact that they are often doing something else whilst listening, 15–34s are 46% more likely than the average adult to agree that they 'Often notice adverts on radio'. (*Source: TGI 2001*)

Why are young audiences so valuable?

- There are nearly 16 million young adults in the UK today, with 15–34s accounting for around a third of the total population. Nearly half of 15–34s work full time, whilst 24% are still studying.

- 'Live for today' is the motto for many young adults – they are more likely to do things on the spur of the moment and less likely to worry about the future.

- Despite having yet to reach their full earning potential, many young adults have a high disposable income, which they spend readily, often spending more than they earn – they are less likely to be worried about being in debt and only 35% have a pension and/or a mortgage.

- Keeping up with the latest fashion is very important to image-conscious young adults – they are nearly 70% more likely than adults in general to claim to spend lots on clothes.

- 15–34s are also early adopters of new technology – 78% have a mobile phone, over half own a PC and they are 35% more likely to own a DVD player.

Why are they so difficult to reach via television?

- Young adults are now spending less time watching television – average hours of commercial television watched per head for 16–34s have fallen 4% since last year, standing at 14.9 hours in Q4 2001. 16–34 impacts continue a downward trend, falling 14% year-on-year in January 2002, with ITV and Channel Four losing 30% and 26%, respectively. (*Source: BARB*)

- The net effect of the long-term decline in audiences, seemingly exacerbated by the introduction of a new BARB panel, is raising even more questions about the cost-effectiveness of using television to talk to young adults.

- Internet usage amongst this audience is high – 15–34s are 40% more likely than adults to be regular users of the Internet. (*Source: RAJAR to December 2001*)

Figure 4.5 *Harnessing the effectiveness of radio for young adults. Source: ROAR 2001 and Radio Days 2, 1999.*

Most advertising agencies have websites (see the *Guardian Media Guide* or The Knowledge, <http://www.theknowledgeonline.com>, for details) that promote their latest and most successful campaigns. Contact one and ask for details of their organisation and some of their campaigns.

Part of the difficulty advertisers face is that quite often we, the audience, are trying to avoid advertisements. We may do this by throwing away direct mail without opening it, by arriving late at the cinema before the main film has started but after the advertisements have been shown, by 'zapping' through advertisements on videos, DVDs or between television programmes, or by 'skimming' through newspapers and magazines. The Radio Advertising Bureau claims that radio is the one medium where we do not actively avoid the advertisements (see case study on p. 257). We may not like them and may get bored with them, but they suggest that the advertisements are treated largely like the rest of the radio output. Radio, according to the Radio Advertising Bureau, is a good 'auxiliary' medium to complement campaigns running in other 'primary' media such as television (see p. 140 for an explanation of primary and secondary media).

Choose a well-known company such as Marks & Spencer, Gap or Levis Strauss & Co., or one that is currently running a particular campaign. Try to 'deconstruct' the campaign:

- Using the categories identified in Part 2, on media audiences (p. 107), try to identify who the target audience is and what the 'theme' or message behind the campaign is.
- List all the media where the campaign appears (apart from the more obvious media sources, this may include billboards, the cinema and websites).
- Explain why the advertisements appear where they do.
- If possible, visit the shops and see what 'point-of-sale' advertising is taking place, for example displays in the shop, leaflets by the check-outs.
- Perhaps the company will send you some information if you contact it or it may have a website giving details of the campaign (see, for example, <http://www.rubyourself.co.uk>).
- You may be able to estimate approximately the amount of money the company has spent (although this can be difficult because rates tend to be commercially sensitive).
- Carry out a survey amongst the target audience to see how effective this campaign has been. You may want to consider the audience's awareness of the campaign and products as well as their intention to purchase any of the products.

ADVERTISING AND REGULATION

The degree to which advertising is regulated and controlled gives some idea of the importance, and potential influence, that it is considered to have. There is a range of organisations whose role is to make sure advertisements are not causing offence or breaking the rules. Many parts of the industry also have their own 'advisory' codes on what is acceptable in terms of advertising. The BACC (Broadcast Advertising Clearance Centre, <http://www.bacc.org.uk>), for instance, is a non-statutory body that takes responsibility for 'checking' all television and radio advertisements, although it is Ofcom (the Office of Communication, <http://www.ofcom.org.uk>) that has the legal responsibility for regulating all commercial radio advertising. Up until 2003, when it was replaced by Ofcom (see section on regulation, p. 204), the ITC (Independent Television Commission) regulated advertising on commercial terrestrial television, cable and satellite.

Terrestrial television advertising is limited to an average of seven minutes per hour during the day and 7.5 minutes per hour during the evening peak time. On satellite and cable channels the average is nine minutes per hour. On some types of programming, for example religious services, currently no advertising is allowed.

There have been strict controls on the advertising of health products, medicines and medical services since commercial television was introduced in 1955. However, over the years there has been a gradual loosening of the restrictions. As a result of concerns over AIDS (acquired immune deficiency syndrome) in the 1980s advertisements for condoms became acceptable.

Ofcom is proposing that some of the restrictions on the types of product that can be advertised should be lifted. These include escort agencies, private detectives, treatments for hair loss, pregnancy testing services and hypnotists. It is also considering allowing more 'authoritative' celebrities, for example newscasters, to endorse products and doctors to endorse drugs.

The ASA (Advertising Standards Authority), an industry organisation, regulates advertising in magazines, the cinema, posters and direct mail. It operates a voluntary code (the CAP code, available at <http://www.asa.org.uk>) and is responsible for the 'Legal, Decent, Honest & Truthful' campaign.

BENETTON

Any discussion of advertising has to acknowledge the impact that the campaigns of Benetton have had over the years, whether it be its images of a newborn baby, a dying AIDS patient or Mafia victims.

The AIDS patient advertisement was refused by several magazines, including *Marie Claire*, *Woman's Journal* and *Elle*, as well as *J-17* and *19*. This advertisement, like many others, was referred to the ASA, which recommended that this, like many of Benetton's other advertisements, be withdrawn. However, the controversy itself gave Benetton plenty of publicity.

These campaigns have succeeded in making Benetton a household name, which was the intention of Luciano Benetton and Oliviero Toscani, the founders of the campaigns. Their advertisements have generated a lot of debate, and you can make your own contribution to this debate via the Benetton website (<http://www.benetton.com>).

CHILDREN

One of the most tightly regulated and controversial areas of advertising concerns children. There are many restrictions on the content of advertising aimed at children, the types of advertising that can be seen by children, as well as guidelines on how children may be portrayed in advertisements.

Ofcom stipulates that advertisements should not mislead, particularly in relation to games and toys. Advertisements must not make 'direct exhortations' to children to ask their parents to buy products for them and should not imply that a child will be 'inferior in some way or liable to be held in contempt or ridicule' if they do not own the product.

Many of these rules are the result of parents complaining about 'pester power', the amount of pressure put upon them as a result of advertising aimed at children, particularly in the run-up to Christmas. Toys may be demonstrated 'in action' on television but in real life often require additional components or perhaps need expensive batteries to operate in the manner shown on television.

There are restrictions on the types of advertisements that may be transmitted around children's programmes. Products that may not be advertised at these times include alcohol, liqueur chocolates, matches, medicines, lotteries, and 15 and 18 certificate films. Ofcom also stipulates that 'children in advertisements should be reasonably well-mannered and well-behaved'.

The advertising industry is aware of these concerns and debates surrounding advertisements aimed at children and there are several industry-based initiatives that attempt to promote a more responsible attitude to children's advertising. (See, for example, Mediasmart <http://www.mediasmart.org.uk> and the Advertising Association's site <http://www.childrensprogramme.org>.) There are also several academic surveys that focus on the issue of advertising and children; see, for example, <http://www.aber.ac.uk/media/Documents/short/toyads.html> or <http://www.cardiff.ac.uk/jomec/research/child/Links.html>.

In October 1999 Barnardo's launched a newspaper campaign that caused some controversy. Figure 4.6 shows one of two advertisements featured in the campaign that were referred to the ASA. The other one, 'Martin Ward', featured a boy on top of a high-rise block of flats about to jump off. According to Barnardo's website at the time:

> the current communications campaign challenges outdated views of Britain's biggest children's charity. It positions the organisation in the forefront of the fight to build better futures for disadvantaged, abused and troubled children. Though the advertisements are hard-hitting, the message is one of hope – that Barnardo's can help children overcome childhood deprivation and avoid futures like these. While Barnardo's work has evolved to encompass all the key issues affecting the

lives of disadvantaged children, young people and their families, the public image of the organisation has not kept pace with this development. Research shows that the majority of people in the UK retain an essentially historical view of Barnardo's. They continue to see it as a charity running 'orphanages', or large-scale residential childcare facilities. The image of the organisation remains rooted in its past, epitomised by the 'cottage collecting boxes' once a feature of millions of homes. (<http://www.barnardos.org.uk>)

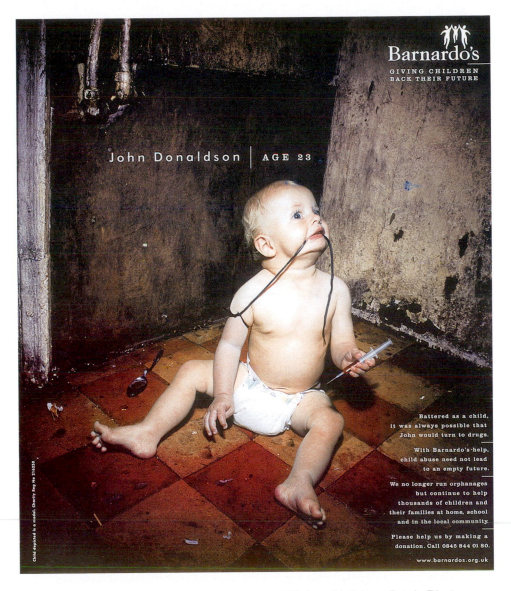

Figure 4.6 *Barnardo's advertisement, 'Giving Children Back Their Future'. Source: Barnado's.*

This is the ASA's adjudication of the Barnardo's advertisement shown in Figure 4.6:

Media: national press

Agency: Bartle Bogle Hegarty

Sector: Non-commercial

Complaints from: Nationwide (28)

Complaint: Objections to an advertisement in the *Guardian*, the *Independent*, the *Independent on Sunday*, the *Observer*, the *Scotsman*, *Scotland on Sunday* and *The Times* for a children's charity. It featured a baby sitting alone in squalid surroundings. Dirt covered the floor and walls; in his teeth the baby held a cord, which was tightened round his right arm to make a tourniquet; in his left hand he held a syringe as if to inject heroin. The headline stated 'John Donaldson Age 23'; the body copy stated 'Battered as a child, it was always possible that John would turn to drugs. With Barnardo's help, child abuse need not lead to an empty future. Although we no longer run orphanages, we continue to help thousands of children and their families at home, school and in the local community'. The complainants objected that the advertisement was shocking and offensive.

The advertisers believed the advertisement complied with the Codes. They said it was part of a campaign to raise awareness of their preventative work with children and young people; the campaign was designed to make people reconsider their opinions about Barnardo's work and the subjects depicted in each advertisement. The advertisers argued that they had not intended merely to shock. They said they had taken the precaution of researching the campaign twice among their target audience of ABC1 adults aged 35 to 55 and their supporters, staff and service users. They submitted the research findings, which they believed showed most people understood the advertisement's message and found its approach effective in changing opinions about Barnardo's work. The advertisers maintained that, because the consequences of drug addiction were potentially devastating, the stark image was justified as a means of raising public awareness of the potential dangers for disadvantaged children; they believed it was an effective way of making the point that Barnardo's could help keep them safe. Their consumer research acknowledged that some people found images of alcoholism or drug abuse upsetting. They nevertheless maintained that an image based on the innocence of a child and potential pain in adult life communicated the message that Barnardo's was a contemporary charity with modern perspectives on child development. The advertisers submitted extracts from published research, which showed that disadvantaged and abused children were particularly vulnerable to emotional and behavioural problems in later life; they provided recent survey results that showed that parents and children found drugs worrying and frightening. They asserted that the child depicted had not been put at risk and that the advertisement was made with full parental awareness and consent. The advertisers said they had monitored public responses to their advertisement; they had received more supportive responses than complaints. The *Independent* said they had received less than five complaints and considered that the advertisement would not cause serious or widespread offence to their readers. the *Guardian* said they believed their readers would understand the advertisers' message and they had received no complaints. The *Scotland on Sunday* said they regarded drugs very seriously but considered that Barnardo's advertisement was compelling and justified. They said they had received no complaints. *The Times*, the *Scotsman*, the *Independent on Sunday* and the *Observer* did not respond. The Authority noted the advertisement had offended or distressed some readers. It nevertheless acknowledged that the advertisers had intended to convey a serious and important message. The Authority considered that they had acted responsibly by conducting research among their target audience to ensure the message was understood and unlikely to shock or offend. The Authority noted the picture of drug abuse was directly related to the advertisers' preventative work with children and considered that the target audience was likely to interpret the image in the context of the accompanying text. The Authority accepted the advertisers' argument that they had not intended merely to shock. It considered that, because the advertisers had used the image to raise public awareness of the seriousness of drug abuse and the action that could be taken to prevent it, the advertisement was unlikely to cause either serious or widespread offence or undue distress and was acceptable.

Adjudication: Complaints not upheld.

ACTIVITY . . .

Access the Ofcom website (<http://www.ofcom.org.uk>) and look through the Ofcom code of practice. You can then look at some of the recent cases reported and the decisions reached.

ADVERTISING EFFECTS

One of the most important debates surrounding advertising is the influence that advertisements may have both on us, the audience, and on those who rely on advertising for their income, namely the media producers.

It is very difficult to assess the effect of advertising and the extent to which people are affected by the advertisements to which they are exposed. In the section on media audiences we looked at some of the difficulties that arise in the case of moral panics and in trying to isolate the effect the media may have from other influences on us – such as parents, education, peer groups or religion. This is perhaps even more difficult in the case of advertising, as we often are not consciously aware of advertisements – they are frequently a tertiary medium (see p. 140) that we may skim past in a magazine or newspaper or fast-forward through on a video.

One of the pieces of evidence to suggest that advertising works is the fact that companies spend so much money on advertising. According to some commentators, up to one-third of the cost of a bar of soap or up to 40 per cent of the price of a tube of toothpaste may represent advertising costs. Remember that, for example, £17 billion is spent on marketing and advertising each year.

ARGUMENTS IN SUPPORT OF ADVERTISING

- It finances a whole range of media (see Part 2, media audiences, p. 107) and provides us with a wide range of choice in terms of the media available to us.
- It can be seen as an essential part of a modern-day, consumerist society and is a very effective way of informing us about new products.
- It stimulates consumption, which benefits industry, increases employment and leads to economic growth.
- Over the years advertising has been a very effective way for government and its various agencies to provide public information about safe sex and the use of condoms, the dangers of drinking and driving or, more mundanely, changing telephone codes. The government is one of the major advertisers in this country.
- Sponsorship is an important source of funding for many sporting and artistic events.
- The advertising industry provides many people with employment.

The media fix their advertising rates according to the size of their audience and its age and social profiles. The rates are highly negotiable depending on numerous factors, including possible large discounts. Figure 4.7 gives some examples of 2001 rates.

ARGUMENTS USED TO CRITICISE ADVERTISING

These are perhaps a little more subtle and complicated, as the following list suggests:

- Advertising creates false hopes and expectations.
- It works on our insecurities.
- It promotes unrealistic and dangerous role models.
- It can influence the content of media texts.
- Advertising revenue can direct programming.
- Advertising revenue is the foundation of new newspapers.

Let us examine each of these allegations in turn.

Figure 4.7 *Sample advertising rates at November 2001. Source: Advertising Association Information Sheet no. 6.*

Daily Mail full page (black and white)	£31,500
Daily Mail full page (colour)	£45,612
Daily Telegraph full page (black and white)	£41,500
Daily Telegraph full page (colour)	£50,750
Sunday Times full page (black and white)	£54,500
TV Times full page (black and white)	£13,700
TV Times full page (colour)	£18,500
J-17 full page (black and white)	£4,900
J-17 full page (colour)	£7,930
Yorkshire Post full page (black and white)	£6,904
Carlton 30 second weekday peak time spot (19.26hrs–23.30hrs)	£30,500
Grampian TV 30 second weekday peak time spot (17.15hrs–23.00hrs) 30 second spot (each day, one week) in London Cinemas (530 screens) 30 second spot (each day, one week) in Lancashire Cinemas (250 screens)	£870 £25,256 £7,000
BRMB (Birmingham Radio) 30 second spot, Wednesday–Friday (16.00hrs–19.00hrs)	£140
Virgin FM (London) 30 second spot, Thursday (16.00hrs–19.00hrs)	£173
Virgin Radio (AM/National) 30 second spot, Thursday (16.00hrs–19.00hrs)	£560

'Advertising creates false hopes and expectations'

Commentators such as C. Wright Mills in the 1950s (see p. 137) and organisations such as Adbusters (<http://www.adbusters.org>) today are critical of the consumerist nature of our society for this reason. They suggest that advertising excludes the less wealthy and creates a 'must-have' society (advertising on children's television is often cited as one of the main examples of this). Advertising, combined with easily available credit, means that some people may buy products they cannot afford. This then may lead them into debt or criminal action to try to obtain those goods that are made desirable to us through advertising (ram-raiding is cited as an example).

'Advertising works on our insecurities'

> The purpose of publicity is to make the spectator marginally dissatisfied with his present way of life. Not with the way of society, but with his own life within it. It suggests that if he buys what it is offering, his life will become better. It offers him an improved alternative to what he is.
>
> All publicity works upon anxiety. The sum of everything is money, to get money is to overcome anxiety.
>
> (Berger 1972)

The work of John Berger (1972) has been used by many people to explain the way in which advertising works upon the individual. Berger suggests that advertising works upon our insecurities and our need to feel 'esteemed' in the eyes of others by implying we are less than perfect if we do not own a particular product or look like the models in the advertisements. The advertisement implies that if we buy that product we will look like the models or lead the type of life shown in the advertisements. Advertising is always working on our insecurities and making us constantly aspire to something new.

'Advertising promotes unrealistic and dangerous role models'

There has been a considerable amount of debate in recent years over the effects of 'super-waif' and 'heroin-chic' images of models in glossy magazines. It is claimed that the constant representation of ultra-thin models in both fashion spreads and advertisements has led to an undermining of girls' self-esteem and to eating disorders. An article published in the *British Medical Journal* in 2000 by Jones and Smith suggests that between 1 and 2 per cent of women between the ages of fifteen and thirty suffer from some kind of eating disorder and that this is directly attributable to the images that appear in fashion and 'lifestyle' magazines. (See also p. 61 on representation and p. 152 on lifestyle magazines.)

(We had wanted to show an illustration of an advert for Kellogg's Cornflakes that used a 'super-waif' type of model and suggested that eating Kellogg's Cornflakes was a way of staying slim but also remaining healthy. However, perhaps because of criticism that Kellogg's received as a result of this advertisement and because of the sensitivity of the whole issue, the company would not grant permission for us to use the advertisement.)

ACTIVITY . . .

Look through back copies of newspapers and magazines and collect examples of these types of advertisements and articles about the issue of female representation.

Advertisements are selling us something more than consumer goods. In providing us with a structure in which we and those goods are interchangeable, they are selling us ourselves.

(Williamson 1978)

ACTIVITY . . .

Choose one particular product or service and illustrate the range of ways in which advertisers have attempted to make it desirable for consumers.

'Advertising can influence the content of media texts'

Some commentators suggest that advertisers can influence the content of media texts, although there is very little direct evidence that this takes place in the British media. One notable example is from the 1960s when *The Sunday Times* Insight team were investigating the links between cigarettes and cancer. Tobacco companies threatened to cancel their advertising with *The Sunday Times* if the investigations were published. The then editor, Harold Evans, published the investigations and the cigarette companies did pull their advertising (a considerable amount in those days) but eventually returned to *The Sunday Times* because it was a particularly effective means of targeting their desired group.

What is perhaps of more concern is the relationship between programme content and sponsors of programmes. This is an acknowledged issue in America but generally has not been seen to be an issue in this country.

It is undeniable that advertisers do have considerable power over the media in which their advertising appears. In the 1980s the *Sport* and the *Star* ran a joint newspaper but the *Star*'s main advertisers, household names including Tesco and Sainsbury's, were unhappy at being associated with the types of stories, features and pictures that appeared in the *Sport*. They threatened to cancel their advertising if the joint venture continued. The *Star* then pulled out of the venture with the *Sport* to safeguard its advertising revenue.

'Advertising revenue can direct programming'

Many commentators feel that Channel Four has become less radical and adventurous over the years and suggest that this may be the influence of advertising revenue. When Channel Four started broadcasting it had a number of quite (for the time) radical programmes, some with fairly small audiences, and could not fill all its advertising space. Gaps would appear on the screen in the commercial breaks with a notice saying that 'Programmes will continue shortly'. Since Channel Four has been allowed to keep all its advertising revenue instead of having to pass it on to the other commercial television companies, some commentators suggest that there has been a general shift towards more popular programmes that attract younger audiences and so raise advertising income.

ACTIVITY . . .

Look at the schedules for Channel Four. Can you identify the way in which different audience 'segments' are packaged together? To what extent do you think that the present Channel Four schedules offer something that is 'innovative'?

Most commercial radio stations tend to offer the same mix of music and presenter 'chat' because they know that this will attract the largest number of the fifteen- to twenty-five-year-olds that advertisers want to target. A commercial station that initially attempts to offer something different, as did London's X-FM or Kiss, often quickly changes its format to reach a more popular market.

ACTIVITY . . .

Carry out a survey of the radio stations that are available in your area.

- Group them under particular types of programming and the audiences that they are aimed at.
- Think about which groups (if any) are not represented by these radio stations. Why do you think this is?

'Advertising revenue is the foundation of new newspapers'

Newspapers such as *Today*, the *Post* and the *Sunday Correspondent* all started up in the 1980s but folded in the 1990s because they could not attract sufficient income from advertising. This may have been as a result of fierce competition in the newspaper market or because the products were not good enough to attract high circulation figures, but in the case of the *Sunday Correspondent*, a left-wing newspaper founded in 1989 and lasting less than one year, it is possible to argue that there was a conspiracy behind its demise, which happened after advertisers withdrew their support. Other radical magazines such as *Red Pepper* or the *Big Issue* struggle to survive because of the lack of advertisers willing to invest their money in these publications.

In Part 2, on media audiences (p. 107) we looked at the case of *News at Ten*, where the need to increase audience ratings and thereby advertising revenue was an issue.

ACTIVITY...

Carry out research asking people what effects they think advertising has on our society.

- Do different groups of people have different views?
- To what extent do people feel that advertising helps consumer choice?
- Do people think that advertising is 'legal, decent, honest and truthful'?

POLITICAL 'SPIN'

In 2000 the Labour government was the fourth largest advertiser (after Unilever, Proctor & Gamble and British Telecom), spending over £100 million on advertising (compared to £43 million in 1997 when it came to power). Much of this government spending falls into the category of public information and has included the drink/drive campaigns and information about the new children's tax credits.

However, it is the unofficial government advertising and marketing that cause the most concern. In Britain there has been a Ministry of Information since the First World War. Especially during the Second World War, the Ministry of Information was responsible for both public information (for example about food rationing) and also more general promotional activities (such as J.B. Priestley's talks on BBC radio) that were aimed at raising morale. It was, however, during the Margaret Thatcher years in the 1980s that the distinction between public and party interests became blurred. The government spent large sums of money advertising privatisation campaigns (such as the Gas Board's 'Tell Sid'), which many commentators felt were advertisements for Thatcherism as much as they were telling the public about share-buying opportunities. Bernard Ingham, Margaret Thatcher's press secretary, eventually became head of the government's Information Service.

When Labour came to power in 1997 a Strategic Communications Unit was established under the leadership of Alastair Campbell, an ex-journalist. Both Alastair Campbell and Peter Mandelson have gained reputations as 'spin doctors', people who try to control the flow of information between politicians and the media and in particular the way in which the government is presented within the media. To 'spin' a story means to highlight its positive aspects at the expense of those that might potentially be harmful or critical. This is done by using a variety of means such as off-the-record briefings, or 'leaking' stories, to favoured journalists and excluding those journalists who are critical of Labour policies and leaders. Spin doctors such as Alastair Campbell will often insist on being present at, or approving beforehand, any interviews that take place between journalists and politicians. They will also write speeches for politicians ensuring that there is a suitable 'soundbite'.

Part of the role of the spin doctor is to try to control the news agenda and this can include trying to suppress stories that are unfavourable to the government. Alastair Campbell, like Bernard Ingham before him, has gained a fierce reputation as someone who will stand up to journalists and has been described by many journalists as 'intimidating'. Alastair Campbell was particularly forthright in his criticism of the BBC's coverage of the war in Iraq in 2003, particularly the BBC's allegations that the government, and Alastair Campbell in particular, had 'sexed up' an intelligence report to justify going to war.

The increasing numbers and power of spin doctors reflect the growing importance of promotion and presentation in politics, whereby political parties and their representatives are marketed in the same way that a soap powder or other product would be. Style, presentation and image become central to a type of 'designer' politics that in America means that, instead of discussing policy, politicians spend millions of dollars running television campaigns that are no different in style and intention to other television advertisements for soft drinks, motor cars or deodorant. Some commentators suggest that this is part of a 'promotional' culture in which a growing proportion of daily life is seen to be constructed around the marketing, advertising and lifestyle discourses of consumer society.

> We now inhabit an information and consumer society, where the manufacture and dissemination of information and image [have] become an essential facet of modern democratic and commercial processes. The media and cultural industries now encompass multinational corporations, government agencies and

departments, political parties, advertisers, public relations firms and many other forms of corporate, private and public organization. These are locked into increasingly sophisticated networks of information gathering, management, manipulation and distribution. In the specific sphere of institutionalized politics, for example, elections have virtually ceased to have a social significance to the general public, outside of their construction and mediation as 'media events'.

(O'Sullivan *et al.* 2003: 13)

ACTIVITY . . .

Identify and analyse one particular public-information campaign that is currently taking place. How successful is it? Who is it targeting?

FURTHER WORK . . .

1   Using your own examples, consider the extent to which advertisers in magazines and television use and manipulate the self-image of potential customers.

2   Carry out content analyses of two different newspapers or magazines (for example the *Sun* and the *Daily Telegraph*, or *Loaded* and *Cosmopolitan*). Identify the range of advertisements that appear in each of them and then compare and contrast the two publications. What differences can you identify and how do you account for these differences? Draw up an audience profile (see p. 122) for each publication.

3   Consider the consequences, both positive and negative, of the BBC taking advertising.

4   (a) Read the section on the *Wiltshire Times* (p. 123) and then look through your local newspaper and 'measure' the amount of space that is taken up with advertising. Identify different types of advertising, for example classified, block advertisements, and 'advertorial' that looks like editorial but is in fact advertising.

(b) Look in *Benn's Media* (see p. 124) or contact the newspaper to see if they will give you some idea of their advertising rates. You can then work out the approximate income that the newspaper receives through advertising revenue.

continued

5   Look through the regulation and controls of advertising. Do you think there is too much, or not enough, control and regulation of advertising? How would you change it?

6   How has advertising changed in the last ten years? What are the main reasons for these changes?

7   Evaluate the success of a particular advertising campaign.

8   Imagine you are creating a marketing campaign for a film, television series, radio station or magazine shortly to be launched. Decide on what you think would be appropriate promotional material. Which media would you use for advertising and promotion?

9   Choosing a particular example, examine the ways in which advertisers use covert techniques such as sponsorship, events, tie-ins, use of celebrities, news management or product placement to promote their products.

10 'A great brand taps into emotions and emotions drive most if not all our decisions' (Scott Bedbury, Marketing Chief, quoted in the *Guardian*, January 2001). Describe and evaluate the emotional appeal of advertising and/or marketing techniques from campaigns you have studied. (AQA Media Studies Unit 2 exam, January 2003.)

11 Many organisations have, in recent years, undertaken an 'image makeover' involving changes in name, logo, advertising style or corporate identity in general. Sometimes all of these have been changed. Using examples, discuss the reasons why organisations may consider changes of this kind. (AQA Communication Studies Unit 5 exam, June 2002.)

FURTHER READING

Berger, J. (1972) *Ways of Seeing*, Penguin.

Dyer, G. (1982) *Advertising as Communication*, Methuen.

Klein, N. (2001) *No Logo*, Flamingo.

Meech, P. (1999) 'Advertising' in Stokes, J. and Reading, A. (eds) *The Media in Britain: Current Debates and Developments*, Macmillan.

Myers, G. (1985) *Understains: The Sense and Seduction of Advertising*, Comedia.

—— (1998) *Ad Worlds – Brands, Media, Audiences*, Arnold.

O'Sullivan, T., Dutton, B. and Rayner, P. (2003) *Studying the Media*, 3rd edn, Arnold.

Packard, V. (1979) [1957] *The Hidden Persuaders*, Penguin.

Wernick, A. (1991) *Promotional Culture: Advertising, Ideology and Symbolic Expression*, Sage.

Williamson, J. (1978) *Decoding Advertisements: Ideology and Meaning in Advertisements*, Boyars.

Other resources

<http://www.adbusters.org>
Adbusters (the organisation responsible for 'Turn Off TV Week').

<http://www.adassoc.org.uk> (Includes <http://www.childrensprogramme.org>, which aims to promote 'responsible' advertising to children.)
Advertising Association 'Promoting and Protecting the Rights, Responsibilities and Role of Advertisers'.

<http://www.asa.org.uk/index.asp>
Advertising Standards Authority website with annual report and details of complaints and adjudications.

<http://www.bacc.org.uk>
Broadcast Advertising Clearance Center.

<http://www.btaa.co.uk/flash.html>
British Television Advertising Awards site, which allows you to see/play award-winning advertisements.

<http://www.isba.org.uk> (Includes Mediasmart (<http://www.mediasmart.org.uk>), 'helping children to watch wisely'.)
Incorporated Society of British Advertisers. ISBA's remit is to help its members to advertise as effectively, efficiently and economically as possible.

<http://www.ipa.co.uk>
Institute of Practioners in advertising with lots of industry information, including careers and awards.

<http://www.theknowledgeonline.com>
The Knowledge, an on-line version of the database of over 17,500 companies and services operating in the British film, television, commercial and video production community.

▼ CASE STUDY 3: THE HORROR GENRE

In this section we look at:

- the nature of the horror genre
- the development of the genre
- representational and audience issues connected with the genre.

[Our] . . . interest in fearsome fantasies cannot be completely explained as the result of a desire to understand the unknown. Still, the legends of the past provided many of the monsters that haunt the literature of the present, and part of the modern enthusiasm for the macabre may be attributed to ancestral memories of the days when demons were almost expected to put in an occasional appearance.'

(L. Daniels, *Fear: A History of Horror in the Mass Media*, Paladin, 1977, p. 8)

There can be little doubt that the horror genre – most particularly the horror film – has now become far more popular with audiences than perhaps at any other time in its history. If its beginnings were rooted in literature – Mary Shelley's *Frankenstein* (1818) and Bram Stoker's *Dracula* (1897) are the titles that seem to spring to everyone's mind – we also know that stories have always been told about ghosts, monsters, witches and the dark. It is now the case that almost every week the local multiplex is showing one or more films that might be considered horror films. Television has repeated showings of horror films, and series abound on television that pit teenagers against mythical monsters. Bookshops are stacked with horror novels and graphic novels.

Figure 4.8 *Scene from the film* Frankenstein. *Source: British Film Institute © Universal Pictures.*

ACTIVITY...

Make a close study of the complete television listings of any given week as well as the film listings in your area. Pick out all the media texts that you would consider to be horror. You might also visit local bookshops or research the sales of horror novels and the like. Spend some time watching a variety of the music channels on television and noting carefully the instances of videos that contain iconic references to the horror genre. Make a list of all the horror texts that you can find. Try to follow the lifespan of horror texts. For instance:

- How long did a horror film last at the local cinema?
- How quickly afterwards did it come out on video or DVD?

Track the trends of horror texts on television:

- What channel do they tend to be on?
- What time of day do they tend to be shown?
- Are they one-off dramas or series?
- Can you establish an audience based on your research?

Compile a list of the elements that *you think* constitute a horror text. You should compare the list you have made with those belonging to other members of your media group in an attempt to create a loose-fitting definition of the term 'horror'. It is likely that some difference of opinion will emerge during your discussion of this definition. Is a ghost story a horror story? At what point does a text about a serial killer become a horror rather than a psychological thriller?

Horror is the stuff of legend and the basis for all our nightmares. The well-worn cliché of a group of people sitting around a camp-fire and telling ghost stories is possibly rooted in ancient practices. Perhaps this is why the opening scene from many a film or television series begins with someone starting to tell a story, often at night, whilst sitting around the ubiquitous camp-fire. An audience will recognise this as one of the first signals that we are about to be told something frightening. An example of this technique can be seen in *The Fog* (directed by John Carpenter, 1979).

Carry out research into people's attitudes to the horror genre. You could ask them:

- Do you enjoy the genre?
- Why do you enjoy the genre?
- If you do not enjoy the genre, why not?
- In which medium do you consume most horror – films, television programmes, books, comics or other?
- What aspects of horror do you most enjoy?
- When you watch horror films and/or programmes at the cinema or on television, do you do so alone or with a group of people?
- What are your favourite horror texts?

Far be it from us to predict the outcome of your research, but it will not come as a great surprise if you discover that the horror genre tends to create two very distinct camps – those who love it and those who would never dream of watching or reading anything in the genre – though it might be interesting to note why people who do not enjoy the genre frequently know so much about it! Once you have discovered who are the horror aficionados you should ask them what exactly they anticipate when watching or reading a horror text.

How do we as an audience recognise horror? As was discussed in the section on genre (p. 53), audiences come to expect certain codes and conventions in any given genre – and at the same time expect some variation on this, otherwise the genre is in danger of becoming stale.

CODES AND CONVENTIONS

Every genre – and we are talking cross-media here – has a set of codes and conventions that have developed throughout the course of its lifespan. Horror is no different. But despite the fact that the horror genre is considered to be fairly static in terms of certain constituent elements, it can be argued that few genres have developed and changed more in relation to wider contexts and audience tastes than has the horror genre.

ACTIVITY . . .

Think carefully about your own list of favourite horror texts. Make a list of the elements within each of your favourite texts that make it possible for you to place each text under the label of 'horror'.

- Are there elements that each of the texts has in common?
- Are there elements that are unique to one particular medium?

These familiar elements are called the codes and conventions and are used in two ways. First, they permit audiences to recognise a genre, and it is often based on this recognition that a member of an audience will decide to purchase a particular text. There is a whole world of choice out there – whatever the medium – and classification by genre and the associated codes and conventions makes our choices easier. These codes and conventions also allow short cuts to be made. Familiar plots, characters, and so on do not need time spent on explanation – we already know what is going on and settle down to explore the finer points.

Second, for similar reasons, the notion of genre is also very useful for media producers. It may not guarantee success but some knowledge and understanding of the genres that are popular at any given time allow producers to adopt and adapt what they consider to be winning formulas that seem popular with audiences. For instance, the popularity of the space/star-wars genre was quickly utilised by producers, who managed to combine the horror genre with the space genre and revive the horror film.

The iconography (codes and conventions and recognisable signs) of the horror genre are worth exploring – and it is also interesting to see how they have developed and altered over the decades. To help you understand this you should try the following activity.

ACTIVITY . . .

Horror is a genre that has long been associated with a set of codes and conventions that seldom change. To what extent is this true? Look at an early example of the horror genre – *Frankenstein* (directed by James Whale, 1931) is a

continued

Unlike the western or gangster film, where there are a few fairly hard and fast rules in terms of the environment that the action might take place in, or indeed the nature of the characters that are ranged against one another, the horror genre can encompass an extraordinarily wide range of environments, characters, threats and subtexts. This is perhaps one of the major reasons that the horror film has remained popular – or has been able to reinvent itself when its popularity seemed to be on the wane. But what exactly does the horror genre consist of?

A SENSE OF THE HISTORICAL

From the 1930s to the 1970s, most horror films were considered very much the poor brethren of the film world. Horror programmes on the television were far and few between and horror novels were generally considered to be trashy paperbacks. Frequently horror films were made cheaply and packaged together in double bills for a supposedly teenage/young-adult audience to go and see (often in late-night showings), to scream and laugh their way through. This notion is captured brilliantly in the film *Matinee* (directed by Joe Dante, 1993), which shows affectionately yet perceptively the cathartic power of horror and also how horror films were watched almost exclusively by young people and looked down upon by adults. There were, of course, exceptions – perhaps the most notable being two films by Alfred Hitchcock, *Psycho* (1960) and *The Birds* (1963), both of which helped change critical perspectives on the horror film over time. Both were released in a decade when the most popular horror movies in the UK were the films that came out of the Hammer studio with titles such as *Frankenstein Must Be Destroyed* (1969) and *Dracula, Prince of Darkness* (1965). They conformed to the popular model, featured monsters and werewolves, and were all set in the dim and distant past – gothic in atmosphere – and so, removed from any sense of reality, audiences felt secure even while they were jumping up and down with fright. Admittedly the 1950s had seen a strand of the horror genre that dealt loosely with reality, in films such as *Them* (directed by Gordon Douglas, 1954), which suggested that the horror film did actually take on board contemporary contexts. Thus the ants in this particular film are mutated by a hefty dose of radiation from atomic testing – mirroring, without a doubt, the anxieties of the Cold War period and the after-effects of the dropping of the atomic bomb. But even then – and aliens did pop down too in a variety of films in the 1950s – there was always the sense that the screen managed to distance the audience from the fictional events that were placed in front of them.

Not so in the mid 1960s with Alfred Hitchcock's P*sycho*, which firmly brought the horror genre into some sort of critical view and into a proper contemporary setting. Despite the sly humour, the over-acting and the tricks played on the audience (the heroine disappears about a quarter of the way into the film), P*sycho* was important in changing the general critical and audience attitude towards the horror film. Whereas Hammer films had not received reviews when they came out at the local cinema or got a central London showcase release, P*sycho* did. It was perhaps one of the first horror films to be treated seriously.

Two other horror films are noteworthy in terms of their impact on film critics and their acceptance by mainstream audiences. *Jaws* (directed by Steven Spielberg, 1975) and *The Exorcist* (directed by William Friedkin, 1973) both made an impact on the film world, but most importantly they signalled that horror as a genre could achieve a significant place in the box-office. Inevitably both films spawned sequels (indeed *The Exorcist V* is in pre-production at the time of writing).

It is surely not a coincidence that the advent of the horror film as a Hollywood product that could (and still can) make large profits is mirrored by the new-found respectability of the horror novel – as exemplified by the popularity of authors such as Stephen King, Peter Straub and Clive Barker. A new generation in the 1970s was prepared to open its mind to new experiences. The barriers between high culture and popular culture were lowered and the horror genre was the genre to profit – in all media.

 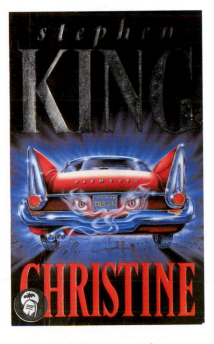

Figure 4.9 *Stephen King book covers for* Carrie *and* Christine. *Source: Hodder & Stoughton © 1975 and 1983.*

ACTIVITY . . .

Investigate the popularity of the horror genre at the present time.

- Look at your local listings magazine for information about films currently showing.
- Look in a television listings magazine to see exactly what is showing on television.
- Visit your local video store and discover what proportion of videos and DVDs borrowed are from the horror genre.
- Find a list of current best-selling books.
- Visit your local library and ask a librarian about popular horror writers. Do the same at a major stationery shop.

A similar trajectory occurred with the American crime novel, since both the crime text and the horror text are perfect frameworks for a serious investigation (sometimes not so serious) and/or critique of the social, political, economic and ethical contexts of the time. For instance, the theme of a horror text is frequently the sins of the fathers being revisited on their sons. This theme might be a cliché but it is not that different from the morality subtext of a Shakespearean play – just less subtle.

The very latest contemporary manifestation of the horror film is aimed at an audience that is more knowing than any other horror audience ever has been – an audience who, because of video, DVD and television, has supped on the history of the horror film, watches *Buffy* on television, reads Stephen King novels and graphic novels and watches music videos that pay reference to the horror genre – a tradition that began with Michael Jackson's *Thriller*.

ACTIVITY . . .

Select a television programme that is considered to be a horror text and watch it carefully.

- What elements of the horror genre did it contain?
- Were there elements from other genres contained within it as well? Why do you think these other generic elements were contained in the programme?
- What clues as to the content of the programme were given by the title sequence?
- Who do you think is the target audience for the programme?
- What elements of the programme made you consider the nature of the target audience?
- Is the programme you selected a popular programme? If so, suggest the reasons for its popularity.

What we have now is a genre that is so aware that the audience know the codes and conventions almost backwards that it has started to become self-referential and postmodern in its approach. Thus we are told in *Scream* (directed by Wes Craven, 1996) that virgins are safe, only to discover that they are not. We are told that anyone who leaves the room will die, only to discover that they do not. We watch Buffy fight werewolves, yet are aware that the series is about much more than simply the fight between good and evil. We read novels that describe over four pages the act of disembowelling and we laugh – or smile – because we are aware that the author is playing with our own fantasies. We watch documentaries on the television about serial killers.

ACTIVITY . . .

There are several examples of horror films that are remade and refashioned. Perhaps the most interesting example is *Invasion of the Bodysnatchers*.

The original film – a genuinely frightening warning about the dangers of conformity – was directed by Don Siegel in 1956 and is stuffed with subtly integrated subtexts (post-war paranoia, for example). The film was remade in 1978 by Phil Kaufmann, who turned it into a study in alienation of a society in transition, with references made to the social and political landscape of the time. In 1994 the film was remade again, this time as *Bodysnatchers* (directed by Abel Ferrara, 1994), transposed to a military base in the USA and revolving around the nuclear family coming apart. In 1998 *The Faculty* (directed by Robert Rodriguez) boasts virtually the same plot but is transposed to a high school and the central heroes and heroines are misfit college students with dialogue that acknowledges the debt to all three *Bodysnatcher* films.

■   Watch all four films. In so doing you will observe the way the horror film changes and develops – how the themes it deals with change even though the central premise remains the same. It will not take long for you to work out how the audience for such films has changed and how the appeal to an audience changes over time.

It is the ability of media producers to adapt and develop any generic text that is what allows it to last and to continue in popularity. The gangster film genre was revived by *The Godfather* in 1971 when a fundamentally ordinary gangster story was given a new angle – the gangsters were humanised, given families and problems and were no longer simply the 'bad guys'. This is something that the western has failed to do – though it

Figure 4.10 *Scene from* Invasion of the Bodysnatchers. *Source: British Film Institute © Associated British Pathé Ltd.*

can be argued (and frequently is) that the space text is in fact the western in a different location. Similarly the horror text has constantly been reinvented There are now so many subdivisions and cross-generic links that the whole field is very difficult to generalise about.

The following elements can all be found in current horror texts:

- **The monster** Texts still exist about monsters from the deep, alien invasions, mutation. The monster can represent the id, the offspring from foul scientific experimentation gone wrong, can act as a warning that man must know his place, or can simply be hungry!
- **The gothic** There are still texts that revisit the horrors of old, *Frankenstein* and *Dracula*. It is interesting to note how there are frequent attempts to bring traditional gothic monsters into a contemporary setting – with varied levels of success.
- **The devil incarnate** The child of the anti-Christ and the spawn of the devil. There has always been a sub-genre of the battle between good and evil; the battle for our souls.
- **Aliens from outer space** The threat of the ultimate unknown. We know they are out there and they surely are not friendly.

- **The horror character** Characters who have created a franchise as they slaughter their way through the narrative and seem never to die. Somehow they have become more popular than conventional heroes.
- **The horror comedy** Our knowledge of the genre is such that we can now parody and pastiche it to our hearts' content.

NOTEBOX

If the gothic horror text had had its day in the 1960s, it was reinvented in the 1970s and 1980s. It was taken into outer space – *Alien*, for example – or brought back home fair and square – *Halloween*, *Friday the 13th* and *Nightmare on Elm Street*, in which notions of reality began to bring the horror home.

Horror is now popular with all ages and viewed/read by people of all ages; it is no longer predominantly an adult genre. The majority of the horror audience now consists of teenagers, yet there is an audience that is much younger. There exists a whole range of texts aimed at children that ostensibly fit into the horror genre. *Count Duckula* and all the *Ghostbusters* cartoons and films are examples, as are television shows such as *Goosebumps* that are shown at 5 p.m. on children's television. In many ways the horror text has become family viewing – it is a rare horror text that is now shown late at night or is rated 18.

REPRESENTATION IN HORROR

When Shakespeare wrote *Macbeth* he did so with the understanding that the audience honestly believed in the existence of witches.

Now that the great majority of present-day audiences no longer believe in witches and monsters, and now that we live in a world in which we are more and more distanced from the horrible events that do happen, it is perhaps the horror film that serves to keep us aware of the intrinsic fragility and despair of life.

KEY TERM

CATHARSIS A purging of the emotions through pity and terror, leaving an audience less likely to behave horribly because they have experienced the results vicariously.

The early horror film was a male-dominated domain. Women were victims and/or the object of desire. Dracula represented the strong silent man who developed a power over women, who then became his slaves – with a sexual undertone that few films have managed to capture but which literature has achieved. The predominantly male audience sat and watched as women were threatened and killed but at the same time may well have had a woman sitting next to them, since horror films are stereotypically considered to be the ultimate date movies.

Figure 4.11 DVD cover of Ring 2.
Source: Tartan Terror.

Refer back to the section on representation (p. 61), and then refer back to the list you made earlier in the activity on p. 293 and look in particular at the characters you noted down and the roles that they play. If we are to agree that all forms of popular culture do in fact mirror and reflect the nature of the society and culture prevalent when they were made – in other words the 'wider contexts' – the horror genre is particularly interesting in its presentation of the role of women.

ACTIVITY . . .

Look again at the four versions of the *Invasion of the Bodysnatchers* films that spread over a period of nearly fifty years (p. 299).

■ Look closely at the way in which women are represented. Compare the main female protagonist in the 1956 version most particularly with the main female(s) in the last two versions. What are the differences?
■ At one extreme we have the woman in distress, saved by her man, but also displaying a fatal feminine weakness. Fifty years later we have younger women who are capable of taking control and fighting back. How did these changes take place?

Figure 4.12 *Sigourney Weaver in* Alien 3. *Source: British Film Institute © Twentieth Century Fox.*

ACTIVITY . . .

At this point it would be useful to look at *Alien* and *Halloween*. Both texts represent important moments in the portrayal of women in the latter part of the twentieth century, though it could be said that one was a step forward and the other was a step back.

- Look carefully at Ripley (Sigourney Weaver) and then look carefully at Laurie (Jamie Lee Curtis). Analyse the look, the clothes, the attitude, the reaction to events, the relationship with others and the way that each character deals with the 'threat'.

It is interesting to note the masculinisation of female characters in the horror genre that has happened over time and is particularly evident in the examples above. It is also interesting to look at the nature of the female victims in the genre.

Since the horror genre is so popular at present you should be taking the opportunity to watch and read as many contemporary texts as you can. Every time you look at or read a horror text you should make sure that you examine closely two important aspects – the representation of women and the representation of the threat.

- Is it possible to make a generalisation about the representation of women in horror texts of the present day?
- Can the same generalisation be made about the threats so common in horror texts?
- Have contemporary horror texts moved away from the stereotypes of earlier horror texts or not?

Many critics have claimed that the horror genre is essentially misogynist and can be said to reflect a perceived hatred of women, especially the post-feminist woman. Thus the victims are often women who are sexually active, whilst those who survive are commonly thought of as 'good girls'. This is particularly true of a sub-genre – the 'slasher' – in which women in peril are the focal point of the narrative. The slasher movie is an interesting phenomenon because there is definitely a contextual undercurrent going on in the genre that may be a reaction to feminism.

Look at a selection of horror texts from the 1970s and examine the number of stock characters that you can identify.

- How easy is it to identify the victims before anything actually happens?
- Examine the heroes and/or survivors?
- What do these two groups of characters have in common with one another?
- What do we have now? A new breed of woman who will take on the monster? Or is it more complicated than that? Are the victims and survivors still so easy to identify?

AUDIENCE AND HORROR

Look back at the subsection on the media 'effects' theory (p. 145). Often consumption of the horror genre is cited as an example of the effects theory in action. There have been many instances of a particular horror film being banned from cinema exhibition because of the effect film classifiers assume that it might have on an audience. This was particularly true of the 'video nasties' (such as *Child's Play 3*) that are referred to elsewhere in this volume (p. 146). Most recently the teenage killers at Columbine were said to be followers of Marilyn Manson, who borrows heavily from the iconography of the horror film in his videos. It is interesting to note how quickly some media organisations and politicians try to blame the horror text whenever certain outrages occur (this is known as a 'moral panic') but how frequently these are found to be red herrings. Michael Ryan, who went on a killing spree in Hungerford in 1987, was accused of being influenced by repeated viewings of the *Rambo* video – although at the inquest it was discovered he did not possess a video player. The list of 'video nasties' was very long at one stage and contained several notorious titles, though interestingly most of them are now available for home consumption.

ACTIVITY . . .

Investigate the audience theories that are available elsewhere in this book (p. 145). Bearing in mind the horror texts that you have consumed in your lifetime, what relevance do you think these theories have when discussed in relation to the horror genre? The horror genre will always outrage certain members of the community. In many cases the creators of horror texts set out quite deliberately to offend and to shock. There are entire sub-genres within the horror genre, such as 'splatter flicks' that are designed only for the strong-hearted (and those with strong stomachs too). There is much debate about the attitude of an audience when confronted with a horror text.

- Do we identify with the killer or the victim?
- What do you think of the anti-hero?
- Why do we admire Hannibal Lecter?
- How many people take a horror text seriously and how many can distance themselves from what they are watching or reading?

The problem with all audience theory is that it is almost impossible to prove – nor is there much point in trying to prove it. If all human beings reacted in exactly the same way to any stimulus then life might be more predictable but very boring. The amount of research that is carried out on media effects is considerable. Most research manages to prove the views held by the researcher in the first place. But it is a controversial area that merits discussion and debate.

FURTHER READING

Jancovich, M. (ed.) (2001) *Horror Film Reader*, Routledge.

Miller, T. (ed.) (2002) *Television Studies*, BFI.

Neale, S. (ed.) (2002) *Genre and Contemporary Hollywood*, BFI.

Newman, K. (ed.) (2002) *Science Fiction/Horror: A Sight and Sound Reader*, BFI.

PART 5: ESSENTIAL MEDIA SKILLS

▼ RESEARCH SKILLS

In this section we:

- look at what is meant by research in the context of Media Studies
- offer some guidelines about what you need to do to carry out effective research
- look at different types of research and some of the difficulties that you may encounter, and offer advice on how to carry out your own original research
- suggest where you may be able to access the results of other people's research.

WHAT IS RESEARCH?

There is a considerable amount of media-related research carried out in this country. This research is undertaken for academic purposes, mainly by universities, and for commercial purposes by many commercial media organisations.

In the sections on media audiences (p. 107) and advertising and marketing (p. 257) much of the material that we looked at was produced as a result of research carried out by a wide range of different researchers over long periods of time. Although they may have been looking at different things, all these researchers were generally interested in one thing – how audiences interact with the media that they consume. Many of their results have been widely discussed and used to help shape policy either by media organisations themselves, by governments or by other media-based trade and industry bodies who set up codes of practice. In the subsection on the 'effects' debate (p. 145) we looked at some of the criticisms that have been levelled at some of this research. We saw that it can be a difficult and complex task to carry out research that will stand up to close scrutiny.

As the media become more fragmented and competitive, commercial organisations – from media producers to advertisers – increasingly try to monitor consumption and anticipate our interests and desires. They all therefore undertake a large amount of

research, or commission others such as companies like Key Note to do the research on their behalf (see box on 'The grey consumer' below). This research is perhaps less academic or policy-based but has great commercial value. It will help producers and advertisers target their products more effectively and identify new niche markets.

The grey consumer

In 2001, 39.2 per cent of the total UK population was aged over 45; this is forecast to rise to 40.8 per cent by 2006. In terms of the adult – over 15 – population, nearly half (48.2 per cent) were aged over 45 in 2001. There is an over-representation of women within this age group, especially among the over 75 year-olds – this is due entirely to the fact that women have a greater life expectancy than men. However, improvements in healthcare have meant that men have begun to narrow the gap – by 2001, 36.5 per cent of all over 75 year-olds were male, compared with 34.8 per cent in 1996.

Marketing and advertising to this age group can be problematic, not least because these consumers can be sensitive about the way they are portrayed in advertising, especially of the type which lumps all 'older people' together without taking account of the considerable differences between them. The fact that creative staff in advertising and marketing agencies are often aged in their 20s may also make it difficult for them to empathise with these consumers. The importance of this age group, and the unique problems in targeting it, have led to the formation of a number of agencies specialising in the mature market.

The original consumer research commissioned by Key Note for this report found that adults over the age of 45 are more likely than average to buy newspapers or magazines, garden products, insurance policies, and holidays (both in the UK and abroad). They are just as likely as other consumers to spend their money on books, savings/investments and medications, and only slightly less likely to spend on home improvements, and on things for friends and family.

This generation has not grown up with new technology, but many over 45 year-olds are competent Internet users. However, Internet access in households headed by those aged over 55 is still relatively low. Key Note's research found that the over 45 year-olds who have used the Internet in the last 3 months are more likely than those who have not to spend regularly on many of the items covered in the survey, and are especially more likely to spend on holidays abroad, and on eating and drinking out. What is perhaps even more surprising is that recent Internet users over 45 are more likely than all recent Internet users to spend regularly on holidays – both abroad and in the UK – and on a wide variety of other items, including savings and investments, gardening and home improvements. Only in the case of CDs, records and tapes are they significantly less likely than other Internet users to be buyers.

(Key Note, <http://www.keynote.co.uk>)

Research is usually trying to 'test' a hypothesis. For example, 'Does the advertising of alcoholic drinks on television reinforce images of male superiority?' or 'Is the idea of public service broadcasting out of date in the age of digital radio?' Getting your hypothesis right is important and requires a considerable amount of thought and discussion.

> **HYPOTHESIS**   An assumption or question about something that the research will investigate and, it is hoped, either prove or disprove.

KEY TERM

WHY UNDERTAKE RESEARCH?

One reason is to pass exams, as most Media Studies examinations have a requirement that you should undertake some kind of independent research activity. However, there are other, more positive, reasons for undertaking research:

- You will gain a greater in-depth knowledge and understanding of the topic that you are researching.
- You will develop your research skills and learn about the processes and methodologies of research. These skills will be useful to you if you go on to higher education or in many work situations.
- The more research you carry out, and with your developing understanding of how research works, the more able you will be to criticise and evaluate research carried out by other people.
- There is a sense of excitement and achievement in the knowledge that you are carrying out original research, doing something that no one else has done before, and actually creating 'new' knowledge.

ACTIVITY...

Look at the credits on a range of television broadcasts and see how often the role of researcher comes up. Suggest reasons why particular programmes may need researchers. What sort of experience and qualifications are these researchers likely to have? Many of the television companies publish guides to careers in television that detail the various roles in television production and the skills and background required.

DIFFERENT TYPES OF RESEARCH

Although there are many different types of research, they are generally divided into two methods, one using primary data and the other using secondary data. We can also identify two main categories of research: quantitative and qualitative.

QUANTITATIVE RESEARCH A type of research, usually based on numbers, statistics or tables, that attempts to 'measure' some kind of phenomenon and produce 'hard' data. It often involves working with large groups of people.

QUALITATIVE RESEARCH A type of research that attempts to explain or understand something and may necessitate much discussion and analysis of people's attitudes and behaviour. It usually involves working with small numbers of people or 'focus groups'.

Carrying out primary research is when you conduct your own original research; perhaps by conducting interviews or doing your own content analysis. Secondary research is when you use research already carried out by other people, such as the study discussed by Cumberbatch (see p. 316) or organisations such as BARB (see p. 127) or the Glasgow University Media Group.

In terms of the different categories of research, quantitative research is usually larger scale and may involve large amounts of data that are 'measured'. Its 'value' lies more in the large sample of data that is looked at than in the depth of the research. This type of research usually requires a lot of resources in terms both of time and access to the material being researched. Most students are likely to rely upon secondary sources for this type of data. BARB uses a panel of 5,100 homes to represent the viewing of the twenty-four million households in Britain. Every television set, video, cable and satellite decoder in each of the 5,100 homes is electronically monitored by a 'people meter'. The meters record when sets are switched on, to which channel and who is viewing. The system will download its information to the main computer overnight so that advertising agencies and media buyers will have the data on their desks the follow-ing morning. Adjustments are then made for 'time-shifting', where video recorders have been used. These metered households 'mirror' the demographic profile of the country's population. BARB can therefore make assumptions by extrapolation on the basis of its sample, for example that fourteen million people watched last Tuesday's episode of *EastEnders*. (For more information on BARB see its website <http://www.barb.co.uk>.)

One of the attractions of using this kind of data is that it looks 'official' and authoritative and is usually easy to understand. However, it can also sometimes be rather limited. It may be interesting to know that eighteen million people watched *EastEnders* last Tuesday but it would be more interesting to know why and how (for example what else the viewers were doing at the same time as watching *EastEnders*); this type of quantitative research generally cannot answer such questions.

Qualitative research, on the other hand, probably could answer the questions 'why' and 'how' but only for a small number of that eighteen-million-strong *EastEnders* audience. Qualitative research is where a smaller range of research is carried out but it is looked at in greater depth. Much of the work of people such as Ien Ang and David Morley that we looked at in the section on media audiences attempts to answer the questions 'why' and 'how' and is therefore smaller in scope. Ien Ang's *Watching Dallas: Soap Opera and the Melodramatic Imagination* is a study based upon forty-two people who replied to her advertisement in a magazine.

Figure 5.1 *BARB Top 20 ratings for terrestrial channels, week ending 28 September 2003. Source: Broadcast Magazine.*

	Title	Day	Time	Viewers (millions)	Broadcaster/ producer	Last year
1	Coronation Street	Mon	19.30	15.09	Granada	2
2	Coronation Street	Mon	20.30	14.82	Granada	1
3	EastEnders	Mon	20.00	13.72	BBC One	3
4	EastEnders	Tues	19.30	13.30	BBC One	4
5	EastEnders	Fri	20.00	12.59	BBC One	6
6	Coronation Street	Wed	19.30	12.59	Granada	7
7	Coronation Street	Fri	19.30	12.47	Granada	8
8	EastEnders	Thurs	19.30	12.46	BBC One	5
9	Coronation Street	Sun	20.55	11.38	Granada	11
10	Emmerdale	Mon	19.00	10.74	ITV1 YTV	9
11	Emmerdale	Tues	19.00	10.74	ITV1 YTV	10
12	Casualty	Sat	20.15	9.51	BBC One	12
13	Emmerdale	Thurs	19.00	9.27	ITV1 YTV	13
14	Emmerdale	Wed	19.00	9.25	ITV1 YTV	14
15	Monarch of the Glen	Sun	20.00	9.20	BBC One Ecosse	22
16	Emmerdale	Fri	19.00	9.12	ITV1 YTV	15
17	EastEnders: The Return of Dirty Den	Sun	19.00	8.18	BBC One	16
18	The Bill	Wed	20.00	7.88	ITV1 Thames	17
19	Waking the Dead	Mon	21.00	7.75	BBC One	20
20	The Bill	Thurs	20.00	7.46	ITV1 Thames	23

CARRYING OUT YOUR OWN PRIMARY RESEARCH

Questionnaires and surveys

One of the main methods of undertaking primary research is by asking people questions. This may be in the form of one-to-one interviews with a small number of people who have particularly relevant experience. They are often more 'in-depth' than other interviews or surveys that may be shorter in terms of each piece of data produced but be answered by a wider range of people. Another popular method of asking people questions about the media is through surveys. These are usually carried out by asking a relatively large number of people to fill in a form or some sort of questionnaire. Surveys are a popular method for students to carry out research because they seem relatively easy and demand little in terms of resources. However, if they are not thought through carefully, surveys can often produce little of real use and end up being a waste of time and effort.

If you are going to use a questionnaire, you need to think carefully about the number and type of questions that you are going to include. (If you make the questionnaire too long, people will be reluctant to spend the time answering it or it will take you too long to collate the answers.) Asking the right type of questions is just as important. Closed questions are easier to collate but open questions may give you more information.

Open questions are those that start with 'what', 'where', 'why', 'when', 'how' or 'who' and encourage the interviewee to 'open up' and talk. Closed questions are those that require a very limited answer, often just yes or no. Another method for questionnaires is to use tick boxes, making the responses easy to collate and making it possible to process them through software packages such as Microsoft's Excel.

The advantage of closed questions is that they are easier to quantify if you are carrying out a large number of interviews. The results can usually be easily transferred to visual images such as pie-charts or bar-charts. Open questions are usually used in qualitative research, such as David Morley's *Family Television* (1986), in which a small number of people are being interviewed and the research is trying to gather more detailed information. Morley interviewed the members of eighteen households about the manner in which they consumed television and the 'uses' they made of it (see p. 141).

Think about the logistics of undertaking a survey and also try to imagine yourself as a respondent. If someone you did not know came up to you in the street and asked you to fill in a questionnaire several pages long, how keen would you be? It is probably easier to ask people you know to fill in questionnaires but then there is the danger that you are only researching amongst a small and particular group and so your sample does not have any value or reliability (see discussion on Morley, p. 313).

ACTIVITY . . .

Design two small questionnaires dealing with the same topic. Each questionnaire should have about five or six questions, one with open questions and the other with closed questions. After you have done your research, list the advantages and disadvantages of the two questionnaires and decide which is more useful for your research.

Researchers are often limited by lack of time and other resources and so cannot always carry out exercises on as large a scale as they would wish. Instead, like BARB (see p. 127), they collect information from a smaller group, or sample, in such a way that the information gained is representative of the larger group.

When using questionnaires, should you ask people to complete the questionnaires while you wait or should you let people take them away and hope that they will return them when you ask? If you want people to fill them in while you wait, this implies several things:

- the location is suitable for people to stop
- they have something to write with (you may need lots of pens)
- there is something for them to lean on (try writing without anything to lean on!)
- they will have the time and inclination to stop and complete the questionnaire.

It is also useful to pre-test your questionnaire or survey with a few people to check that none of your questions is ambiguous or confusing. Other people may also notice any bias that is inherent in your questions, for example 'Why do you think *The Royle Family* is so funny?' or 'In what ways does *Coronation Street* portray a negative representation of ethnic minorities?'

All these factors are part of the logistics of carrying out surveys and questionnaires. Perhaps more importantly, you need to think about why you are doing this, the purpose of this particular piece of research and how it will help you test your hypothesis. Do not be tempted to undertake surveys and questionnaires just because they look easy or because they are a popular methodology with other students.

METHODOLOGY The system or manner used to carry out research; the different ways in which 'data' can be captured.

KEY TERM

Interviews

Interviews can play a large part in research and can be conducted as part of your primary research or as a secondary resource by using the interviews carried out by someone else, for instance Morley in *Family Television*. His methodology included conducting in-depth interviews, many with open-ended questions that allowed the individual members of the households to talk about their television consumption. Although much of this data was difficult to put into numerical form or to construct generalisations from, it has been a very influential piece of research. It has helped our understanding

of how individuals interact with the television programmes they are watching and the importance of the circumstances, or 'situated culture', in which most people consume the media.

Morley did not claim that his sample of eighteen households was representative of the population as a whole. He recognised its limitations. If you are carrying out interviews, you also need to think of how representative your sample will be. Interviewing every-one in your Media Studies class will not be representative of the population as a whole, or even of all students, but only of those students who are studying the media in your locality and who may have similar social backgrounds. This does not mean that your sample will be wasted because it may support other, more quantitative, research. You do need, however, to recognise and acknowledge the limitations of your sample.

Although the amount of time you have to devote to your research is probably limited, it can be a useful check if you carry out more than one type of research. This will enable you to check the sets of results against each other. This should make your findings more reliable as well as possibly giving an extra dimension to your work. For example, Janice Radway in *Reading the Romance* (1984) used a variety of methodologies, including structured questionnaires, open-ended group discussion, in-depth interviews and content analysis.

Organising interviews

Be prepared. Think about the type of interview you want to carry out and have a clear idea of its purpose. To draft a set of questions, it is helpful first to make a list of the points that need to be covered. Good questions are simple and direct. You should, however, be prepared to deviate from the prepared questions if other relevant issues come up.

Interviews are usually arranged well in advance, as most people are unwilling or unable to stop what they are doing and immediately answer questions in any meaningful or useful way. Interviewees sometimes ask to see the questions in advance, too, as they want time to prepare their answers or are nervous about being interviewed.

Wherever an interview takes place it should allow both you and the person being interviewed to relax, as it is usually when people are relaxed that they start to talk more openly and naturally. Body language is a good indication of how people are feeling. Part of your role as an interviewer is to make sure that your interviewees are feeling comfortable.

People being interviewed often prefer to conduct the interview on familiar territory where they feel in control. If you are recording an interview, perhaps for future reference, try to use an environment that does not have any disturbing background noises, such as traffic noises or crowds of people (school or college corridors are NOT a good idea). Your recording equipment should be as unobtrusive as possible as it can sometimes have an intimidating effect on those being interviewed.

One of the difficulties in carrying out interviews is that often you are asking people to remember something, for instance what they listened to on the radio yesterday or last week, what adverts they saw at the cinema or who made the decision about last night's television viewing.

One of the tricks used by professional researchers is to include a series of prompts to help respondents remember particular programmes, products, and so on. Perhaps have a copy of the television schedules to hand or a list of films as a means of jogging people's memory. Often professional researchers will also include a fictitious name to check the accuracy of people's responses. It is surprising how often people remember watching programmes that never existed or seeing adverts for products that were never shown.

ACTIVITY . . .

To test how accurately we can recall information, think about the last time you went to the cinema or the last magazine that you read.

- Can you recall the advertisements that were shown before the film started or that appeared in the magazine?
- Ask others to do the same exercise.
- How reliable do you think their (and your) memory is?
- Can you think of any ways in which you might be able to help people remember more accurately?

One of the ways around this problem is to ask your interviewees to keep a record or diary of their media consumption. (See section on how to study the media, p. 15.) This can, however, be quite burdensome for them to keep and quite time-consuming to read through and summarise unless it is very well designed.

Some people are unwilling to be open about their media consumption. They do not want to admit that they watch particular television programmes because they feel that the programmes are considered 'trashy'. They may be unwilling to admit to the number of soap operas they watch or that they read tabloid newspapers because they feel that they should be reading broadsheets. It is therefore very important that you do not appear to be judgemental. You may also need to reassure them that the results will remain anonymous.

Focus groups

Professional organisations such as advertising or marketing agencies will often use focus groups or panels. These are pre-selected groups of people who represent particular interests or habits or are a sample of larger groups. When new advertising campaigns or magazines are being launched they often employ these methods to research the responses of their 'target' groups. If you want to run focus groups you need to think about how you are going to manage the group, prompt discussion and record what is said. You may wish to record the group's discussion using video or audio, but again this needs to be discreet otherwise it may inhibit some of the participants. You should, however, warn them that the meeting is going to be recorded and check that they are willing to co-operate and give their permission.

Academics sometimes use simulations or observations where they monitor people's behaviour. These, like focus groups, are quite time-consuming to set up and carry out, and if you do not have the time and resources to undertake this type of primary research yourself you might be able to use someone else's results as part of your secondary data.

Content analysis

This is often a popular method of carrying out research into the content of media texts as it can be a relatively simple process. However, as significant or reliable results need large numbers to substantiate them, content analysis is often very time-consuming and sometimes does not provide the 'quality' of results that the effort involved suggests.

Content analysis involves the 'counting' of the number of times a particular phenomenon may appear in a selected range of media texts. For instance, Cumberbatch and his collegues at Aston University, Birmingham, carried out a contents analysis for the Broadcasting Standards Council in 1990 looking at gender representation in tele-vision advertising. Part of their research involved 'counting' the number of times women appeared in advertisements (twice as often as men), the number of advertise-ments that had male voice-overs (80 per cent), and the different roles in which men and women were shown. Cumberbatch and his collegues looked at 500 prime-time advertisements taken from a two-week period. Prime-time was defined by them as between 4 p.m. and 10 p.m. They also looked at some pre-recorded material from an earlier period in the same year. (See also the reference to Gerbner in the section on representation, p. 61.)

One of the main problems with content analysis is in deciding the categories that you are going to 'count'. For instance, in the Cumberbatch research one finding was that 64 per cent of the women appearing in television advertisements were 'attractive', compared to only 22 per cent of men. Another finding was that 50 per cent of the women were aged between twenty-one and thirty-nine, compared to 30 per cent of men.

ACTIVITY . . .

Consider what difficulties a researcher might encounter in trying to use these categories. Can you suggest any other strategies that could be used to try to reach the same results?

One of the best-known examples of content analysis is the work carried out by the Glasgow University Media Group and published in books such as *Bad News*, *More Bad*

News, *Really Bad News* and *War and Peace News*. They researched television news bulletins to see the manner in which various news items (such as the 1984 miners' strike) were presented, who spoke and the type of language used. Their data was then analysed by computer and they claimed to show how news reporting was 'biased' against the miners.

Content analysis can be an effective way of making comparisons between different media – for instance the types of articles and news stories that appear in broad-sheet and tabloid newspapers. It is also a useful methodology if you want to look at changing patterns over time; for example Marjorie Ferguson's (1983) study of themes in popular women's magazines since the Second World War, *Forever Feminine: Women's magazines and the Cult of Femininity*.

If you are using secondary sources, then content analysis can be quite useful, especially if as in the Ferguson or Cumberbatch cases someone has already carried out quite detailed quantitative work. However, you need to be aware that one of the main criticisms of content analysis is that, like the hypodermic needle theory (see p. 136), it concentrates too much on the text itself and does not take into account the audience's interaction with and interpretation of the text's meaning.

How to undertake your own content analysis project

1   The first stage of any research exercise is to clarify and define what it is you are trying to do, what it is you are trying to research, the basic patterns you are aiming to measure, and why. At this stage you should be able to establish a hypothesis or argument to test in your research.
2   Once you have decided what it is that you want to uncover, then that should determine the next stage of your research. This is to decide upon the range of media texts that you are going to look at. At this point it is important to be realistic in terms of the time and resources you have available. If, like Cumberbatch, you are looking to do research that focuses on television advertising, then you need to think about how you are going to 'capture' your raw data – the television advertisements:

- What timespan will you cover? A 'typical' twenty-four hours (what is 'typical'?) or just peak viewing time but across a range of days? Will you include weekends or focus on weekdays?
- Will you record the complete output, programmes as well as advertisements? This will require a large amount of video tape. You will also have many more hours of tape to look through.
- Will you instead just record the commercial breaks? In which case someone will need to be present to switch on and off the video recorder as the times of these breaks cannot be set beforehand.
- Will you record all the television channels that carry advertising, just the main terrestrial ones, or some of the satellite/cable/digital channels as well? Your decision will have an impact on the technology that you will require to carry out these recordings.

3   The next stage is to decide upon the categories that you are going to 'count' when you have captured and looked through all this data. Your categories should be clear and easy for others to understand and identify. You should avoid the more subjective categories such as the 'attractive' example in the Cumberbatch exercise mentioned earlier. As you can see, there are many decisions that you are required to make, each of which has an impact on your findings. You also need to be clear what your reasons are for the decisions that you reach, as they often reflect certain assumptions that you are making (perhaps unconsciously) about television consumption, advertising and its content.

4   This is where you actually carry out your research, recording and logging the material that you will be looking at.

5   Now you reach the most interesting stage of your content analysis, namely analysing the results. Has your hypothesis been supported? Are there any additional results that you had not anticipated? Does your study support or contradict the findings of other similar research?

6   This is the last stage of your content analysis. You should reflect upon the process that you have carried out, what you have learnt about this method of undertaking research, and make suggestions on how the exercise might be improved in the future.

ACTIVITY...

Content analysis as a methodology has many critics. What do you think are the problems with this type of research? Consider some of these suggestions and design your own contents analysis exercise.

Issues of representation are often good topics for content analysis and can cover subjects such as gender, age, class, race or sexuality and, in terms of texts, you can focus on, for example, soap operas, television situation comedy, television dramas, children's comics or magazines.

The study can be based on contemporary texts or can be a comparison between historical texts (assuming you can gain access to them – see the end of this section, p. 320) and similar texts of today. Consider the difficulties that you may encounter and the extent to which these might detract from the value of your research.

USING SECONDARY DATA

Many commercial media organisations undertake their own research, usually for commercial reasons such as to identify market share or size of audience, or to help inform scheduling decisions or the place and price of advertisements. Much of this research has a commercial value but sometimes, when it is out of date, companies may be willing to make it available to students.

Other organisations provide information regarding their work and often have some up-to-date facts and figures about the industry that may be useful. Sometimes, however, there is a tendency to use this material just because it comes from an 'official' source rather than because of its relevance to your research area. It is important therefore to make sure that any data you use are relevant and necessary and not included just to make your work seem more impressive.

Below we have listed some organisations that provide free information as well as websites that might be useful. There are, however, some drawbacks to using material from the Internet (see p. 25). You also need to be sure for copyright reasons that you accurately reference any material that you use.

The bibliography

A bibliography is where you list all the information sources that you have used in your research. You should provide all the details necessary for someone else to be able to trace and look up the original data. For books and articles from magazines, you should use the Harvard system, listing the author, date, title and publisher. Many books also give the place of publication. If you look at the further reading sections of this book you will see how the Harvard system is set out. It is useful to keep a record of the details of any books or articles that you look at as you go along because it is sometimes difficult at the end to remember where a particular piece of data came from. (See the section on how to study the media, p. 15.)

The rules for referencing non-print-based material are a little less clear. Again it is important to provide enough information for the original data to be traced. For data from the Internet you should include the URL and the date you accessed it to allow for any subsequent modifications. If you use video or television programmes you should, where possible, provide details of:

■ director (if appropriate)
■ title of the film or programme
■ broadcasting channel
■ series title
■ date of broadcast.

If you have undertaken your own primary research, then you will probably discuss the main findings and their implications in the body of your work. However, you need to include details of the methodology used, probably in appendices that are placed at the end of your work. This is also where you might include copies of questionnaires, details and results of surveys, transcripts of interviews, and other supporting material.

Finally, here are some key points:

■ Be aware of the difficulty of being truly 'objective' and avoid trying to 'prove' a particular result that suits your own ideas.
■ Make sure that you have a clear focus and hypothesis. Quantity is no substitute for quality.
■ Be realistic and recognise and acknowledge the limitations of your research.

- Always explain to your respondents who you are and the purpose of your research.
- Explain what will happen to their responses, who will see the information and whether it will be anonymous or not. Ask their permission to use the material.
- Reflect on your methodology and the processes you have undertaken. There is always something new to learn.
- Always keep a record of your contacts and sources and make sure that you acknowledge your sources for secondary data.

FURTHER READING

Cumberbatch, G. (1990) *Television Advertising and Sex Role Stereotyping: A Content Analysis*, Broadcasting Standards Council.

Kirchner, D. (ed.) (1997) *The Researcher's Guide to British Film and Television Collections*, 5th edn, British Universities Film & Video Council.

Morley, D. (1986) *Family Television*, Comedia.

O'Sullivan, T., Dutton, B. and Rayner, P. (2003) 'Media investigation and research' in *Studying the Media*, 3rd edn, Arnold.

Stokes, J. (1999) 'Use it or lose it: sex, sexuality and sexual health in magazines for girls' in Stokes, J. and Reading, A. (eds) *The Media in Britain: Current Debates and Developments*, Macmillan.

—— (2003) *How to Do Media and Cultural Studies*, Sage.

Trowler, P. (1996) 'Approaches to media research' in Trowler, P. *Investigating Mass Media*, 2nd edn, Collins.

▼ PRODUCTION SKILLS

In this section we:

- explore the important area of the practical production
- guide you through the very important area of pre-production and planning
- suggest successful ways of going about the actual production process
- look at what is required in the post-production and evaluation section.

This section is necessarily general since everyone will have their own ideas as to the nature of their production, but most of what is suggested is relevant for all the media that you may wish to use.

This practical production module can be the most rewarding, the most fun, but also the most frustrating and, occasionally, the most disappointing. Production work has a place in all current media courses for several reasons:

- the hands-on approach can teach a great deal about the realities of real-life media production
- you can grapple with the key concepts and methods of production within a real framework, rather than just a theoretical one
- you can demonstrate what you have learnt about the media in a practical context
- there is also room for creativity and imagination.

Perhaps the most difficult aspect of the whole process is the first one.

PLANNING

This part of the process can be quite worrying to start with. You have to produce a piece of work that is going to be marked and looked at by external moderators. Perhaps you do not feel very confident with the equipment, you certainly are not an actor and you have no idea what your production project will be. This part of the process has to be considered as a holistic exercise. But three interlinked points require investigation and decision-making: the medium, the audience and the subject matter.

The medium

First, find out which media you are allowed to work in and what sort of equipment is available to you. Discuss this with your teacher.

- Which media have you had experience of working in before?
- Which did you feel most comfortable and confident with?
- Are you most likely to work on the production *only* in lesson/school time or also outside school/college time?
- How much time do you have available to you?
- What media have you studied previously, and do you feel that you have a working awareness of those media in terms of technique, genre, narrative and so on?

Depending on which examination board's specification you are studying you may find that the choice of media text is restricted by the areas that you have studied in the other modules of the course.

Once you have decided on the medium you will need to consider the next aspect of the practical production process.

The audience

Who is your target audience? It is no use saying that you will make a magazine about stock-car racing based on the fact that you go every week and really enjoy it. Market research may suggest that there is insufficient demand for such a magazine as fans of stock-car racing prefer watching it to reading a magazine about it. Equally it is not necessarily a good idea to aim your product at a young teenage audience – it is likely to be the case that you are too close to that market and objective decision-making might become difficult. In many cases it is in fact far better to isolate a specific audience that you are not a part of so that you can remain that much more objective and then personal taste and opinion are less likely to get in the way of your decision-making. Again this is linked with the medium you use and the subject matter (see below, p. 323), but you must:

- attempt to identify a target audience
- research their likes, dislikes and media-consumption habits.

Ideally through your research you will discover an area that you feel is not well represented at present.

ACTIVITY . . .

Create a questionnaire that you can distribute widely across a spectrum of people. Consider carefully the type of questions you need to ask them about their media consumption. But also consider the personal information that you require to make the survey worthwhile. Remember, even if you are looking at a teenage

One example of a media product aimed at a particular audience is the 'grey' magazines aimed specifically at the over-sixties. Such magazines can be difficult to find since they tend not to be on newsagents' shelves but are ordered specially – either by a newsagent for known customers (and therefore kept under the counter) or directly by the readers themselves on a subscription basis. However, if you were to look at these magazines you would find that they make certain presumptions about the over-sixties, which may prompt you to think about the (possibly enormous) market of over-sixties who are not catered for by these magazines.

Equally, research into magazines aimed at teenage girls may suggest that all of these magazines are in fact very similar. So it may be an interesting challenge to produce a magazine for this audience that is totally different from all the others already available. It is not for us to suggest what the contents of such a teenage-girl magazine might be but just to suggest that you examine that area.

You may find it worth your while to interview your family and friends about their media consumption and ask them to suggest ways in which they feel they are not being catered for by existing media products.

The subject matter

The subject material of your production is inevitably linked with its target audience and so must obviously appeal to its intended audience and be in an appropriate medium for this audience. It must also be possible to produce the material within the constraints of the medium that you have decided to employ. For instance, you are unlikely to be able to make a video about a wartime submarine since your ability to create realistic sets and costumes will be severely limited in a school/college context. However, the possibilities offered by a radio play are almost endless.

You also have to be realistic about the time, money and energy that you have. Do not be over-ambitious – be realistic. For example, if you have decided to target forty-year-old sci-fi film enthusiasts then it is fundamentally unrealistic to decide to make a fiction film, largely because you are unlikely to have the equipment and budget necessary to do so. But if you think around the problem then you might:

- make a television or radio magazine programme that is about sci-fi films
- make a trailer/advertising campaign for a new sci-fi film
- make a parody of a sci-fi film of the 1950s (though note that parody/pastiche is actually a sophisticated skill).

This is a good time to conduct a brainstorming session. Sit down with your group and jot down all the ideas that you have about a possible production. Allow yourself around fifteen to twenty minutes to do this. Then take a fifteen-minute break. Return and discuss carefully what you have written down and begin to examine the links between the various ideas.

One other point at this stage is important – how many people are to work on your production.

Individual vs group

In the real media world very few people work in total isolation. The reality is that most media productions are the result of teamwork – someone may well make the primary decisions but essentially the product is made by a group of people, all with different well-defined roles within the organisation. This should be the way that you choose to work – in an ideal world within your classroom.

However, it may be the case that you do want to strike an individual path, for all sorts of reasons. Certainly other people can be unreliable and perhaps not as committed as you are. You may well have a particular interest in a medium, subject or audience that no one else shares. If you are not prepared to compromise then perhaps you should go it alone – whilst remaining aware of the fact that this puts all the responsibility on you. There will be no one else to rely on. Equally there will be no one else to let you down.

This can be a very difficult decision and one you need to think about carefully. At this point you have probably made all the choices that are possible. You now enter the second stage, which is where you actually set about producing the artefact or media product.

The production process can be broken down into three stages: pre-production, production and post-production.

PRE-PRODUCTION

Having made all the decisions about the nature of your product, you now enter the phase that is absolutely necessary to all media products. In the real world it is a rare individual who is allowed a completely free rein to go out and do whatever s/he sees fit at the time 'because it feels right'. Nowadays, whatever the product, an awful lot of work goes into the pre-production stage.

Researching similar media

Whatever the media you are working in it is almost inevitable that there are other products out there covering the same area. You need to investigate your 'rivals' and 'competitors' to see what they are doing, investigate their subject material, research how well they seem to target their audience, and look at what works and what does not. Look particularly at how rival products are presented to the audience – study the opening sequences if visual, the front pages if print. What assumptions are the producers making about their audience? Do you want to alter these assumptions and, if you do, then how are you going to do this?

For instance, it seems that children's television presenters are required to be fairly 'wacky' and shout a lot, whilst the camera never stops moving. Children's television also seems to assume that the majority of children are interested only in boy bands and computer games and, it would appear, very little else.

So what would you change if your area was children's television? Again, you would need to watch a considerable amount of this genre before you could begin to form any conclusions – but remember that you should not be afraid to accept the things that work and rethink the things that seem to you not to work.

This is really the area of genre expectations (see section on genre, p. 53) and, whilst accepting the importance of these expectations, it is also important to confront and challenge them (and to be able to articulate the reasoning behind any decision that you make).

Researching the audience

We tend to assume that we know what is best for everyone and also that public taste is fairly uniform throughout the country. The truth is that even large-scale media productions can have varying success throughout different regions in the country. What works in London will not necessarily work in Taunton or Doncaster. It is also the case that not all teenage girls necessarily enjoy the same things – and the same is true of teenage boys.

You could say that at present the teenage magazine market tends to play safe by creating an identikit picture of a typical teenager (see section on representation, p. 61) and then creating magazines based on that image. This works to an extent – sales figures are high – but there are still many teenagers nationwide who do not buy magazines because there is simply nothing that caters for them. This could be an interesting area for you to explore.

Having decided upon your medium, subject material and audience you now have to go out and investigate the real nature of your target audience.

- What media texts do they consume?
- What in particular do they enjoy about them?
- Which aspects of their favourite texts do they most appreciate?
- But most fundamentally – what more do they want?

- How could the product(s) be improved?
- What other types of texts would they like to be created for them?

This is very much what happens in the real media world. Media producers tend to build a profile of their consumers and it can be a very detailed profile, based not just on sex, age and class but also encompassing such things as location, family circumstances, jobs, consumption patterns and preferences.

It is important to ensure that this research does not just take place in your classroom or indeed school. Whatever the nature of your target audience, you should spread your net as far and as wide as possible in an attempt to get a truly representative feel for the subject. This has pitfalls none the less, but as broad a survey as possible gives you more evidence upon which to format and create your eventual product.

Researching the subject matter

This might seem to be stating the obvious, but no one can just produce a media artefact without researching the subject matter in the first place. Whatever the nature of the production you are developing it is absolutely essential that you have thought about and planned exactly what the subject matter and content will be. It is often the case that students use material that they have found and borrowed from other sources – for instance, those who decide to create a girls' magazine often think it is enough simply to copy out articles that they have found in existing publications. This of course under-cuts everything that we have discussed above. It suggests to the readers (and ultimately these are the examiners) that you have not really thought about the nature of your audience nor considered the results of all the research that you should have done.

This is even more the case when creating an audio-visual product. Your job is not simply to copy what is already out there, but to develop it and take it further.

There are secondary sources – by which we mean finding out information from books in the library or perhaps from interesting websites on the Internet – but to make any production come alive you also need to investigate primary sources – interviewing people who are prepared to debate the issues that you are investigating in your production, for example. And all this needs careful planning and advance preparation.

Organising

Now you have to get organised. Prepare yourself and your group so that everyone has a job to do. It is very important that everyone else knows what exactly that job involves. It is also vital that everyone knows when each of the different tasks is going to be done *and* the final date for completion of the project. This holds true for whatever medium you have decided to work in. All of this information needs to be itemised on paper and distributed throughout the group (as well as a copy being ready for submission at the end of the course).

Whatever the eventual product you have decided to create, there is still yet more planning to do. It is important that you do not start work without having a clear idea of what the finished product will look like. This involves serious consideration of the actual contents and the look of the final product. For instance, a front cover of a magazine does not just happen. It involves taking into account all the research work that has gone on before and attempting to create a cover that will:

- appeal to the target audience
- give an idea about what is contained within the front cover
- demonstrate awareness of the generic rules of the sort of magazine it is
- have some immediate visual appeal – always remember that in theory you are competing with all the magazines that are already out there.

Similarly you will need to produce a mock-up of the magazine – as you would in real life – in which you are able to demonstrate what will actually be in it, and also suggest the order in which the editorial material, advertisements and illustrations will appear. This is also your opportunity to start experimenting with the look/style/format of the magazine.

If you are making a video then what you should *not* do is just go out and start filming. You will need to produce a script, and an accompanying series of shot-sheets so that you have a basic idea of what the final product will look like. You will also need to prepare careful plans of what will be shot, when and where, who in your group will be needed, when people will be available (especially if you are interviewing members of the public) and what will be needed (props, costumes, equipment).

While this may not necessarily all be true of a documentary, even then there are only a few documentary film-makers who simply go out with a camera and see what happens. They are much more likely to have decided in the first place who they want to interview, where, when, what they want to ask them, and also (if the truth be told) what sort of light they want to show them in.

This preparation work may not be the most exciting part of the production process – and there will be always members of the group who just want to get on and do it – but at the end of the day all your planning will save you a great deal of time, and also prevent you from making a lot of mistakes. It should mean that the final product is delivered on time – which of course in the real media world is incredibly important.

PRODUCTION

There are two very important primary stages to the production process. Perhaps the most important is that of familiarisation with the technology available to you, to discover exactly what the equipment you are using is capable of doing for you. This may be a little depressing because most schools and colleges cannot afford the newest 'state of the art' technology. But this should not stand in your way. Far too many students have the idea that they need the very best of everything to complete the process and in fact nothing could be further from the truth.

You are not being judged on the technology that you have been using but on what you have managed to produce with the technology that is available to you. The beneficial aspect of this is that you will often be forced into being far more creative and imaginative than you might have been if you had relied on the technology to do everything for you. This familiarisation process involves an element of 'play'.

Figure 5.2 *In the same way as professionals, students may find themselves filming sequences either on location or in the studio. Source: BBC Picture Archive.*

- Experiment with the software on your computer to see exactly what it is capable of.
- Walk around your school or college for an hour or two with the video camera and see what you can do with it – how good the picture quality is in a dark corridor, for instance, and whether the auto-focus is a hindrance or a help.
- Find out what sound effects you can create on your tape recorder and how much extraneous sound the microphone picks up.

Things are likely to happen that you might not have taken into consideration – for instance:

- Can the end of lesson bell be heard when you record?
- Do other students tend to mug to the camera as they pass?
- Can your computer save the complicated graphic that you have created?

When you feel comfortable with the equipment, when you know its capabilities and your own limitations, when everyone has agreed on their tasks, when everyone knows what they are doing and when everyone feels confident and prepared . . . then you can begin!

You will have been given some kind of a deadline – do everything that you can to keep to this. In the best of all possible worlds you will have constructed a plan that is built around the deadlines set by your teacher/lecturer. Stick to it wherever possible.

However, things will not always go strictly according to plan. Computers will crash. The video player will eat video tapes. It will be raining on the day that you have organised to shoot outside. The music department will have double-booked the recording studio in which you were going to record the soundtrack. These are the kinds of things that can lead to total despondency. However, if you have a well-organised plan then it is not too difficult to look forward and work out exactly what you can do in the meantime. There is always too much to do and not enough time to do it in. So if the item you were going to work on on any given day suddenly becomes impossible to do, then there should always be an alternative section or task that you can be working on.

Remember, too, to hold frequent 'progress-report meetings'. These are important for several reasons. You should constantly assess how things are going, give everyone an opportunity to come up with new ideas or complaints and also ensure that the entire production is still on track.

You may well have a plan but there is another important point to make at this stage. There is always the possibility that, no matter how good your plan, things will not necessarily work out as you had thought they might. No matter how you see things in your head, in reality they might not be a success. There can be any number of reasons for this. Perhaps the sun was shining in the wrong direction. Maybe the colour printer did not have sufficient contrast, thereby making the shades of the same basic colour

merge into one. Or an actor vital to the scene you have prepared to shoot did not turn up.

In cases like these you will have to be prepared to improvise, and maybe alter direction completely. Interestingly, this can sometimes work to your advantage – often what you had least expected turns out to be the best option. This flexibility is important. You have a plan but something better turns up. When it does, seize the opportunity (but remember to note it down because it will be very relevant for your commentary).

Here are some other tips to bear in mind whilst working on your production:

1   Keep everything. That front cover might not seem right at the time but you may change your mind after you have tried and failed to improve on it. It will also be very useful as evidence when you explain the developmental process in your commentary. Equally all the video material you create may come in useful when editing. Shoot, watch and log it all, every day if possible.
2   Bear in mind at all times that it is your ideas, and your attempts to get your ideas into concrete form, that matter. You are not professionals working full time on the job. You will be rewarded for making a genuine attempt at something, even though it might seem to you to be a failure (as long as it is recorded in your log/commentary).
3   Never lose sight of the pre-production research that you did – and which should in any case have taken up much of your time. You will almost certainly be working within a genre – keep in mind at all times the conventions of that genre and its likely audience. Your audience needs to be entertained and challenged, otherwise your product has failed.
4   Even though you might be striving for originality the chances of achieving it are pretty slight. For instance, if you are working within a particular magazine genre and want to create a product that is totally original (and has the potential to be a fantastic financial success) you should always bear in mind that there are people employed in the media world who are paid thousands of pounds a year to try to dream up similar ideas. And they rarely succeed either. It is a good idea to be as ambitious as possible, but that ambition needs to be tempered with a dose of reality. This is a cruel way of suggesting that even though your end product might not be all you had hoped it might be, it will probably have a great deal of merit – and why give all your best ideas to an examiner for nothing? Save the really good ones until you are working!
5   Keep a log/diary. You will forget what happened six weeks ago. The practicalities of media production are important. It is not simply about ideas but also about technique and about coping with external pressures to get the whole thing finished. This process needs to be articulated in your commentary. If corners are cut because of budgetary or time constraints then you will need to explain how you coped and how it affected what you achieved.

POST-PRODUCTION

All media products need to be marketed and advertised. They do not sell themselves. Many candidates simply produce an artefact and leave it at that. It is very important that you consider the presentation of your product very carefully. There is little point in working very hard on your video production and then delivering the finished product in a shabby, unmarked video case. The same is often true of a radio production. Similarly, do not present a magazine that is unkempt, badly bound or a second-generation copy that is hard to read.

First appearances count for a great deal – and not only on the high street. If the product has been well packaged and looks clean and smart then it is much more likely to be considered a success. Therefore, if you have made a video, package it in a new plastic cover and create a proper video cover that fits the genre of the piece and gives suitable information about the product on the back for those who need to know. Bear in mind that the video should look as if it could compete with all the other videos on the shelf in the local video hire shop.

Equally, if your product is print-based then it needs to look good so that people browsing in a newsagent will be tempted to pick it up. At all times bear in mind the opposition on the newsagent's shelves and think carefully about the audience that you are trying to attract.

You will have spent a long time considering the look of your front page. But the product as a whole needs to be kept pristine. Think very carefully about the different forms of binding available to you. Consider laminating each page and creating a rather firmer wrap-around front cover so that it always stays in one piece. (Remember that you are not being marked for the type of binding that you employ.) Indeed, some candidates in the past have dispensed completely with the pretence of binding their product and have simply placed each page within a plastic folder – and explained why they have done so in their rationale. This ensures that your product will be marked looking its best.

THE COMMENTARY/RATIONALE

The practical production means very little unless it is accompanied by a commentary. This is where you have the opportunity to write a commentary, usually about 1,000 words or so, explaining the rationale behind the product, how you went about it and how you would evaluate the finished product.

Everybody who works on a production team will have to produce their own commentary. It is your chance to articulate how your product illuminates your understanding of the key concepts of the Media Studies syllabus that you are following. As a guide, it is probably a very good idea to divide your piece of writing into three distinct parts: intention, process and outcome.

Intention

This section is very similar to the idea of a brief. You should explain what it is that you have set out to do and the ideas behind it. Explain why you have chosen the particular product and the subject material of that particular product, as well as suggesting the target audience that you are aiming for and how you intend to attract them. When doing this you should also explain the research that you have undertaken whilst planning your production. Refer to real media texts that you have studied. Show how your production will be linked to them in some way – either in terms of form or ideas. You should refer to the key concepts of the course and it is here that you should reveal your engagement with those very key concepts and how your practical production puts that engagement into concrete form. Thus if you have decided to create a short horror-film trailer then this is where you have the opportunity to discuss the media language found in such texts and also any issues of representation that you might decide to tackle. Media theory into media practice!

Process

In this section you should explain the actual technical process of getting your media product made. There is a danger here of going into far too much detail. With this in mind, you should watch the word count very carefully. What is *not* needed is a day-by-day, blow-by-blow account of the minutiae of the production process. But you do need to explain the reasons why the product has turned out the way it has – what decisions were made and the rationale behind them. It is also an opportunity to discuss any technical and other problems you encountered and how you overcame them. There will have been technical hitches. Explain how and why they occurred and how you dealt with them. Do not dwell on how one particular character kept on letting you down because this often ends up sounding like sour grapes. As your teachers and lecturers should be monitoring your production at all times, it is likely that they will already know who is doing what and, more importantly, who is doing very little.

Outcome

In this part of the commentary you should do to your production what you have been doing to other media products since you started the course. In other words, you should try, as objectively as possible, to evaluate the effectiveness of your product in terms of its use of the chosen media, its subject matter and its suggested target audience. Try to be as honest as you can. Do not be overcritical, but at the same time try not to be too bland. Marks are not given for the following phrases: 'and I really enjoyed making it', 'I don't think it could be improved on' or 'all in all I think it's pretty good'.

It is important that you refer to the key concepts and show how they have illuminated your understanding of the production process and how, too, you have attempted to show your understanding of them in the final product. Where the specification asks that the production is linked in some way to areas studied in other modules, you must make those links obvious in your evaluation.

In all three parts of the rationale it is important to avoid description and concentrate on showing how you have got to grips with media concepts through the practical process. In other words, you need to be as critical and analytical of your own production as you have been with every other media product you have studied over the course. It is also an opportunity for you to reflect on your own learning and the relevance of what you think you have learnt in the past.

It will not be a perfect production – although it may well be very close to perfection – but the important thing is that the production will be assessed as positively as is possible. With this in mind, anyone looking at the production and rationale should respond to a healthy dose of self-criticism in a flexible and encouraging way.

Finally, do not simply leave this part of the process to the last minute. It is a piece of work that has to be shaped and considered in exactly the same way as the product itself and can earn you a substantial rise in your marks. Keep to the word length, type the essay, spell-check what you have written and, again, ensure that it is well presented and relevant to the production that you have submitted.

▼ PREPARING FOR EXAMS

The chances are you have worked hard all year on your Media Studies course. Now it is time for the exams. Remember that exams are your opportunity to show off what you have learnt and to convert this knowledge into a good grade. You will find that in general Media Studies exams are not about finding out what you do not know. They are more likely to be an opportunity for you show off precisely what you do know and to demonstrate how well you have grasped the concepts that underpin a study of the media. If you approach your exams with this in mind, you are more likely to do well than if you go into the exam room in a state of fear and loathing. Try to see the exam as your opportunity to let the world know just what you can do.

NOTEBOX

As we pointed out in the section on how to study the media (p. 15), there are very few, if any, 'right' answers in this discipline. Media Studies is about the skills of analysis and evaluation. You must be willing to accept that there are few set rules or set patterns. In fact, much of the intellectual reward in studying the media lies in the ambiguity of the issues they raise. The debate about the need to regulate the media is a good example. For you to say that there is too much regulation of the media is neither right nor wrong. Indeed it is unlikely that any position on such a complex issue can be adopted successfully or convincingly. What examiners are looking for is your ability to show you have understood the complexity of the debate. You should do this by rehearsing the key issues that surround it and supporting these with appropriate examples.

DRAWING UP A REVISION PLAN

A revision plan is the essential first step towards preparing yourself for your Media Studies exam. You may find the following steps a useful way to guide you in drawing up such a plan.

1   Make sure you know what you need to revise. Either check the specification or syllabus yourself, or ask your teacher what you need to do. In some cases you may

find that there is a choice of topic areas and you may have to decide how many of these you are going to prepare for the exam.

2   Make a list of the topics you have decided you need to cover. Check where you can best find the information you need on these topics. Start with your own notes and then look at how textbooks, such as this one, may be able to help you.

3   Draw up a revision timetable devoting a suitable amount of time to each topic. Be realistic about how many hours you can devote to this. There will almost certainly be other subjects making demands on your time, as well as all of those diversions you will have to succumb to.

4   Put together a list of up-to-date examples that you can draw upon to illustrate your answers. If you have made good notes throughout your course, you should have a good range of texts such as films, television and radio programmes, newspaper and magazine articles that you can call upon. It is also worth thinking in advance about how you may be able to use these in the exam. Remember, too, to keep an eye on such sources as the *Media Guardian* for up-to-date information on key media issues and debates.

5   Remember that revision you do at the very last minute may be of little use. Revising is like preparing yourself for a sporting event. A sustained programme of preparation will always be more effective than a last-minute panic.

UNSEEN PAPERS

Most exam boards set a paper that requires you to write about a media text you will see for the first time in the exam itself. This is often called the 'unseen' paper. Typically the exam will consist of a video or sound extract that will be played to you once you are in the exam room. Alternatively you may be asked to look at a print-based text such as a magazine article. Usually you are asked to respond to the text in around an hour and a half to two hours. The type of text, video, sound and print will vary, as will the precise instructions telling you what to do. The principles for approaching this type of exercise, however, remain very similar. In fact it is likely you will have had a go at some practice papers in class to help you get the hang of them.

NOTEBOX

A good way of practising for the unseen paper is to look at texts you have chosen yourself. Magazine covers, radio advertisements, extracts from television programmes and cinema trails are all good examples. Then try to get down some notes as quickly as you can on what specific aspects of the text you would want to point out if you were writing an analysis. This way you will help prepare yourself mentally for the task of unseen analysis in the exam itself.

The current trend in unseen papers is to provide you with at least some information advising you what you should look for in your commentary on the text. (See sample papers in the appendix.) This guidance provides a potential checklist of points to cover. It is important to bear in mind that it may not be a good idea to work mechanically through any such list trying to get something down under each heading. Each text that you will be asked to consider is unique. As such it needs an individual response. Your ability to identify the unique qualities of the text and base your commentary on these is the real test of your ability in such a paper. You should not, for example, spend time on an issue such as narrative if you feel that this is a relatively unimportant aspect of the text. Rather focus on those elements that you feel are significant and be prepared to highlight these in your analysis. The checklist is, however, a useful mechanism for ensuring that you have not disregarded a key element of the analysis.

Organising your response is an important aspect of this question. A brilliantly perceptive textual analysis is of little use if it is confused and difficult to follow. The guidance or checklist may come in useful here as a way of suggesting to you headings under which to organise your response. However you decide to organise what you have to say, make sure that it is both logical and user-friendly for the examiner. The easier it is for someone to digest what you have to say, the more likely you are to be rewarded for it.

▼ APPENDIX
SAMPLE EXAM PAPERS

EXAM PAPER 1

All GCE Media examinations now include a module that asks candidates to provide a textual analysis of a media text. Frequently that media text is a print piece but the moving image is becoming increasingly popular since most centres have learnt to deal with the complexities of the new multi-exam experience!

Whatever the media text that you might have to confront, the process is very much the same. GCE Media Studies specifications are based around a series of Key Concepts and although they might all have slightly different emphases (and indeed might be called something completely different) they are essentially the same thing. The Key Concepts in the AQA specification, for example, are:

■ Media Language – the differing ways that media texts use the language of style and form to communicate with their audience.
■ Media Representations – the different ways in which the media present to us aspects of the world, particularly people and places.
■ Media Audiences – the target audience and what the text will provide it with.
■ Media Institutions – who produced, distributed and broadcast the text, and possibly why.
■ Values and Ideologies – the beliefs and political ideas suggested by the text in question.

It will be important to tackle the text by utilising these Key Concepts. However, it is also important to remember that each Key Concept does not stand alone. It is not simply a matter of writing a paragraph on each as if they are not related to one another. Better answers will always be cognisant of the fact that any media text should really be looked at holistically – all of the Key Concepts are inter-related. Thus, for instance, the media language utilised in any text will have some bearing on the representations to be found within it and will also give the reader some clues as to the likely target audience.

But how to tackle the exam? First of all ensure that you use any reading time as effectively as possible. No matter what the media form, you will be given an opportunity to read or view the text and make notes. At first simply read the text as a whole. Exactly as it was created to be read or viewed by an audience. Then, and only then, should you begin to break the text down into its constituent parts and also begin to look at it under the various Key Concept headings. You may find that the examination question does not necessarily list these Key Concepts as it might have done in the past. However it will almost certainly suggest the areas that you should pay attention to.

It is probably not a good idea to begin writing your response until the full reading time has been used up. Then – when you begin – do NOT waste time by describing the text. Remember that the examiner has the text in front of him/her and will know it well – indeed will have discussed it with colleagues. You will gain no marks for an accurate denotation. None whatsoever. But you will waste a lot of time.

What will gain you marks is analysis. Analysis involves asking the important questions 'how?' and 'why?' and then attempting to answer them whilst referring to the text in question as closely as possible. If you want to make a statement about the text you are 'reading' then find an example within the text of what it is you are trying to point out. Avoid generalisations. In the rubric for the examination you may well find the statement 'you will be rewarded for specific reference to the text' or something very similar. Don't ignore that advice.

You will also gain marks by evaluating the text. Ask yourself how it works and how it compares with similar texts, how successful a text you believe it is and how the target audience may respond to it.

Do not be afraid to use your imagination. You may well 'see' things in the text that had not occurred to the examiners. If you back up any statement you make with evidence from the text then feel confident enough to put it down.

Above all – and even though this may seem absurd considering we are talking about an examination – have fun. Any unseen paper is designed to give examination candidates the opportunity to show engagement, reveal what they have learnt over the period of the course and also to reveal a sense of critical autonomy.

ACTIVITY . . .

Here is the text set for analysis by AQA in January 2004. Look carefully at both the text and the question paper and then prepare notes under the Key Concept headings to show how you would answer the paper.

Answer the **one** compulsory question below.
The question carries 60 marks.

QUESTION

Provide an analysis of the text: the front cover and contents pages of *Computer Active*, issue 131, published 20 February – 5 March 2003 by VNU Business Publications.

- You have **15 minutes** to read and make notes on the question and the accompanying print text.

- You will then have **one hour** to write your analysis.

- You will be rewarded for making detailed references to the text.

- You should focus your analysis upon the Key Concepts of Media Language, Representation and Media Audiences.

- You may also wish to comment upon Values and Ideology and Media Institutions.

Source: Assessment and Qualifications Alliance (AQA), General Certificate of Education, January 2004, Advanced Subsidiary Examination. With kind permission.

£1.30 ONLY

THE ONLY PLAIN ENGLISH COMPUTER MAGAZINE

UK'S **BEST-SELLING** COMPUTER MAG

computer act!ve

ISSUE **131**

FORTNIGHTLY

www.computeractive.co.uk

Bag a bargain
You can buy PC gear for less
p38

Screened out
We test PCs without monitors
p60

A Wizard idea
How Windows' Wizards can help you
p30

WIN!
Ten broadband kits from Tiscali and access for a year
p84

WORKSHOPS
15 step-by-step pages **p43**

* **Fit documents on one page**
  Shrink and fit lots of text in Word
* **Divide and conquer**
  Split your hard disk for neat filing
* **Connect more devices**
  Add ports to your PC the easy way
* **Sort out pictures and video**
  Use Microsoft Clip Organizer
* **Give your documents style**
  Use Word's Styles to format text
* **Hints & Tips**

L👁👁K OUT!

Protect your family against internet filth

NEW!

MCAFEE SPAMKILLER
Is this the answer to junk email?

HP PHOTOSMART 230
Great prints - and you don't need a PC

9 771461 621028

Approved by the Plain English Campaign

2003
Supported by VMU Business Publications and Computeractive
The European Year of People with Disabilities

UK'S BEST-SELLING COMPUTER MAG

computer act!ve

Crystal Mark
Clarity
approved by
Plain English Campaign

ISSUE 131: 20 FEB - 5 MAR 2003

FROM THE EDITOR

Concerns about porn, the safety of children and the proliferation of spam are putting people off the internet. Don't worry, as Computer*active* is here to help. Our piece on filtering and online safety should put you at ease. If you want to upgrade your PC but are happy with your monitor, we've tested a range of PCs that come without displays, and we've also revealed where you can find new, working products at bargain prices. Finally, look out for the next issue of Computer*active* on the news-stands in a fortnight. We'll publish a special fifth birthday edition with extra editorial pages, a free supplement and some great competitions.

James Harding

Web act!ve The UK's best-selling internet monthly

The next issue of Web*active* is out now, available at most good independent newsagents and supermarkets, including Tesco, Dillons and Spar. In this issue are features on keeping viruses and hackers at bay and home improvement ideas online. Web*active* only costs 99p so why not give it a try? For subscriptions, contact 01858 438881. Annual subscriptions cost £12 for 13 issues, including P&P

WORKSHOPS

Split your hard disk   **44**
Organise files and folders by splitting up your hard disk with PartitionMagic

Fit several pages into one   **47**
Use Microsoft Word's Shrink to Fit feature to put several pages of text into one

Fit more USB ports   **48**
Make your computer more expandable by adding extra USB ports

Use Microsoft Clip Organizer   **52**
Organise your photos, music and video files

Use Styles in Microsoft Word   **54**
Format text easily using Word's Style feature

Hints & Tips   **58**

contents

TISCALI BROADBAND   P84

P76

AIRGUN   SKS

For details of subscriptions, back issues, email addresses, our technical helpline or how to contact us for any other reason, read the box on the next issue page - facing the inside back cover.

Features

P30

P38

cover story

LOOK OUT!

Protect your family against internet filth

On test

P60

P73

P22

P21

P20

P24

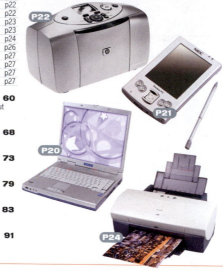

EXAM PAPER 2

Consider the exam paper on p. 344. It was set for the AS Level examination by AQA in January 2004. Candidates were allowed one and a half hours to complete the two questions required. The paper is typical of an essay-based examination set by all the boards at AS/A Level.

Let us consider some of the issues you would need to take into account if you were in the exam room about to sit this paper. First you would need to think about timing. Assuming that you allow yourself five minutes' thinking time at the beginning and five minutes to check your work at the end, that means 80 minutes to work on the questions or 40 minutes for each.

In preparing yourself for the exam, you should have explored at least two of the topic areas identified for each of the questions. It makes sense, therefore, to focus your attention on these. Of course, if you have prepared more than two areas, then you need to consider all possibilities. This is not, however, a good time to decide that you can answer a question on an area that you have not explored, even if it does look an attractive option. If you have not studied an area, you may not be aware of the particular issues that the examiner will be expecting you to discuss.

Note that on this paper each topic area has two options. You need to read *each* of these carefully. It is common under the pressure of an exam to jump in and decide to write on one option without first considering the other fully. Spend a little time deciding which is the better choice for you. It is probably worth noting down a few ideas for both and then choosing the one that you feel most confident about.

Let us look in more detail at question 1 on the topic of Film and Broadcast Fiction. To some extent the nature of your preparatory work on this topic might decide which option to tackle. As you can see, question (a) calls for knowledge of two broadcast fiction texts, whereas option (b) requires you to have looked at a range of texts drawn from either film, broadcast fiction or both. Both tasks require you to make a detailed response, but in slightly different ways. Option (a) specifically asks you to focus your answer on differences in narrative structure and techniques in two broadcast fiction texts. This means you must know about narrative theory if you are going to tackle this question. You might find it useful to look back at the section on narrative on p. 42 to remind yourself of some of the key points you would need to know. It is also important that you are able to call upon two texts that will provide a significant contrast in their use of narrative as you are being asked to look at the 'differences' in order to describe and illustrate these. You might, for example, like to consider how far a soap opera and a sitcom would provide sufficient opportunity to explore such differences.

ACTIVITY . . .

Draw up a plan for a response to this essay. Make your notes under these headings:

- Narrative structure devices
- Text 1
- Text 2
- Differences

Answer **two** questions, each from a different topic area.
All questions carry 30 marks.

1 Film and Broadcast Fiction

Either (a) Describe and illustrate the main differences in the narrative structure and techniques used in **two** broadcast fiction texts of your choice.

Give reasons for the differences.

Or (b) Do you think that film and television fiction does more than simply entertain?

Support your views by referring to a range of film **AND/OR** broadcast fiction texts.

2 Documentary

Either (a) Explain how documentaries can only give their viewers a mediated view of 'real life'.

Or (b) Analyse **two** documentaries, one of which must be contemporary, that you believe to be of particular interest in the development of the documentary genre.

3 Advertising and Marketing

Either (a) Describe, giving detailed examples, some of the potential advantages for advertisers and marketeers of **one or more** of the following media outlets:

- Television
- Radio
- Print media
- Outdoor advertising
- Cinema
- Internet and new media technologies.

Or (b) "Standing out from the crowd is an essential part of any advertising campaign." (Meg Carter in *The Guardian* 28/01/02)

Discuss this statement with detailed reference to a recent campaign of your choice.

4 British Newspapers

Either (a) By referring to examples of news stories and features from **one or more** British newspapers, show how these reveal the values of the newspapers concerned.

Or (b) A visiting American actress said that the British press is out of control. Do you agree?

Support your answer with examples.

(*In your discussion you may like to consider some of the following issues: privacy; sensationalism; inaccuracy; fabrication; regulation.*)

Source: Assessment and Qualifications Alliance (AQA), General Certificate of Education, January 2004, Advanced Subsidiary Examination. With kind permission.

As you can see, choosing appropriate texts is important for this question. You will no doubt have spent time in class looking at texts your teacher has introduced. Many other members of the class are likely to use these. It may well be in your interests to choose your own texts rather than relying on those you have considered in class. This way you should bring a freshness and personal engagement to your response in a way that would be lacking if you rely heavily on the ideas of the teacher and the rest of the class. Do not worry too much about choosing text that you think an examiner will consider 'appropriate'. What is important is to provide evidence of your ability to engage with the texts in the way we have suggested. Do, however, make sure that your chosen text meets the requirements of being a *fictional* text.

Finally do not forget that this question is inviting you to demonstrate your awareness of broader media theory. A good response will show that you have a detailed understanding of narrative theory allied to the skill to use this theory to elucidate how narrative is used in the construction of broadcast fiction texts.

Option (b) looks on the surface a much wider question; it does not limit you to narrative analysis of two texts. Note also that it does not limit you to one media form. You can tackle film, television or both. You are being asked to produce a response that invites you to express an opinion about the function of film and television texts. In the end your opinion is unlikely to matter a great deal. What is important is the quality of the argument you put forward and your ability to illustrate and support the points you make by making reference to a 'range' of texts. So again the best approach would be to use texts which are personal to you rather than relying on examples provided by your teacher to the whole class. Ideally you will choose texts that can illustrate the different facets of your argument.

Now look again at the question. There is no 'right' answer. Nor is there an argument that your examiner particularly wants to hear. You can argue that that these texts do nothing more than simply entertain. Equally you could argue that texts are also there to educate and to uplift us morally and fulfil us spiritually. There again you may say that a lot depends on the text.

So it is up to you to decide which of the questions you feel better equipped to tackle. Now consider how you might apply this kind of thinking process to the other topic area you have prepared.

ACTIVITY…

Working in pairs, choose another topic area and give careful consideration to each of the alternative questions. You do not need detailed knowledge of the topic area to do this. Working together, write down what you consider to be the key points you need to take into account in choosing your question. Then individually provide a brief essay plan for the question you prefer.

When you have finished, compare your essay plan with your partner's. Identify and discuss similarities and differences.

 **RESOURCES**

USEFUL DATA SOURCES

Advertising Association
Abford House
15 Wilton Road
London SW1V 1NJ
☎ 020 7828 2771
<http://www.adassoc.org.uk>

Advertising Standards Authority (ASA)
2 Torrington Place
London WC1E 7HW
☎ 020 7580 5555
<http://www.asa.org.uk>

BBC
Television Centre
Wood Lane
London W12 7RJ
☎ 020 7743 8000
<http://www.bbc.co.uk>

British Board of Film Classification (BBFC)
3 Soho Square
London W1V 5DE
☎ 020 7440 1570
<http://www.bbfc.co.uk>

Broadcasting Standards Commission (BSC)
7 The Sanctuary
London SW1P 3JS
☎ 020 7233 0544
<http://www.bsc.org.uk>

Channel Four Television
124 Horseferry Road
London SW1P 2TX
☎ 020 7396 4444
<http://www.channel4.com>

Community Media Association
5 Paternoster Square
Sheffield S1 2BX
☎ 0114 279 5219
<http://www.commedia.org.uk>

Film Education
Alhambra House
27–31 Charing Cross Road
London WC2H 0AU
☎ 020 7976 2291
<http://www.filmeducation.org>

The Institute of Practitioners in Advertising (IPA)
44 Belgrave Square
London SW1X 8QS
☎ 020 7235 7020
<http://www.ipa.co.uk>

Market Research Society
15 Northburgh Street
London EC1V 0AH
☎ 020 7490 4911
<http://www.marketresearch.org.uk>

Northern Ireland Film Commission
21 Ormeau Avenue
Belfast BT2 8HD
☎ 028 9023 2444
<http://www.nifc.co.uk>

Ofcom
Office of Communications
Riverside House
2A Southwark Bridge Road
London SE1 9HA
☎ 020 7981 3000
<http://www.ofcom.org.uk>

The Publishers Association
1 Kingsway
London WC2 6XF
☎ 020 7565 7474
<http://www.publishers.org.uk>

Press Complaints Commission (PCC)
1 Salisbury Square
London EC4Y 8AE
☎ 020 7353 1248
<http://www.pcc.org.uk>

Radio Authority
Holbrook House
Great Queen Street
London WC2B 5DG
☎ 020 7430 2724
<http://www.radioauthority.org.uk>

Scottish Screen
249 West George Street
Glasgow G2 4QE
☎ 0141 302 1700
<http://www.scottishscreen.com>

Voice of the Listener
101 King's Drive
Gravesend
Kent DA12 5BQ
☎ 01474 352835
<http://www.vlv.org.uk>

South Wales Film Commission
The Media Centre
Culverhouse Cross
Cardiff CF5 6XJ
☎ 02920 590240
<http://www.focuswales.co.uk/swfc.
html>

ARCHIVES

British Film Institute (BFI)
21 Stephen Street
London W1P 1PL
☎ 020 7255 1444
<http://www.bfi.org.uk>

British Library Newspaper Library
Colindale Avenue
London NW9 5HE
☎ 020 7412 7353
<http://www.bl.uk/collections/
newspapers.html>

East Anglian Film Archive
University of East Anglia
Norwich NR4 7TJ
☎ 01603 456161
<http://www.uea.ac.uk/eafa>

**National Museum of Photography,
Film and Television (NMPFT)**
Bradford
West Yorkshire BD1 1NQ
☎ 01274 202030
<http://www.nmpft.org.uk>

National Sound Archive
British Library
96 Euston Road
London NW1 2DB
☎ 020 7412 7436
<http://cadensa.bl.uk>

North West Film Archive
Manchester Metropolitan University
Minshull House
47–9 Chorlton Street
Manchester M1 3EU
☎ 0161 247 3097
<http://www.nwfa.mmu.ac.uk>

North West Sound Archive
Old Steward's Office
The Castle
Clitheroe
Lancashire BB7 1AZ
☎ 01200 427897
<http://www.gmcro.co.uk/other/NWSA/
nwsa.htm>

Scottish Screen Archive
1 Bowmont Gardens
Glasgow G12 9LR
☎ 0141 337 7413
<http://www.scottishscreen.com>

South East Film and Video Archive
University of Brighton
Grand Parade
Brighton BN2 2JY
☎ 01273 643213
<http://www.brighton.ac.uk/sefva>

Wales Film and Television Archive
Unit 1, Science Park
Cefn Llan
Aberystwyth
Ceredigion SY23 3AH
☎ 01970 626007
<http://www.movinghistory.ac.uk/
archives/wa/region.html>

Wessex Film and Sound Archive
Hampshire Record Office
Sussex Street
Winchester SO23 8TH
☎ 01962 847742
<http://www.hants.gov.uk/record-
office/film>

▼ GLOSSARY

action code A narrative device by which a resolution is produced through action, for example a shoot-out.

actuality Recordings of images and sounds of events made on location as they actually happen for inclusion in news reports or documentaries.

ADSL (asymmetric digital subscriber line) A telephone network that turns an ordinary telephone copper wire into a high-speed connection for Internet, broadcasting and video-on-demand services.

anchorage The fixing or limiting of a particular set of meanings to an image. One of the most common forms of anchorage is the caption underneath a photograph.

anti-narrative A text that seeks deliberately to disrupt narrative flow in order to achieve a particular effect, such as the repetition of images or the disruption of a chronological sequence of events.

breaking news A news story, the details of which are unfolding as the story is being reported.

bricolage The way signs or artefacts are borrowed from different styles or genres to create something new.

broadsheet A large rectangular newspaper, such as the *Daily Telegraph* or *The Times*. Broadsheets are visually associated with serious journalism, reporting important events at home and abroad. They are targeted at an upmarket, professional readership.

catharsis A purging of the emotions through pity and terror, leaving an audience less likely to behave horribly because they have experienced the results vicariously.

closed questions These demand a very limited answer, often just yes or no.

codes Rules or conventions by which signs are put together to create meaning.

connotation The meaning of a sign that is arrived at through the cultural experiences a reader brings to it.

content analysis A method of collecting, collating and analysing large amounts of information about the content of media products, such as television advertisements, in order to draw conclusions about such issues as the representation of gender roles.

convergence The coming together of different communication technologies such as the telephone, the computer and the television.

denotation What an image actually shows and what is immediately apparent, rather than opposed to the assumptions an individual reader may make about it.

dissolve Film term for the transition between two images whereby one 'dissolves' into the next.

docu-soap A hybrid genre in which elements of documentary and soap opera are combined to create a series about the lives of real people.

encoding A process by which the media construct messages.

end credits At the end of a film or television production, a detailed list of all the people who contributed to the production, from producers and directors to actors and technical, administrative and support crews.

enigma A narrative device that teases the audience by presenting a puzzle or riddle to be solved.

feature In newspapers this is generally an article that concerns itself with a topical issue while not having any hard news content.

genre The term used for the classification of media texts into groups with similar characteristics.

hard news News that is important and is happening at the time it is reported. A rescue attempt on a cross-Channel ferry, the death of an important national figure or a rise in mortgage interest rates could all be classified as hard news.

hegemony The concept used by the Marxist critic Antonio Gramsci to describe how people are influenced into accepting the dominance of a power elite who impose their will and worldview on the rest of the population. Gramsci argues that this elite is able to rule because the rest of the population allow it to do so. It can be argued, therefore, that the ideological role of the media is to persuade us that it is in our best interests to accept the dominance of this elite.

horizontal integration This involves the acquisition of competitors in the same section of the industry. It might be possible for one company to seek to control all of the market – a monopoly position – but most capitalist countries have laws to prevent this happening.

hypodermic needle theory A theory that suggests that the media 'inject' ideas into a passive audience, like giving a patient a drug.

hypothesis An assumption or question about something that the research will investigate and, it is hoped, either prove or disprove.

icon A sign that works by resemblance.

iconography Those particular signs that we associate with particular genres, such as physical attributes and dress of actors, the settings and 'tools of the trade' (for example cars, guns).

ideology A system of beliefs that determines how power relations are organised within a society.

independents Companies (usually relatively small ones) that maintain a status outside the normal big-business remit and therefore tend to focus on minority-interest products.

index A sign that works by a relationship to the object or concept it refers to; for example, smoke is an index of fire.

interpellation The process by which a media text summons an audience in much the same way as a town crier would ring a bell and shout to summon an audience for an important announcement.

intertextuality The way in which texts refer to other media texts that producers assume audiences will recognise.

linear narrative A plot that moves forward in a straight line without flashbacks or digressions.

media imperialism The idea that powerful and wealthy countries can exercise economic, cultural and social control over others through control of media industries.

media saturation A term used to describe the extent to which our experience of the world is dominated by the media, not only at an individual level but also nationally and globally.

mediation The process by which a media text represents an idea, issue or event to us. This is a useful word as it suggests the way in which things undergo change in the process of being acted upon by the media.

methodology The system or manner used to carry out research; the different ways in which 'data' can be captured.

mode of address The way in which a particular text will address or speak to its audience.

moral panic A mass response to a group, a person or an attitude that becomes defined as a threat to society.

multiplex A cinema that contains several screens under one roof, usually with one projection booth servicing all screens. The number of screens can vary; the new Warner Village in Birmingham contains thirty screens.

multi-tracking The process whereby different instruments and voices are recorded separately and then mixed together in a recording studio.

narrative The way in which a story is told in both fictional and non-fictional media texts.

narrowcasting The opposite of broadcasting. Where texts are aimed at very small, special-interest groups.

niche market A small target audience with specific interests, for example DIY, classic cars or royalty.

open questions Those that start with 'what', 'where', 'why', 'when', 'how' or 'who'. These encourage the interviewee to 'open up' and talk freely.

parallel action A narrative device in which two scenes are observed as happening at the same time by cutting between them.

polysemic The way in which a text has a variety of meanings and the audience is an important component in determining those meanings.

postmodernism The social, political and cultural attitudes and images of the late twentieth and early twenty-first century.

primary media Where we pay close attention to the media text, for instance in the close reading of a magazine or newspaper, or in the cinema where we concentrate on the film in front of us.

process model This model considered the audience's interaction with the media as part of a linear process (sender–channel–message–receiver) in which the meaning of the message is thought to be 'fixed' by the producer.

PSB (public service broadcasting) Introduced in the UK in the 1920s by Lord Reith, later Director General of the BBC, with a remit to 'inform, educate and entertain'. The yearly licence fee was payable first to cover radio sets and then, after the Second World War, to include televisions, too. This form of financing meant that the service was not reliant on outside commercial backing and could therefore, in principle, remain unbiased. PSB is designed to ensure a balanced coverage of different types of programme.

qualitative research A type of research that attempts to explain or understand something and may necessitate much discussion and analysis of people's attitudes and behaviour. It usually involves working with small numbers of people or 'focus groups'.

quantitative research A type of research, usually based on numbers, statistics or tables, that attempts to 'measure' some kind of phenomenon and produce 'hard' data. It often involves working with large groups of people.

realism Representation by the media of situations or ideas in such a way that they seem real.

representation The process by which the media present to us the 'real world'.

secondary media Where the medium or text is there in the background and we are aware that it is there but are not concentrating on it.

semiotics The study of signs and sign systems.

sign The sign consists of two components: the signifier and the signified. The signifier is a physical object, for example a sound, printed word or advertisement. The signified is a mental concept or meaning conveyed by the signifier.

simulacra Simulations or copies that are replacing the 'real' artefacts.

situated culture A term used to describe how our 'situation' (daily routines and patterns, social relationships with family and peer groups) can influence our engagement with and interpretation of media texts.

soundbite A snappy and memorable quotation that can easily be assimilated into a broadcast news story (for example Tony Blair's 'Education, education, education').

spin doctor A person who tries to create a favourable slant to an item of news such as a potentially unpopular policy.

structuralism This approach argues that identifying underlying structures is all-important in undertaking analysis. In linguistics, for example, it can be argued that all languages have a similar underlying grammatical structure, which we are born with the capacity to learn. Similarly, certain social structures, such as the family unit, may be common to many cultures.

symbol A sign that represents an object or concept solely by the agreement of the people who use it.

tabloid A compact newspaper, half the size of a broadsheet, designed to appeal to a mass audience. Tabloids, particularly at the lower end of the market, are associated with sensationalising trivial events rather than with comprehensive coverage of national and international news.

tertiary media Where the medium is present but we are not at all aware of it. The most obvious examples are advertising hoardings or placards that we pass but do not register.

text In Media Studies this term is used to refer to all media products.

uses and gratifications theory The idea that media audiences make active use of what the media offer. The audience has a set of needs, which the media in one form or another meet.

utopian solution The fantasy element and escapism from daily routines and problems provided by entertainment genres.

vertical integration This involves the ownership of every stage of the production process (production + distribution + exhibition), thereby ensuring complete control of a media product.

▼ BIBLIOGRAPHY

Allen, S. (2000) *News Culture*, Open University Press.

Ang, I. (1985) *Watching Dallas: Soap Opera and the Melodramatic Imagination*, Methuen.

—— (1991) *Desperately Seeking the Audience*, Routledge.

Armes, R. (1988) *On Video*, Oxford University Press.

Baehr, H. and Dyer, G. (eds) (1987) *Boxed In: Women and Television*, Pandora.

Barker, M. (1989) *Comics, Ideology, Power and the Critics*, Manchester University Press.

Barker, M. and Petley, J. (eds) (2001) *Ill-Effects: The Media/Violence Debate*, Routledge.

Barnard, S. (2000) *Studying Radio*, Arnold.

Barrass, R. (1984) *Study!*, E & F.N. Spon.

Barthes, R. (1993) [1957] *Mythologies*, Vintage Classics.

Bell, A., Joyce, M. and Rivers, D. (1999) *Advanced Level Media*, Hodder & Stoughton.

Berger, J. (1972) *Ways of Seeing*, Penguin.

Blumler, J. and Katz, E. (eds) (1975) *The Uses of Mass Communications: Current Perspectives on Gratification Research*, Sage.

Bordwell, D. and Thompson, K. (1979) *Film Art: An Introduction*, McGraw-Hill.

Boyd, A. (1994) *Broadcast Journalism: Techniques of Radio and TV News*, Focal Press.

Branston, G. and Stafford, R. (1999) *The Media Student's Book*, 2nd edn, Routledge.

Buckingham, D. (1987) *Public Secrets: EastEnders and its Audience*, BFI Publishing.

Chambers, E. and Northedge, A. (1997) *The Arts Good Study Guide*, Open University Press.

Cohen, S. (1972) *Folk Devils and Moral Panics: The Creation of Mods and Rockers*, MacGibbon & Kee.

Cohen, S. and Young, J. (1973) *The Manufacture of News: Deviance, Social Problems and the Mass Media*, Constable.

Corner, J. (ed.) (1991) *Popular Television in Britain*, BFI Publishing.

—— (1996) *The Art of Record: A Critical Introduction to Documentary*, Manchester University Press.

Crisell, A. (1994) *Understanding Radio*, Routledge.

—— (1997) *An Introductory History of British Broadcasting*, Routledge.

Cumberbatch, G. (1990) *Television Advertising and Sex Role Stereotyping*: A Content Analysis, Broadcasting Standards Council.

Curran, J. and Seaton, J. (1997) *Power Without Responsibility*: The Press and Broadcasting in Britain, Routledge.

Daniels, L. (1977) *Fear: a history of Horror in the Mass Media*, Paladin.

Deacon, D. *et al.* (1999) *Researching Communications*: A Practical Guide to Methods in Media and Cultural Analysis, Arnold.

Drew, S. and Bingham, R. (1997) *The Student Skills Guide*, Gower.

Dutton, B. (1995) *Media Studies: An Introduction*, Longman.

Dyer, G. (1982) *Advertising as Communication*, Methuen.

Dyer, R. (1977) 'Entertainment and utopia', *Movie*, vol. 24.

Dyja, E. (ed.) (1999) *Film and Television Handbook 2000*, BFI Publishing.

Evans, H. (1986) *Pictures on a Page*, Heinemann.

Ferguson, M. (1983) *Forever Feminine: Women's Magazines and the Cult of Femininity*, Heinemann.

Fiske, J. (1987) *Television Culture*, Methuen.

—— (1990) *Introduction to Communication Studies*, 2nd edn, Routledge.

Fiske, J. and Hartley, J. (1978) *Reading Television*, Methuen.

Franklin, B. (ed.) (2001) *British Television Policy: A Reader*, Routledge.

—— (2003) 'Media institutions and production' in O'Sullivan, T., Dutton, B. and Rayner, P., *Studying the Media*, Arnold.

Frith, S. and Goodwin, A. (eds) (1990) *On Record*, Routledge.

Fry, R. (1999) *The Great Big Book of How to Study*, Career Press.

Galtung, J. and Ruge, M. (1973) 'Structuring and selecting news' in Cohen, S. and Young, J. (eds) *The Manufacture of News: Deviance, Social Problems and the Mass Media*, Constable.

Gauntlett, D. (2002) *Media, Gender and Identity*, Routledge.

Geraghty, C. (1991) *Women and Soap-Opera*, Polity Press.

Glasgow University Media Group (1985) *War and Peace News*, Open University Press.

Goodwin, A. and Whannel, G. (eds) (1990) *Understanding Television*, Routledge.

Gray, A. (1992) *Video Playtime*, Routledge.

Halloran, J. (1970) *The Effects of Television*, Panther.

Hartley, J. (1982) *Understanding News*, Routledge.

Hebdige, D. (1988) *Hiding in the Light: On Images and Things*, Routledge.

Herman, E.S. and Chomsky, N. (1994) *Manufacturing Consent*, Vintage.

Hobson, D. (1982) *Crossroads: The Drama of a Soap Opera*, Methuen.

Hollows, J. and Jancovich, M. (1996) *Approaches to Popular Film*, Manchester University Press.

Jancovich, M. (ed.) (2001) *Horror Film Reader*, Routledge.

Katz, E., Blumler, J. and Gurevitch, M. (1974) 'Utilisation of mass communication by the individual' in Blumler, J. and Katz, E. (eds) *The Uses of Mass Communications: Current Perspectives on Gratifications Research*, Sage.

Keeble, R. (2001) *The Newspapers Handbook*, 3rd edn, Routledge.

Kirchner, D. (ed.) (1997) *The Researcher's Guide to British Film and Television Collections*, 5th edn, British Universities Film & Video Council.

Klein, N. (2001) *No Logo*, Flamingo.

Livingstone, S. (1998) *Making Sense of Television*, Routledge.

McLuhan, M. (1964) *Understanding Media*, Routledge & Kegan Paul.

McLuhan, M. and Fiore, Q. (1997) [1967] *The Medium Is the Massage*, Wired Books.

McMahon, B. and Quinn, R. (1986) *Real Images*, Macmillan.

—— (1988) *Exploring Images*, Macmillan.

McRobbie, A. (1983) 'Teenage Girls, *Jackie* and the ideology of adolescent femininity' in Waites B. *et al.*, *Popular Culture: Past and Present*, Croom Helm.

—— (1994) '*More!* New sexualities in girls' and women's magazines' in Curran, J., Morley, D. and Walkerdine V. (eds) *Cultural Studies and Communications*, Arnold.

—— (1995) *Feminism and Youth Culture – From Jackie to Just Seventeen*, 2nd edn, Macmillan.

Meech, P. (1999) 'Advertising' in Stokes, J. and Reading, A. (eds) *The Media in Britain: Current Debates and Developments*, Macmillan.

Messenger Davis, M. (1989) *Television Is Good for Kids*, Hilary Shipman.

Miller, T. (ed.) (2002) *Television Studies*, BFI.

Mitchell, C. (2000) *Women and Radio*, Routledge.

Monaco, J. (1977) *How to Read a Film*, Oxford University Press.

Moores, S. (1993) *Interpreting Audiences: The Ethnography of Media Consumption*, Sage.

Morley, D. (1980) *The Nationwide Audience*, BFI Publishing.

—— (1986) *Family Television*, Comedia.

Mulvey, L. (1975) 'Visual pleasure and narrative cinema', *Screen*, vol. 16, no. 3.

Myers, G. (1985) *Understains: The Sense and Seduction of Advertising*, Comedia.

—— (1998) *Ad Worlds – Brands, Media, Audiences*, Arnold.

Neale, S. (ed.) (2002) *Genre and Contemporary Hollywood*, BFI.

Nelmes, J. (ed.) (1999) *An Introduction to Film Studies*, 2nd edn, Routledge.

Newman, K. (ed.) (2002) *Science Fiction/Horror: A Sight and Sound Reader*, BFI.

Nixon, S. (1996) *Hard Looks (Masculinities, Spectatorship and Contemporary Consumption)*, St. Martins Press.

O'Sullivan, T., Dutton, B. and Rayner, P. (1994) *Key Concepts in Communication and Cultural Studies*, Routledge.

—— (2003) *Studying the Media*, 3rd edn, Arnold.

O'Sullivan, T. and Jewkes, Y. (eds) (1997) *The Media Studies Reader*, Arnold.

Packard, V. (1979) [1957] *The Hidden Persuaders*, Penguin.

Paget, D. (1998) *No Other Way to Tell It: Dramadoc/Docudrama on Television*, Manchester University Press.

Peak, S. and Fisher, P. (eds) (Annual) *Guardian Media Guide*, Fourth Estate.

Perkins, T. (1979) 'Rethinking stereotypes' in Barratt, M., Corrigan, P., Kuhn, A. and Wolff, V. (eds) *Ideology and Cultural Production*, Croom Helm.

Price, S. (1997) *The Complete A–Z Media and Communication Handbook*, Hodder & Stoughton.

Radway, J. (1984) *Reading the Romance: Women, Patriarchy and Popular Literature*, Verso.

Saussure, F. de (1983) [1916] *Course in General Linguistics*, Gerald Duckworth.

Schlesinger, P. (1987) *Putting Reality Together*: BBC News, Methuen.

Selby, K. and Cowdery, R. (1995) *How to Study Television*, Macmillan.

Shingler, M. and Wieringa, C. (1998) *On Air: Methods and Meanings in Radio*, Arnold.

Stacey, J. (1994) *Star Gazing: Hollywood Cinema and Female Spectatorship*, Routledge.

Stokes, J. (1999) 'Use it or lose it: sex, sexuality and sexual health in magazines for girls' in Stokes, J. and Reading, A. (eds) *The Media in Britain: Current Debates and Developments*, Macmillan.

—— (2003) *How to Do Media and Cultural Studies*, Sage.

Storey, J. (1993) *An Introductory Guide to Cultural Theory and Popular Culture*, Harvester Wheatsheaf.

Strinati, D. (1995) *An Introduction to Theories of Popular Culture*, Routledge.

Strinati, D. and Wagg, S. (eds) (1992) *Come On Down: Popular Media Culture in Post War Britain*, Routledge.

Taylor, K. (2000) 'Girl Power! How an audience perceives the teenage girl through various media forms'. Unpublished dissertation, Cheltenham & Gloucester College of Higher Education.

Taylor, L. and Willis, A. (1999) *Media Studies: Texts, Institutions and Audiences*, Blackwell.

Tilley, A. (1991) 'Narrative' in Lusted, D. (ed.) *The Media Studies Book: A Guide for Teachers*, Routledge.

Trowler, P. (1996) *Investigating Mass Media*, 2nd edn, Collins.

Tunstall, J. (1983) *The Media in Britain*, Constable.

Watson, J. and Hill, A. (1996) *A Dictionary of Communication and Media Studies*, Arnold.

Watts, H. (1982) *On Camera*, Aavo.

Wernick, A. (1991) *Promotional Culture: Advertising, Ideology and Symbolic Expression*, Sage.

Whelehan, I. (2000) *Overloaded: Popular Culture and the Future of Feminism*, The Woman's Press.

Wilcock, J. (2000) *Documentaries*, Auteur.

Williams, K. (1997) *'Get Me a Murder a Day'*: A History of Mass Communication in Britain, Arnold.

—— (2003) *Understanding Media Theory*, Arnold.

Williams, R. (1974) *Television: Technology and Cultural Form*, Routledge.

Williamson, J. (1978) *Decoding Advertisements: Ideology and Meaning in Advertisements*, Boyars.

Winship, J. (1987) *Inside Women's Magazines*, Pandora.

Winston, B. (1995) *Claiming the Real: The Documentary Film Revisited*, BFI Publishing.

Wright Mills, C. (2000) [1956] *The Power Elite*, Oxford University Press.

▼ INDEX

Note: page numbers in italics denote illustrations or tables